PROPHECIES OF THE BIBLE

God's Word
for the
Biblically-Inept™ SERIES

Daymond R. Duck

CARTOONS BY
Reverend Fun
(Dennis "Max" Hengeveld)
Dennis is a graphic de-
signer for Gospel Films and
the author of *Has
Anybody Seen My Locust?*
His cartoons can
be seen worldwide at
www.reverendfun.com.

STARBURST PUBLISHERS®

P. O. Box 4123, Lancaster, Pennsylvania 17604

To schedule author appearances, write:
Author Appearances
Starburst Publishers
P.O. Box 4123
Lancaster, Pennsylvania 17604
(717) 293-0939

www.starburstpublishers.com

CREDITS:
Cover design by David Marty Design
Text design and composition by John Reinhardt Book Design
Illustrations by Melissa A. Burkhart and Bruce Burkhart
Cartoons by Dennis "Max" Hengeveld

Unless otherwise noted, or paraphrased by the author, all Scripture quotations are from the New International Version of The Holy Bible.

Scripture taken from the HOLY BIBLE: NEW INTERNATIONAL VERSION® (NIV®). Copyright © 1973, 1978, 1984 by International Bible Society.

Reverend Fun cartoons ©Copyright Gospel Films Incorporated.

To the best of its ability, Starburst Publishers® has strived to find the source of all material. If there has been an oversight, please contact us, and we will make any correction deemed necessary in future printings. We also declare that to the best of our knowledge all material (quoted or not) contained herein is accurate, and we shall not be held liable for the same.

First Printing, February 2000

ISBN: 1-892016-22-2
Library of Congress Number 99-67257

Printed in the United States of America

READ THESE PAGES BEFORE YOU READ THIS BOOK . . .

Welcome to the *God's Word for the Biblically-Inept™* series. If you find reading the Bible overwhelming, baffling, and frustrating, then this Revolutionary Commentary™ is for you!

Each page is organized for easy reading with icons, sidebars, and bullets to make the Bible's message easy to understand. *God's Word for the Biblically-Inept™* series includes opinions and insights from Bible experts of all kinds, so you get various opinions on Bible teachings—not just one!

There are more *God's Word for the Biblically-Inept™* titles on the way. The following is a partial list of upcoming books. We have assigned each title an abbreviated **title code**. This code along with page numbers is incorporated in the text *throughout the series*, allowing easy reference from one title to another.

Prophecies of the Bible—God's Word for the Biblically-Inept™

Daymond R. Duck   TITLE CODE: GWPB

God has a plan for this crazy planet, and now, understanding it is easier than ever! Best-selling author and end-time prophecy expert Daymond R. Duck explains the complicated prophecies of the Bible in plain English. Read with wonder as Duck shows you all there is to know about the End of the Age, the New World Order, the Second Coming, and the Coming World Government. Includes useful commentary, expert quotes, icons, sidebars, chapter summaries, and study questions! Find out what prophecies have already been fulfilled and what's in store for the future!

(trade paper) ISBN 1892016222 $16.95   AVAILABLE NOW

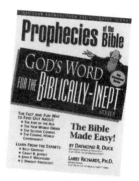

Genesis—God's Word for the Biblically-Inept™

Joyce L. Gibson   TITLE CODE: GWGN

Joyce L. Gibson breaks the Bible down into bite-sized pieces making it easy to understand and incorporate into your life. Readers will learn about Creation, Adam and Eve, the Flood, Abraham and Isaac, and more. Includes chapter summaries, bullet points, definitions, and study questions.

(trade paper) ISBN 1892016125 $16.95   AVAILABLE NOW

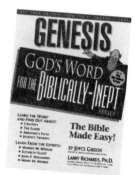

The Bible—God's Word for the Biblically-Inept™

Larry Richards   TITLE CODE: GWBI

Get serious about learning the Bible from cover to cover! Here is an overview of the Bible written by Larry (Lawrence O.) Richards, one of today's leading Bible writers. Each chapter contains select verses from books of the Bible along with illustrations, definitions, and references to related Bible passages.

(trade paper) ISBN 0914984551 $16.95   AVAILABLE NOW

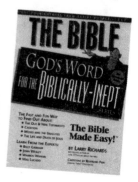

Revelation—God's Word for the Biblically-Inept™

Daymond R. Duck   TITLE CODE: GWRV

Revelation—God's Word for the Biblically-Inept™ includes every verse of the book of Revelation along with quotes from leading experts, icons, sidebars, and bullets. Learn and enjoy as end-time prophecy expert Daymond R. Duck leads us through one of the Bible's most confusing books.

(trade paper) ISBN 0914984985 $16.95 AVAILABLE NOW

Daniel—God's Word for the Biblically-Inept™

Daymond R. Duck   TITLE CODE: GWDN

Daniel is a book of prophecy and the key to understanding the mysteries of the Tribulation and end-time events. This verse-by-verse commentary combines humor and scholarship to get at the essentials of Scripture. Perfect for those who want to know the truth about the Antichrist.

(trade paper) ISBN 0914984489 $16.95 AVAILABLE NOW

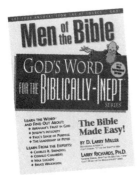

Men of the Bible—God's Word for the Biblically-Inept™

D. Larry Miller   TITLE CODE: GWMB

Benefit from the life experiences of the powerful men of the Bible! Learn how the inspirational struggles of men such as Moses, Daniel, Paul, and David parallel the struggles of men today. It will inspire and build Christian character in your walk with the Lord.

(trade paper) ISBN 1892016079 $16.95 AVAILABLE NOW

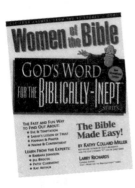

Women of the Bible—God's Word for the Biblically-Inept™

Kathy Collard Miller   TITLE CODE: GWWB

Finally, a Bible perspective just for women! Gain valuable insight from the successes and struggles of such women as Eve, Esther, Mary, Sarah, and Rebekah. Interesting icons like "Get Close to God," "Build Your Spirit," and "Grow Your Marriage" will make it easy to incorporate God's Word into your daily life.

(trade paper) ISBN 0914984063 $16.95 AVAILABLE NOW

Health & Nutrition—God's Word for the Biblically-Inept™

Kathleen O'Bannon Baldinger TITLE CODE: GWHN

The Bible is full of God's rules for good health! Kathleen O'Bannon Baldinger reveals scientific evidence that proves that the diet and health principles outlined in the Bible are the best for total health. Experts include Pamela Smith, Julian Whitaker, Kenneth Cooper, and T. D. Jakes.

(trade paper) ISBN 0914984055 $16.95 AVAILABLE NOW

Life of Christ, Volume 1—God's Word for the Biblically-Inept™

Robert C. Girard TITLE CODE: GWLC

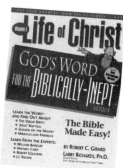

Girard takes the reader on an easy-to-understand journey through the gospels of Matthew, Mark, Luke, and John tracing the story of Jesus from his virgin birth to his revolutionary ministry. Icons, illustrations, chapter overviews, study questions, and more make learning about Jesus' baptism, the Sermon on the Mount, and his miracles and parables easier than ever.

(trade paper) ISBN 1892016230 $16.95 AVAILABLE MARCH 2000

Purchasing Information

www.starburstpublishers.com

Books are available from your favorite bookstore, either from current stock or special order. To assist bookstores in locating your selection, be sure to give title, author, and ISBN. If unable to purchase from a bookstore, you may order direct from STARBURST PUBLISHERS. When ordering please enclose full payment plus shipping and handling as follows:

Post Office (4th class)
$3.00 with a purchase of up to $20.00
$4.00 ($20.01–$50.00)
5% of purchase price for purchases of $50.01 and up

Canada
$5.00 (up to $35.00)
15% ($35.01 and up)

United Parcel Service (UPS)
$4.50 (up to $20.00)
$6.00 ($20.01–$50.00)
7% ($50.01 and up)

Overseas
$5.00 (up to $25.00)
20% ($25.01 and up)

Payment in U.S. funds only. Please allow two to three weeks minimum (longer overseas) for delivery. Make checks payable to and mail to:

Starburst Publishers® • P.O. Box 4123 • Lancaster, PA 17604

Credit card orders may be placed by calling 1-800-441-1456, Mon.–Fri., 8:30 A.M. to 5:30 P.M. Eastern Standard Time. Prices are subject to change without notice. Catalogs are available for a 9 x 12 self-addressed envelope with four first-class stamps.

New Titles Are Coming!

Starburst Publishers plans to continue adding to the *God's Word for the Biblically-Inept*™ series. Look for the following future titles:

- **Romans**
- **Acts**
- **Mark**
- **Ezekiel**

What's in the Bible for . . .™

From the creators of the *God's Word for the Biblically-Inept™* series comes the innovative *What's in the Bible for . . .™* series. Scripture has certain things to say to certain people, but without a guide, hunting down *all* of what the Bible has to say to you can be overwhelming. Borrowing the user-friendly format of the *God's Word for the Biblically-Inept™* series, this new series spotlights those passages and themes of Scripture that are relevent to particular groups of people. Whether you're young or old, married or single, male or female, this series will simplify the very important process of applying the Bible to your life.

What's in the Bible for . . .™ Women

Georgia Curtis Ling

TITLE CODE: WBFW

What does the Bible have to say to women? Women of all ages will find biblical insight on topics that are meaningful to them in six simple sections including Faith, Family, Friends, Fellowship, Freedom, and Femininity. This book uses illustrations, bullet points, chapter summaries, and icons to make understanding God's Word easier than ever!

(trade paper) ISBN 1892016109 $16.95   AVAILABLE NOW

What's in the Bible for . . .™ Mothers

Judy Bodmer

TITLE CODE: WBFM

Is home schooling a good idea? Is it okay to work? At what age should I start treating my children like responsible adults? What is the most important thing I can teach my children? If you are asking these questions and need help answering them, *What's in the Bible for. . .™ Mothers* is especially for you! Simple and user-friendly, this motherhood manual offers hope and instruction for today's mothers by jumping into the lives of mothers in the Bible (e.g., Naomi, Elizabeth, and Mary) and by exploring biblical principles that are essential to being a nurturing mother.

(trade paper) ISBN 1892016265 $16.95   AVAILABLE MAY 2000

What's in the Bible for . . .™ Teens

TITLE CODE: WBFT

Mark and Jeanette Littleton

What's in the Bible for. . .™ Teens contains topical Bible themes that parallel the challenges and pressures of today's adolescents. Learn about Bible Prophecy, God and Relationships, and Peer Pressure in a conversational and fun tone. Helpful and eye-catching "WWJD?" icons, illustrations, and sidebars included.

(trade paper) ISBN 1892016052 $16.95   AVAILABLE OCTOBER 2000

• **Learn more at www.biblicallyinept.com** •

What Readers Tell Us . . .

"Congratulations on an outstanding piece of work! I look forward to seeing the entire *Biblically-Inept™* series. I absolutely love it!"

—Ken Abraham, *best-selling author*

"Fantastic! What a fascinating approach to presenting the book of Revelation. It makes studying Bible prophecy easy, exciting, and interesting for everybody. Good content, great quotes, dynamic graphics. This book has more 'bells and whistles' than anything I've ever seen. It's user-friendly to the max!"

—Dr. Ed Hindson, *Assistant Pastor,*
Rehoboth Baptist Church, and best-selling author

"I am currently involved in studying the book of Revelation and find your study guide very informative, concise, and helpful. It makes reading and understanding the book of Revelation easier . . ."

—Jeffrey, *Bloomington, Indiana*

"The Revelation book arrived this morning. I spent a few minutes glancing through it and am confident that you have a winner. The layout—the artwork—the interaction are marvelous. . . . I AM IMPRESSED!"

—Dan Penwell, *Manager, Trade Products,*
Hendrickson Publishers

"I am writing to voice my approval of Starburst Publishers' *God's Word for the Biblically-Inept™* series. I have three books in the series: THE BIBLE, DANIEL, and REVELATION. . . . I hope Starburst Publishers continues to add to the *God's Word for the Biblically-Inept™* series. Ideally, I would like the series to include 67 books—one for each book of the Bible, plus your already published [books] . . . May I compliment you for this new, interesting, and easy-to-understand series."

—Wayne, *Burr Oak, Kansas*

CHAPTERS AT A GLANCE

Part I: Prophecies in the Old Testament

Part II: Prophecies in the New Testament

ILLUSTRATIONS

INTRODUCTION

Welcome to *Prophecies—God's Word for the Biblically-Inept*. This is the third book by Daymond R. Duck (**Revelation** was his first; **Daniel** was his second) in a new series that takes the Bible and makes it fun and educational. This is not the usual book on Bible prophecy. It is a REVOLUTIONARY COMMENTARY™ that will change your outlook on Bible prophecy forever. You *will* Learn the Word™!

Let's Get Started

(Let's Get Started)

To Gain Your Confidence

Dr. Bob Jones Sr. said, "Simplicity is truth's most becoming garb." I wholeheartedly agree. Complicated speech is an unnecessary barrier that often stands in the way of my comprehension. Nothing is more worthless to me than a book filled with big theological terms and words I do not understand.

Prophecies—God's Word for the Biblically-Inept is for those who are not interested in all that complicated stuff. You can be sure that I have tried to take an educational approach, but much effort has gone into keeping things simple. Accuracy is my first consideration, but naturalness and simplicity ranks right up there with it. I don't want the truth to be hidden by speech that only theologians use.

> **Genesis 1:1** In the beginning God created the heavens

(Verse of Scripture)

A Word About Prophecy

Prophecy is what God says about the future. He is the only one who can predict things to come before they happen. Prophecy is unique because it reveals God's plans. He is unique because he can and will do what he says. There is something he wants us to know about this. He says, *"Remember the former things, those of long ago; I am God, and there is no other; I am God, and there is none like me. I make known the end from the beginning, from ancient times,*

THE BIG PICTURE

> **Genesis 1:1–2:3** The Bible begins, "In the beginning..."

(The Big Picture)

☞ **GO TO:**

Matthew 9:14–15
(fasting)

(Go To)

what is still to come. I say: My purpose will stand, and I will do all that I please" (Isaiah 46:9–10). Simply put, God knows the future. It is in his hands. What he says is prophecy. And what he says cannot be altered.

During Bible times God called men of high character to write down his words. These special men had a very close relationship with him. What they wrote flowed from God through them by the Holy Spirit's power. Their words are nothing more and nothing less than the inspired or dictated Word of God. God was the originator and men were the recorders. And the parts that deal with future events are called prophecy.

The Bible was recorded by approximately forty different writers over a period of several hundred years. They recorded it in sixty-six volumes, called books, which are broken down into two sections: an "Old" Testament of thirty-nine books and a "New" Testament of twenty-seven books. Centuries later, scholars took what the writers had recorded and divided the text into chapters and verses.

All of those who recorded God's words were Jews except possibly Luke. He was definitely a scholar in Jewish matters, but some authorities believe he was Greek by ancestry. As much as forty percent of what they wrote is prophecy. In this book I have addressed the issues that seem to be of most interest to people today.

KEY POINT

When we acknowledge our guilt and trust Jesus as Savior, God forgives our sins freely and completely.

(Key Point)

A Word About Prophets

There is a plague of false prophets today and we must not trust these false prophets to give us the truth or even a valid interpretation of the truth. Unfortunately, many who claim to speak for God do more to hide the truth than to reveal it. Some pose as theologians, seminary professors, and even preachers, but their prophetic understanding appears to be no greater than that of the average newspaper astrologer or the local tabloid psychic.

We should always keep in mind the stern biblical warning not to add to or take anything away from what it says (Deuteronomy 4:2; 12:32; Proverbs 30:6; Revelation 22:18–19). Those who are not careful to do this violate a fundamental teaching of the Bible. A person speaking from a deep understanding of God will say nothing to contradict the Word of God. But a person speaking for the wrong reason will say much that runs counter to the truth. As the Bible says, God *"frustrates the words of the unfaithful"* (Proverbs 22:12).

"What is truth?" Pontius Pilate asked Jesus (John 18:38). This is

RELATED CURRENT EVENTS

(Related Current Events)

a good question, but Pilate was not asking Jesus because he wanted to know the answer. Pilate was a cynic, and he was implying that truth is whatever those in authority want it to be. But truth is not what a high-profile person or what those in authority say it is. Truth is the Bible. When Jesus prayed, he said, *"Your word is truth"* (John 17:17). And the bottom line is that the only modern-day prophet worth listening to is the one who sticks to the Bible. Such a speaker or teacher believes the Word and glorifies God.

A Word About Timing

When we think about prophecy, we usually think of the future. But first there are four important questions worth exploring.

    *First, are prophecies fulfilled **literally**?* I interpret the Bible literally in its plain sense. Others who write or speak on prophecies may interpret the Bible in **symbolic or allegorical** ways. Such people believe the prophetic passages are just great ideas or timeless truths, and they wonder what the fuss is about.

    Second, what prophecies have already been fulfilled? Some prophecies, such as the First Coming of Jesus, have been fulfilled. I believe other prophecies, such as the Church Age, are being fulfilled now, and still other prophecies are for the future. Some Bible experts disagree; they believe all prophecy has already been fulfilled.

    Third, what prophecies have not been fulfilled? The Second Coming of Christ is one prophecy that has not yet happened. I believe the Tribulation Period has not yet occurred. Other Bible scholars think the famines, earthquakes, and floods we are experiencing today are those predicted in the Bible. Still other scholars believe nothing is currently being fulfilled. For them, it's all about the future.

    Fourth, when and how will the unfulfilled prophecies be fulfilled? I believe that on some occasions the Bible gives enough information to know the exact time a prophecy was, or will be, fulfilled. On other occasions it provides enough clues to place the prophecy in a certain time period—even if we don't know the exact day or hour that time period will arrive.

    One other thing about timing: some prophecies are referred to as "double fulfillment" or "double reference" prophecies. This does not mean they will be fulfilled more than once or over and over again, nor does it mean they have more than one meaning or can be interpreted in more than one way. Rather, double fulfillment or double reference means that part of the prophecy refers to one event or time period and part of it refers to a different event or time period. There is wide agreement among conservative proph-

KEY Symbols:

Dry Bones
Jews in foreign lands

One Stick
Israel will not be divided

(Key Symbols)

literally: understanding words to mean exactly what they say

symbolic or allegorical: understanding words to refer to something other than their usual meaning

(What?)

Fulfillment

(Fulfillment)

What Others are Saying:

(What Others Are Saying)

ecy experts that every prophecy will be totally fulfilled, but some prophecies will go through phases or stages before that happens. We also agree that one phase may be in one time period and another phase in a different time period, and the length of time between the two may range from the blink of an eye to thousands of years.

The Fulfillment Feature

This book moves from one prophecy to the next from Genesis to Revelation. At the end of my discussion about each prophecy, I have used something called the Fulfillment feature. The Fulfillment feature does two things.

(Remember This)

1. It tells you whether the prophecy is fulfilled, unfulfilled, partially fulfilled, or continuously being fulfilled.

2. It gives you more detail about when the prophecy was, is being, or will be fulfilled.

Continuously Being Fulfilled
First Coming
Second Coming
Millennium

The fulfilled prophecies confirm that God inspired the Scriptures. They can also be cited as evidence that the remaining prophecies will be literally fulfilled at God's chosen time.

Symbols, Symbols, And More Symbols

The Bible is filled with symbols, but we don't have to guess what they mean because they are often interpreted for us. Some symbols are explained within the context of the prophecy. Others are explained in a different passage of Scripture. I believe God did this to make us study the entire Bible. You do not need a Ph.D. to understand symbolism. You only need to search the Scriptures.

Something to Ponder

(Something to Ponder)

Why Use The New International Version (NIV)?

I have looked at the prophecies in the Bible as the experts would, but I have also written this book in an easy-to-understand manner. That's why I chose to use the *New International Version* (NIV) of the Bible, a scholarly translation that accurately expresses the original Bible in clear and contemporary English, while remain-

WARNING

(Warning)

Remember This . . .

ing faithful to the thoughts of biblical writers.

Why Study Bible Prophecy?

We are living in perilous times. Quite often, the explanations of New Age astrologers, channelers, mystics, and psychics are being treated with respect. With regularity, the false doctrines and false prophecies of cults are valued more than the true doctrines and true prophecies of Christianity. Here are ten good reasons to study *Prophecies—God's Word for the Biblically-Inept*:

1. The Bible prophets received their messages from God, so what they said is the Word of God.
2. The accuracy of Bible prophecy proves the divine inspiration of the Scriptures.
3. Bible prophecy teaches us many things about God, politics, and faith.
4. Bible prophecy gives us assurance and hope in difficult or uncertain times.
5. Bible prophecy promotes evangelism, causes us to witness, and moves us to pray.
6. Bible prophecy aids perseverance during trials.
7. Bible prophecy causes us to watch for things to be fulfilled.
8. Knowing Bible prophecy increases our ability to help others.
9. Because so much Bible prophecy has already been literally fulfilled, we can logically expect the rest to be literally fulfilled.
10. If we do not study Bible prophecy, our understanding of the entire Bible will remain biblically inept.

How To Use *Prophecies—God's Word for the Biblically-Inept*

This book is divided into two main parts corresponding to the two main divisions of the Bible: Prophecies in the **Old Testament** and Prophecies in the **New Testament**. Part One is subdivided into five chapters: Prophecies in the Pentateuch, Prophecies in the Books of History, Prophecies in the Books of Poetry, Prophecies in the Major Prophets, and Prophecies in the Minor Prophets. Part Two is subdivided into four chapters: Prophecies in the Gospels and Acts, Prophecies in the Letters Written by the Apostle Paul, Prophecies in the Letters Written by Other Apostles, and

Dig Deeper

(Dig Deeper)

Study Questions

(Study Questions)

Old Testament: a collection of the first 39 books of the Bible, the oldest section of the Bible

New Testament: a collection of the last 27 books of the Bible, all written in the 60 years following Jesus' death

Prophecies in Revelation (see GWBI, pages 2, 148).

The Features

This book contains a number of features that will help you learn. They're illustrated in the sidebar of this introduction. Here is a list of descriptions for each of them.

Sections and Icons	What's It For?
CHAPTER HIGHLIGHTS	the most prominent points of the chapter
Let's Get Started	a chapter warm-up
Verse of Scripture	what you came for—the Bible
THE BIG PICTURE	summarizes passages and shows where they fit in the Bible
Commentary	my thoughts on what the verses mean
GO TO:	other Bible verses to help you better understand (underlined in text)
What?	the meaning of a word (bold in text)
KEY POINT	major point of the chapter
What Others are Saying:	if you don't believe me, listen to the experts
Illustrations	a picture is worth a thousand words
Remember This . . .	don't forget this
Something to Ponder	interesting points to get you thinking
Warning	red lights to keep you from danger
Dig Deeper	find out more from the Bible
RELATED CURRENT EVENTS	tidbits from today's news
KEY Symbols	quick guide to the symbols
Fulfillment	lets you know when and how a prophecy is fulfilled.
Study Questions	questions to get you discussing, studying, and digging deeper
CHAPTER WRAP-UP	the most prominent points revisited

A Word About Words

There are several interchangeable terms: Scripture, Scriptures, Word, Word of God, God's Word, Book, etc. All of these mean the same thing and come under the broad heading called the Bible. I will use each one at various times, but I will use "Bible" most of the time.

The word "Lord" in the Old Testament refers to Yahweh, God, whereas in the New Testament it refers to God's Son, Jesus Christ.

Tips To Help You

The Bible was written for all people, and God wants everyone to understand it. He even wants everyone to understand Bible prophecy. The Holy Spirit can do wonders to help you. Here are ten tips:

1. Begin with prayer.
2. Do not forget that God is infallible, and he does not make mistakes.
3. Do not forget that God is all-powerful, and he can do anything he wants to do.
4. Do not forget that God cannot lie, so what he says will be fulfilled exactly as he says.
5. Unless it is clear that symbols are being used, the prophecy should be interpreted literally.
6. When it is clear that a symbol is being used, find another passage of Scripture that interprets the symbol.
7. Look for normal, common sense interpretations, not bizarre explanations.
8. Remember that some prophecies are about individuals (e.g., the Antichrist), some are about groups (e.g., the 144,000), some are about cities (e.g., Bethlehem), some are about nations (e.g., Russia), and some are about world empires (e.g., Babylon). But most prophecies are about one of three main groups: Israel (the Jews), the Gentiles (the non-Jews), and the **Church** (Christians). The common thread in most prophecies is the Messiah (Jesus).
9. Remember that there are several different gatherings and destructions of Israel, several different rises and falls of Gentile nations, and two comings of Jesus.
10. Remember that some prophecy is sealed up and cannot be understood until God is ready to reveal it.

Church: the followers of Jesus Christ, as opposed to the building where people meet to worship

Bible Quote: This is where you'll read a quote from the Bible.

James 1:5 If any of you lacks wisdom, he should ask God, who gives generously to all without finding fault, and it will be given to him.

Decisions, Decisions: In Or Out?

James, the brother of Jesus, is writing to the new believers who were scattered about the Roman world (see GWBI, pages 213–214) when they fled from persecution. James knows that godly wisdom is a great gift. He gives a simple plan to get it: if you n~~eed~~ wisdom, ask for it. God will give it to us.

Up 'til now we've concentrated on finding the wind ~~to fill the~~ sails of your drifting marriage and overcoming marital pro~~blems.~~ But you may be the reader who is shaking her head, thinking ~~that~~ I just don't understand what you're going through. You can't take the abuse any longer; you've forgiven the **infidelity** time after time; and in order for you and your children to survive, you see no alternative but divorce.

So let m~~e~~

husband ~~...~~ get out a~~nd~~ ~~...~~ your abuse sec~~...~~ ~~...conti~~nues, ing to you; they are also harmful to your children's physical and emotional state.

Commentary: This is where you'll read commentary about the biblical quote.

"What?": When you see a word in bold, go to the sidebar for a definition.

infidelity: sexual unfaithfulness of a spouse

Go To: When you see a word or phrase that's underlined, go to the sidebar for a biblical cross-reference.

☞ **GO TO:**

Psalm 111:10 (source)

When you feel you've depleted all of your options, continue to ask God for wisdom in order to have the knowledge to make the right decisions. Wise women seek God. God is the <u>source</u> of wisdom and wisdom is found in Christ and the Word.

Remember This . . .

Gary Chapman, Ph.D.: Is there hope for women who suffe~~r~~ physical abuse from their husbands? Does reality living offer ~~any~~ genuine hope? I believe the answer to those questions is y~~es~~.[6]

Give It Away

You don't have to be a farmer to understand what the Apostle Paul wrote to the Corinthian church (see illustration, page 143). A picture is worth a thousand words, and Paul is painting a master-piece. He reminds us of what any smart farmer knows: in order to produce a bountiful harvest, he has to plan for it.

What Others are Saying:

What Others Are Saying: This is where you'll read what an expert has to say about the subject at hand.

MEN OF POWER: LESSONS IN MIGHT AND MISSTEPS 9

127

Feature with icon in the sidebar: Throughout the book you will see sections of text with corresponding icons in the sidebar. See the chart on page xx for a description of all the features in this book.

Part One

PROPHECIES IN THE OLD TESTAMENT

Reverend Fun

When God stopped communicating through burning bushes.

☞ **GO TO:**

Revelation 6:1–7 (famine)

1 Thessalonians 4:13–18 (still alive)

Two Kinds Of Prophecy

This book is about prophecies—**fulfilled** and **unfulfilled**. The fulfilled prophecies are identified and we know when their fulfillment took place. The unfulfilled prophecies are identified too, but we only have a general idea about when they will be fulfilled. We don't know the day or the hour, but we do know when they will be fulfilled in relation to other events. These events have special names: **Tribulation Period**, **Rapture**, **Second Coming**, and **Millennium**.

Tribulation Period

Jesus was prophesying about the end of the age when he said, *"For then there will be great distress, unequaled from the beginning of the world until now—and never to be equaled again"* (Matthew 24:21). Contrary to what some say, the world is not moving toward a **New World Order** characterized by peace, cooperation and prosperity. It is plunging toward distress characterized by calamities such as war, famine, **pestilence**, natural disasters, and death. This future period of distress is called the Tribulation Period. According to the Bible, the Tribulation Period will be seven years long and the last 3½ years are called the **Great Tribulation Period** (**KJV**) or the period of great distress (**NIV**). More is said about this later under the discussion of Daniel's prophecies (see also GWDN, pages 256–257).

Rapture

There is wide agreement among those who study Bible prophecy that several passages of Scripture teach a future resurrection of deceased church members, a sudden gathering of those who are still alive at that time, and a "catching away" of these people into heaven. This expected "catching away" is usually called the Rapture. Some call it the Rapture of the Church. But while there is wide agreement that the Rapture will happen, there are different opinions about when it will happen in relation to the Tribulation Period. Most experts believe the Rapture will occur before the Tribulation Period. Their belief is called the Pre-Tribulation Rapture Theory. A small minority of experts believe the Rapture will occur at the middle of the Tribulation Period and their belief is called the Mid-Tribulation Rapture Theory. Another group believes the Rapture will occur at the end of the Tribulation Period and their belief is called the Post-Tribulation Rapture Theory. This book

Rapture Theories

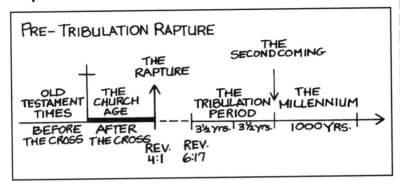

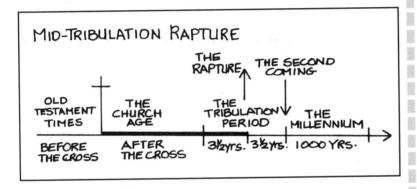

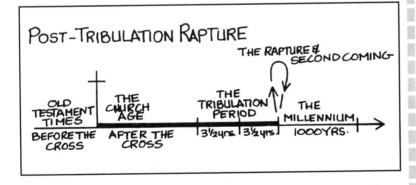

agrees with the majority by taking the Pre-Tribulation Rapture position. The diagrams on this page should help you understand these concepts.

KEY POINT

The word *Rapture* is
not in the English
translations of the
Bible, but the concept
is.

☞ **GO TO:**

John 1:29
(sin of the world)

John 14:1–4; Acts 1:11
(back)

*Premillennialism: Christ
will return before his
thousand-year reign*

☞ **GO TO:**

Revelation 20:1–7
(thousand)

The word *Rapture* is not in the English translations of the Bible, but the concept is. The first New Testament texts were written in Greek, and the Greek word *harpazo*, meaning "suddenly taken away by an irresistible force," was used. When the Greek texts were translated into Latin, *harpazo* was replaced by the Latin word *rapere*. When the Latin texts were translated into English, a problem arose: *harpazo* and *rapere* wouldn't translate into just one English word. So instead of using an awkward combination, they have taken the Latin word *rapere* and Anglicized it into the word *Rapture*.

Second Coming

Two of the most important events mentioned in the Bible are the two comings of Jesus: the first to die for the <u>sin of the world</u>, and the second to put an end to all sin. That's right, Jesus is coming <u>back</u> to put an end to Satan's influence here on earth. He will bind Satan, restore Israel, renew this creation, and reign here on earth for awhile. Earth will be a wonderful place to live once again.

Millennium

It is important to know what the Millennium is because this book discusses prophecies being fulfilled in relation to that period of time. But understanding the Millennium gets confusing because there are three different beliefs about it: Premillennialism, Amillennialism, and Postmillennialism. All three include the Second Coming of Christ and believe the saved will spend eternity with God.

Premillennialism was the first belief to appear, historically speaking. The word millennium is Latin and it means "a thousand years." A <u>thousand</u>-year reign of Christ is mentioned six times in the book of Revelation. Putting "Pre" in front of millennium suggests Christ will return before the thousand-year reign. By interpreting the Scriptures literally, the early Church came to the conclusion that Jesus will return to earth, destroy Israel's enemies, establish a kingdom, sit on the throne of David in Jerusalem, and rule over the world for a thousand years. Under his rule, all of the covenants with Israel will be literally fulfilled during that thousand-year reign; and peace, justice, and righteousness will prevail over the earth. Premillennialists believe that in the distant future

Millennium Theories	Church Age	Rapture	Tribulation	Millennium
Premillennialism	Now	Before Tribulation	After Rapture	Second Coming ushers in kingdom with Jesus on throne in Jerusalem
Amillennialism	Now	Occurs with Second Coming	Not applicable	No earthly kingdom
Postmillennialism	Now and getting better	None	Not applicable	Before the Second Coming

after the kingdom is purged of sin, Jesus will turn it over to the Father, and it will be merged with his kingdom. This is the view of many conservative Protestants and is the one set forth in this book.

Amillennialism appeared about three hundred years after Premillennialism. Putting an "A" in front of the word millennium means "no millennium" or "no thousand years." Those who embrace Amillennialism believe all the prophecies about Israel refer to the Church, that the kingdom is the Church, that the Millennium is the Church Age, and that the New Earth is heaven. They believe Satan was bound at the first coming of Jesus. Instead of Jesus coming to sit on the throne of David in Jerusalem to rule over the world, they believe we are in the Millennium (Church Age) now and Jesus is ruling over the earth through the Church. For them the Rapture is the Second Coming. This is the view of most Catholics and liberal Protestants.

Postmillennialism did not surface until the seventeenth century. This belief ignores or explains away most prophecies. Postmillennialsim suggests that the world is constantly getting better, that the whole world will eventually be **Christianized**, and that Christ will not come back until it is. Postmillennialism means Christ will return after the Millennium, after the world is Christianized. Instead of Christ coming to establish his kingdom, Postmillennialists believe the church is building that kingdom. This belief almost died out in the mid-twentieth century, but is making a comeback under the names of Dominion Now, Dominion Theology, and Reconstructionism.

Amillennialism: the thousand-year reign has been replaced by the Church Age

Postmillennialism: Christ will return after his thousand-year reign (Church Age)

Christianized: converted to Christianity

1 PROPHECIES IN THE PENTATEUCH

CHAPTER HIGHLIGHTS

- Corruption on Earth
- Covenants with the Patriarchs
- The Coming Ruler
- Choices for Israel
- The Coming Tribulation Period

Let's Get Started

The first five books of the Old Testament are often called the **Pentateuch**. The word Pentateuch is a combination of two Greek words meaning five books or five scrolls. These five books are the oldest books in the Bible. Most authorities believe God gave the information contained therein to an Israelite leader named **Moses** (see illustration, page 8). Moses recorded the information in the form of a continuous story beginning with Creation and ending with his death.[1]

Some other names for the Pentateuch are the Law, the Law of Moses, the Mosaic Law, and the **Torah**. The word Torah is Hebrew and it means instruction, guidance, or Law. Devout Jews believe the Pentateuch contains laws given by God. Devout Christians believe it also contains prophecies given by him. Christians also believe Moses was a prophet and every little detail of what he prophesied will be fulfilled. Jesus says, *"Do not think that I have come to abolish the Law or the Prophets; I have not come to abolish them but to fulfill them. I tell you the truth, until heaven and earth disappear, not the smallest letter, not the least stroke of a pen, will by any means disappear from the Law until everything is accomplished"* (Matthew 5:17–18).

Pentateuch: the first five books of the Old Testament

Moses: the first prophet

Torah: Pentateuch, Law of Moses, Mosaic Law

☞ **GO TO:**

Exodus 3:1–22 (Moses)

Luke 24:44 (Law of Moses)

Deuteronomy 34:10–12 (prophet)

BIRTH | MOSES IN PHAROAH'S PALACE | MOSES IN EXILE IN MIDIAN | MOSES IN THE WILDERNESS | DEATH

1525 B.C.   1485 B.C.   1445 B.C.   1405 B.C.

The Life of Moses

Moses' life may be divided into three periods of forty years. He spent each period in a different place.

What Others are Saying:

KEY POINT

Every detail of Moses' prophecies must be fulfilled.

Something to Ponder

☞ **GO TO:**

Deuteronomy 34:1–12 (died)

Mark 10:27 (possible)

Larry Richards: The Old Testament is a collection of 39 books, which were written between 1450 B.C. and 400 B.C. They tell the story of God's special relationship with one human family, the family of Abraham, Isaac, and Jacob, which became the Jewish people. Through this people God revealed himself to all mankind. And through this people God set in motion a plan to save all who would believe in him from the terrible consequences of sin.[2]

Some critics say Moses could not be the author of the first five books of the Bible because the fifth book provides information about things that happened after he <u>died</u>, for example the inclusions about Moses' death. But Jesus told us things about his own death before he died, that he would be killed and raised from the dead three days later. It is possible that Moses was able to foresee his own death experience. Jesus said, *"all things are <u>possible</u> with God."* This doesn't prove Moses wrote the first five books of the Bible, but it does mean the critics could be wrong.

GENESIS

Genesis 3:14–19 So the LORD God said to the serpent, "Because you have done this, Cursed are you above all the livestock and all the wild animals! You will crawl on your belly and you will eat dust all the days of your life. And I will put enmity between you and the woman, and between your offspring and hers; he will crush your head, and you will strike his heel." To the woman he said, "I will greatly increase your pains in childbearing; with pain you will give birth to children. Your desire will be for your husband, and he will rule over you."

> To Adam he said, "Because you listened to your wife and ate from the tree about which I commanded you, 'You must not eat of it,' Cursed is the ground because of you; through painful toil you will eat of it all the days of your life. It will produce thorns and thistles for you, and you will eat the plants of the field. By the sweat of your brow you will eat your food until you return to the ground, since from it you were taken; for dust you are and to dust you will return."

Life In A Nutshell

Some call this the first prophecy in the Bible. When God <u>created</u> Adam and Eve, he placed them in a beautiful place called the <u>Garden of Eden</u>. He had created many different trees and he told them they could eat from any tree in the garden except <u>the Tree</u> of the Knowledge of Good and Evil (see GWHN, page 4). They disobeyed and that is sin; sin always has a price. God decreed seven **judgments** because of <u>sin</u>:

1. Satan is cursed for as long as he lives.
2. Satan's head will ultimately be crushed.
3. Throughout history there will be conflict between the serpent's **offspring** and the woman's offspring, between good and evil.
4. Throughout history women will undergo pain during childbirth.
5. Throughout history women will have to <u>submit</u> to their husbands.
6. Throughout history men will have to work to feed themselves.
7. Throughout history human beings will die.

☞ GO TO:

Genesis 2:4–7 (created)

Genesis 2:15 (Garden of Eden)

Genesis 2:16–17 (the Tree)

Romans 5:12 (sin)

Ephesians 5:24 (submit)

judgments: acts of God intended to punish

offspring: children, descendants, that which comes from something

Wayne Barber, Eddie Rasnake, and Richard Shepherd: Sin had shattered the oneness with God that they had experienced. Instead of a oneness with God there was division and running away from God. Instead of honesty between themselves and their Creator, there was blame and excuses. The oneness between Adam and Eve was gone as well. In its place were separation, accusations, and disharmony. With Adam's disobedience, sin entered the human race. Instead of life and oneness with God, they experienced death and separation.[3]

What Others are Saying:

Ed Hindson: Satan's doom is already assured, but the battle is far from being over. He still "prowls around like a roaring lion looking for someone to devour" (1 Peter 5:8). He has fallen from heaven (Isaiah 14:2). He was condemned in Eden (Genesis 3:14). He accuses the believers (Revelation 12:10). Eventually he will be cast out of heaven permanently and will expend his wrath on earth (Revelation 12:7–12). Ultimately he will be defeated at **Armageddon** and cast into the abyss (Revelation 19:11–20:3). Finally he will be thrown into the lake of fire (Revelation 20:10). . . . He may be a defeated foe, but he has every intention of keeping up the fight to the very end.[4]

Armageddon: a great battle between good and evil at the Second Coming

In the NIV this passage reads, "woman's offspring," but the KJV says "woman's seed." Men have seed (sperm), but there is no such thing as a "woman's seed." Therefore, many scholars say the "woman's seed" predicts a miracle birth. And the miracle birth they have in mind is the virgin birth of Jesus. This is why this prophecy is called "the first **messianic** prophecy in the Bible."

Remember This . . .

messianic: having to do with the Messiah

Because we have anesthetics, painkillers, well-equipped hospitals, etc., childbirth is less painful in this country than it once was. But these modern conveniences have only been available for the last few decades. Most are not available at all in many foreign countries. After thousands of years, this prophecy is still true.

Something to Ponder

Fulfillment: This prophecy is continually being fulfilled, but it will not be completely fulfilled until some point after the Millennium. Satan suffered a major defeat when Jesus died on the cross to take away our sin. The curse will be suspended during the thousand years of the Millennium when Satan is bound (Revelation 20:2), but he will be set free again for an unspecified length of time (Revelation 20:3). Following that, Satan will die the second death when he is thrown into the Lake of Fire and this prophecy will be completely fulfilled (see GWRV, page 34).

Continuously Being Fulfilled
After the Millennium

It is encouraging to know that Jesus will ultimately defeat Satan. But we should also know that the struggle between good and evil, the woman's offspring and Satan's offspring, will be a long drawn-out affair. The judgment of God is sure, but he is very patient.

☞ **GO TO:**

Revelation 20:14
(second death)

Revelation 20:10 (Lake)

KEY POINT

Satan will die the second death.

> **Genesis 6:11–13** Now the earth was corrupt in God's sight and was full of violence. God saw how corrupt the earth had become, for all the people on earth had corrupted their ways. So God said to Noah, "I am going to put an end to all people, for the earth is filled with violence because of them. I am surely going to destroy both them and the earth."

In The Days Of Noah

Adam and Eve's sin was the beginning of a moral crisis on earth. Their son Cain <u>killed</u> his brother Abel. Cain left the <u>presence</u> of God and moved away and society worsened. When Cain's great-great-great-grandson Lamech came on the scene, he was a **polygamist** married to <u>two women</u>. And by Noah's day, almost two thousand years after Adam, great **wickedness** covered the earth. So God decided to destroy his creation with a flood (see GWBI, pages 9–11).

Bruce A. Tanner: Sin is not only a degenerative disease but also a contagious one. Like gravity, sin can be expected to exert a continuous downward pull on individuals and on society. It did not take fallen man long to learn the ways of sin.[5]

Wayne Barber, Eddie Rasnake, and Richard Shepherd: Noah was not a perfect man, but he revered God, and out of that reverence flowed obedience. Out of Noah's obedience came Noah's stake in the righteousness of faith. It really is a remarkable thought that it is not my good moral behavior that shapes my righteousness, but my faith—my willingness to trust God, and take Him at His word.[6]

Robert T. Boyd: There are no fewer than thirty-three separate records from distinctly different people groups that tell of a world-wide flood. The similarities between these accounts and Moses' description of the flood in Noah's time are remarkable.[7]

Some say the flood was a local flood limited just to the Middle East. If that is true, how is it that Noah's Ark came to rest near the top of a 17,000 foot mountain called <u>Ararat</u>?

☞ **GO TO:**

Genesis 4:8 (killed)

Genesis 4:16 (presence)

Genesis 4:19 (two women)

Genesis 6:5 (wickedness)

What Others are Saying:

polygamist: one who has more than one mate

wickedness: all sin

Something to Ponder

GO TO:

Genesis 8:1–4 (Ararat)

Remember This . . .

depraved: wicked, corrupt

☞ **GO TO:**

Numbers 14:18 (guilty)

Proverbs 6:16–19 (hates)

Fulfilled
Tribulation Period

KEY POINT

This promise applies to the entire world, not just to the nation of Israel.

sacrifice: death of a substitute in payment for sin

faith: trust in God

☞ **GO TO:**

Hebrews 11:6–7 (faith)

Revelation 21:1 (earth)

God is very loving, but he is also holy. He is very patient, but man is not free to do any evil thing he wants to do. God cannot and will not overlook the sin of a **depraved** society forever. He will punish the guilty. Here are seven things God hates:

1. Haughty eyes
2. A lying tongue
3. Hands that shed innocent blood
4. A heart that devises wicked schemes
5. Feet that are quick to rush into evil
6. A false witness who pours out lies
7. A man who stirs up dissension among brothers

Fulfillment: The flood portion of this prophecy has been fulfilled, but Jesus drew a comparison between the wickedness on earth during the days of Noah and that which will exist during the Tribulation Period just before the Second Coming. He said, *"As it was in the days of Noah, so it will be at the coming of the Son of Man. For in the days before the flood, people were eating and drinking, marrying and giving in marriage, up to the day Noah entered the ark; and they knew nothing about what would happen until the flood came and took them all away. That is how it will be at the coming of the Son of Man"* (Matthew 24:37–39). The bad news is that humankind is going to become more and more evil. But the good news is that Jesus is going to return and put an end to it.

> **Genesis 8:22** "As long as the earth endures, seedtime and harvest, cold and heat, summer and winter, day and night will never cease."

A Promise To Remember

Following the flood, Noah's first act was to build an altar and offer a **sacrifice** to God. He was specifically humbling himself, giving thanks to God for saving him and his family, and declaring his **faith**. God was pleased with this and promised that as long as the earth exists, there will always be seasons (see GWBI, pages 35–37).

We sometimes hear that one of the signs of the Second Coming will be, "winter the same as summer except for the budding of the trees," but the Bible does not say this. Furthermore, Genesis 8:22 contradicts it.

Fulfillment: This prophecy is continuously being fulfilled and it will continue to be fulfilled until the earth is destroyed sometime after the Millennium. Here God promises that seasons will always be distinct.

WARNING

Continuously Being Fulfilled

After the Millennium

> **Genesis 12:1–3** The Lord had said to Abram, "Leave your country, your people and your father's household and go to the land I will show you. I will make you into a great nation and I will bless you; I will make your name great, and you will be a blessing. I will bless those who bless you, and whoever curses you I will curse; and all peoples on earth will be blessed through you."

God's Covenant With Abram (Abraham)

God's **covenant** with <u>Abraham</u> is also called the Abrahamic Covenant. God said to Abraham:

- Leave your country (<u>Ur of the Chaldeans</u>).
- Leave your people (friends, relatives).
- Leave your father's house.
- Go to the land I will show you.

If Abraham would do these four things, God promised he would do seven things. Some scholars break these promises down into the following categories:

National Promise

- "I will make you into a great nation."

Personal Promises

- "I will bless you."
- "I will make your name great" (i.e., make you famous).
- "You will be a blessing" (i.e., a benefit to others).

World Promises

- "I will bless those who bless you."

covenant: an agreement between two parties

 GO TO:

Galatians 3:6–16 (Abraham)

Genesis 11:31 (Ur of the Chaldeans)

- "I will curse those who curse you" (the people and nations in the world who do evil to Abraham and his nation).
- "I will bless the whole world through you" (the Messiah will be a descendant of Abraham).

Dig Deeper

God's Covenants	Scripture
Edenic Covenant	Genesis 1:28–30; 2:15–17
Adamic Covenant	Genesis 3:14–19
Noahic Covenant	Genesis 8:20–9:17
Abrahamic Covenant	Genesis 12:1–3; 13:14–15, 17
Mosaic Covenant	Exodus 20–23
Davidic Covenant	2 Samuel 7:4–17; Psalm 89:3–4
Palestinian Covenant	Deuteronomy 30:1–10
New Covenant	Jeremiah 31:31–40; Hebrews 8:6–13

What Others are Saying:

grace: *undeserved favor from God*

prophets: *people through whom God speaks and guides choices*

Scripture: *verses in the Holy Bible*

apostles: *people who have personally seen Jesus*

Wayne Barber, Eddie Rasnake, and Richard Shepherd: One would look in vain for an explanation of why he [Abraham] was selected for God's purposes. The only answer we have is that by **grace**, God sought him out. God had a unique purpose for Abraham's life. He called him from a pagan culture to make a new nation—one that would follow God.[8]

John F. Walvoord: Blessing has come to Israel and to the world as a whole through the **prophets**, through the writers of **Scripture**, through the **apostles**, and preeminently through Jesus Christ. Blessings which God has promised Abraham have been showered on the recipients through many centuries up to the present time and will continue until the end of human history.[9]

Henry M. Morris with Henry M. Morris III: The nations that have befriended the Jews (notably the United States and, to a lesser degree, England, France, and others) have indeed been blessed. Those that have persecuted the Jews (Egypt, Babylon, Assyria, Rome, Spain, Nazi Germany, and others—Russia's time is coming!) have eventually gone down to defeat and humiliation.[10]

☞ **GO TO:**

Genesis 12:6–7 (Canaan)

Canaan: *Israel*

Russell L. Penney: Abraham was truly blessed just as God had promised. As well, a great nation emerged from Abraham (Genesis 12:2), and to that nation God gave the promise of the land of **Canaan** (Genesis 12:7; 13:5; 15:18–21; 17:7–8). Through

Abraham have also come blessings to all nations. In addition to giving us God's Word, it was Abraham's descendant Jesus Christ who died on the cross to **atone** for the sins of mankind.[11]

Abraham and Noah are both recognized in the New Testament for their great <u>faith</u> because they trusted in God when he asked them to do something unusual. Noah believed God when he said he was going to destroy the world with a flood, so Noah built an Ark and was saved. Abraham believed God when he made all those promises, so he moved to Canaan and they started coming true. How should we respond to the prophecies of God?

The covenants reveal what God plans to do in the future. By keeping his covenants, God gives us evidence of his existence and how he moves in history.

First, he binds himself to do specific things. Then, he views his covenants as promises he is obligated to keep because his honor and reputation are at stake. Finally, he fulfills them in every detail because he wants his people to know he can be trusted. Prophecy is a record of promises made and promises kept.

THE JACKSON SUN, DECEMBER 4, 1994 . . .

"Faith needs greater role in TV," Network exec. says. "TV talks about rediscovering faith, but more needs to be done," John Roos says. . . . And for INSP [The Inspirational Network], it's an ambitious effort. "Love Stories of the Holy Land" airs Saturdays. Love stories? "We're trying to do it in an entertaining way," Roos says. "This is an ideal way to get into the Bible in a different way. The series started Sept. 12 with Abraham and Sarah. More are on the way.[12]

This covenant was made with Abraham, not the Church. The Church is a recipient of the spiritual blessings because God by his grace included it. As a party of the covenant he can do that. But the Church has not replaced Israel. The material blessings (land, its size, etc.) belong to that nation only.

atone: make reconciliation with God

Something to Ponder

☞ **GO TO:**

Hebrews 11:7–19 (faith)

Remember This . . .

RELATED CURRENT EVENTS

KEY POINT

God's blessings will fall on those who are kind to the Jews and his curses will fall on those who mistreat them.

WARNING

☞ **GO TO:**

Genesis 12:4
(seventy-five)

Genesis 16:1–16
(Ishmael)

Genesis 17:1–27 (Isaac)

Matthew 1:1
(Abraham)

forever: until the earth is destroyed

KEY POINT

The land belongs to
Israel forever.

**Something
to Ponder**

Fulfillment: Abraham left the place where he lived and went to the land of Canaan (see illustration, page 17). He was <u>seventy-five</u> years old when he departed. Ten years after he arrived, a servant of his wife bore him a son named <u>Ishmael</u>. Fourteen years later, when Abraham was one hundred years old, his wife Sarah bore him a son named <u>Isaac</u>. It is clear that God intended for his covenant with <u>Abraham</u> to pass through this son. Isaac's descendants would become the great nation of Israel and they would be the instruments of blessing and curses in the world. This prophecy is continuously being fulfilled through the existence of Israel. It was partially fulfilled at the First Coming of Jesus and it will be completely fulfilled after the Millennium when Satan is cast into the Lake of Fire.

> **Genesis 13:14–17** The LORD said to Abram after Lot had parted from him, "Lift up your eyes from where you are and look north and south, east and west. All the land that you see I will give to you and your offspring forever. I will make your offspring like the dust of the earth, so that if anyone could count the dust, then your offspring could be counted. Go, walk through the length and breadth of the land, for I am giving it to you."

Forever Is A Long Time

The Lord appeared unto Abraham a second time and on this occasion God told Abraham he would give the land of Canaan to him and his descendants **forever**. God was saying, "I will not give you and your descendants the land and expect to get it back at a later date." The land of Canaan is Israel's forever.

God also told Abraham he would have a great number of descendants. They would number more than anyone could count.

God gave the land to Israel, but there is a problem. Muslims do not believe Israel's God is God. They worship Allah and believe he gave the land to them. This makes the land conflict a theological conflict. The question is, Whose god is God or who worships the true God? The media and multitudes are lining up against Israel, and at the same time setting themselves against God. It will take the Tribulation Period and the Second Coming of Christ to settle the issue. But make no mistake, the Word of God says he will do just that.

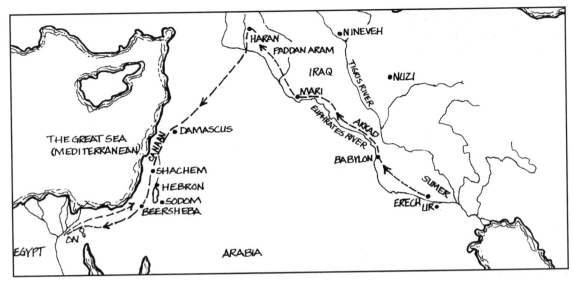

Abraham's Travels

Abram and his wife Sarai traveled from Ur of the Chaldeans, through Haran and Egypt, to Canaan.

Some teach that the people of God (Israel and the Church) began with the Abrahamic Covenant, but God's people date back to the beginning of creation (Adam, Eve, Seth, Enoch, Noah).

Fulfillment: Israel has occupied the land several times, but because of sin God has allowed them to be removed for temporary periods of time. So the land portion of this prophecy is continuously being fulfilled, but it will not be fully realized until the Millennium. The great number of descendants portion of the prophecy has already been fulfilled.

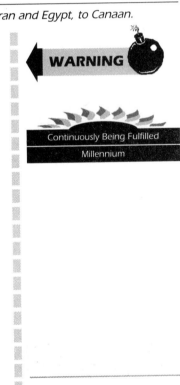

Continuously Being Fulfilled
Millennium

> **Genesis 15:18** On that day the LORD made a covenant with Abram and said, "To your descendants I give this land, from the river of Egypt to the great river, the Euphrates . . ."

Lots And Lots Of Land And A Covenant To Boot

God appeared unto Abraham a third time and on this occasion he spelled out the boundaries of the land he was giving to Abraham and his descendants. It covers an area that runs from the river of Egypt, which is a reference to the Nile River, to the river Euphrates.

☞ **GO TO:**

1 Kings 4:21; 8:65 (Egypt)

Some say this is more land than Israel has ever occupied. It includes all of modern Israel, all of the West Bank territories, part of Egypt, and part of Iraq (see illustration, page 19). But more importantly, God made a covenant with Abraham. He bound himself to give the land of Canaan to Abraham and his descendants.

What Others are Saying:

Robert T. Boyd: We need to keep in mind that all is not recorded about possession of the *whole* land, but when we read that David's dominion was established by the Euphrates River (1 Chronicles 18:3) and that Solomon's border was to the border or "river of Egypt," we must conclude that the **Promised Land** was extended to its fullest. It is wrong to say that Israel never possessed all her land.[13]

Promised Land: another name for the land of Israel

Unfulfilled
Millennium

Fulfillment: Among scholars there are differences of opinion about whether or not Israel has ever possessed all the land God promised. But they are not divided about the fact that Israel will possess all of the Promised Land during the Millennium. So this is designated unfulfilled with reservations.

KEY POINT

When God makes a covenant, he sets up a standard by which he can be measured. He exposes himself to being evaluated.

> **Genesis 17:7–8** "I will establish my covenant as an everlasting covenant between me and you and your descendants after you for the generations to come, to be your God and the God of your descendants after you. The whole land of Canaan, where you are now an alien, I will give as an everlasting possession to you and your descendants after you; and I will be their God."

KEY Symbols:

River of Egypt
Nile River

Israel's God

The Lord repeated his promise to give all the land of Canaan to Abraham and his descendants and, once again, he added something else. He would be the God of Abraham and his descendants throughout all generations. No matter what, he would keep his covenant and never turn his back on Abraham's descendants.

☞ **GO TO:**

Daniel 9:4 (covenant)

Something to Ponder

At times Israel has been an evil nation. Idolatry and unbelief have filled the land. On at least two occasions, God let foreigners destroy the nation (Babylon and Rome). But God is faithful and has never ceased to be Israel's God.

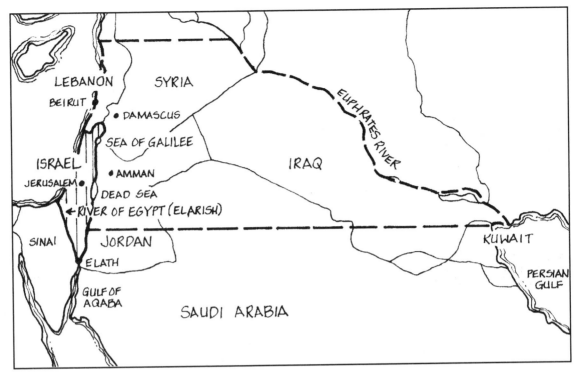

The Promised Land

The shaded area indicates present-day Israel. The area encompassed by the dashed line indicates the area Jews will occupy in the millennial reign of Christ.

God gave "the whole land of Canaan" to Israel. The Arabs and their Palestinian allies are trying to take control of Israel and Jerusalem piece by piece and many world leaders are helping them. But God said all the land belongs to Abrahamic offspring (Israel).

Fulfillment: In spite of the fact that Israel has returned to the land in unbelief, this prophecy is constantly being fulfilled. The relationship between God and Israel is not what it should be, but things will change when the Jews accept Jesus as the Messiah at his Second Coming. That will start the Millennium and they will occupy all the land God promised to them.

Remember This . . .

Continuously Being Fulfilled
Second Coming
Millennium

KEY POINT

God will always be Israel's God.

> **Genesis 17:19** Then God said, "Yes, but your wife Sarah will bear you a son, and you will call him Isaac. I will establish my covenant with him as an everlasting covenant for his descendants after him."

Announcing A New Arrival

God's promise to give the land of Canaan to Abraham and his descendants could only be fulfilled by Abraham having a child. When his wife Sarah decided she could not conceive, she suggested that Abraham father a child by her maidservant <u>Hagar</u>. Abraham did as she suggested and <u>Ishmael</u> was born. That was a great thing for an eighty-six-year-old man, but it was not what God had intended. He appeared to Abraham and announced that his wife Sarah would indeed have a baby, it would be a male child, his name would be <u>Isaac</u>, and God's covenant would be renewed with this child and his descendants (see GWWB, pages 30–31, 34–41).

Abraham fathered several <u>sons</u> by his wives, his **concubines**, and their servants. God blessed all of them, but the covenant he made with Abraham passed through Isaac.

Some suggest that God approves of polygamy and extramarital sex because what Abraham did is in the Bible, but he does not. Notice that he refused to renew his covenant with any of Abraham's children except Isaac.

Fulfillment: When Abraham was one hundred years old and Sarah was <u>ninety</u>, the portion of this prophecy that pertains to Isaac was fulfilled. The remainder is continuously being fulfilled from generation to generation.

> **Genesis 18:17–18** Then the LORD said, "Shall I hide from Abraham what I am about to do? Abraham will surely become a great and powerful nation, and all nations on earth will be blessed through him."

A Blessing For All

The inhabitants of two cities that existed in Abraham's lifetime were particularly **evil** so God decided to destroy them. But he had

---

☞ **GO TO:**

Genesis 16:1–4 (Hagar)

Genesis 16:15–16 (Ishmael)

Genesis 21:12; 25:1–7 (Isaac)

Genesis 16:10–12; 21:1–8 (sons)

concubines: *secondary wives*

Remember This . . .

Continuously Being Fulfilled

Fulfilled in Old Testament

☞ **GO TO:**

Genesis 17:17 (ninety)

evil: *sinful, wicked*

a special relationship with Abraham and that prompted a question, "Should I hide my intentions from Abraham since I have promised that he will become a great nation and a source of <u>blessing</u> to all people?"

W. H. Griffith Thomas: How beautiful is the suggestion made by the Divine **soliloquy**! "Shall I hide from Abraham that thing which I do?" God's friends are permitted to know His secrets because they are His friends. Abraham is regarded by God as having a right to know what was about to be done (Psalm 25:4; Amos 3:7).[14]

Fulfillment: God revealed his plan to Abraham and then destroyed the cities of <u>Sodom</u> and Gomorrah. Abraham's descendants eventually became the nation of Israel. During the Millennium, Israel will be the great nation predicted in the Bible. All the earth was blessed when Abraham's descendant named Jesus died for the sins of the <u>world</u>. More blessings will be realized at Jesus' Second Coming.

> **Genesis 22:15–18** The angel of the LORD called to Abraham from heaven a second time and said, "I swear by myself, declares the LORD, that because you have done this and have not withheld your son, your only son, I will surely bless you and make your descendants as numerous as the stars in the sky and as the sand on the seashore. Your descendants will take possession of the cities of their enemies, and through your offspring all nations on earth will be blessed, because you have obeyed me."

Abraham Passes With Flying Colors

God had a special relationship with Abraham, but he still decided to <u>test</u> him by asking him to sacrifice his son Isaac as a burnt offering. With simple childlike faith Abraham was about to obey when God stopped him. God could see that Abraham was willing to go all the way and that was enough. He hadn't intended for Isaac to be killed. The angel of the Lord appeared and told Abraham that his willingness to obey God would be rewarded: Israel would become a very powerful nation, one that would occupy the territory of its enemies.

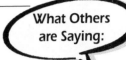 **GO TO:**

Acts 3:24–26 (blessing)

What Others are Saying:

soliloquy: talking to oneself

| Continuously Being Fulfilled |
| Fulfilled in Old Testament |
| First Coming |
| Second Coming |
| Millennium |

KEY POINT

Those in <u>covenant</u> with God have a special relationship with God.

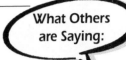 **GO TO:**

Psalm 25:14 (covenant)

Genesis 19:27–28 (Sodom)

John 3:16–18 (world)

Genesis 22:1 (test)

KEY POINT

God rewards people who have faith.

W. H. Griffith Thomas: Faith in the case of Abraham, as indeed in every other instance, is taking God at His word. True faith is nothing more, as it is nothing less, than this. God speaks: man believes. This is the true idea involved in the phrase "implicit trust," a trust that relies upon God without having his reasons "unfolded" to us. This simple faith, taking God at His word, is always at the foundation of the believer's peace and restfulness, strength and progress.[15]

| Continuously Being Fulfilled |
| First Coming |
| Second Coming |
| Millennium |

Fulfillment: The number of Abraham's descendants is constantly growing. All the nations were blessed at the First Coming of Jesus. Israel will possess the promised cities and territories at the Second Coming of Jesus and continue through the Millennium.

> **Genesis 26:3–4** "Stay in this land for a while, and I will be with you and will bless you. For to you and your descendants I will give all these lands and will confirm the oath I swore to your father Abraham. I will make your descendants as numerous as the stars in the sky and will give them all these lands, and through your offspring all nations on earth will be blessed."

God's Covenant With Isaac

☞ **GO TO:**

Genesis 12:10; 26:1
(famine)

Not long after Abraham moved to the land of Canaan there was a <u>famine</u> in the Promised Land. God did not tell Abraham to relocate, but Abraham had family, servants, and animals to feed so he temporarily moved to Egypt. The event in this passage of Scripture took place about seventy to eighty years after Abraham returned to the land of Canaan.

Abraham had died and his son Isaac was a grown man. When a second famine came to the land, God did not want Isaac to do what his father had done. So God appeared to Isaac and asked him not to go to Egypt. God wanted Isaac to stay in the Promised Land and he promised to

- be with him
- bless him
- give the land to him
- carry out the covenant he made with Abraham
- give him a great number of descendants
- give the land to his descendants
- make one of his descendants a blessing to the whole earth

W. H. Griffith Thomas: Trials are permitted to come into the life of the best and holiest of men, and it is by this means that God sometimes teaches His most precious lessons. . . . Egypt was not the promised land, and there were dangers there to body and to soul from which it was necessary that Isaac should be safeguarded.[16]

Fulfillment: God blessed Isaac by giving him the land and many descendants. All the earth was blessed many generations later when his descendant Jesus came into the <u>world</u> the first time. More blessings will be realized at Jesus' Second Coming. Abraham's descendants will possess all the land during the Millennium.

> **Genesis 28:13–15** "I am the LORD, the God of your father Abraham and the God of Isaac. I will give you and your descendants the land on which you are lying. Your descendants will be like the dust of the earth, and you will spread out to the west and to the east, to the north and to the south. All peoples on earth will be blessed through you and your offspring. I am with you and will watch over you wherever you go, and I will bring you back to this land. I will not leave you until I have done what I have promised you."

God's Covenant With Jacob (Israel)

Isaac had twin sons named <u>Jacob and Esau</u>. The one born first was Esau and that gave him a **birthright** to inherit the covenant God made with Abraham and Isaac. But Esau was foolish. The birthright meant very little to him and he sold it to Jacob for a bowl of stew. Several years later, Jacob deceived his father and tricked him into giving him his **blessing** as the head of the family. When Esau learned about it, he planned to kill Jacob, but Jacob fled the country. On his first night away from home God appeared to Jacob and said he was giving him everything he promised to Abraham and Isaac. Thus the all-important covenant land went to Jacob.

What Others are Saying:

Continuously Being Fulfilled
Fulfilled in Old Testament
First Coming
Second Coming
Millennium

☞ **GO TO:**

John 1:29; 11:27 (world)

☞ **GO TO:**

Genesis 25:19–26 (Jacob and Esau)

Genesis 25:29–34 (birthright)

Genesis 27:1–40 (blessing)

birthright: *the oldest son's right to inherit*

blessing: *an oral last will and testament*

patriarchs: early fathers, head of the family

KEY POINT

Jacob's name was
changed to Israel.

☞ **GO TO:**

Genesis 32:1
(handmaids)

Genesis 35:1, 6 (Bethel)

Genesis 32:22–30
(Israel)

handmaids: servants

Wayne Barber, Eddie Rasnake, and Richard Shepherd:
Jacob experienced seven revelations from the Lord in his jour-
neys, and in those revelations we discover Jacob learning to follow God—to hear His word and obey. Those revelations occurred
around five significant turning points in Jacob's life, turning points
designed by God to fulfill the destiny He had for Jacob. But not
only for Jacob, they were also part of God's destiny for His people
Israel, for His Son the Messiah, and for all His redeemed throughout the ages—all those who have been, are now, or ever will be on
the journey of following God.[17]

Abraham, Isaac, and Jacob are sometimes called the **patriarchs**. As such, each was the male head of their family or
clan. The Jews recognize them as the beginning of the nation of Israel.

Fulfillment: God blessed Jacob (Israel) with twelve sons and
this is continuously being fulfilled because their descendants
eventually became the nation of Israel. Jesus came from this
nation. More blessings will be realized at his Second Coming. They will possess all the land during the Millennium.

> **Genesis 35:10–12** God said to him, "Your name is
> Jacob, but you will no longer be called Jacob; your name
> will be Israel." So he named him Israel. And God said
> to him, "I am God Almighty; be fruitful and increase in
> number. A nation and a community of nations will come
> from you, and kings will come from your body. The
> land I gave to Abraham and Isaac I also give to you,
> and I will give this land to your descendants after you."

Jacob Gets A New Name

Jacob was out of the land for about twenty years. He returned to
the land of Canaan with two wives, two **handmaids**, and eleven
children, and moved around until God told him to settle in Bethel.
At that point God told him not to go by the name of Jacob anymore—his new name would be Israel. God said a nation and kings
would descend from him and God repeated his promise that the
land given to Abraham and Isaac now belonged to Jacob and his
descendants.

Fulfillment: Jacob's name became Israel and his descendants became the nation of Israel. Some even became kings. The nation of Israel occupied the land at various times during the Old Testament period. They occupy part of it today, will receive all of it at the Second Coming, and will occupy all of it during the Millennium.

Continuously Being Fulfilled
Second Coming
Millennium

> **Genesis 49:10** The scepter will not depart from Judah, nor the ruler's staff from between his feet, until he comes to whom it belongs and the obedience of the nations is his.

The Coming Ruler

When he was dying, Israel called his twelve sons together to reveal things about their future. One of his sons was named <u>Judah</u>. Israel called Judah a <u>lion's cub</u>. Israel said the **scepter** will belong to the tribe of Judah *"until he who comes to whom it belongs and the obedience of the nations is his."* This means God's Messiah and coming Ruler of the nations will be from the tribe of Judah. In verse 24, God's Messiah is called the Mighty One of <u>Jacob</u>, the Shepherd, and the <u>Rock</u> of Israel.

The King James Version of this passage reads, *"The sceptre shall not depart from Judah, nor a lawgiver from between his feet, until Shiloh come."* Among scholars there is wide agreement that Shiloh means rest or peace. Adam's sin brought the curse of **<u>enmity</u>** and <u>toil</u>. Hence there will be no peace on earth and people will be required to labor for a living until the Second Coming of Jesus.

The twelve tribes of Israel are named after the descendants of Jacob (Israel). Jacob had twelve sons. One son was named Levi and his descendants are called the Tribe of Levi (or Levites). The Levites were selected to be the priests, so they were not counted among the twelve tribes. Omitting them left eleven tribes. One son was named Joseph. He was sold into slavery in Egypt. Joseph married an Egyptian, so his descendants were part Egyptian. He had two sons, Ephraim and Manasseh, who were made heads of tribes instead of their father. Omitting Joseph left ten tribes, but adding his two sons made twelve tribes. The tribe of Judah was selected to be the leader of all the tribes.

scepter: the rod or staff carried by a king or sovereign ruler

☞ **GO TO:**

Genesis 49:1–2, 8–12 (Judah)

Genesis 49:9 (lion's cub)

Isaiah 49:26 (Jacob)

1 Corinthians 10:4 (Rock)

Genesis 3:15 (enmity)

Genesis 3:17–19 (toil)

enmity: hostility or animosity

Something to Ponder

Continuously Being Fulfilled

Second Coming

Millennium

☞ **GO TO:**

Revelation 5:5 (Lion)

John 10:11
   (good shepherd)

Revelation 19:6
   (King of kings)

Revelation 2:27
   (iron scepter)

☞ **GO TO:**

Exodus 1:1–22 (Egypt)

Exodus 7:14–12:30
   (plagues)

Exodus 2:1–4:17
   (Moses)

Deuteronomy 28:12
   (rain)

Deuteronomy 28:23–
   25 (enemies)

plagues: something that
causes a great deal of
suffering

Pharaoh: a title given to
the main ruler in Egypt

Fulfillment: Some of the names of Jesus are <u>Lion</u> of the tribe of Judah, Mighty One of Jacob, and the <u>good shepherd</u>. Jesus is the <u>King of kings</u> and Lord of lords who will rule with an <u>iron scepter</u> during the Millennium.

LEVITICUS

THE BIG PICTURE 🔎

Leviticus 25:1–26:46 The twelve sons of Israel (Jacob) multiplied and moved to Egypt. During a span of several hundred years, Israel's descendants had become slaves. So God raised up Moses to lead them out of the land of Egypt to Mount Sinai. There God gave the land of Canaan to them, but they had to let the land rest every seventh year, help the poor, observe the Sabbaths, etc. If they obeyed, he would bless them. If they disobeyed, he would punish them. If the punishment did not work, he would eventually put them off the land and let it rest one year for each seventh year they wrongfully planted a crop. But he would not cancel his covenant or permit all of the people to be destroyed. After the land rested the proper number of years, he would restore the nation.

The Big If . . . (The Mosaic Covenant)

Another famine came and the descendants of Israel wound up in <u>Egypt</u>. The Israelites stayed in Egypt for 430 years and their numbers increased to several hundred thousand, some say perhaps as many as two million. This population explosion troubled the Egyptians. They were afraid the Israelites would soon outnumber and overpower them. So the Egyptians took the Israelites as slaves. God responded by sending **plagues** to force **Pharaoh** to let them leave, and by raising up an Israelite named <u>Moses</u> to lead them.

Moses led his people to Mount Sinai and it was there that God made a special covenant with the nation. *If* Israel would obey him, God promised to bless the nation with <u>rain</u>, good crops, fruit, peace, victory over her enemies, and safe dwelling. *If* Israel would not obey, God would make the nation afraid, send diseases, and let the nation's <u>enemies</u> defeat her. *If* the nation continued to disobey, God would punish the people seven times more with poor crops. *If* that did not work, God would punish them seven times more with plagues of wild animals. *If* that failed,

God would punish them seven times more with diseases and famine. *If* they still disobeyed, God would punish them seven times more, they would cannibalize their children, the <u>land</u> would become desolate, the people would be scattered among the nations, and the land would rest to make up for all those years they wrongfully planted crops.

• • •

From the days of Moses to the days of Jeremiah, Israel went through many cycles. Beginning with Moses, Israel served God for several years and enjoyed the <u>blessings</u> he promised. But in spite of his goodness, a new generation arose who began to rebel. When God called for repentance, the people did not respond. So he withdrew his help and his blessings evaporated—times were hard. Then the reeling nation sought out God. He restored her, and the blessings returned. Israel repeated this cycle over and over again. By the time Jeremiah came along, Israel was divided. The Northern Kingdom of Israel had been destroyed and the Southern Kingdom of Judah was in dire circumstances. The chosen people were unwilling to obey God and stopped their ears to what true prophets were saying. They worshiped false gods and did not let the soil rest as God instructed them. Their sins provoked his wrath.[18]

• • •

Letting the land rest every seventh year was a great test for the nation. If the people trusted God enough to not plant crops, God would bless them. If they did not trust him enough to do that, God would afflict them. The message for us today is trust God and he will take care of us.

Fulfillment: Israel broke the covenant again and again. Finally, <u>Jeremiah</u> warned the people to repent or God would put them off the land. When the people refused to heed the warning God let King <u>Nebuchadnezzar</u> of Babylon defeat them. Multitudes of Jews were killed. Others were taken to foreign lands. Seventy years later, more than forty thousand returned. In A.D. 70 the Romans conquered the land. Multitudes were killed again, but not everyone. In A.D. 135 those who were left were scattered and their property was sold. This prophecy has been fulfilled.

☞ **GO TO:**

Deuteronomy 28:33–37 (land)

Deuteronomy 28:1–8 (blessings)

Remember This . . .

KEY POINT

God told the Jews to let the land rest every seventh year.

Fulfilled

☞ **GO TO:**

Jeremiah 25:1–13 (Jeremiah)

2 Chronicles 36:11–21 (Nebuchadnezzar)

> **Numbers 24:14–19** "Now I am going back to my
> people, but come, let me warn you of what this people
> will do to your people in days to come." Then he ut-
> tered his oracle: "The oracle of Balaam son of Beor, the
> oracle of one whose eye sees clearly, the oracle of one
> who hears the words of God, who has knowledge from
> the Most High, who sees a vision from the Almighty,
> who falls prostrate, and whose eyes are opened: I see
> him, but not now; I behold him, but not near. A star
> will come out of Jacob; a scepter will rise out of Israel.
> He will crush the foreheads of Moab, the skulls of all
> the sons of Sheth. Edom will be conquered; Seir, his
> enemy, will be conquered, but Israel will grow strong.
> A ruler will come out of Jacob and destroy the survi-
> vors of the city."

☞ **GO TO:**

Genesis 49:10 (scepter)

Micah 6:5 (Balaam)

2 Peter 2:13–16 (loved)

Jude 11 (error)

Revelation 2:14
(taught)

Moab and Edom: *two
small kingdoms in
southern Jordan*

**Remember
This . . .**

idolatry: *worshiping false
gods*

sexual immorality:
sexual wrongdoing

Remember Balaam

The story of Balaam is one of the strangest in the Bible. He was a
living contradiction who knew a lot of Scripture but set most of it
aside. He was an unusual prophet who mixed divine revelation
with pagan practices, a man of faith who sold out to Satan. He
said something we often hear at Christmas, *"A star will come out
of Jacob; a scepter will rise out of Israel."* Among scholars there is
wide agreement that this is a prophecy about Jesus. Some even
believe the wise men who went to Jerusalem and Bethlehem at his
birth went there because of this prophecy. At Jerusalem they asked
King Herod, *"Where is the one who has been born king of the Jews?
We saw his star in the east and have come to worship him"* (Matthew
2:2). Balaam also prophesied the destruction of **Moab and Edom**.

Balaam is a man to be remembered. The Bible says:
1. Remember what Balaam said (Numbers 22–25).
2. Remember what Balaam loved—he loved the wages of
   wickedness and accepted money to do wrong.
3. Remember Balaam's error—he was greedy.
4. Remember what Balaam taught—**idolatry** and **sexual
   immorality**.

Fulfillment: Balaam said what he saw was "not near." In the future, Israel's ungodly neighbors in southern Jordan will be destroyed and the kingdoms of the world will be subdued. <u>Morning Star</u> is one of the names of Jesus. He appeared almost two thousand years ago and he will appear again near the end of earth's darkest hour (Tribulation Period). His light will overcome the darkness.

☞ **GO TO:**

Revelation 22:16
(Morning Star)

DEUTERONOMY

> **Deuteronomy 4:26–31** I call heaven and earth as witnesses against you this day that you will quickly perish from the land that you are crossing the Jordan to possess. You will not live there long but will certainly be destroyed. The LORD will scatter you among the peoples, and only a few of you will survive among the nations to which the LORD will drive you. There you will worship man-made gods of wood and stone, which cannot see or hear or eat or smell. But if from there you seek the LORD your God, you will find him if you look for him with all your heart and with all your soul. When you are in distress and all these things have happened to you, then in later days you will return to the LORD your God and obey him. For the LORD your God is a merciful God; he will not abandon or destroy you or forget the covenant with your forefathers, which he confirmed to them by oath.

Israel's History Foretold

Moses led the children of Israel out of Egypt, through the wilderness, and to the east bank of the Jordan River. They were ready to enter the Promised Land, but before they did, Moses had some final words of warning. He spoke in the name of the Lord calling heaven and earth to witness against them. He predicted **apostasy** would grip the new nation, that it would soon **backslide**, that the people would be killed or removed from the land, that the survivors would be few in number, and that they would be compelled to commit idolatry in foreign lands. He also said if the people would repent and seek God, the Lord would forgive them.

For the first time in the Bible, the Tribulation Period is referenced here: "a day of <u>distress</u>." It will occur in the "***later days***."

apostasy: *rebellion against God*

backslide: *slip back into sin*

later days: *the days just prior to the end of a period (e.g., Church Age, Tribulation Period)*

☞ **GO TO:**

Zephaniah 1:14–17
(distress)

☞ **GO TO:**

Deuteronomy 7:9–10
(covenant)

Remember This . . .

fathers: *in this case,
Abraham, Isaac, and
Jacob*

Something to Ponder

Unfulfilled

Second Coming

☞ **GO TO:**

Matthew 24:15–16
(flee)

When the Tribulation Period arrives, if people repent, our merciful God will not forsake them; he will not forget the <u>covenant</u> he made with their **fathers**. The same love, mercy, and power that he makes available to others will be available to them.

We know the following about the Israelites in the later days:

1. God's chosen people will backslide.
2. If backsliders do not repent, God will punish them.
3. If backsliders do repent, God will forgive them.

As long as the nation of Israel remained faithful to God, they would be special to him, he would not forsake them, and he would let them dwell in the Promised Land. If they broke their relationship with him, they would be no different than anyone else, and he would no longer let them dwell in the Promised Land. Removing them would be a judgment designed to bring self-examination and repentance. This will happen during the Tribulation Period—God will remember his covenants and the relationship will be restored.

Fulfillment: Israel is notorious for backsliding and because of that, the nation has been destroyed more than once. God's chosen people will once again return to the land, but they will have to <u>flee</u> to the mountains in the future during the Tribulation Period. They will remember this prophecy and repent, and God will remember his covenants and restore them.

STUDY QUESTIONS

1. Why is knowledge of prophecy so important to understanding the Bible?
2. Does God permit evil?
3. Why is understanding God's covenants so important to understanding the Bible?
4. What do the covenants with Abraham, Isaac, and Jacob have to do with Christians?
5. What clues do we have as to the identity of the Messiah?

CHAPTER WRAP-UP

• Satan's corruption of Adam and Eve brought curses upon the first couple and the serpent. His corruption of the whole earth brought a flood, but as long as the earth exists, there will be crops and seasons. (Genesis 3:14–19; 6:11–13; 8:22)

- God made covenants with Abraham, Isaac, and Jacob promising to give the land of Canaan to them and their descendants, to make them into a great nation, and to bless all the earth through them. (Genesis 12:1–3; 13:14–17; 17:7–8; 17:19; 18:17–18; 22:15–18; 26:3–4; 28:13–15; 35:10–12)

- God promised that the one who will rule the nations will come from the tribe of Jacob. (Genesis 49:10; Numbers 24:14–19)

- If Israel kept the covenants, God promised many blessings, plus he would let Israel stay on the land. If Israel broke the covenants, God promised to chastise the nation, and if the chastisement did not work, he would put the people off the land for awhile. (Leviticus 25:1–26:46)

- Moses said Israel would backslide in the later days (at the end of the age), but God will not forsake them. If the people repent, he will forgive them. (Deuteronomy 4:26–31)

2 PROPHECIES IN THE BOOKS OF HISTORY

CHAPTER HIGHLIGHTS

- A Woman's Prayer
- A Covenant for David
- A Warning for Solomon
- A God Who Remembers
- King Is Coming

Let's Get Started

The second division of the Old Testament, beginning with the book of Joshua and ending with the book of Esther, contains twelve books chronicling the history of Israel. The twelve books do not appear in chronological order in the Bible, so neither will they here. Finally, it should be noted that only four of the books contain prophecies of interest to this study.

1 SAMUEL

> **1 Samuel 2:10** "Those who oppose the LORD will be shattered. He will thunder against them from heaven; the LORD will judge the ends of the earth. He will give strength to his king and exalt the horn of his anointed."

A Messiah And King

The first book of Samuel begins with a barren woman named Hannah praying for a child. When her prayer is answered a few months later, she names her newborn son **Samuel**. When he is old enough to be weaned, Hannah takes Samuel to the Lord's house at Shiloh and presents him to Eli the priest for a life of service to God. She begins to pray and ends her prayer with this verse:"*He* [God] *will give strength to his king and exalt the horn of his anointed*" (1 Samuel 2:10). The word <u>anointed</u> is translated "Messiah" in Hebrew and "Christos" in Greek. This is the first use of the word Messiah in the Bible. Hannah rejoices because God's enemies will

Samuel: a Hebrew name meaning "heard of God"

☞ **GO TO:**

Daniel 9:25–26 (anointed)

---

be shattered. He will move against them from heaven. He will empower his <u>king</u> and exalt his Messiah. God will set up a <u>kingdom</u>, and his Messiah and King will rule over it.

What Others are Saying:

impostors: false Christs

Unfulfilled

Second Coming

☞ **GO TO:**

Jeremiah 23:3–8; Ezekiel 37:1–28; John 19:19 (king)

Luke 1:32–33 (kingdom)

King David: a great king of Israel who loved God

David's people: Israel

David's house: the dynasty or house of David, David's descendants

David's son: Solomon

God's house: the Temple

throne: authority

☞ **GO TO:**

Luke 2:4 (house)

1 Chronicles 17:11–14 (kingdom)

Lee Strobel: Hundreds of years before Jesus was born, prophets foretold the coming of the Messiah, or the Anointed One, who would redeem God's people. In effect, dozens of these Old Testament prophecies created a fingerprint that only the true Messiah could fit. This gave Israel a way to rule out **impostors** and validate the credentials of the authentic Messiah.[1]

Fulfillment: This prophecy will be fulfilled at the Second Coming of Christ.

2 SAMUEL

THE BIG PICTURE 🔍

> **2 Samuel 7:4–17** At a time of peace in Israel, King David wanted to build a house for God. But before he got started, God sent Nathan the prophet to remind David that it was God who made him great. God promised through Nathan: to make David's name great, to provide a place for Israel, to provide a house for David, to raise up one of David's offspring (a son named Solomon) to succeed him, to let Solomon build God's house, to establish Solomon's throne forever, to punish Solomon's sin but never stop loving him, and to establish David's house, kingdom, and throne forever.

God's Covenant With David

God's covenant with **King David** is usually called "the Davidic Covenant" (see GWBI, page 65). It contains seven promises that God made to David:

1. David's name will be revered.
2. **David's people** will have a land forever.
3. **David's <u>house</u>** will exist forever.
4. **David's son** will succeed him.
5. David's son will build **God's house**.
6. David's son will be punished for his sins.
7. David's <u>kingdom</u> and **throne** will last forever.

Henry H. Halley: Here, in the 7th chapter of 2 Samuel, begins the long line of promises that DAVID'S FAMILY should reign FOREVER over God's people; that is, there should come from David an Eternal Family Line of Kings, culminating in ONE ETERNAL KING.[2]

John F. Walvoord: In these promises God has made clear that the Davidic covenant is not subject to human conditions and that God has vowed on the basis of his own trustworthiness that he will fulfill the covenant. It is also clear that the promise was given to David, not to someone else, though it will be fulfilled by Christ as the descendant of David, and that the fulfillment relates to the people of God, in this context the people of <u>Israel</u>.[3]

King Solomon built the first <u>Temple</u> and the Babylonians destroyed it. The Jews rebuilt it and the Romans destroyed it. Several prophecies teach that it will be rebuilt again before the Second Coming of Christ.

The destruction of Israel and Judah does not cancel this covenant. God simply removed the family from the throne to await a suitable, faithful descendant. Some of King David's descendants survived the destruction of Israel and Judah, and the right to reign passed on through them. Then Jesus was born and it is through him that the throne of David will be established forever.

Fulfillment: David became famous in his lifetime and even today the Jews revere him as Israel's greatest king. Two cities, Bethlehem and Jerusalem, have become known as "the city of David." David's son Solomon succeeded him as king of Israel. He built the first Temple. He also worshiped other gods. Solomon's sin made God angry, so God allowed Israel to be divided into **two nations** following Solomon's death. When Jesus was born, his genealogy was traced back to David through both his legal father, Joseph, and his biological mother, Mary. Thus Jesus is the legal heir to David's throne, and he will sit on the earthly throne of David during the Millennium.

What Others are Saying:

☞ **GO TO:**

2 Samuel 7:24–29 (Israel)

1 Kings 5:5 (Temple)

Remember This . . .

WARNING

Partially Fulfilled
Millennium

two nations: *Northern Kingdom, called Israel, and Southern Kingdom, called Judah (see illustration, page 65)*

> **2 Samuel 23:3–7** "The God of Israel spoke, the Rock of Israel said to me: 'When one rules over men in righteousness, when he rules in the fear of God, he is like the light of morning at sunrise on a cloudless morning, like the brightness after rain that brings the grass from the earth.' "Is not my house right with God? Has he not made with me an everlasting covenant, arranged and secured in every part? Will he not bring to fruition my salvation and grant me my every desire? But evil men are all to be cast aside like thorns, which are not gathered with the hand. Whoever touches thorns uses a tool of iron or the shaft of a spear; they are burned up where they lie."

KEY POINT

A covenant with God ensures our salvation.

A Sure Thing

King David was on his deathbed when God revealed these things. God told David that a **righteous** leader who **fears God** is like sunshine on a cloudy day; God notices him. Such a leader is also a blessing to others. They will prosper and grow under his reign.

David knew that he had not lived up to this. Not many leaders do. But he also knew that he was leaving office in a right relationship with God. He had an everlasting covenant that secured his future. Evil leaders cannot make that same claim. They will be cast aside and <u>burned</u>.

righteous: *just*

fears God: *has respect for God*

☞ **GO TO:**

John 15:1–8 (burned)

Something to Ponder

What are your priorities in life? Are you prioritizing first things first? Does righteousness and the fear of God play a part? It is a dangerous thing to come to the end of one's life without a right relationship with God.

Unfulfilled
Second Coming
After the Millennium

☞ **GO TO:**

Daniel 12:1–3 (raised)

Revelation 20:5, 11–14 (Lake of Fire)

Fulfillment: God's coming King is both Savior and Judge. David will be <u>raised</u> from the dead and enjoy God's blessings at the Second Coming of Christ. The wicked will be raised and cast into the <u>Lake of Fire</u> after the Millennium. This should motivate us to prepare. We will all appear before one of the judgment seats. There will be no way to avoid it. When we get there, we will need a Savior, but it will be too late for some. It is absolutely necessary to resolve this before we stand in his presence. The Lake of Fire awaits those who do not.

1 KINGS

> **1 Kings 9:3–9** The LORD said to him: "I have heard the prayer and plea you have made before me; I have consecrated this temple, which you have built, by putting my Name there forever. My eyes and my heart will always be there. "As for you, if you walk before me in integrity of heart and uprightness, as David your father did, and do all I command and observe my decrees and laws, I will establish your royal throne over Israel forever, as I promised David your father when I said, 'You shall never fail to have a man on the throne of Israel.' But if you or your sons turn away from me and do not observe the commands and decrees I have given you and go off to serve other gods and worship them, then I will cut off Israel from the land I have given them and will reject this temple I have consecrated for my Name. Israel will then become a byword and an object of ridicule among all peoples. And though this temple is now imposing, all who pass by will be appalled and will scoff and say, 'Why has the LORD done such a thing to this land and to this temple?' People will answer, 'Because they have forsaken the LORD their God, who brought their fathers out of Egypt, and have embraced other gods, worshiping and serving them—that is why the LORD brought all this disaster on them.'"

If, And, But . . . : Blessings Galore Or Judgment

In the <u>fourth</u> year of his reign, King Solomon started construction on the Temple (see illustration, page 38), and it was completed <u>seven</u> years later. He spent the next <u>thirteen</u> years constructing his palace. Then God appeared to Solomon and assured him that he had heard his prayer, that he had **consecrated** the Temple, that he had **put his name on** the Temple, and that **his eyes and heart** would be at the Temple. God added that if Solomon would have **uprightness** and **integrity** of heart and would keep his **commandments**, the kingdom would be secure and Solomon's descendants would continue to reign. But if Solomon or his descendants <u>turned away</u> from God, and if they worshiped idols, God would put <u>Israel</u> off the land, turn his back on the Temple, and cause the Jews to be ridiculed in the world.

☞ **GO TO:**

1 Kings 6:1 (fourth)

1 Kings 6:38 (seven)

1 Kings 7:1 (thirteen)

2 Chronicles 7:19–22 (turned away)

2 Kings 14:27 (Israel)

consecrated: accepted it as a special place

put his name on: agreed to let it be called God's house

his eyes and heart: God's presence

uprightness: a desire to live by God's rules

integrity: faithfulness to God

commandments: all the commandments of God including the Ten Commandments

Something to Ponder

Remember This . . .

Fulfilled

☞ **GO TO:**

2 Kings 19:30–31 (remnant)

2 Kings 17:20 (Judah)

2 Kings 21:12–15 (Jerusalem)

KEY POINT

Being faithful to God brings blessings, but forsaking God brings judgment.

☞ **GO TO:**

2 Kings 22:15–17 (forsaking)

God expects rulers to follow him and to be an example for his people. Unfaithful rulers lead people astray. Straying people will be held responsible for their sins.

God did not say he would cancel his covenant with David. He said he would remove those who rejected him from the land. This was a threat to temporarily set the covenant aside. He could reactivate it with a remnant of faithful people at some point in the future.

Fulfillment: Solomon and his descendants turned their backs on God and the nation was divided into a Northern Kingdom (Israel) and a Southern Kingdom (Judah). Eventually both kingdoms, the Temple, and Jerusalem were destroyed and the Jews have been ridiculed all over the world ever since (see GWDN, pages 18–20, 36).

Solomon's Temple

Solomon's lavish Temple would be worth five billion dollars today.

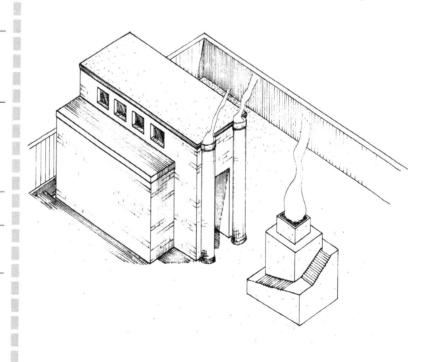

KINGS OF THE DIVIDED KINGDOM

THE NORTHERN KINGDOM (ISRAEL)				THE SOUTHERN KINGDOM (JUDAH)			
Name	Reign B.C.	Character	Scripture	Name	Reign B.C.	Character	Scripture
Jeroboam I	931–910	Bad	1 Kings 12–14	Rehoboam	931–913	Bad	1 Kings 12–14
Nadab	910–909	Bad	1 Kings 15	Abijah	913–911	Bad	1 Kings 15
Baasha	909–886	Bad	1 Kings 15–16	Asa	911–870	Good	1 Kings 15
Elah	886–885	Bad	1 Kings 16	Jehoshaphat	870–848	Good	1 Kings 22
Zimri	885	Bad	1 Kings 16	Jehoram	848–841	Bad	2 Kings 8
Omri	885–874	Bad	1 Kings 16	Ahaziah	853–852	Bad	2 Kings 8
Ahab	874–853	Bad	1 Kings 16–22	Athaliah	841–835	Bad	2 Kings 11
Ahaziah	853–852	Bad	1 Kings 22; 2 Kings 1				
Joram (or Jehoram)	852–841	Bad	2 Kings 3–8	Joash	835–796	Good	2 Kings 12
Jehu	841–814	Bad	2 Kings 9–10	Amaziah	796–767	Good	2 Kings 14
Jehoahaz (or Joahaz)	814–798	Bad	2 Kings 13	Azariah (or Uzziah)	767–740	Good	2 Kings 15
Jehoash (or Joash)	798–782	Bad	2 Kings 13	Jotham	740–732	Good	2 Kings 15
Jeroboam II	782–753	Bad	2 Kings 14	Ahaz	732–716	Bad	2 Kings 16
Zechariah	753–752	Bad	2 Kings 15	Hezekiah	716–687	Good	2 Kings 18–20
Shallum	752	Bad	2 Kings 15	Manasseh	687–642	Bad	2 Kings 21
Menahem	752–742	Bad	2 Kings 15	Amon	642–640	Bad	2 Kings 21
Pekahiah	742–740	Bad	2 Kings 15	Josiah	640–608	Good	2 Kings 22
Pekah	740–732	Bad	2 Kings 15	Jehoahaz	608	Bad	2 Kings 23
Hoshea	732–721	Bad	2 Kings 17	Jehoiakim	608–597	Bad	2 Kings 23
				Jehoiachin	597	Bad	2 Kings 24
				Zedekiah	597–586	Bad	2 Kings 24

Israel Destroyed by Assyria in 722 B.C.   Judah Destroyed by Babylon in 586 B.C.

valid: *binding or true*

oath: *solemn pledge or vow*

decree: *official decision, mandate, or command*

everlasting: *eternal, forever, never-ending*

☞ **GO TO:**

Genesis 12:1–3 (Abraham)

Genesis 26:3–4 (Isaac)

Genesis 28:13–15 (Jacob)

Something to Ponder

Remember This . . .

Continuously Being Fulfilled

Second Coming

Millennium

1 CHRONICLES

> **1 Chronicles 16:15–18** He remembers his covenant forever, the word he commanded, for a thousand generations, the covenant he made with Abraham, the oath he swore to Isaac. He confirmed it to Jacob as a decree, to Israel as an everlasting covenant: "To you I will give the land of Canaan as the portion you will inherit."

God Remembers

God does not, will not, and cannot forget his covenants. His covenants are as **valid** today as they were thousands of years ago. The covenant God made with <u>Abraham</u> and the **oath** he swore to <u>Isaac</u> were confirmed to <u>Jacob</u> as a **decree** and to Israel as an **everlasting** covenant. Israel will inherit the land of Canaan.

God has made some precious promises to Christians (2 Peter 1:4), and all his promises to us will be kept. He promised forgiveness of sins, to raise us from the dead, to give us eternal life. It is good to remember God's promises and, like Israel, we should remain faithful to God.

That God has made distinct promises to Israel isn't the point here. That God remembers his promises to Israel forever isn't the point either. The point is: Israel and the world should know that the Jews will get the land of Canaan. God is always mindful of his covenants; they will be fulfilled.

Fulfillment: God's covenants to give Abraham, Isaac, and Jacob many descendants are constantly being fulfilled. His covenants to give them all the land of Canaan will be fulfilled at the Second Coming. And Israel will occupy all their land during the Millennium.

Notice the words "I will" and "you will." They indicate God's determination to bring these things to pass. Many people don't know about these covenants, many don't think they are important, and many doubt they will be kept, but God never goes back on his word.

> **1 Chronicles 16:31–33** Let the heavens rejoice, let the earth be glad; let them say among the nations, "The LORD reigns!" Let the sea resound, and all that is in it; let the fields be jubilant, and everything in them! Then the trees of the forest will sing, they will sing for joy before the LORD, for he comes to judge the earth.

There's A Great Day Coming

King David had brought the Ark of the Covenant to Jerusalem and the Jews were celebrating (see GWRV, pages 166–167). It was a great day in Israel and as the people rejoiced they began to focus on the greater day that is coming. It will be a sad day for the lost, but it will be a great day of celebration for God's people. The Lord will reign and judge the earth. The lost will be purged from the earth and the saved will enter into the Millennium.

Thomas Ice and Timothy Demy: Though we often hear the phrase "judgment day," it is not biblically accurate because there are several future judgments in God's prophetic plan. These judgments will occur at various times between the rapture and the end of the millennium. The judgments are certain; no one will escape them. They will make manifest God's justice and righteousness to all the world and will silence all who have scoffed at or denied God.[4]

What Others are Saying:

The Bible says, *"if we judged ourselves, we would not come under judgment"* (1 Corinthians 11:31). Christians believe they will not be judged for their sins because they have practiced a form of self-examination. They have considered their sins, searched their hearts, repented, examined their faith, seen their need for a Savior, and accepted Jesus. Jesus says, *"For God so loved the world that he gave his one and only Son, that whoever believes in him shall not perish but have eternal life. For God did not send his Son into the world to condemn the world, but to save the world through him. Whoever believes in him is not condemned, but whoever does not believe stands condemned already because he has not believed in the name of God's one and only Son"* (John 3:16–18).

Something to Ponder

Jesus talked about a <u>time</u> when everyone will be judged. There will be no place to run, no place to hide, no way to escape. Every person will <u>reap</u> what they have sown. Every <u>deed</u> will be brought into judgment. Seven groups to be judged are:

	What Judged	When Judged	Why Judged
Deceased Christians	Works	After the Rapture	For Rewards
(Reference: 1 Corinthians 3:11–15; 10:31; Romans 8:1; 2 Corinthians 5:10; Ephesians 6:7)			
Deceased O.T.* Saints	Faith in Messiah	Second Coming	For Rewards
(Reference: Daniel 12:1–3)			
Deceased T.P.* Saints	Faith in Christ	Second Coming	To Raise Believers
(Reference: Revelation 20:4–6)			
Living Jews	Faith in Christ	Second Coming	To Purge Unbelievers
(Reference: Ezekiel 20:33–38)			
Living Gentiles	Faith in Chirst	Second Coming	To Purge Unbelievers
(Reference: Joel 3:1, 2; 1 Corinthians 11:31, 32; Matthew 25:31–46; Revelation 3:21)			
Satan and Fallen Angels	Rejecting God	Rejecting Christ	After Millennium
(Reference: Matthew 25:41; 2 Peter 2:4; Jude 6; Revelation 20:10; 1 Corinthians 6:3)			
Unbelievers	After Millennium	Destroy Fallen Angels	Degrees of Punishment
(Reference: Revelation 20:11–15; Luke 12:47, 48)			

* "O.T." stands for Old Testament and "T.P." stands for Tribulation Period.

Unfulfilled

Second Coming

Millennium

☞ **GO TO:**

John 5:25–29 (time)

Galatians 6:7 (reap)

Ecclesiastes 12:13–14 (deed)

Fulfillment: Jesus will judge the nations at his Second Coming and he will reign on earth during the Millennium.

> **1 Chronicles 17:11–14** "'When your days are over and you go to be with your fathers, I will raise up your offspring to succeed you, one of your own sons, and I will establish his kingdom. He is the one who will build a house for me, and I will establish his throne forever. I will be his father, and he will be my son. I will never take my love away from him, as I took it away from your predecessor. I will set him over my house and my kingdom forever; his throne will be established forever.'"

A Double Prophecy

David wanted to build a <u>house</u> (Temple) for God, but God would not let him because David was a <u>warrior</u> who had shed the blood of men. But God assured David that after his death, one of his "sons" (or "descendants") would succeed him on the <u>throne</u> in Israel. God said <u>David's</u> son would build him a house, God would establish his kingdom, and David's son would rule over it forever.

Since Old Testament times scholars have said this is a double prophecy (i.e., it has a double meaning). In one sense, it refers to David's son Solomon who succeeded David on the throne and built the first earthly Temple. But in a greater sense, it refers to David's descendant Jesus who is building a spiritual <u>temple</u> and kingdom for God. It is his kingdom and reign that will be established forever.

H. Wayne House: At times, a given prophecy may have reference to more than one future event. When this is the case, the term often used to describe this phenomenon is *double fulfillment* or *double reference*. Other terms, dependent on the particulars, might be *multiple fulfillment*, with more than two instances in view, or *progressive fulfillment*, indicating that the prophecy is not static but finds fulfillment in a succession of events.[5]

Fulfillment: In the sense that this prophecy refers to Solomon and the earthly Temple, it has been fulfilled. Solomon succeeded David on the throne and he built the first Temple. But in the greater and more significant sense that it refers to Jesus, the spiritual temple he is building for God, and the eternal kingdom God is building, this prophecy is yet to be fulfilled.

STUDY QUESTIONS

1. What is so significant about the last verse of Hannah's prayer?
2. What is David's house and how can it last forever?
3. Why would God allow the Temple to be destroyed?
4. When will God's covenants with Abraham, Isaac and Jacob be forgotten and why?
5. Is the Second Coming of Christ a reason to celebrate or a reason to weep?

☞ **GO TO:**

2 Samuel 7:4–17 (house)

1 Chronicles 28:3 (warrior)

Acts 2:29–36 (throne)

Jeremiah 23:3–8; Acts 13:34 (David)

What Others are Saying:

☞ **GO TO:**

1 Corinthians 6:19 (temple)

| Unfulfilled |
| Fulfilled |
| Second Coming |
| Millennium |

KEY POINT

The Temple and kingdom that will last forever is the one that Jesus will rule over.

- Hannah's request for a child was answered by God when Samuel was born. She turned him over to Eli the priest to raise in service to God. Her prayer of thanksgiving ends with a prophecy about the Second Coming of Christ. He is God's anointed or God's Messiah and King. (1 Samuel 2:10)

- God made a covenant with David to let his descendants succeed him, to make them a dynasty, and to let one of his sons (Jesus) rule over the kingdom forever. While on his deathbed, David said that he had not always been faithful to God, but he knew that God would keep the covenant because it is an everlasting covenant. (1 Samuel 7:4–17; 23:3–7)

- Solomon built the first earthly Temple and God was pleased. He even assured Solomon that his kingdom was secure if he and his descendants remained faithful. But God warned Solomon that if he or his descendants turned away, the kingdom and the Temple would be destroyed and the Jews would be ridiculed all over the world. (1 Kings 9:3–7)

- Those who think God forgets his covenants are wrong. He will never forget them so the promises he made to Abraham, Isaac, Jacob and the others will be fulfilled. A thousand generations can pass, but God's faithfulness will not change. (1 Chronicles 16:15–18)

- A kingdom requires a king—a king is coming to reign over an earthly kingdom. He will be a descendant of King David and his kingdom will last forever. (1 Chronicles 16:31–33; 17:11–14)

3 PROPHECIES IN THE BOOKS OF POETRY

CHAPTER HIGHLIGHTS

- The Resurrection of the Dead
- The Second Coming of Christ
- The First Coming of Christ
- The Tribulation Period
- The Millennium

Let's Get Started

Poetry permeates the Bible. It has been suggested that perhaps as much as one-third of the Old Testament is **Hebrew** poetry. In fact, five of the Old Testament books—Job, Psalms, Proverbs, Ecclesiastes, and Song of Songs—are almost entirely poetry and are often called the Poetic Books or the Books of Poetry. It's relevant to note that Hebrew poetry is not a series of verses that rhyme. Rather than ending lines with similar sounding words, Hebrew poetry instead repeats thoughts in varying ways.

Hebrew: another name for the Israelites, the Jews

JOB

> **Job 19:25–27** I know that my Redeemer lives, and that in the end he will stand upon the earth. And after my skin has been destroyed, yet in my flesh I will see God; I myself will see him with my own eyes—I, and not another. How my heart yearns within me!

Job Knows A Thing Or Two

Job lost everything he had. He was very sick, and some of his friends were trying to encourage him by suggesting he concentrate on regaining his wealth and health. But Job was not thinking about **temporal** things. He was thinking about a **resurrection** of the dead (see illustration, page 71), and he reminded his friends of some very important truths. He was full of hope because he **knew** he had a living **Redeemer**, one who at some point in the

temporal: worldly or secular

resurrection: the dead coming back to life

knew: was convinced

Redeemer: a deliverer, Jesus

☞ **GO TO:**

1 Peter 1:18–19 (Redeemer)

Our bodies will be destroyed, but we will receive new ones.

What Others are Saying:

revelation: a hidden truth that has been revealed

Something to Ponder

Unfulfilled

Second Coming

latter days will stand upon this earth. Job expected to die, to have his soul and spirit leave his body, and to have his flesh turn to dust. But after all that, he expected his soul and spirit to be in his flesh again and to see God with his own eyes. Job longed for this (see GWDN, pages 320–321 and GWRV, pages 298–299).

Charles Stanley: Of course, we grieve when someone we love is taken in death. But we grieve differently from the way the world does. We do not grieve as those who have no hope. We can look forward to a wonderful reunion someday with them and with the One who died—and lives—for us!

If He had remained dead, we would have nothing.

Nothing.

No hope. No faith. No comfort.

But we have a living Savior, who transcended the laws of death and smashed them forever.[1]

How did Job know that he would be raised, that he has a Redeemer? Could it be that he had a **revelation** from God? If not, it must have been common knowledge among believers in his lifetime.

Fulfillment: Job will be raised from the dead with the Old Testament saints in the resurrection of life.

PSALMS

THE BIG PICTURE

Psalms The book of Psalms contains 150 different poems covering a variety of subjects, such as the creation, the history of Israel, the birth of Christ, the Second Coming, the Millennium, praise, thanksgiving, and repentance. Psalms are used in the rituals of both Judaism and Christianity. And they are quoted 186 times in the New Testament.

More Than Just Another Book Of Poems

The book of Psalms is not an ordinary book. It contains a number of verses that are widely recognized by scholars as prophecies relating to the first coming of Christ. Because the verses are scattered throughout the book, a list of first coming prophecies and their New Testament fulfillment is provided below.

Prophecy: " . . . *because you will not abandon me to the grave, nor will you let your* **Holy One** *see decay*" (Psalm 16:10).

Fulfillment: "*Seeing what was ahead, he spoke of the resurrection of the Christ, that he was not abandoned to the grave, nor did his body see decay. God has raised this Jesus to life, and we are all witnesses of the fact*" (Acts 2:31–32).

Holy One: Jesus

Prophecy: "*My God, my God, why have you forsaken me? Why are you so far from saving me, so far from the words of my* **groaning**?" (Psalm 22:1).

Fulfillment: "*And at the ninth hour Jesus cried out in a loud voice, 'Eloi, Eloi, lama sabachthani?'—which means, 'My God, my God, why have you <u>forsaken</u> me?'*" (Mark 15:34).

groaning: pain, suffering

☞ **GO TO:**

Matthew 27:46
(forsaken)

Prophecy: "*But I am a worm and not a man, scorned by men and despised by the people. All who see me mock me; they hurl insults, shaking their heads: "He trusts in the* LORD; *let the* LORD *rescue him. Let him deliver him, since he delights in him*" (Psalm 22:6–8).

Fulfillment: "*Those who passed by hurled <u>insults</u> at him, shaking their heads and saying, 'You who are going to destroy the temple and build it in three days, save yourself! Come down from the cross, if you are the Son of God!' In the same way the chief priests, the teachers of the law and the elders mocked him. 'He saved others,' they said, 'but he can't save himself! He's the King of Israel! Let him come down now from the cross, and we will believe in him. He trusts in God. Let God rescue him now if he wants him, for he said, "I am the Son of God"'*" (Matthew 27:39–43).

☞ **GO TO:**

Luke 23:35–37 (insults)

Prophecy: "**Dogs** *have surrounded me; a band of evil men has encircled me, they have pierced my hands and my feet. I can count all my bones; people stare and gloat over me. They divide my <u>garments</u> among them and* **cast lots** *for my clothing*" (Psalm 22:16–18).

Fulfillment: "*and, as another scripture says, 'They will look on the one they have pierced'*" (John 19:37).

"*When they had crucified him, they divided up his clothes by casting lots*" (Matthew 27:35).

Dogs: evil people, like unclean animals

cast lots: using chance to determine an outcome or settle an issue

☞ **GO TO:**

Luke 23:34–35
(garments)

Prophecy: *"Into your hands I commit my spirit; redeem me, O L*ord*, the God of truth"* (Psalm 31:5).

Fulfillment: *"Jesus called out with a loud voice, 'Father, into your hands I commit my <u>spirit</u>.' When he had said this, he breathed his last"* (Luke 23:46).

GO TO:

Matthew 27:50 (spirit)

Prophecy: *"He protects all his bones, not one of them will be broken"* (Psalm 34:20).

Fulfillment: *"But when they came to Jesus and found that he was already dead, they did not break his legs. Instead, one of the soldiers pierced Jesus' side with a spear, bringing a sudden flow of blood and water. The man who saw it has given testimony, and his testimony is true. He knows that he tells the truth, and he testifies so that you also may believe. These things happened so that the scripture would be fulfilled: 'Not one of his bones will be broken'"* (John 19:33–36).

Prophecy: *"Ruthless witnesses come forward; they question me on things I know nothing about"* (Psalm 35:11).

Fulfillment: *"Then some stood up and gave this false testimony against him: 'We heard him say, "I will destroy this man-made <u>temple</u> and in three days will build another, not made by man"'"* (Mark 14:57–58).

☞ **GO TO:**

John 2:19 (temple)

Luke 23:49 (distance)

Prophecy: *"My friends and companions avoid me because of my wounds; my neighbors stay far away"* (Psalm 38:11).

Fulfillment: *"Many women were there, watching from a <u>distance</u>. They had followed Jesus from Galilee to care for his needs. Among them were Mary Magdalene, Mary the mother of James and Joses, and the mother of Zebedee's sons"* (Matthew 27:55–56).

Prophecy: *"Even my close friend, whom I trusted, he who shared my bread, has lifted up his heel against me"* (Psalm 41:9).

Fulfillment: *"When evening came, Jesus was reclining at the table with the Twelve. And while they were eating, he said, 'I tell you the truth, one of you will betray me.' They were very sad and began to say to him one after the other, 'Surely not I, Lord?' Jesus replied, 'The one who has dipped his hand into the bowl with me will betray me. The Son of Man will go just as it is written about him. But woe to that man who betrays the Son of*

Man! It would be better for him if he had not been born.' Then Judas, the one who would betray him, said, 'Surely not I, Rabbi?' Jesus answered, 'Yes, it is you'" (Matthew 26:20–25).

Prophecy: "I am worn out calling for help; my throat is parched. My eyes fail, looking for my God" (Psalm 69:3).

"They put gall in my food and gave me vinegar for my thirst" (Psalm 69:21).

Fulfillment: "There they offered Jesus wine to drink, mixed with **gall**; but after tasting it, he refused to drink it" (Matthew 27:34).

gall: a bitter juice usually made from herbs

"Immediately one of them ran and got a sponge. He filled it with wine vinegar, put it on a stick, and offered it to Jesus to drink" (Matthew 27:48).

Prophecy: "In return for my friendship they accuse me, but I am a man of prayer" (Psalm 109:4).

Fulfillment: "He who hates me hates my Father as well. If I had not done among them what no one else did, they would not be guilty of sin. But now they have seen these miracles, and yet they have hated both me and my Father. But this is to fulfill what is written in their Law: 'They hated me without reason'" (John 15:23–25).

Prophecy: "My knees give way from fasting; my body is thin and gaunt. I am an object of scorn to my accusers; when they see me, they shake their heads" (Psalm 109:24–25).

Fulfillment: "Those who passed by <u>hurled</u> insults at him, shaking their heads" (Matthew 27:39).

☞ **GO TO:**

Mark 15:29 (hurled)

Luke 20:42–43 (feet)

Prophecy: "The LORD says to my Lord: 'Sit at my right hand until I make your enemies a footstool for your feet'" (Psalm 110:1).

Fulfillment: "The Lord said to my Lord: 'Sit at my right hand until I put your enemies under your <u>feet</u>'" (Matthew 22:44).

Arno C. Gaebelein: Our Lord used the Psalms in His public ministry. He silenced the tempting Pharisees by asking them a question from the One Hundred and Tenth Psalm. Most likely in the nights spent in prayer He poured out His heart in the language of the Psalms. When He came to Jerusalem He was welcomed by the glad shout, "Hosannah to the Son of David," and

What Others are Saying:

when His enemies murmured He referred them to the prediction of the Eighth Psalm. The last word addressed to Jerusalem was a quotation from the Book of Psalms: "Blessed is he that cometh in the name of the Lord" (Psalm 118:26).[2]

RELATED CURRENT EVENTS

THE JACKSON SUN, NOVEMBER 29, 1998 . . .

During the joyous harvest celebration of Tabernacles (Sukkot), Jews recite the Hallel Psalms, numbers 113 to 118, which are also good readings at the Thanksgiving dinner table. As for Christians, the Liturgical Press' new International Bible Commentary says the Psalms have always been central for public prayer in church and for private devotionals. The commentary says that the Psalms of national thanksgiving include the grouping of Psalms 65, 66 and 67, also appropriate readings for Thanksgiving. These Psalms all follow the same general structure of a call to give thanks, a declaration of God's saving actions, a recalling of past national distress and God coming to rescue the people. Psalm 65 expresses thanks especially for deliverance from drought. In Psalm 66, the people of Israel remember that God enabled them to escape from bondage. Psalm 67 sees a plentiful harvest as an occasion for not only Israel but all peoples to praise the divine Provider. Its poetic lines echo across thousands of years.[3]

Fulfilled

First Coming

Fulfillment: These were all fulfilled at the first coming of Christ.

THE BIG PICTURE 🔍

Psalm 2 This poem divides into four stanzas of three verses each. Verses 1–3 question why the nations, rulers and peoples of the earth would rebel against God and his Anointed One—Christ. Verses 4–6 picture God laughing, scoffing, rebuking, and terrifying earth's rebels for opposing him and Christ. Verses 7–9 quote Christ as saying he is God's Son and he will crush earth's rebels. Verses 10–12 command the rebels to be wise, be warned, serve the Lord, and kiss the Son or be destroyed.

Wake Up And Smell The Coffee

The question is, "Why would people <u>conspire</u> against God and his **Anointed** One?" The prophecy is that there will be a great worldwide movement to discredit and destroy those who serve God and believe in Christ, that this movement will try to break the **chains and fetters** of Christianity, throw them aside and set up its own world government. God will laugh at this conspiracy, then he will scoff at it, then he will get <u>angry</u>. Christ will establish a kingdom and rule the <u>world</u> on God's behalf. When the time comes, God will issue a decree and his Son will come and crush the rebellion. Christ is <u>King</u>; he will establish a <u>kingdom</u> and rule the world with an <u>iron scepter</u>. Society's rebellious unbelievers are going to be destroyed.

J. R. Church: God is determined to set His King upon His holy hill of **Zion**. Messiah will establish a worldwide kingdom, be given the nations for His inheritance and the uttermost parts of the earth for His possession. He will come at the end of a series of great wars to *break them with a rod of iron and dash them in pieces like a potter's vessel* (Psalm 2:9).[4]

Thomas Ice and Timothy Demy: The New Testament pictures the condition within the professing church at the end of the age by a system of denials.

- Denial of GOD—Luke 17:26; 2 Timothy 3:4–5
- Denial of CHRIST—1 John 2:18; 4:3; 2 Peter 2:6
- Denial of CHRIST'S RETURN—2 Peter 3:3–4
- Denial of THE FAITH—1 Timothy 4:1–2; Jude 3
- Denial of SOUND DOCTRINE—2 Timothy 4:3–4
- Denial of THE SEPARATED LIFE—2 Timothy 3:1–7
- Denial of CHRISTIAN LIBERTY—1 Timothy 4:3–4
- Denial of MORALS—2 Timothy 3:1–8, 13; Jude 18
- Denial of AUTHORITY—2 Timothy 3:4[5]

DESTINY BULLETIN, NOVEMBER 1998 . . .

Religious liberalism, which denies the inspiration of the Bible, the deity of Christ, and other precious truths, is continuing to work in our world. Philosophies such as neo-orthodoxy are working their way into many of our churches. When

---

Anointed One: Jesus

chains and fetters: laws, truths, teachings

☞ **GO TO:**

Acts 4:23–30 (conspire)

1 Samuel 2:10 (Anointed)

Psalm 18:7–15 (angry)

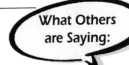
What Others are Saying:

☞ **GO TO:**

Psalm 24:1–10 (world)

Psalm 10:15, 16; Jeremiah 30:8–9; Ezekiel 37:1–28; Hosea 3:4–5; Zechariah 14:9, 16–17 (King)

Psalm 45:6 (kingdom)

Numbers 24:14–19; Revelation 19:15 (iron scepter)

Zion: a poetic name for Jerusalem

RELATED CURRENT EVENTS

KEY Symbols:

Iron Scepter
God's standards

| Unfulfilled |
| Second Coming |

Battle of Armageddon:
the last and greatest war before the Millennium

☞ **GO TO:**

Psalm 9:7–9 (judge)

Psalm 22:27–31
   (nations)

Dig Deeper

leaders turn from the Gospel to another heretical form of Christianity, it is not long before total deterioration sets in. In America in our time, there are thousands of empty churches where once the Gospel sounded, but now there is a haunting silence. An eerie irresponsibility has settled upon the minds of many who should be giving a loud and forceful presentation of the Gospel.[6]

Apostasy, rebellion, and unbelief angers God and in due time he will deal with them.

Fulfillment: The conspiracy of unbelievers against God and Jesus began with the persecution of Jesus and his disciples, and it will lead to a one-world government with a one-world religious system at the end of this age. In short order, the world will experience the Tribulation Period, the **Battle of Armageddon**, and the Second Coming of Christ. Jesus will judge the nations, the Millennium will begin, the kingdom of righteousness will be established, and Jesus will rule with a rod of iron.

The Tribulation Period	Scripture
The nations will fall beneath his feet.	Psalm 45:1–6
There will be no mercy for the wicked.	Psalm 59:5–8
The enemies of Christ will cringe.	Psalm 66:3
The wicked will perish.	Psalm 68:1–2
The proud will get what they deserve.	Psalm 94:1–4

> **Psalm 46:6–11** Nations are in uproar, kingdoms fall; he lifts his voice, the earth melts. The LORD Almighty is with us; the God of Jacob is our fortress. Come and see the works of the LORD, the desolations he has brought on the earth. He makes wars cease to the ends of the earth; he breaks the bow and shatters the spear, he burns the shields with fire. "Be still, and know that I am God; I will be exalted among the nations, I will be exalted in the earth." The LORD Almighty is with us; the God of Jacob is our fortress.

When "Peace On Earth" Becomes A Fact

In this poem, the writer looks back on history to the Tribulation Period. He saw the <u>nations</u> in an uproar. War and rumors of war prevailed in many places. Mighty kingdoms fell. All God had to do was lift his voice and the <u>flesh</u> of his enemies dissolved; he won a great victory. Though the world was in turmoil, the God of Jacob (i.e., the God of Israel, Jehovah) protected his people, the **remnant** of Israel. The writer asks us to come and see the works of the Lord and the terrible blow he dealt to the wicked on earth. He used a great battle to bring an end to <u>war</u>, breaking the weapons of his enemies. The writer asks us to be calm and know God, to not fret over the turmoil in the world, to acknowledge what God can do, and to watch him do it. God will be exalted on earth and he will protect his people.

Ed Hindson: Armageddon! The mere mention of it causes us to tremble. Armageddon is the ultimate biblical symbol for the great war at the end of the age. Its very name conjures up visions of global destruction, worldwide devastation, and indescribable human suffering. It is the war to end all wars![7]

At the Tribulation Period midpoint, a remnant of Israel will flee Jerusalem (Revelation 12:6). Near the end of the Tribulation Period, a great war called the Battle of Armageddon will take place (Revelation 16:12–16). That will trigger the Second Coming of Jesus—he will win a great victory for God and deliver his people.

Fulfillment: This prophecy will be fulfilled in the future. Believers will be able to look back on the Tribulation Period and review what happened. We will understand that God used that terrible time to deal with the wicked on earth and to establish his kingdom here.

The Second Coming	Scripture
The King of glory is coming.	Psalm 24:7–10
Jesus will judge his people.	Psalm 50:3–5
Jesus will judge righteously.	Psalm 96:10–13
Kings and leaders will be crushed.	Psalm 110:1–7

☞ **GO TO:**

Matthew 24:7 (nations)

Zechariah 14:12–15 (flesh)

Revelation 19:11–21 (war)

remnant: those Jews who are in a right relationship with God

What Others are Saying:

Remember This . . .

Unfulfilled
Millennium

Dig Deeper

> **Psalm 47** Clap your hands, all you nations; shout to God with cries of joy. How awesome is the LORD Most High, the great King over all the earth! He subdued nations under us, peoples under our feet. He chose our inheritance for us, the pride of Jacob, whom he loved. God has ascended amid shouts of joy, the LORD amid the sounding of trumpets. Sing praises to God, sing praises; sing praises to our King, sing praises. For God is the King of all the earth; sing to him a psalm of praise. God reigns over the nations; God is seated on his holy throne. The nobles of the nations assemble as the people of the God of Abraham, for the kings of the earth belong to God; he is greatly exalted.

exuberance: *great joy*

King: *Jesus*

Something to Ponder

Remember This . . .

☞ **GO TO:**

Psalm 2:1–12 (chains)

Matthew 2:2; 27:11, 37 (King of the Jews)

Revelation 19:16 (King of kings)

Joy To The World!

This psalm presents a prophetic picture of an event that will take place on earth during the Millennium. People on earth are encouraged to show **exuberance**: to clap, shout, and rejoice. Our **King** is awesome and great. He has subdued the nations, established his kingdom, and elevated Israel to a place of prominence in the world. He has occupied his holy throne amidst shouting and trumpet sounds. Praises are given to him. He is King of all the earth. World leaders are gathered before him. Leaders of his people are there. Control of the earth is in his hands, and he is greatly praised.

Every person on earth belongs to a kingdom: one is God's and the other is Satan's. Ultimately God's kingdom will prevail and Satan's kingdom will be destroyed.

Almost two thousand years ago, Jewish leaders conspired against Jesus and had him crucified. Now world leaders conspire against him and try to break his <u>chains</u>. But he is <u>King of the Jews</u> and King of all the earth. God has made him <u>King of kings</u> and Lord of lords, and the day will come when he is established as absolute ruler over all things.

The God who kept his promises by sending Jesus to the cross, by raising him from the dead, by reuniting Europe, by bringing Israel back into existence, and by causing the city of Jerusalem to be rebuilt will surely bring this to pass too. It will be like a bombshell exploding in the face of an unbelieving world. Jesus will reign, and we will be able to rejoice.

Fulfillment: This worship service will take place during the Millennium. Its purpose will be to celebrate the things Jesus has done to accomplish God's will for the world. It will be a time of applause, song, and praise.

The Millennium	Scripture
Everyone on earth will turn to Christ.	Psalm 22:27–31
Jerusalem will be the city of God.	Psalm 48:1–3
Righteousness will prevail.	Psalm 72:1–20
Jesus will reign.	Psalm 93:1, 2
Jesus is God's salvation.	Psalm 98:1–9
God will remember his covenants.	Psalm 105:8–11
The throne of David will be in Israel.	Psalm 132:11–18
The Jews will return to Israel and Jerusalem.	Psalm 147:2, 3

Dig Deeper

THOSE WHO WILL LIVE ON EARTH DURING THE MILLENNIUM

1. The saved Israelites who are alive at the end of the Tribulation Period.
2. The saved Gentiles who are alive at the end of the Tribulation Period.
3. Children born to saved survivors of the Tribulation Period during the Millennium.
4. The Old Testament saints who trusted God and looked forward to the coming Messiah.
5. Christians who went in the Rapture and return with Jesus at his Second Coming.
6. Those who accept Christ and are killed between the Rapture and the Second Coming.

THOSE WHO WILL NOT LIVE ON EARTH DURING THE MILLENNIUM

1. All unbelievers who die before the Second Coming.
2. All unbelievers who are alive at the Second Coming. (They will be removed.)

Edom: *an area in ancient Jordan*

Ishmaelites: *descendants of Ishmael*

Moab: *an area in ancient Jordan*

Hagrites: *descendants of Hagar (Sarah's handmaid)*

Gebal: *a city in ancient Lebanon*

Ammon: *a city in ancient Jordan*

Amalek: *descendants of Esau (Jacob/Israel's brother)*

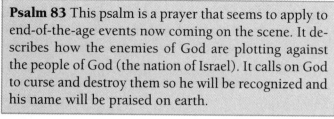

Psalm 83 This psalm is a prayer that seems to apply to end-of-the-age events now coming on the scene. It describes how the enemies of God are plotting against the people of God (the nation of Israel). It calls on God to curse and destroy them so he will be recognized and his name will be praised on earth.

An Evil Alliance

In this prayer, God is asked not to be silent, quiet, or still. It is said that his enemies are busy conspiring against his people, that they want to destroy the nation of Israel. The enemies are identified as **Edom**, the **Ishmaelites**, **Moab**, the **Hagrites**, **Gebal**, **Ammon**, **Amalek**, **Philistia**, **Tyre**, **Assyria**, and the descendants of **Lot**. God is asked to make them dust, like a tumbleweed blown by the wind, to make them run as terrified creatures before a fire, to shame and disgrace them. He is asked to do this so they will know that he is God and he alone rules the earth.

What Others are Saying:

Philistia: *Palestinians, PLO*

Tyre: *a city in ancient Lebanon*

Assyria: *an ancient empire including Syria, Iraq, and part of Egypt*

Lot: *a nephew of Abraham*

☞ **GO TO:**

Isaiah 14:28–32 (Philistia)

Tribulation Period

Charles Halff: The amazing thing about this prophecy is that it could never have been fulfilled until our present-day generation. Why not? Simply because Israel hasn't existed as a sovereign nation since the 8th century B.C., when the Babylonian oppression began, resulting with the Captivity in 586 B.C. It was not until A.D. 1948 that a nation in the Middle East once again became known as "Israel." The prophets actually foresaw the re-establishment of Israel as a nation in the last days.[8]

Arno C. Gaebelein: Behind it all stands the murderer from the beginning, that sinister being who knows that God's redemption program is inseparably linked with Israel, that salvation is of the Jews. And therefore he tries to cut them off as a nation, so that their name be no longer remembered. That enemy also knows all about the glorious future promised to Israel. As the time approaches when that future is to be realized, the enemy will make the final assault. Then comes the supreme effort to exterminate the nation and blot out the name of Israel forever.[9]

Fulfillment: The underlying causes of this prayer are now coming on the scene. It will be answered because God will defend his people and his name. One purpose of the Tribulation Period is to deal with Israel's enemies.

STUDY QUESTIONS

1. How does Hebrew poetry differ from American poetry?
2. What did Job believe about his own resurrection?
3. How does God respond to the conspiracy of unbelievers against him and his Christ?
4. According to the Psalms, how will people react to the First Coming of Christ?
5. Who will worship Christ during the Millennium? What city is called the city of God? Where will the throne of David be?

CHAPTER WRAP-UP

- Job lost everything, but he was not discouraged. He was full of hope, believed he had a Redeemer, believed he would be raised from the dead, and believed he would have a new body. (Job 19:25–27)

- Rebellion and conspiracy against God and Jesus will be a characteristic of the end of this age. This will anger God. Jesus will return, crush the rebellion, deal harshly with the conspirators, establish a kingdom of righteousness, and reign on earth as King. (Psalm 2:1–21; see also Psalm 24, 50, 96, and 110)

- The Psalms are quoted 186 times in the New Testament. Many quotes are about Jesus and his crucifixion and resurrection. (See also Psalm 16, 22, 31, 34, 35, 38, 41, 69, 109, and 110)

- A time of national upset and war is coming. The enemies of Israel will plot to destroy the nation. God will judge them, nations will fall, and the wicked will perish. (Psalm 46:6–11; 83:1–18; see also Psalm 45, 59, 66, 68, and 94)

- Jesus is King. He will establish a kingdom on earth and sit on the throne of David in Jerusalem. He will be worshiped. Righteousness will prevail. (Psalm 47:1–9; see also Psalm 22, 48, 72, 93, 98, 105, 132, and 147)

4 PROPHECIES IN THE MAJOR PROPHETS

CHAPTER HIGHLIGHTS

- Isaiah
- Jeremiah
- Lamentations
- Ezekiel
- Daniel

Let's Get Started

The book of Isaiah begins a series of five Old Testament books that are sometimes **collectively** called the Major Prophets. But they are not major in the sense that their messages are more important than those of the other books in the Bible. They are major in the sense that their messages are long. All of the messages in the Bible are important because they are nothing less than the inspired Word of God. But this section is referred to as major because it is so **extensive**.

collectively: taken together, as a group

extensive: covers so many things

ISAIAH

Isaiah 1:24–31 Therefore the Lord, the LORD Almighty, the Mighty One of Israel, declares: "Ah, I will get relief from my foes and avenge myself on my enemies. I will turn my hand against you; I will thoroughly purge away your dross and remove all your impurities. I will restore your judges as in days of old, your counselors as at the beginning. Afterward you will be called the City of Righteousness, the Faithful City." Zion will be redeemed with justice, her penitent ones with righteousness. But rebels and sinners will both be broken, and those who forsake the LORD will perish. "You will be ashamed because of the sacred oaks in which you have delighted; you will be disgraced because of the gardens that you have chosen. You will be like an oak with fading leaves, like a garden without water. The mighty man will become tinder and his work a spark; both will burn together, with no one to quench the fire."

redemption: the payment of a price to free sinners

repent: to turn away from wrong and toward God

☞ **GO TO:**

2 Kings 17:7–23 (sins)

Unfulfilled

Tribulation Period

Millennium

calamities: war, disasters, etc.

KEY Symbols:

The City of Righteousness
Jerusalem in the future

The Faithful City
Jerusalem in the future

☞ **GO TO:**

Ezekiel 43:10–12;
   Micah 4:1–7 (Temple)

Judgment Of Judah And Jerusalem

God identified himself in three ways: he is the Lord, he is the Lord Almighty, and he is the Mighty One of Israel. He is an all-powerful supreme being who is a force not to be trifled with. His judgment will come to Judah and Jerusalem to accomplish two things: to purge the wicked and to restore the nation. Upon completion, Jerusalem will be known as the City of Righteousness and also as the Faithful City. God's judgment will lead to the **redemption** of the godly because they will **repent** of their sins. The ungodly will be destroyed because they have forsaken him. They will reap shame and disgrace because of their false religion. They will deceive themselves into thinking they are strong, but they will perish.

Fulfillment: The Jews have returned to the land and Jerusalem has been rebuilt, but the Jews have not accepted Jesus as the Messiah. God is a force to be reckoned with and he will deal with them. He will send **calamities** during the Tribulation Period to separate the righteous from the unrighteous. Afterward, during the Millennium, Jesus will reign in Jerusalem and the city will be known as the City of Righteousness, the Faithful City.

THE BIG PICTURE

> **Isaiah 2:1–22** Concerning Judah and Jerusalem in the last days, the Temple will be rebuilt. It will be higher than the surrounding area, it will become the religious center of the world, multitudes will go there to learn God's ways, Jesus will rule over the nations, war will end, there will be peace on earth, and all Israel will be encouraged to follow him. God forsook Israel and its Temple because the people embraced pagan customs and practiced divination, piled up treasures and committed idolatry. He forced them out of the country, scattered them among the nations, and set aside a time of judgment. When this happens the proud will be humbled, Jesus will be exalted, idols will be destroyed, men will hide in caves, earthquakes will shake the earth, and Israel will stop trusting in mortal men.

The Times, They Are A-changin'

The Temple will be rebuilt in the last days. It will be elevated above the surrounding area and transformed into a worldwide religious center, called the house of Israel's God. Jesus will sit on the throne of David, rule the nations, decide national issues, and arbitrate disputes. Weapons will be destroyed and war will cease. Military preparation will end.

God forsook Israel and its former Temple because the people forsook him. They took up the customs of **unregenerate** people, customs forbidden in the Bible: they practiced **divination**, <u>coveted</u> wealth, and worshiped <u>idols</u>. Thus, sin is the reason why the Jews were scattered all over the world and why God said there will be a Tribulation Period. The wealthy who suffer from <u>pride</u> and the idolaters who suffer from arrogance will be humbled. Many Jews will abandon their idols and turn back to God.

Randall Price: When the Millennium begins, topographical changes will occur that will cause the city itself to be elevated above the surrounding land, which will be flattened into a vast plain (Zechariah 14:10). This will be done so that the Temple Mount will occupy the highest elevation in the region, making Jerusalem the new center of the Land.[1]

Dave Hunt: Of particular interest is the fact that, as the *Smithsonian* article documents, dowsing is now being used to uncover all sorts of information—answers to virtually every question one could ask. Dowsing, then, is simply another form of "divination" (any occult technique for obtaining information and help from the spirit world through a physical device). It is strictly forbidden in the Bible. Other divination devices commonly used include crystal balls, tarot cards, Ouija boards, tea leaves and pendulums.[2]

There is nothing wrong with acquiring wealth unless it is acquired illegally, used to glorify oneself instead of God, or used as a substitute for trusting in God (see Proverbs 10:4, 22, 28).

Fulfillment: The Jews will rebuild their Temple by the middle of the Tribulation Period, but that Temple (sometimes called the Tribulation Period Temple) is not the one that will become the religious center of the world. The glorious Temple in this passage that Jesus will rule from is often called the Millennial Temple. The set time of judgment is the Tribulation Period. Repentance and true worship will be a result.

unregenerate: *unsaved*

divination: *trying to predict the future through omens*

☞ **GO TO:**

Exodus 20:17 (coveted)

Exodus 20:4–5 (idols)

Proverbs 8:13 (pride)

What Others are Saying:

KEY POINT

God's people should not be like everyone else in the world.

KEY Symbols:

Temple
The house of Israel's God

Something to Ponder

Unfulfilled

Tribulation Period

Millennium

The Scattering of the Jews	Scripture

Dig Deeper

Judah was made desolate, cities were burned, the fields were stripped. .... Isaiah 1:7–9

The people spoke against God. .... Isaiah 3:8

The land was filled with injustice and unrighteousness. .... Isaiah 5:1–10

The people did not understand the Word of God. .... Isaiah 6:9–12

The women were complacent about spiritual matters. .... Isaiah 32:9–14

The people would not follow God or obey his laws. .... Isaiah 42:23–25

All their leaders from the first to the last sinned. .... Isaiah 43:26–28

The people failed to respond to God. .... Isaiah 50:1–2

Their sleeping, spiritually blind children would not be able to lead them. .... Isaiah 51:17–20

Sin separated the people from God. .... Isaiah 59:1–2

The people blindly turned their back on God. .... Isaiah 59:9–15

The Millennium	Scripture

Dig Deeper

The government will be upon the shoulders of Jesus. .... Isaiah 9:6–7

Righteousness and peace will prevail. .... Isaiah 11:1–13

It will be a time of praise, singing, and thanksgiving. .... Isaiah 12:1–6

In love, Jesus will sit on the throne of David. .... Isaiah 16:5

God will put an end to death and tears. .... Isaiah 25:6–9

Judah will be strong and will rejoice. .... Isaiah 26:1–17

It will be a time of abundance and restoration in Israel. .... Isaiah 27:1–13

The sun and moon will be brighter. .... Isaiah 30:23–26

God's people will have spiritual understanding. .... Isaiah 32:1–4

There will be no sickness or sin in Jerusalem. .... Isaiah 33:20–24

The Millennium	Scripture
The desert will bloom, the blind will see, the deaf will hear, and the lame will walk.	... Isaiah 35:1–10
The Jews will be regathered.	Isaiah 43:5–7
God will pour out his Spirit.	Isaiah 44:3
Gladness and joy will prevail.	Isaiah 51:3–4; 9–16
Everyone will know Jesus.	Isaiah 52:6–10
Israel will be enlarged.	Isaiah 54:1–17
Gentiles will share the blessings.	Isaiah 56:6–8
Gentiles will worship Jesus.	Isaiah 60:1–9
Israel will be blessed.	Isaiah 61:4–11
Jesus will delight in Israel.	Isaiah 62:1–12
There will be a new heaven and a new earth.	.... Isaiah 65:17–25
God will deal with his enemies.	Isaiah 66:1–24

Dig Deeper

> **Isaiah 4:1–6** In that day seven women will take hold of one man and say, "We will eat our own food and provide our own clothes; only let us be called by your name. Take away our disgrace!" In that day the Branch of the LORD will be beautiful and glorious, and the fruit of the land will be the pride and glory of the survivors in Israel. Those who are left in Zion, who remain in Jerusalem, will be called holy, all who are recorded among the living in Jerusalem. The Lord will wash away the filth of the women of Zion; he will cleanse the bloodstains from Jerusalem by a spirit of judgment and a spirit of fire. Then the LORD will create over all of Mount Zion and over those who assemble there a cloud of smoke by day and a glow of flaming fire by night; over all the glory will be a canopy. It will be a shelter and shade from the heat of the day, and a refuge and hiding place from the storm and rain.

Wanted: A Few Good Men

This passage begins with a verse about the Tribulation Period and moves on to some comments about the Millennium. War will **decimate** the male population of the earth during the Tribulation Period. So many <u>men</u> will be <u>killed</u> that seven women will be willing to share each male survivor. Women will be so desperate

decimate: kill many

☞ **GO TO:**

Isaiah 3:25 (men)

Revelation 6:7–8; 9:15 (killed)

☞ **GO TO:**

Isaiah 4:2; 11:1–5;
Jeremiah 23:5;
Zechariah 3:8; 6:12
(Branch)

Exodus 33:9 (cloud)

Exodus 40:34–38 (fire)

Unfulfilled

Tribulation Period

Millennium

☞ **GO TO:**

Matthew 24:22
(survive)

*Dig
Deeper*

KEY Symbols:

Branch
Jesus

☞ **GO TO:**

2 Kings 16:5 (besieged)

to marry and have children, they will offer to work to support themselves. During the Millennium, the <u>Branch</u> (Jesus) will be the pride and glory of the survivors in Israel. He will be honored by those Jews who make it through the Tribulation Period and they will be called holy. The city of Jerusalem and women who have sinned will be judged and cleansed by fire. God will be present in a <u>cloud</u> of smoke and flaming <u>fire</u>. He will be the defense, shelter, shade, refuge, and hiding place of the Jews and they will be safe (see GWRV, pages 94–95).

Fulfillment: This will be fulfilled during the Tribulation Period and Millennium. Were it not for the Second Coming of Christ no one would <u>survive</u> the Tribulation Period. But he will come back, put an end to war and restore the earth.

The Tribulation Period	Scripture
A remnant of Jews will rely on the Lord.	Isaiah 10:20–23
Many Palestinians will be destroyed.	Isaiah 14:28–32
The Ethiopian (Cush) army will be destroyed.	Isaiah 18:1–7
Fear will grip the earth.	Isaiah 24:1, 3, 6, 17–22
Jesus will prevail against his enemies.	Isaiah 42:13–16
God's enemies will know his name.	Isaiah 64:1–4

> **Isaiah 7:14** "Therefore the Lord himself will give you a sign: The virgin will be with child and will give birth to a son, and will call him Immanuel."

The Virgin Birth

It was a time of trouble. The nation of Israel had divided (see illustration, page 65) into a Northern Kingdom (called Israel) and a Southern Kingdom (called Judah). The Northern Kingdom formed an alliance with a third nation (Syria) and the two <u>besieged</u> Judah along with Jerusalem in an effort to overthrow King Ahaz of Judah. They thought they would prevail, but they did not. When they continued to plot against King Ahaz, God sent the prophet Isaiah to tell King Ahaz not to be afraid. King Ahaz

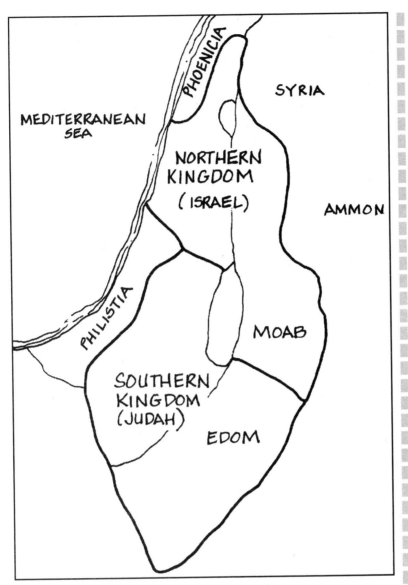

Northern and Southern Kingdoms

Israel was divided into two kingdoms: Israel in the north and Judah in the south.

was skeptical, so God sent Isaiah to him with a second message. God would give the king a sign if he would ask for it. King Ahaz refused God's generous offer, so God decided to give one to the whole **house of David**: a virgin would give birth to a son and he would be called Immanuel.

KEY POINT

The virgin birth of Jesus is a sign.

house of David: the Jews

What Others are Saying:

Herbert Lockyer: Is it not somewhat remarkable that whenever the birth of the Messiah is spoken of in prophecy, reference is made to His mother, or to the womb, never to a human father, which, of course, Jesus did not have.[3]

**Remember
This . . .**

extraordinary: unusual

WARNING

Fulfilled
First Coming

**Dig
Deeper**

☞ **GO TO:**

Matthew 1:18–23; Luke
1:26–38 (virgin)

Matthew 22:29
(Scriptures)

banner: flag

*day of the Lord: another
name for the Tribulation
Period*

☞ **GO TO:**

Genesis 19:1–29
(Sodom and
Gomorrah)

Isaiah said, *"The Lord himself will give you a sign."* According to Webster's, a sign is something **extraordinary**. For a young woman to bear a child isn't extraordinary. Young women bear children every day. But it would be extraordinary if a virgin bore a child—that would be a sign.

The Hebrew word *almah* can be translated two ways: <u>virgin</u> or young woman. Here it is translated virgin, but many unbelievers say it should be translated "young woman." They clearly do not know the <u>Scriptures</u> or the power of God.

Fulfillment: This was fulfilled several hundred years later when the virgin Mary gave birth to Jesus. When Mary questioned it an angel said, *"Nothing is impossible with God."*

The First Coming	Scripture
The people will see a great light.	Isaiah 9:2
The characteristics of God's servant.	Isaiah 42:1–4
Jesus will be beaten, mocked, and spit upon.	Isaiah 50:6
Jesus will suffer.	Isaiah 52:13–15; 53:1–12
The ministry of Jesus.	Isaiah 61:1–2

THE BIG PICTURE 🔍

Isaiah 13:1–22 God will bring many nations with the weapons of his wrath from faraway lands to fight against Babylon. When the Tribulation Period arrives, the land will be made desolate, the universe will experience great cosmic upheavals, multitudes will die, Babylon will be destroyed like Sodom and Gomorrah, and it will never be inhabited by people again.

Iraq

This prophecy calls for a **banner** to be raised on a bare hilltop (where it can be clearly seen) to summon a great army against Babylon. This army will gather under God's influence and be used to pour out his wrath like he did on <u>Sodom and Gomorrah</u>. Troops from many nations and faraway lands will be assembled during the **day of the Lord** to destroy the whole country. People will become helpless and terrified when they see this awesome force gathered against them. Confusion will grip them. They will realize that they are being punished for their sins. The stars will not shine, the sun will be <u>darkened</u>, and the moon will give no light. The population will be decimated. A <u>man</u> will be worth more than precious commodities. People will scatter. Those who are captured will be killed. Even children will be killed. Houses will be plundered. Women will be raped. There will be no mercy, no compassion, no place to hide. The beautiful city of Babylon will be seen <u>burning</u> to the ground. People will never live there again (see GWRV, pages 263–277).

☞ **GO TO:**

Matthew 24:29 (darkened)

Isaiah 4:1–6 (man)

Revelation 18:1–24 (burning)

Noah Hutchings: The subject of Isaiah 13 is total destruction; the object of destruction is the entire land Babylon (modern Iraq); the time period is the day of the Lord.[4]

What Others are Saying:

Grant R. Jeffrey: The prophets warn that Babylon will be utterly destroyed by God and that the fire and smoke will ascend from her ruins forever. As indicated in my *MESSIAH* book, the city of Babylon is being rebuilt by Saddam Hussein beside the ancient ruins at a cost of over $850 million to date. The city lies on top of an ancient lake of asphalt and oil that will burn forever when God destroys her as "Sodom and Gomorrah" on the "day of the Lord."[5]

There are those who say this prophecy refers to the capture of Babylon by the Medes and Persians. But that attack was a two-nation assault by neighboring countries, while this will be a multination assault by enemies from faraway places.

WARNING

Fulfillment: It is plainly stated that this prophecy will take place in the day of the Lord.

Unfulfilled
Tribulation Period

THE BIG PICTURE 🔍

Isaiah 17:1–14 Damascus will be destroyed and its suburbs will be abandoned. Many cities in the northern part of Israel will also be destroyed and Israel will be greatly weakened. Jews will go hungry. But a remnant of Jews will repent and accept Jesus. Meanwhile, many Syrian cities will be abandoned because they have forgotten God. A number of nations will rage against Israel, but God will rebuke them.

Syria And Northern Israel

It is not hard to find commentators who say this prophecy has been fulfilled, but because **Damascus** has been destroyed so many times, there is much doubt about who fulfilled it and when it happened. There are others who believe this has never been fulfilled because Damascus has always been rebuilt and it has never ceased to exist as a city. There may have been an initial partial fulfillment, but a greater, more complete fulfillment is yet to come.

Thus, we see that Damascus will be permanently destroyed sometime in the future. The cities of **Aroer** will be abandoned. Fortified cities in **Ephraim** will be destroyed. The power of Damascus will be broken. The cities of **Aram** will disappear.

When this happens, the glory of **Jacob** will diminish and Israel will be weakened. Many Jews will have to glean for food and large cities will be abandoned because the Jews will have forgotten the God of their salvation. As a result, some Jews will abandon their idols and false religion, turn from their sins, and accept Jesus.

At that time, nations will rage and threaten Israel, but God will intervene on Israel's behalf and silence the opposing nations.

What Others are Saying:

Gary Stearman: This prophecy calls for the complete destruction of Damascus. . . . Will there be some kind of military exchange between Israel and Syria? Will it destroy parts of both countries? The territory of Ephraim is the heart of Israel, from the River Jordan to the Mediterranean Sea. In the days of Israel's original land grant, it extended from just north of Jerusalem, northward to the region of Shechem. It would encompass all of today's Samaria, plus more land to the west and north. Put in another way, it is the northern half of the contested West Bank Territories.[6]

DISPATCH FROM JERUSALEM, SEPTEMBER/OCTOBER 1998 . . .

RELATED CURRENT EVENTS

It is known Syrians are now arming themselves with two brigades of mobile SCUD missiles (see illustration, page 69), the SCUD-B, which can reach Tel Aviv, and the SCUD-C, which can reach as far south as Dimona. Combined with their short-range missiles, Syria will soon have the capability to hit all parts of Israel with nearly 50 missiles at one time. Intelligence sources report Syria has begun placing SCUDs into deep underground bunkers in mountains south and east of Damascus, which cannot be penetrated by even the newest and most modern weapons.[7]

SCUD Missile

SCUD missiles like this one are easy to move and retarget.

☞ **GO TO:**

Genesis 35:21–29
(Judah)

Genesis 41:50–52
(Ephraim)

Remember
This . . .

Unfulfilled

Church Age

☞ **GO TO:**

Ezekiel 38–39
(Gog and Magog)

KEY Symbols:

Southern Kingdom
Judah

Northern Kingdom
Israel or Ephraim

One of Jacob's sons was named <u>Judah</u>. When the nation of Israel divided into a Northern Kingdom and a Southern Kingdom, the Southern Kingdom called itself Judah. Another one of Jacob's sons was named Joseph. He had two children named Manasseh and <u>Ephraim</u>. When the nation of Israel divided, the Northern Kingdom called itself Israel, but there were times when it was called Ephraim.

Fulfillment: Scholars are divided on when this battle will take place. Some, including me, think war between Israel and Syria could break out any moment, while others think this will trigger the Battle of <u>Gog and Magog</u> and they usually place that in the Tribulation Period.

> **Isaiah 26:19–21** But your dead will live; their bodies will rise. You who dwell in the dust, wake up and shout for joy. Your dew is like the dew of the morning; the earth will give birth to her dead. Go, my people, enter your rooms and shut the doors behind you; hide yourselves for a little while until his wrath has passed by. See, the LORD is coming out of his dwelling to punish the people of the earth for their sins. The earth will disclose the blood shed upon her; she will conceal her slain no longer.

KEY POINT

Shedding blood (unjust war, murder, abortion) will be exposed and punished.

☞ **GO TO:**

Matthew 27:52 (bodies)

1 Thessalonians 4:13–18; John 5:28–29 (rise)

Daniel 12:2 (dust)

Matthew 24:15–16 (flee)

Zephaniah 1:14–18 (wrath)

What Others are Saying:

Remember This . . .

Some Encouraging Words

God's people have much to look forward to. Those who have died will not be put in the grave and forgotten. God will remember his people and restore their bodies (see illustration, page 71). Moreover, wickedness won't consume the earth. Jesus will come from heaven to punish the unrighteous for their sins. Those who have shed the blood of the innocent who cry out to God will be exposed. Isaiah points out several things that will happen:

1. The dead will live (death is not the end of a person).
2. Their <u>bodies</u> will <u>rise</u> (the resurrection will be a resurrection of the body).
3. Those who dwell in the <u>dust</u> will wake up and rejoice (we will be Raptured to heaven).
4. God's people on earth are warned to seek shelter ("go" and "hide" or <u>flee</u>).
5. God's <u>wrath</u> will be poured out on the earth (the Tribulation Period).
6. God's wrath will be a punishment for sin (this will be the high cost of low living).
7. The sins of those who have shed blood will be exposed (secret sins will be revealed).

Tim LaHaye: Deliverance of Christians from the world's greatest period of wrath is a gift of God for His church. It is not something she deserves, but something He gives because He loves His church. . . . Scripture and the love of Christ seem to favor the pretribulationist view of the rapture.[8]

Among Christians there are differences of opinion about when the Rapture will occur in relation to the Tribulation Period, but most believe the church will not go through that terrible time. Notice the sequence of events in this passage. The dead will be raised first (Rapture). God will pour out his wrath on the earth later (Tribulation Period).

Fulfillment: There will be a resurrection of life with four phases and a resurrection of condemnation. The resurrection in this passage refers to Phase 2—the resurrection of the Church at the Rapture (see illustration, page 71).

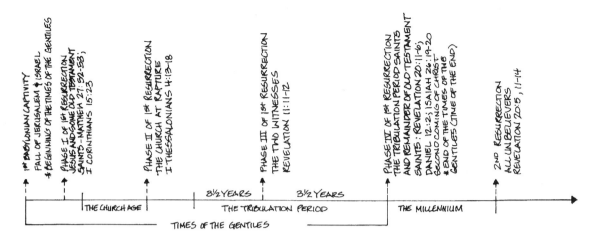

Time Line of the Two Resurrections

Pictured here is a time line of the resurrection of life (for believers) and the resurrection of death (for unbelievers). See John 5:28–29.

JEREMIAH

Jeremiah 3:14–18 "Return, faithless people," declares the LORD, "for I am your husband. I will choose you—one from a town and two from a clan—and bring you to Zion. Then I will give you shepherds after my own heart, who will lead you with knowledge and understanding. In those days, when your numbers have increased greatly in the land," declares the LORD, "men will no longer say, 'The ark of the covenant of the LORD.' It will never enter their minds or be remembered; it will not be missed, nor will another one be made. At that time they will call Jerusalem The Throne of the LORD, and all nations will gather in Jerusalem to honor the name of the LORD. No longer will they follow the stubbornness of their evil hearts. In those days the house of Judah will join the house of Israel, and together they will come from a northern land to the land I gave your forefathers as an inheritance.

We Will Renew Our Marriage Vows

The people in both the Northern Kingdom (Israel) and the Southern Kingdom (Judah) believed they were the people of God, but because they were unfaithful, God compared them to an adul-

☞ **GO TO:**

Jeremiah 31:32; Hosea 2:16–23 (husband)

Psalm 23:1–6 (shepherds)

Exodus 25:10–22 (Ark)

RELATED CURRENT EVENTS

Remember This . . .

Unfulfilled
Millennium

☞ **GO TO:**

Exodus 20:14; Leviticus 20:10 (adultery)

terous wife. This prophecy reminds his **faithless** people that they have broken their **marriage vows**. It calls upon them to return to their **husband**. God assures them that they will be a nation again. He tells them he would prefer to bring them back into the land as a group, but he will choose to bring them back as individuals: "*one from a town and two from a* **clan**." When they return, he will give them faithful **shepherds**. He will cause them to multiply. They will forget about the **Ark of the Covenant** and not need it because the Lord will sit on his throne in Jerusalem (Jeremiah 30:8–9; Zechariah 14:9, 16–17). Gentiles from all nations will go there, honor Jesus, and repent of their sins. The Northern Kingdom will be united with the Southern Kingdom and the two will be one nation again (see GWRV, pages 166–167).

***DISPATCH FROM JERUSALEM*, NOVEMBER/DECEMBER 1998 . . .**

On the occasion of the Jewish New Year 5759 [September 21, 1998], the Central Bureau of Statistics released a report reviewing population growth over the last year. Israel's population today is estimated to be over 6,000,000, of whom 4,756,000 (79.4%) are Jews, and 887,000 (14.8%) are Muslims and 125,853 (2.1%) are Christians. Over the year, Israel's population has grown by 133,000.[9]

God compares unfaithful people to an adulterous or unfaithful wife. Adultery violates the Ten Commandments. It is a sin so serious that God said violators must be dealt with in the harshest of manners. They must be put to death (Deuteronomy 22:22–24).

Fulfillment: The Jews are currently returning to the land. They are returning not as a nation, but as individuals and families from all over the world. They are returning not to a divided kingdom, but to a united kingdom. But this is just preparation for an ultimate future fulfillment. Not until the Millennium will Jesus sit on the throne in Jerusalem and be worshiped by all people.

> **Jeremiah 12:14–17** This is what the LORD says: "As for all my wicked neighbors who seize the inheritance I gave my people Israel, I will uproot them from their lands and I will uproot the house of Judah from among them. But after I uproot them, I will again have compassion and will bring each of them back to his own inheritance and his own country. And if they learn well the ways of my people and swear by my name, saying, 'As surely as the LORD lives'—even as they once taught my people to swear by Baal—then they will be established among my people. But if any nation does not listen, I will completely uproot and destroy it," declares the LORD.

An Offer That Can't Be Refused

God has a message for those wicked people who seize the land he gave to his chosen people. What they have done to Israel will be done to them. He will drive them out of their own lands. But then he will have mercy on them and allow them to return home. If they will learn the ways of Israel and accept Jesus as the Messiah, their <u>nations</u> will be restored. But if they refuse, they will be completely destroyed.

☞ **GO TO:**

Psalm 2:1–12;
Revelation 12:5;
19:15 (nations)

> The good of the world transcends the right of nations to choose their own government. The time is coming when God will no longer let nations exist if their governments do not honor him. Everything will be done in order. First, God will cause the Jews to repent of their sins and accept Jesus as the Messiah. After that, he will restore the nation. Then, he will offer restoration to Israel's neighbors, and then to all the other nations on earth.

Remember This . . .

Unfulfilled
Millennium

Fulfillment: Israel's neighbors will be driven out of their land during the Tribulation Period. They will be given the opportunity to accept Jesus and be restored during the Millennium. Some nations will do that and they will have a glorious future. Other nations will reject Christ and they will cease to exist. Just as individuals are responsible for how we respond to Jesus, so are the nations.

Dig Deeper

The Millennium	Scripture
Every Jew will return to Israel.	Jeremiah 16:14–15
The Jews will return to God with all their heart.	Jeremiah 24:4–7
The Jews will pray and seek God.	Jeremiah 29:12–14
Anti-Semitism will end and the Jews will have a king.	Jeremiah 30:8–9
Israel will prosper, sing, rejoice, build cities, have their own leaders.	Jeremiah 30:18–22
God will make a new covenant with Israel.	Jeremiah 31:31–34
The new covenant will be an everlasting covenant.	Jeremiah 31:37–41
The Jews will be cleansed, forgiven, and have peace.	Jeremiah 33:8–11
Moab and Ammon (Jordan) will be restored.	Jeremiah 48:46–47; 49:6
Elam (a mountainous area in Iran) will be restored.	Jeremiah 49:39
The Jews will be guiltless and sinless.	Jeremiah 50:19–20

Jeremiah 23:3–8 "I myself will gather the remnant of my flock out of all the countries where I have driven them and will bring them back to their pasture, where they will be fruitful and increase in number. I will place shepherds over them who will tend them, and they will no longer be afraid or terrified, nor will any be missing," declares the LORD. "The days are coming," declares the LORD, "when I will raise up to David a righteous Branch, a King who will reign wisely and do what is just and right in the land. In his days Judah will be saved and Israel will live in safety. This is the name by which he will be called: The LORD Our Righteousness. "So then, the days are coming," declares the LORD, "when people will no longer say, 'As surely as the LORD lives, who brought the Israelites up out of Egypt,' but they will say, 'As surely as the LORD lives, who brought the descendants of Israel up out of the land of the north and out of all the countries where he had banished them.' Then they will live in their own land."

The King Is Coming

God <u>scattered</u> the Jews all over the world, but that was not permanent. This is his promise to bring every one of them back into the land, to make them fruitful and cause them to increase in number, to give them faithful leaders and make them unafraid. The time will come when God will send a <u>descendant</u> of King <u>David</u>, a righteous <u>branch</u> of the royal family, a wise <u>King</u> who will rule justly. When he comes the Jews will be saved, they will dwell safely in the land, and they will call him The Lord Our **Righteousness**. One thing is for sure: this return from the north and from the other countries will be so great it will make the Jews forget the exodus from Egypt (see Jeremiah 16:14–15; Exodus 12:31–42).

This is a most amazing prophecy. The Jews recognize the exodus from Egypt as the greatest single event in their history. But God is saying it is a mere shadow of what will happen in the future. Every Jew on earth will return to Israel.

John Hagee: The Jews from the north country (Russia) have returned to Israel by the tens of thousands, as have Jewish people from around the globe. We have seen them on CNN disembarking from planes in Tel Aviv. We have read it in every form of print media. They do live in their own land, just as Jeremiah predicted. Their return to their homeland is another sign of the terminal generation.[10]

Thomas Ice and Timothy Demy: Modern Israel is prophetically significant and is fulfilling Bible prophecy. Readers of God's Word need to be careful to distinguish which verses are being fulfilled in our day and which references await future events. In short, there will be *two* end–time regatherings—one before the tribulation and one after the tribulation.[11]

Fulfillment: The Jewish return to the land of Israel is now underway, but they are not saved and not dwelling safely. That will happen after the Second Coming of Jesus when he is sitting on the throne in Jerusalem. The ultimate return will occur during the Millennium.

☞ **GO TO:**

Ezekiel 34:11–16 (scattered)

Romans 1:1–4 (descendant)

2 Samuel 7:14–17; Jeremiah 33:14–16; Ezekiel 34:22–31; 37:1–28; Hosea 3:4–5; Luke 1:32–33 (David)

What Others are Saying:

☞ **GO TO:**

Isaiah 4:2; 11:1; Zechariah 3:8; 6:12 (branch)

Zechariah 14:9, 16–17; Ezekiel 37:1–28 (King)

1 Corinthians 1:26–31 (Righteousness)

Unfulfilled
Millennium

Righteousness: our right standing with God

The Scattering of the Jews	Scripture
They brought it on themselves by forsaking God.	Jeremiah 2:14–17
God divorced them for committing spiritual adultery (worshiping false gods).	Jeremiah 3:6–8
They lacked understanding and did not know God.	Jeremiah 4:19–22
They forsook God and served foreign gods.	Jeremiah 5:19
The least to the greatest (people, prophets, leaders) were greedy and deceitful.	Jeremiah 6:11–15
They tried to provoke God, but it backfired.	Jeremiah 7:17–20
They refused to repent.	Jeremiah 8:4–7
They were not ashamed of their sins.	Jeremiah 8:12
They forsook the law of God and their hearts were stubborn.	Jeremiah 9:13–16
Their leaders would not pray.	Jeremiah 10:17–22
They refused to be bound to God.	Jeremiah 13:8–11
They were so accustomed to doing evil they could not do good.	Jeremiah 13:22–27
They rejected God and continued to backslide.	Jeremiah 15:1–9
They were made to serve their enemies.	Jeremiah 17:4
They forgot God.	Jeremiah 18:15–17
Jerusalem was burned, people were captured, many were killed.	Jeremiah 21:8–10

Dig Deeper

KEY Symbols:

The Lord Our Righteousness
Jesus

Jeremiah 30:5–7 "This is what the Lord says: 'Cries of fear are heard—terror, not peace. Ask and see: Can a man bear children? Then why do I see every strong man with his hands on his stomach like a woman in labor, every face turned deathly pale? How awful that day will be! None will be like it. It will be a time of trouble for Jacob, but he will be saved out of it.'"

☞ **GO TO:**

Daniel 9:27 (covenant)

Trouble, Trouble, Trouble

The Tribulation Period will begin with a <u>covenant</u> of peace, but it will quickly turn into a time of crying, fear, and terror. The impact of humankind's sin and God's judgments will be worse than anything the <u>world</u> has ever experienced. But in spite of everything that happens, Israel will survive as a nation.

☞ **GO TO:**

Matthew 24:21–22 (world)

What Others are Saying:

Charles Halff: It will involve the Jewish people, the nation Israel and Jews all over the world. Many are in their promised land now, mostly in unbelief. It will also be connected with the horrendous judgments upon Gentile civilization, because of their wickedness, anti-Semitism and rejection of the Gospel.[12]

Many commentators refer to the Tribulation Period as *"the time of Jacob's trouble"* (Jeremiah 30 KJV) or *"a time of trouble for Jacob"* (NIV). Jacob was one of the twin sons of <u>Isaac</u>. As long as he was an unbeliever, he was called Jacob. But when he became a believer, God changed his name to <u>Israel</u>. "A time of trouble for Jacob" refers to a time of trouble for unbelieving Israel.

Some people teach that the Church will go through part of the Tribulation Period. Others teach that the Church will go through all of it. But the Church is never mentioned in the Bible in connection with that terrible time. That is one reason many authorities believe in a Pre-Tribulation Rapture.

Fulfillment: The return of Israel to the land, the rebuilding of Jerusalem, the peace movement, and many other occurrences indicate that this time of trouble is drawing near. But this is a reference to the Tribulation Period.

Remember This . . .

☞ **GO TO:**

Genesis 25:24–26 (Isaac)

Genesis 32:24–30 (Israel)

WARNING

Unfulfilled
Tribulation Period

The Tribulation Period	Scripture
The nations cannot endure God's wrath.	Jeremiah 10:10
God's anger will not cease until his purposes are accomplished.	Jeremiah 23:19–20
The unburied dead will be like garbage lying all over the earth.	Jeremiah 25:29–33
God will completely destroy the nations.	Jeremiah 46:27–28

Dig Deeper

> **Jeremiah 31:1–11** God says he will be the God of all the families of Israel. He will gather the Jews who were scattered and give them rest in the land. He loves the Jews with an everlasting love and will draw them back to the land of Israel. He will rebuild the nation—they will plant crops and Jerusalem will be rebuilt. God says rejoice, shout among the foremost of the nations, cry out for God to save his people. He will bring them from the land of the north and from the ends of the earth. He will bring the blind and the lame, expectant mothers and women in labor. They will cry and pray. It will be made known all over the world that he who scattered Israel will deliver them.

The Shout In Russia

There are those who say the Northern Kingdom of Israel has been wiped out or lost and only a remnant of Jews from the Southern Kingdom are left in the world. Then there are nations that once refused to release their Jewish citizens. There are skeptics who said most of the Jews will never leave the land of their birth to live in Israel. But God said he is the God of all the Jews. They will be reunited as one nation and regathered back in the land. In spite of their sins, God loves the Jews with a love that will never cease. He will draw them back into the land, rebuild the nation, rebuild Jerusalem, and give them crops.

For several years, Russia was one of those nations that would not release Jews, but God said he would "*bring them from the land of the north and gather them from the ends of the earth*" (Jeremiah 31:8). He said he would gather all of them, including the handicapped and pregnant, and they would return with great **elation**. God wants the nations to notice this because he wants everyone to know him and to know that the same God who scattered the Jews is regathering and protecting them.

Hundreds of thousands of Jews have returned to Israel, causing a population explosion in the Promised Land. The population, which stood at approximately 800,000 in 1948, today exceeds six million. Most have moved from Russia, which lies to the north of Israel, but records show Jews have moved from 120 different nations and speak more than eighty different languages.

☞ **GO TO:**

Jeremiah 16:14–15 (north)

elation: joy

Something to Ponder

Notice who is speaking these words:

Verse 1: *"At that time," declares the LORD . . .*
Verse 2: *This is what the LORD says: . . .*
Verse 3: *The LORD appeared to us in the past, saying: . . .*
Verse 7: *This is what the LORD says: . . .*
Verse 10: *Hear the word of the LORD . . .*

Now ask two questions: (1) Why is this prophecy so accurate? and (2) How should people respond?

Remember
This . . .

MIDNIGHT CALL, NOVEMBER 1998 . . .

```
Israel's population is the 95th biggest in the
world, ahead of countries such as Finland, Den-
mark, Norway and Holland. Births in Israel rose by
three percent in 1997 as 124,500 babies were born.
Registered Jewish mothers gave birth to 86,100
babies. Of the 66,000 people who made aliya in
1997, 58.7% were Jewish, 1.6% were Christian and
39.7% were other. A whopping 54,600 (83%) of the
aliya came from the former Soviet Union.¹³
```

**RELATED
CURRENT
EVENTS**

aliya: "going up" to Israel

Fulfillment: The fulfillment of this prophecy has started, but all the Jews will not be back in the land until the Millennium. In the words of David Ben Gurion, the first Prime Minister of modern Israel, "The Jews are a miracle of world history. In the course of one generation they have renewed their land, their language and their nationality. The secret of this miracle is found in the Bible."

Unfulfilled

Millennium

LAMENTATIONS

The Scattering of the Jews	Scripture
Jerusalem was deserted, despised, plundered; people were exiled or captured.	Lamentations 1:1–10
The Jews were made destitute.	Lamentations 1:16
God had no pity on them.	Lamentations 2:1–2
God acted like an enemy.	Lamentations 2:5–6
God made the Jews scum and refuse among the nations.	Lamentations 3:45

The Millennium	Scripture
Jerusalem's punishment will come to an end.	Lamentations 4:22

*Dig
Deeper*

> **Ezekiel 34:22–31** The Lord will save and judge his sheep. They will have one shepherd—his servant David—to tend them. The Lord will be their God and David will be their prince. The Lord will make a new covenant with them; he'll send showers, fruit, and good crops. They will know him and will no longer be plundered or afraid. They will live safely and have plenty to eat.

The Golden Age

corrupt shepherds:
corrupt priests and
prophets

The Lord had been addressing the **corrupt shepherds** of Israel when his thoughts turned to his own people. Many will die during the Tribulation Period, but he will not let all of them be destroyed. He will rescue a large number of them. The corrupt shepherds favored the rich and powerful, but the Good Shepherd will judge everyone alike. Instead of many corrupt shepherds, Israel will have only one shepherd, his servant David. The Lord will be their God and David will be their prince. The Lord will make a new covenant with them. He will rid the land of wild beasts and will send rain when needed. He will cause the trees to yield fruit and make the crops grow. The people will know him. He will set them free and make them safe. They will know that he is with them and that they are his people.

What Others are Saying:

Arnold G. Fruchtenbaum: The absolute monarchy of the Messiah will extend to Israel as well as to the Gentile nations. But directly under Christ, having authority over all Israel, will be the resurrected David, who is given both titles of king and prince. He will be a king because he will rule over Israel, but he will be a prince in that he will be under the authority of Christ.[14]

John F. Walvoord: Though many have tried to explain away this passage, it obviously requires the second coming of Christ, the establishment of David's kingdom on earth, the resurrection of David, and David's sharing the throne of Israel as **co-regent** with Christ.[15]

co-regent: a co-ruler, an
acting ruler in the
absence of the main ruler

1. Israel will have a good shepherd.
    Jesus is the good <u>shepherd</u>.

2. Israel's shepherd will be their God.
    Jesus is <u>God</u> (the <u>Father</u>).

3. Israel's shepherd will set them free.
    Jesus came to set people <u>free</u>.

4. Israel's shepherd will judge his people.
    God has entrusted all <u>judgment</u> to Jesus.

5. Israel's shepherd will protect his people.
    <u>No one</u> can harm those Jesus protects.

6. Israel will know their shepherd.
    Jesus' sheep <u>know</u> his voice.

7. Israel will follow their shepherd.
    Jesus' sheep will follow him.

☞ **GO TO:**

John 10:11 (shepherd)

1 Timothy 2:5 (God)

John 10:30 (Father)

Luke 4:16–21 (free)

John 5:22 (judgment)

John 10:29 (No one)

John 10:27 (know)

Based on many prophecies the Jews rightly expect their Messiah to appear and ratify a covenant of <u>peace</u>. But Jesus warns them, *"I have come in my Father's <u>name</u>, and you do not accept me; but if someone else comes in his own name, you will accept him."* Before Jesus returns the Antichrist will appear and produce a worthless <u>covenant</u> of peace. They will accept him and that will begin the Tribulation Period. They will not have true peace until the Millennium.

Fulfillment: Jesus is gathering his sheep back in the land in preparation for this prophecy. But they will have to go through the Tribulation Period before it can be fulfilled. These blessings are reserved for the Millennium.

Remember This . . .

Unfulfilled
Millennium

The Millennium	Scripture
God will give the land back to Israel	Ezekiel 11:17
The Jews will remove all their idols	Ezekiel 11:18
The Jews will receive the Holy Spirit	Ezekiel 11:19
The Jews will keep God's laws	Ezekiel 11:20
God will remember his covenant	Ezekiel 16:60–63
Jews who do not follow God will be purged	Ezekiel 20:33–38
God will require the Jews to offer gifts and sacrifices	Ezekiel 20:40–42
Those who malign Israel will be punished	Ezekiel 28:25, 26

Dig Deeper

☞ **GO TO:**

Ezekiel 37:26–28 (peace)

John 5:43 (name)

Daniel 9:27 (covenant)

> **Ezekiel 36:1–38** God says Israel's enemies will claim the land of Israel, but because they have harmed and ridiculed the Jews and claimed his land as their possession, he will punish them. He will bring the Jews home, cause the land to produce crops, the towns and cities to be rebuilt, and their enemies to be silenced. God says he is aware that the Jews committed many sins and that is why he scattered them. But many people misunderstand this and do not believe the Jews are his people. So for his name's sake, he will regather them, cleanse them, change their hearts, put his spirit in them, make the land produce, and cause them to know him. When he gets through, the remaining nations will know him.

Who Holds The Deed To Israel?

This is what underlies the Palestinian claim to the land of Israel: Satan wants to keep the Jewish people off the land, and before Jesus can come back and establish his earthly kingdom in Israel, the Jewish nation must be restored. As long as someone else possesses the land, Jesus will not return. God says Israel's enemies will brag that the **ancient heights** belong to them. He says to tell Israel's enemies they have mistreated the Jews, that they have **malice** in their hearts. The land belongs to God and he is upset; he will oppose those who oppose Israel.

God says the Jews rebelled against him so he scattered them, but that does not give Israel's enemies the right to claim the land or criticize him. So he is going to do seven things to protect his name: (1) remove the Jews from foreign countries, (2) cleanse their sins, (3) **regenerate** their heart and spirit, (4) cause them to keep his laws, (5) put them on the land he gave to their **forefathers**, (6) make the land fertile, and (7) cause them to repent and turn to him. This will be his way of telling the world who he is.

ancient heights: mountains, Temple Mount, holy places

malice: sin (against God and Israel, they do not believe the Bible)

regenerate: remove their rebellion and give them a new nature

forefathers: Abraham, Isaac, and Jacob

What Others are Saying:

Jimmy DeYoung: Ezekiel 36 refers to the land at least thirty-five times. God's promise to Abraham must be kept. God must give Abraham's descendants the land. Verse 22 says that God will do this, not for the sake of Israel, but for His holy name's sake. Hebrews 6:13 says that, *"when God made promise to Abraham, because he could swear no greater, he sware by himself."* For His holy name's sake He will give all the land promised to Abraham to his descendants.[16]

In 1948, the nation of Israel was reestablished. In the fifty years since that time, more than 2,600,000 Jews have migrated back to Israel. In the last ten years, more than 750,000 have moved from the former Soviet Union alone. Today, the **PLO** claims the land belongs to them. They are demanding immediate control of East Jerusalem and the Temple Mount. This is exactly what the Bible says would happen.

In October 1998, the U.S. pushed the Jews into signing the Wye River Agreement calling for them to turn another thirteen percent of the West Bank over to the Palestinians. But it is not for the U.S., the Arabs, the Europeans, or even the UN to decide who should possess it. To do so is to ignore the sovereignty of God. Why is this worth remembering? Because <u>dividing</u> up the land of Israel is one of the reasons God gives for pulling the nations into the **Battle of Armageddon**.

***DISPATCH FROM JERUSALEM,* NOVEMBER/DECEMBER 1998 . . . KEY PROVISIONS OF THE [WYE RIVER] AGREEMENT ARE:**

- Israel will relinquish an additional 13 percent of territory in Judea and Samaria, putting the total given over to the **PA** thus far at 40% of the territory.
- A Palestinian airport will open in Gaza, and Yasir Arafat can fly in and out without a security inspection by Israel.
- Israel and the Palestinians will jointly consider an additional Israeli pullback. Israel and the Palestinians will start final status talks on issues including the future of Jerusalem.[17]

Fulfillment: These incredible events are proof positive that prophecy is rapidly being fulfilled and the world is quickly moving toward the Tribulation Period. After going through that the Jews will repent and be restored. Everyone should pay close attention. God wants to be known and understood. He does not want to be mischaracterized or misrepresented. He is holy and he will protect his name. Restoring Israel to the land is something he must do. It will cause others to take notice and repent.

Something to Ponder

PLO: *Palestine Liberation Organization*

Remember This . . .

☞ **GO TO:**

Joel 3:2 (dividing)

RELATED CURRENT EVENTS

Battle of Armageddon: *a great battle on earth during the Tribulation Period*

PA: *Palestinian Authority*

Unfulfilled

Millennium

Dig Deeper

The Scattering of the Jews	Scripture
The towns were destroyed, altars devastated, idols smashed, people slain.	Ezekiel 6:6–7
God does not make threats in vain.	Ezekiel 6:10
The Jews were filled with sorrow.	Ezekiel 23:32–34
God would not forgive them until his wrath subsided.	Ezekiel 24:13–14
Survivors were killed by wild animals and plagues.	Ezekiel 33:27–29

THE BIG PICTURE 🔍

Ezekiel 37:1–28 The Spirit of God carried Ezekiel to a valley filled with dry bones and told him to prophesy over them. Ezekiel did what God commanded him to do and the bones came together, were covered with tendons, flesh, and skin in that order. Then Ezekiel was told to prophesy that breath should enter these bodies. He did that and life came into all of them. At that point, God said the bones symbolized the house of Israel. He told Ezekiel to prophesy again and say God will regather the Jews, put his Spirit in them, put them back on the land, and make them his people. He told Ezekiel to take two sticks, write Judah on one and Ephraim on the other, and join them together so they are one stick. God said the joined stick means the Jewish nation would be revived not as two nations, but as one single nation. His servant David will be king over it, the Jews will keep his laws, God will make a covenant of peace with them, and he will put his sanctuary in Israel. He will be Israel's God, the Jews will be his people, and the nations will know him.

Sticks and Bones

This is one of the most famous chapters in the Old Testament because it predicts an end-of-the-age return of Israel as a nation, and because Jewish leaders and conservative Christians both apply this prophecy to events taking place in the land of Israel today. The once horrendous scattering of the Jews has been replaced by an amazing regathering. The nation has been resurrected, and multitudes of orthodox Jews expect a Messiah and King to appear at any moment. According to the prediction here, this new life is

God's doing, and it precedes a grand conversion. The main points of the passage are as follows:

1. The Spirit of the Lord showed Ezekiel a valley filled with dry bones.
2. God said, "Tell the bones they will live."
3. "Tell them they will come back to life in a gradual step-by-step process."
4. "Tell them God will begin with the bones, attach tendons, add flesh, cover that with skin, and put breath in the dead bodies."
5. First, there was a rattling noise; second, the bones came together into skeletons; third, tendons appeared; fourth, flesh appeared; and fifth, skin appeared on the dead bodies.
6. The bodies were assembled, but they were not breathing.
7. God commanded breath to enter into the bodies.
8. The bodies came to life and stood on their feet as a great army.
9. God said, "The bones represent the entire nation of Israel."
10. The people say, "Our bones are dried up, our hope is gone, we are cut off from the land."
11. But God said, "I will raise you from the dead, bring you back into the land of Israel, put my Spirit in you, and you will know me."
12. God told Ezekiel to write **Judah** on one stick and **Ephraim** on another.
13. God told Ezekiel to join the sticks together into one stick.
14. God said this means the Jews will be "one nation in the land, on the mountains of Israel."
15. Israel will have one king.
16. Israel will never again be two nations or be divided into two kingdoms.
17. The Jews will stop sinning, be forgiven, be cleansed, serve God, and be his people.
18. David will be Israel's king.
19. Israel will have a shepherd.
20. The Jews will obey God.

☞ **GO TO:**

Zechariah 12:9–10 (Spirit)

Isaiah 17:1–14 (Judah/Ephraim)

Psalm 2:1–12; Jeremiah 23:3–8; Hosea 3:4–5; Zephaniah 3:15; Zechariah 14:9, 16–17 (king)

1 Chronicles 17:7–15; 2 Samuel 7:14–17; Jeremiah 23:3–8; 33:14–16; Ezekiel 34:21–31; Luke 1:32–33 (David/ shepherd/covenant)

Judah: *Southern Kingdom*

Ephraim: *Northern Kingdom*

21. The Jews will live on the land God gave to Jacob, the land their ancestors lived on.
22. The Jews will live there forever.
23. God will make a <u>covenant</u> of peace with Israel.
24. The covenant of peace will be an everlasting covenant.
25. God will have a dwelling place (Temple) in Israel.
26. The Gentiles will know that God has a special relationship with Israel.

What Others are Saying:

Henry M. Morris with Henry M. Morris III: The "wandering Jews" were without a national home for "many days" (Hosea 3:4–5), and it seemed impossible that such prophecies as these could ever be fulfilled. Even many Bible-believing Christians thought for centuries that God was through with Israel and that all the Old Testament promises to Israel should be spiritualized and applied to the church. But now, with the return of the Jews and the re-establishment of their nation, it is evident in a unique way that God's Word means exactly what it says.[18]

KEY Symbols:

Dry Bones
Jews in foreign lands

One Stick
Israel will not be divided

Randall Price: Ezekiel refers to a "covenant of peace" (Ezekiel 34:25; 37:26) made between the Lord and the "sons of Israel" that will have several provisions: (1) it will involve secure occupation of the Land of Israel; (2) it will be everlasting (Ezekiel 37:26b); (3) it will establish and increase the Israeli population in the Land (Ezekiel 37:26c; compare verses 25 and 36:24, 28); and (4) it will secure the rebuilding of the Temple and return the Divine Presence (Ezekiel 37:26d–27; compare chapters 40–48).[19]

Gary Hedrick: With everything that's happening in the world lately many people are wondering what time it is on God's prophetic calendar. How close are we to that midnight hour of world history when Christ will return? Israel is the clock God has given us so we can tell what time it is. In fact, God's prophetic plan revolves around the nation Israel. So when we want to know what time it is on God's prophetic calendar and we want to know where we are on God's prophetic plan all we have to do is look at the clock. Look at Israel.[20]

In this vision, it was the Holy Spirit that assembled the bones, made them into bodies, and gave them life. With this being the case, who or what is causing the Jews to return to Israel? Is this miracle evidence of the existence and power of God?

God's covenant of peace with Israel will be an everlasting covenant, not a seven-year covenant. Israel's seven-year covenant with the Antichrist will begin the Tribulation Period. Their everlasting covenant with God will begin the Millennium.

Fulfillment: The Northern Kingdom of Israel fell around 721 B.C. (more than 2700 years ago). The Southern Kingdom of Judah fell around 586 B.C. (more than 2500 years ago). The nation was rebuilt, but it was destroyed again in A.D. 70 (more than 1900 years ago). It is truly incredible that the Jews have been able to keep their identity without a nation of their own. But they have and this is exactly what the Bible says would happen. Fulfillment is well underway, but all of these things will not be completed until the Millennium.

Something to Ponder

Remember This . . .

Unfulfilled
Millennium

THE BIG PICTURE

Ezekiel 38:1–39:16 God told Ezekiel to look at Gog, who lives in Magog and is the leader of Rosh, Meshech, and Tubal. Ezekiel is to tell Gog to prepare because God intends to pull Gog, his army, and the armies of many nations with him to the mountains of Israel. Among these nations will be Persia, Ethiopia, Libya, Gomer, and Togarmah. Their armies will be like a great storm. They will think they are attacking an easy prey and are about to seize valuable booty. Sheba, Dedan, and the nations that have come out of Tarshish will protest their invasion, but offer no help to Israel. Gog will come from his place in the far north, advance against God's people—Israel—and many nations will know God is holy when he takes vengeance against Gog. God will get angry, cause a great earthquake, overturn the mountains, cause Gog's troops to fight amongst themselves, and attack them with plagues of rain, hail, and burning sulfur. People in many nations will recognize God's greatness and know him. Gog's army will drop their weapons, die on the mountains, and become a feast for the birds of prey and wild animals. God will put an end to people profaning his name. It will take the Jews seven years to burn Gog's weapons and seven months to bury the remains of his troops.

Russia Invades Israel

Volumes have been written about this prophecy and it is impossible to comment on many of the details. Some of the most significant points are as follows:

Gog: a title that means dictator

title: a name like emperor, Caesar, Pharaoh

Magog: a grandson of Noah

Rosh: the Hebrew word for Russia

Meshech: Moscow, a large Russian city on the European continent

Tubal: Tobolsk, a large Russian city on the Asian continent

☞ **GO TO:**

Genesis 10:2 (Magog)

Genesis 12:3 (curse)

1. Most prophetic scholars agree that **Gog** is a **title** that means dictator or man on top.

2. Gog's territory is the land where **Magog** settled.

3. Gog will be the prince of **Rosh**, **Meshech**, and **Tubal**.

4. Gog will come from his place in the far north.

5. All nations except the four that are north of Israel—Lebanon, Syria, Turkey, and Russia—are ruled out; the one nation in the far north is Russia.

6. God said he is against Russia. He did not say why, but he told Abraham he would <u>curse</u> anyone who curses Israel, and Russia falls into that category.

7. God said he will put hooks in Russia's jaws, which means Russia will lose control of her destiny.

8. Russia's allies will be Persia (Iran), Cush (Ethiopia/Iraq/Sudan), Put (Libya), Gomer (Germany), and Togarmah (Turkey/Armenia).

9. The time of this attack will be *"in the latter years"* and *"in the latter days"* (Ezekiel 38:8, 16 KJV).

10. One precondition for this attack is the regathering of Jews from many nations. (The current population of Israel now exceeds six million.)

11. Another precondition is for Israel to possess silver, gold, livestock, and goods. (She does.)

12. Another precondition is for Israel to be dwelling safely. (The nation has quickly won every war it has been involved in.)

13. Another precondition is for many nations to be living in unbelief.

14. Another precondition is the rebuilding of unwalled villages. They exist.

15. Finally, birds of prey and wild animals will return to the land. (Vultures, buzzards, pelicans, wolves, and jackals are now found in many areas of Israel.)

Randall Price: Israel, at present, fits the description given in Ezekiel 38 of "living securely . . . without walls, and having no bars or gates" (verse 11). Only the old city of Jerusalem is walled, but the majority of Jerusalemites live in the new city outside these walls.[21]

Chuck Missler: God apparently sends "fire" down, not only upon Magog and his allies, but on some distant people living in the "isles" or "coastlands." Who are they "who dwell carelessly [securely] in the Isles"? The word for isles could be an **idiom** for remote continents. Could this be an allusion to the United States? Is the "fire on Magog"—*and these others*—a result of a nuclear exchange?[22]

Grant R. Jeffrey: When Russia is defeated by God's miraculous power, the newly united European Union will emerge as the greatest economic, political, and military power on the planet. These pivotal events will set the stage for the rise of the new European superstate and the emergence of the new leader who will ultimately assume the role of the Antichrist, the final world dictator who will rule the planet during the last seven years leading to the climactic Battle of Armageddon.[23]

DESTINY NEWSLETTER, DECEMBER 1998 . . .

```
Boris Yeltsin is once again in the Hospital and
is fighting a persistent case of pneumonia. At
best, these are the waning days of his leader-
ship. In the Russian scene, the question of his
successor, therefore, becomes quite critical.
Russia is even now in a state of economic ruin
and its one great asset is 22,000 nuclear mis-
siles. These deadly weapons make the Russian
situation the time bomb of the world.24
```

The fact that the Antichrist is not mentioned in these verses is viewed by some as a good indication that the Russian invasion occurs before he arrives on the scene. If the Antichrist were a great world leader at this time, it is not likely that he would stand on the sidelines and leave Russia unchallenged. If this were the middle of the Tribulation Period, he would be in control of some of these nations and they would not be in the Russian coalition. His absence is a good indication of a Pre-Tribulation Period attack.

What Others
are Saying:

idiom: phrase, expression

RELATED CURRENT EVENTS

Something to Ponder

Fulfillment: This combination of nations has never attacked Israel before. When Ezekiel wrote this prophecy, the Northern and Southern Kingdoms had both been destroyed. The nation came back into existence, but we can identify all the powers that controlled Israel until the nation was destroyed again by the Romans in A.D. 70. We also know that Israel did not come back into existence until 1948. Finally, we are aware of all the nations that have attacked the Jews since then. This prophecy has a future fulfillment and all the signs indicate that the time is getting close.

> **Ezekiel 43:10–12** "Son of man, describe the temple to the people of Israel, that they may be ashamed of their sins. Let them consider the plan, and if they are ashamed of all they have done, make known to them the design of the temple—its arrangement, its exits and entrances—its whole design and all its regulations and laws. Write these down before them so that they may be faithful to its design and follow all its regulations. This is the law of the temple: All the surrounding area on top of the mountain will be most holy. Such is the law of the temple."

The Millennial Temple

The last nine chapters of Ezekiel describe the <u>Temple</u> that will be built on earth in Jerusalem and put in use during the Millennium. Both Jews and Gentiles will worship there. The tribe of <u>Levi</u> will serve as priests and handle the daily <u>sacrifices</u> that will be offered. Some sacrifices will be sin <u>offerings</u> and they will be a vivid reminder that all have <u>sinned</u>. The **Temple Mount** will be **holy**.

☞ **GO TO:**

Micah 4:1–7 (Temple)

Ezekiel 43:19 (Levi)

Ezekiel 46:13 (sacrifices)

Ezekiel 43:22–27 (offerings)

Romans 3:23 (sinned)

What Others are Saying:

Randall Price: Jerusalem is enlarged and made glorious by the return of the Divine Presence (Jeremiah 3:17; Ezekiel 43:1–7; Zechariah 8:3–8). It is made the center of the world with the Temple Mount as the source of universal religious instruction and worship (Isaiah 2:2–3; 56:7). The Temple is built by Messiah with Gentile assistance (Zechariah 6:12–15; Isaiah 56:5–6), and the Gentile nations learn **Torah** and worship the One True God (Zechariah 14:16–19).[25]

Temple Mount: the area in Jerusalem where all the Jewish temples were located

holy: separated or set apart for God

Torah: God's instructions

The Old Testament animal sacrifices pointed forward to the future sacrifice of Christ on the cross. New Testament church members do not offer animal sacrifices, but they take part in the Lord's Supper which, in part, looks back to the past sacrifice of Christ. During the Millennium, the animal sacrifices will do the same thing. They will still remind people that Christ died on a cross for their sins.

Something to Ponder

Fulfillment: The adoption of the shekel as a medium of exchange, the manufacture of the vessels for the animal sacrifices, the election of priests from the tribe of Levi, the manufacture of the priests' clothing, the manufacture of the musical instruments for the worship services—these are things that have been done with the Millennial Temple in mind. Unfortunately, the Jews are being deceived because the Tribulation Period Temple will be built first. That Temple will be defiled by the Antichrist. Then the Millennial Temple will be built (see illustration, page 92).

Unfulfilled
Millennium

The Millennial Temple	Scripture
It will have several gates.	Ezekiel 40:6–37
It will have a place to prepare the animal sacrifices.	Ezekiel 40:38–43
It will have rooms for the priests.	Ezekiel 40:44–47; 42:1–17
It will be at least three stories high.	Ezekiel 42:1–20
The presence of God will reside at this Temple.	Ezekiel 43:1–5; 48:35
The throne of God will be in the Temple.	Ezekiel 43:6–7
The system of animal sacrifices will be revived. The shekel will be used for monetary exchanges.	Ezekiel 45:12
The feast of Passover will be observed.	Ezekiel 45:21–24
Worship services will take place on the Sabbaths and New Moons.	Ezekiel 46:1–10
A river of water will flow from the Temple.	Ezekiel 47:1–12
Gentiles will settle in Jerusalem and reproduce.	Ezekiel 47:21–22
The tribe of Dan will be restored.	Ezekiel 48:1–2

Dig Deeper

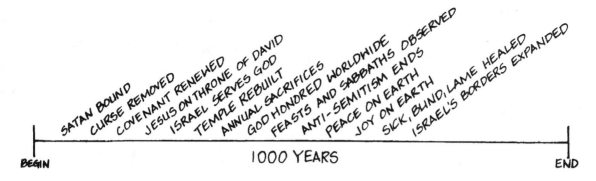

BEGIN   1000 YEARS   END

SATAN BOUND
CURSE REMOVED
COVENANT RENEWED
JESUS ON THRONE OF DAVID
ISRAEL SERVES GOD
TEMPLE REBUILT
ANNUAL SACRIFICES
GOD HONORED WORLDWIDE
FEASTS AND SABBATHS OBSERVED
ANTI-SEMITISM ENDS
PEACE ON EARTH
JOY ON EARTH
SICK, BLIND, LAME HEALED
ISRAEL'S BORDERS EXPANDED

Important Events in the Millennium

Temples in the Bible

Sanctuary	Scripture	Approximate Dates
The Tabernacle	Exodus 26:1–37; 36:8–38; 1 Samuel 4:10–11	Built about 1446 B.C. Probably destroyed (date unknown)
Solomon's Temple	1 Kings 5–8; Jeremiah 32:28–44; Daniel 1:1–2	Built about 960 B.C. Destroyed 586 B.C.
Zerubbabel's Temple	Ezra 3:1–8; 4:1–14; 6:13–15	Built 516 B.C. Desecrated 169 B.C.
Herod's Temple: Remodeled, enlarged; name changed	John 2:20; Matthew 24:12; Daniel 9:26	Started about 19 B.C. Destroyed A.D. 70
Church Age Temple	1 Corinthians 6:10–20; 2 Corinthians 6:16–18	Christians indwelt between First Coming and Rapture
Tribulation Period Temple	Daniel 9:27; 11:31; 12:11; Matthew 24:15–16; 2 Thessalonians 2:4; Revelation 11:1–2	Will be defiled at Tribulation Period midpoint
Millennial Temple	Ezekiel 40–48; Isaiah 2:2–3; 56:7	Millennium

The Millennial Temple	Scripture
The land will be divided among the tribes of Israel.	Ezekiel 48:1–29
Jerusalem will be enlarged.	Ezekiel 48:35

Dig Deeper

DANIEL

> **Daniel 2:38–44** "You are that head of gold. After you, another kingdom will rise, inferior to yours. Next, a third kingdom, one of bronze, will rule over the whole earth. Finally, there will be a fourth kingdom, strong as iron—for iron breaks and smashes everything—and as iron breaks things to pieces, so it will crush and break all the others. Just as you saw that the feet and toes were partly of baked clay and partly of iron, so this will be a divided kingdom; yet it will have some of the strength of iron in it, even as you saw iron mixed with clay. As the toes were partly iron and partly clay, so this kingdom will be partly strong and partly brittle. And just as you saw the iron mixed with baked clay, so the people will be a mixture and will not remain united, any more than iron mixes with clay. In the time of those kings, the God of heaven will set up a kingdom that will never be destroyed, nor will it be left to another people. It will crush all those kingdoms and bring them to an end, but it will itself endure forever.

A Sign Of The Second Coming: World Government

A **Gentile** named Nebuchadnezzar was king of a world government headquartered in Babylon when he had a distressing dream about a great statue with a head of gold, chest and arms of silver, belly and thighs of brass, legs of iron, and feet of iron mixed with clay. His many advisers could not tell him what the dream meant, but God revealed the dream and its interpretation to a young Jewish captive named Daniel. God told Daniel the head of gold on the statue represented the kingdom of Babylon; the chest and arms of silver represented a second world kingdom that would replace Babylon; the belly and thighs of brass represented a third world kingdom; the legs of iron represented a fourth world kingdom; and the feet of iron mixed with clay represented a fifth world king-

Gentile: someone who is not a Jew

☞ GO TO:

Luke 21:24 (Times)

Daniel 1:1–2 (Jerusalem)

Daniel 5:28; 8:1–21
(Medes and Persians)

Times of the Gentiles:
the period of time
Gentiles rule on earth (the
period of time before the
Second Coming)

KEY POINT

The Second Coming of
Christ will occur while
the fifth world king-
dom is in power.

**RELATED
CURRENT
EVENTS**

dom. While this fifth world kingdom is on earth, Jesus will come back and establish a kingdom that will never be destroyed.

God used this statue in Nebuchadnezzar's dream to give us a broad outline of what the Bible calls the **Times of the Gentiles**. It covers that period of time in history that the city of Jerusalem will be under the influence of Gentile governments. It begins with Babylon's capture of the city of Jerusalem in 586 B.C. and extends into the future until the Second Coming of Christ at the end of the Tribulation Period.

History reveals that Babylon's world kingdom (the head of gold on the statue) was replaced by the Medes and Persians (the chest and arms of silver). This kingdom was replaced by the brass kingdom on the statue (the Greek Empire under Alexander the Great). The Greek Empire was followed by the iron kingdom on the statue (the Old Roman Empire). This empire was not replaced; it just broke up. And there has not been a world kingdom since then. But according to Nebuchadnezzar's dream there will be one more before Jesus returns (the kingdom of iron mixed with clay). It seems this will be the United Nations. If so, the Second Coming of Jesus is not long off (see GWDN, pages 35–67).

**What Others
are Saying:**

Marlin Maddoux: There is absolutely no way that you can look to the future and the way it's developing and not see a connection to what the Scriptures have told us.[26]

ENDTIME, JANUARY/FEBRUARY 1999...

Seven years after the Gulf War, the United Nations continues to sanction the people of Iraq
economically, mandate how much oil they can sell,
tell them what they must do with the income from
that oil, and insist on intrusive searches of
military sites by UN arms inspectors. I'm sure if
you asked the people of Iraq if we are in world
government right now, they would emphatically
assure you that we are.[27]

• • •

INTERNATIONAL INTELLIGENCE BRIEFING, OCTOBER 1998...

In the last days, the Bible says there will be
three global institutions in place. The first is
a global economy. Although a truly global economy
has never existed in history prior to this gen-

eration, it's here now. The second institution will be a global government, headquartered in, and led by, the Revived Roman Empire. The UN is in place, and hoping to assume the mantle of global governorship. . . . The third institution is a global religion. America has always maintained a posture of religious freedom without government interference. The UN views religion as an instrument of government—provided it is an all-embracing, global religious world-view that all paths to God are equal.[28]

. . .

INTERNATIONAL INTELLIGENCE BRIEFING, JANUARY 1999 . . .

The UN plans to play a significant role in supervising global crisis spots in a post **Y2K** world. This is a crisis made to order for a global government in waiting, and it's waiting patiently for the chance to prove it is up to the task. Expect to see much more UN involvement as we approach 2000, and don't be surprised to see the 'one worlders' embracing Y2K as evidence of the need for global government.[29]

Y2K: *a symbol for the year 2000*

. . .

WOMEN'S INTERNATIONAL MEDIA GROUP NEWSLETTER, DECEMBER 15, 1998 . . .

In 1998 we attended six key high level conferences which were held outside the country. They were: the World Economic Forum in Davos, Switzerland where the captains, kings and queens of industry on a global basis meet for a week so that the UN, IMF/World Bank, World Trade and other world government agencies can brief them on where the world needs to go; the Summit of the Americas in Santiago, Chile where I witnessed the 34 presidents and prime ministers of the countries in our hemisphere sign the Free Trade Areas of the Americas which integrates us politically, economically, and in all other aspects of government; the Group of Eight in England in which the G–7 countries plus Russia agreed to work together on common DOMESTIC problems; the Bank for International Settlements in Basle, Switzerland where the central bank ministers of the world meet to determine the course of world economics, and the International Criminal Court in Rome where, for the first time in history an international court was set up to try individuals who they say committed various types of war crimes. In the future they will add other types of crimes such as crimes against the environment, narcotics, economics and terrorism. It should be noted that anyone who opposes world government and who is a nationalist could be a "terrorist."[30]

Partially Fulfilled

Tribulation Period

Second Coming

Even though the Jews occupied Jerusalem during the life of Jesus, the city was still under the influence of the Old Roman Empire. And even though the Jews occupy Jerusalem today, sovereignty over the city—especially East Jerusalem—is questioned and its control is still under the influence of the United Nations.

Fulfillment: Four-fifths of this prophecy (gold, silver, bronze, and iron) has been fulfilled. The feet of iron mixed with clay are now forming. The United Nations is already touting itself as the next one-world government. When that happens the Tribulation Period will arrive; it will end seven years later with the Second Coming of Christ.

> **Daniel 7:23–27** "He gave me this explanation: 'The fourth beast is a fourth kingdom that will appear on earth. It will be different from all the other kingdoms and will devour the whole earth, trampling it down and crushing it. The ten horns are ten kings who will come from this kingdom. After them another king will arise, different from the earlier ones; he will subdue three kings. He will speak against the Most High and oppress his saints and try to change the set times and the laws. The saints will be handed over to him for a time, times and half a time. But the court will sit, and his power will be taken away and completely destroyed forever. Then the sovereignty, power and greatness of the kingdoms under the whole heaven will be handed

over to the saints, the people of the Most High. His kingdom will be an everlasting kingdom, and all rulers will worship and obey him.'"

One World Government

It seems that Daniel was asleep when he had a series of visions about the future. He saw what this writer believes will be demonic forces causing a great disturbance in the Middle East. Four kingdoms will arise. Authorities disagree over their identity, but one of two opinions is widely accepted: (1) these kingdoms are the same as those in Nebuchadnezzar's dream (Babylon, Medo-Persia, Greece, the Roman Empire—old and Revived); or (2) these kingdoms are kingdoms that will arise at the end of the age (perhaps England and some allies, Russia and some allies, a coalition of Arab or African nations, and the final Gentile world kingdom).

Daniel told an angel he wanted to know more about the fourth kingdom and he was informed that it will be an earthly kingdom that will devour, **trample and crush** the whole earth. In its early existence this fourth world kingdom will have ten kings which means ten divisions with each one having its own ruler or leader. After the ten divisions appear, an eleventh leader will arise. Other Scriptures teach that this leader will be an evil man who will come straight out of the **Abyss** and have Satanic <u>power</u>. According to the angel, this evil man will speak against God and **oppress his saints**. He will be **anti-Christian** and **anti-Semitic**. This is why Christians call him the **Antichrist**. He will *try to change the set times and laws* probably means he will try to change the Christian calendar and all the laws based upon teachings from the Bible. *The saints will be handed over to him for a time, times and half a time* is a Bible expression which means God will let him get away with persecuting Christians and Jews for 3½ years (the second half of the Tribulation Period). After that God will judge him and Jesus will return. He will capture him and cast him into the <u>fiery</u> lake, establish his own kingdom, and turn it over to his own people.

The United Nations is currently working on a new charter called the Earth Charter or Earth Ethic, which is expected to be enacted into law within the next two years. Although the authors of this charter do not refer to it as a world religion, many prophecy experts believe a world religion will be the outcome. Many prophecy experts believe most of the guiding principles for the charter come from Pantheism.

trample and crush: be brutal and destructive

Abyss: *the place where God holds the most vicious demonic spirits*

oppress his saints: *persecute Christians and Jews*

anti-Christian: *against Christians*

anti-Semitic: *against Jews*

Antichrist: *an enemy of Christ who will come during the Tribulation Period*

☞ **GO TO:**

Revelation 17:8 (Abyss)

Revelation 13:2 (power)

Revelation 19:19–20 (fiery)

 **KEY Symbols:**

time, times and half a time

3½ years

 **Something to Ponder**

What Others are Saying:

J. R. Church: I feel that this beast [the fourth kingdom] represents the New World Order whose power base is built upon the foundation of the United Nations. It is the same beast that John describes in Revelation 13. He writes that it has some of the same features as Daniel's previous three beasts—the body of a leopard, feet of a bear, and mouth of a lion. These three political entities are presently members of the United Nations.[31]

Ed Hindson: Bible prophecies clearly predict the rise of the Antichrist in the end times. Many people believe the great millennial end-game has already begun. As civilization speeds toward its final destiny, the appearance of a powerful world ruler is inevitable. The ultimate question facing our generation is whether he is alive and well and moving into power.[32]

| Unfulfilled |
| Tribulation Period |
| Second Coming |

Fulfillment: Since the identity of these four kingdoms is questionable, it is difficult to say whether some of this is fulfilled or not. But we do know that the United Nations world government is now forming. Thus, it is not unreasonable to believe that the ten divisions will soon appear. But the Antichrist cannot appear until after the Rapture, and he will not be judged until Jesus returns at the end of the Tribulation Period.

Dig Deeper

Daniel's Prophecies About the Antichrist	Scripture
He will have eyes like a man (insight, shrewdness, cunning).	Daniel 7:8
He will have a mouth that speaks boastfully (proud, arrogant).	Daniel 7:8, 11, 20
He will look imposing (impressive, commanding).	Daniel 7:20
He will wage war against the saints (God's people) and defeat them.	Daniel 7:21
He will subdue three kings.	Daniel 7:24
He will speak against the Most High (God).	Daniel 7:25
He will try to change set times and laws.	Daniel 7:25
He will oppress the saints and they will be handed over to him for 3½ years.	Daniel 7:25
His power will be taken away and completely destroyed forever.	Daniel 7:26
He will start small, but grow in power.	Daniel 8:9

His power will grow to the south and to the
east and toward the Beautiful Land. .... Daniel 8:9

He will set himself up to be as great as the
Prince of the host (Jesus or God). .... Daniel 8:11

He will take away the daily sacrifice
(at the Jewish Temple). .... Daniel 8:11

Because of rebellion (by those on earth), the
saints and sacrifice will be given over to him. ... Daniel 8:12–13

He will prosper in all he does. .... Daniel 8:12

He will cast truth to the ground
(use deceit and lies). .... Daniel 8:12

He will be a master of intrigue (occultic or
Satanic plots). .... Daniel 8:23

He will become very strong, but not by his
own power (by Satan's power). .... Daniel 8:24

He will cause astounding devastation and
succeed in whatever he does. .... Daniel 8:24

He will destroy the mighty men and the
holy people. .... Daniel 8:24

He will cause deceit (lies, corruption) to
prosper and consider himself superior. .... Daniel 8:24

When they feel secure, he will destroy many
and take his stand against the Prince of
princes (Jesus). .... Daniel 8:25

He will be destroyed, but not by human
power (by God's power). .... Daniel 8:25

He will confirm a covenant with many for
one *seven* (seven years). .... Daniel 9:27

In the middle of the *seven* (at the Tribulation
Period midpoint), he will put an end to
sacrifice and offering (break the covenant). .... Daniel 9:27

On a wing of the temple he will set up an
abomination that causes desolation
(a statue or image of himself). .... Daniel 9:27; 12:11

He will do as he pleases (possess great
power and authority). .... Daniel 11:36

He will exalt and magnify himself above
every god (be a braggart). .... Daniel 11:36

He will say unheard of things against the
God of gods (be a blasphemer)..................... Daniel 11:36

KEY POINT

He will be Satan's
man.

KEY POINT

He will oppose God
and all those who
follow God.

He will be successful until the time of
   wrath (Tribulation Period) is completed. ..... Daniel 11:36
He will show no regard for the gods of his
   fathers (their New Age religion will be
   meaningless to him). .... Daniel 11:37
He will show no regard for the one desired
   by women (the Messiah). .... Daniel 11:37
He will exalt himself above all gods (claim
   he is greater than every god). .... Daniel 11:37
He will honor the god of fortresses (Satan). ..... Daniel 11:38
He will attack the mightiest fortresses with
   the help of a foreign god (Satan). .... Daniel 11:39
He will make those who honor him rulers
   over many people. .... Daniel 11:39
He will distribute the land for a price
   (swap conquered territory for favors). .... Daniel 11:39
He will invade and sweep through many
   countries (attack many nations). .... Daniel 11:40
He will invade the Beautiful Land (Israel). .... Daniel 11:41
He will conquer Egypt, Libya and Nubia
   (Sudan, Ethiopia, and perhaps Djibouti). ..... Daniel 11:42–43
He will pitch his royal tents between the
   seas (Mediterranean Sea and Dead Sea) at
   the beautiful holy mountain (Jerusalem). .... Daniel 11:45
He will come to his end, and no one will
   help him. .... Daniel 11:45

> **Daniel 9:27** "He will confirm a covenant with many
> for one 'seven.' In the middle of the 'seven' he will put
> an end to sacrifice and offering. And on a wing of the
> temple he will set up an abomination that causes deso-
> lation, until the end that is decreed is poured out on
> him."

God's Decree

☞ **GO TO:**

Nehemiah 2:1–8
(rebuild)

seventy sevens: 70 x 7
years = 490 years

One of the most famous prophecies in the entire Bible is found in
Daniel 9:24–27. God sent the angel Gabriel to tell Daniel, *"Seventy sevens [490 years] are decreed for your people and your holy
city to finish transgression, to put an end to sin, to atone for wickedness, to bring in everlasting righteousness, to seal up vision and prophecy and to anoint the most holy"* (verse 24). He said the **seventy
sevens** would begin with a decree to restore and rebuild Jerusa-

lem. After the decree is issued, a period of seven *sevens* (49 years) and another period of sixty-two *sevens* (434 years) would pass and the **Anointed One** would come (see illustration, page 102). Then the Anointed One would be **cut off** and the people of the ruler who would come would destroy the **city** and the **sanctuary**. It is now widely recognized that he foretold the first coming of Jesus to the exact day, that Jesus would be crucified, that Jerusalem would be destroyed, that the Temple would be destroyed, that he foretold these things more than 483 years before they happened, and that all of these things took place exactly as he said they would (see GWDN, pages 249–258).

This sum of seven ***sevens*** (49 years) plus sixty-two *sevens* (434 years) is sixty-nine *sevens* (483 years). It is one *seven* (7 years) short of the required seventy *sevens* (490 years) decreed by God. This last *seven* is often called the seventieth week or the seventieth week of Daniel. It is also called the Tribulation Period.

Gabriel said, "He [the ruler who will come, the Antichrist] *will confirm a covenant with* **many** *for one 'seven'* [7 years]. *In the middle of the 'seven'* [at the Tribulation Period midpoint] *he will put an end to sacrifice and offering*" (verse 27). This foretells the signing of a <u>peace</u> treaty in the Middle East and it implies the rebuilding of the Temple because that is where ***sacrifices*** and **offerings** were always made. It also implies the existence of priests to conduct the services, tools to sacrifice the animals, furniture for the Temple, and clothing for the priests.

Another important point concerns the "*ruler who will come*." His people are the ones who destroyed Jerusalem and the Temple after Jesus was crucified, and history records that it was the Romans who destroyed Jerusalem and the Temple. This means the "*ruler who will come*" will be someone from the group of nations that made up the Roman Empire. Because the Roman Empire broke up before the arrival of this "*ruler who will come*" came on the scene, the Roman Empire has to come back into existence or be revived in order for this prophecy to be fulfilled. This is why the European Union is so important prophetically—it is the uniting of that group of nations that Gabriel said will produce the "*ruler who will come*"; he will be the Antichrist.

The last thing Gabriel said was that the Antichrist will set up an abomination that causes desolation on a wing of the <u>Temple</u>. This will be something that defiles or contaminates the Temple and most authorities believe it will be an <u>image</u> of the Antichrist. When it happens many of the Jews will abandon everything, including the Temple, and <u>flee</u> into the mountains.

Anointed One: Jesus

cut off: crucified

city: Jerusalem

sanctuary: Temple

sevens: seven years

many: representatives of many nations and groups of nations

sacrifices: animal sacrifices

offerings: gifts, worship

☞ **GO TO:**

1 Thessalonians 5:3 (peace)

2 Thessalonians 2:4 (Temple)

Revelation 13:14–18 (image)

Matthew 24:15–16 (flee)

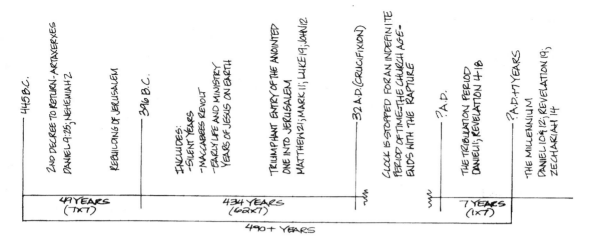

Timeline labels (left to right):
- 445 B.C.
- 2ND DECREE TO RETURN - ARTAXERXES DANIEL 9:25; NEHEMIAH 2
- REBUILDING OF JERUSALEM
- 396 B.C.
- INCLUDES: -SILENT YEARS -MACCABEES REVOLT -EARLY LIFE AND MINISTRY YEARS OF JESUS ON EARTH
- TRIUMPHANT ENTRY OF THE ANOINTED ONE INTO JERUSALEM MATTHEW 21; MARK 11; LUKE 19; JOHN 12
- 32 A.D. (CRUCIFIXION)
- CLOCK IS STOPPED FOR AN INDEFINITE PERIOD OF TIME-THE CHURCH AGE- ENDS WITH THE RAPTURE
- ? A.D.
- THE TRIBULATION PERIOD DANIEL 11; REVELATION 4-18
- ? A.D. +7 YEARS
- THE MILLENNIUM DANIEL 10:4, 12; REVELATION 19; ZECHARIAH 14

| 49 YEARS (7X7) | 434 YEARS (62X7) | 7 YEARS (1X7) |

490 + YEARS

Daniel's Seventy Weeks

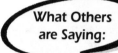

What Others are Saying:

Gary Hedrick: The next event on God's prophetic agenda will be the removal of the Church from planet Earth, an event sometimes called the Rapture, discussed by Paul in 1 Thessalonians 4:13–18. Then, according to Daniel 9, God will call "time in" for Israel. At that point, ". . . *the prince that shall come . . .*" or the Antichrist, will ". . . *confirm the covenant . . .*" with Israel for seven years, marking the beginning of the seventieth "week" (verses 26–27), or the Tribulation Period. But at the midpoint of the seventieth week, or three and one-half years into the seven-year Tribulation, Antichrist will break his treaty with Israel, invade the land, enter the newly rebuilt Temple, and demand to be worshiped.[33]

David Jeremiah with C. C. Carlson: More than anything else in the world, the Jews long for the restoration of their temple and the beginning of temple sacrifice. One day there is going to be this great leader who will sit down at a conference table and say, "My dear friends, it's my desire to help you restore your religious heritage. I have the resources and manpower to rebuild your glorious temple."[34]

Charles H. Dyer: The final three-and-a-half years of this period are a time of unparalleled trouble for the nation of Israel. Jesus Christ described this "abomination that causes desolation" (Matthew 24:15) and indicated that its fulfillment was still in the future.[35]

MIDNIGHT CALL, DECEMBER 1998 . . .

This development [the fact that international pressure caused India and Pakistan to sign an agreement to stop testing nuclear weapons] clearly shows how Israel is again coming under international pressure. Just recently, President Assad of Syria declared that his country is not willing to sign an international treaty as long as Israel possesses nuclear weapons. The consequences for Israel involve placing its security in the hands of an international commission, not being able to rely on its own defense system. This international involvement is impossible to detour and, based on the prophetic Word, will come to pass in the signing of a covenant.[36]

• • •

NEWS FROM ISRAEL, JANUARY 1999 . . .

Israel is being backed into a corner. Peace can only come from the outside, from a power stronger than Israel and the Arab states. That power is Europe. Israel hopes to win peace by placating Europe and the U.S., whose economies are dependent on low oil prices. Translation: Israel must eventually bend to outside dictates in the peace process.[37]

• • •

ENDTIME, JANUARY/FEBRUARY 1999 . . .

On January 1, 1999, eleven of the fifteen countries of the European Union launched a new currency—the Euro. For the first three and one-half years, the Euro will only be used for electronic cashless transactions. In July of 2002, the currencies of the eleven nations are scheduled to be discarded, at which time actual Euro currency will be put into circulation.[38]

• • •

RELATED CURRENT EVENTS

KEY Symbols:

Horn
King or leader

RELATED CURRENT EVENTS

INTERNATIONAL INTELLIGENCE BRIEFING, **NOVEMBER 1998 . . .**

```
At the UN General Assembly this fall in New York,
British Prime Minister Tony Blair promised to
sign an agreement with the UN within six months
to provide British military resources, including
British troops, for UN military actions around
the globe to resolve regional tensions and de-
liver humanitarian assistance. Analysts said that
it was a strong reaffirmation of British commit-
ments to the United Nations and that it could
spark the creation of a permanent standing rapid-
reaction force at the UN's disposal consisting of
troops from multiple nations.³⁹
```

How are we to know the identity of the Antichrist? Here are five clues:

1. He will begin his rise to world power in the European Union (Daniel 9:26).
2. He will rise to power after the world is split into ten regions (Daniel 7:7–8, 24).
3. After rising to power in Europe, he will take over the UN (Daniel 2:40–43).
4. He will sign a covenant with many promising to protect Israel for seven years (Daniel 9:27).
5. He will desecrate the Temple in Jerusalem at the Tribulation Period midpoint (Daniel 9:27).

Something to Ponder

Daniel calls the Antichrist

- another horn (Daniel 7:8; 8:9)
- a little horn (Daniel 7:8)
- another king (Daniel 7:24)
- a stern-faced king (Daniel 8:23)
- the ruler who will come (Daniel 9:26)

Remember This . . .

WARNING

Some people wrongly believe that the Tribulation Period begins with the Rapture, but it actually begins with the signing of a well-publicized covenant. It will be signed by representatives of many nations and it will be a covenant to protect Israel for seven years.

Fulfillment: Things are shaping up for the fulfillment of this prophecy: the UN is being transformed into a world government, the Roman Empire is being revived in the form of the European Union, Israel is back in the land, the quest for a peace treaty in the Middle East is going strong, and preparations for rebuilding the Temple are well underway. But the stage for the seventieth week will not be completely set until after the Rapture and the rise of the Antichrist.

Unfulfilled

Tribulation Period

STUDY QUESTIONS

1. Why will Israel be a testimony to the nations during the Millennium, and what two things will the city of Jerusalem be called?
2. What do Christians call the time of trouble for Jacob, and what will mark its beginning and midpoint?
3. What is the new covenant, what will God do, and when will it expire?
4. In Ezekiel's visions, what did the valley of dry bones and the joined sticks symbolize?
5. What powerful group of nations will attack Israel and be destroyed at the end of the age? What other nations will be destroyed?

CHAPTER WRAP-UP

- Isaiah predicted the defeat of Judah, the destruction of Jerusalem, the regathering of Israel, the building of a Millennial Temple, the reign of Christ on earth during the Millennium, peace on earth during the Millennium, the Tribulation Period, the virgin birth of Christ, the destruction of Babylon (Iraq), the destruction of Damascus (Syria), and the resurrection of the dead. (Isaiah 1:24–31; 2:1–22; 4:1–6; 7:14; 13:1–22; 17:1–14; 26:19–21)

- Jeremiah predicted the restoration of Israel as a nation, the destruction of those nations that seize Jewish land, the Second Coming of Christ, the Millennium, and the Tribulation Period. (Jeremiah 3:14–18; 12:14–17; 23:3–8; 30:5–7; 31:1–11)

- The writer of Lamentations predicted the scattering of the Jews and the Millennium. (Lamentations 1–4)

- Ezekiel predicted that many Jews will survive the Tribulation Period and have a new covenant with God, that Israel will be regathered, that the Jews will repent of their sins and return to God, and that Russia and her allies will invade Israel. He also gave a detailed description of the Millennial Temple. (Ezekiel 34:22–31; 36:1–38; 37:1–28; 38:1–39:16; 40–48)

- Daniel predicted a coming world government at the end of this age, that it will be divided into ten divisions, that it will be ruled by a Satanic person Christians call the Antichrist, and that the Tribulation Period will be in response to a decree from God. (Daniel 2:38–40; 7:23–27; 9:27)

5 PROPHECIES IN THE MINOR PROPHETS

CHAPTER HIGHLIGHTS

- God Loves Unfaithful Israel
- The Worst Is Yet to Come
- God Will Intervene in History
- Anti-Semitism Will Boomerang
- Israel Will Turn to Jesus

Let's Get Started

The Old Testament ends with twelve short books that, because of their length, are often called the Minor Prophets. These twelve prophets lived from about 840 B.C. to 420 B.C., and they were the main moral and spiritual leaders of their time. They spoke to the needs of the people, informing them about God, obedience, faith, love, patience, sin, and judgment, but there were times when they predicted future events and that is where we will concentrate. The messages are widely recognized as being inspired by God, yet critics are surprisingly quiet about the content of these books.

Irving L. Jensen: The books are "minor" only in the sense of being much shorter than such prophecies as Isaiah and Jeremiah (called "major prophets"). Their message is surely not less important today, nor was it when first delivered in Old Testament times. They were minor prophets preaching a major message.[1]

What Others are Saying:

HOSEA

Hosea 1:10–11 "Yet the Israelites will be like the sand on the seashore, which cannot be measured or counted. In the place where it was said to them, 'You are not my people,' they will be called 'sons of the living God.' The people of Judah and the people of Israel will be reunited, and they will appoint one leader and will come up out of the land, for great will be the day of Jezreel."

Hope For The Jews

God told the prophet Hosea to marry an adulterous woman and have children by her to illustrate the fact that the Israelites were *"guilty of the vilest **adultery** in departing from the Lord"* (Hosea 1:2). Hosea's heart would break and that would illustrate that Israel's sin was breaking the heart of God. Hosea's home would be torn apart and that would illustrate that Israel's sin was tearing apart the house of God.

Hosea married an adulterous woman named Gomer (see GWWB, page 227). They had three children and God named all of them. The first was a boy named Jezreel, which means "God sows" or "God scatters," and his name illustrated the fact that God planned to judge Israel's sin and scatter the people. The second was a girl named Lo-Ruhamah, which means "not pitied," and her name illustrated the fact that God was going to stop pitying and forgiving the sinful people. The third was a boy named Lo-Ammi, which means "not my people," and his name illustrated the fact that Israel's sins meant that the Jews were no longer God's people.

These **analogies** meant that God planned to destroy the nation of Israel. Some even want to believe that he planned to put an end to the nation forever. But that goes against the <u>covenants</u> which must be fulfilled and it ignores the prophecies in Hosea 1:10–11. In these verses, God promises that *"the Israelites will be like the <u>sand</u> on the seashore, which cannot be measured or counted."* Although the Jews were no longer his people, the time will come when they will be called *"the sons of the living God."* And although Israel was divided into a Northern Kingdom and a Southern Kingdom, the time will come when they will be <u>one</u> nation. Finally, instead of having separate kings for the two kingdoms, the time will come when they will have one leader.

THE JERUSALEM POST, **NOVEMBER 9, 1998 . . .**

Prime Minister Benjamin Netanyahu said last week he expects up to 150,000 immigrants from Russia and Ukraine during the coming year. He was speaking at a meeting of the Knesset Absorption Committee. "There is a need not just to absorb immigrants, but to encourage immigration," Netanyahu said, promising government funding for projects aimed at bringing Jews to live in Israel.[2]

---

adultery: spiritual adultery (they took up false religions)

KEY POINT

Sin has consequences.

analogies: comparisons, illustrations

☞ **GO TO:**

Genesis 17:7–8 (covenants)

Genesis 22:17 (sand)

Ezekiel 37:15–22 (one)

RELATED CURRENT EVENTS

KEY Symbols:

Living God
*The giver of life
The one who is alive
(not dead like an idol)*

Unfulfilled
Second Coming
Millennium

...destroyed. Many of ... happened over and ...ver been completely ...owing nation again, ...But they will not be ...til the Millennium, ...a reference to their ...hat will occur at his

...ake a covenant for ...the birds of the air ...e ground. Bow and ...the land, so that all ...you to me forever; ...and justice, in love ...in faithfulness, and ...that day I will re-...espond to the skies, ...; and the earth will ...e and oil, and they ...er for myself in the land, I will show ... ...ne I called 'Not my loved one.' I will say to those called 'Not my people,' 'You are my people'; and they will say, 'You are my God.'"

You Are My People

God's <u>covenant</u> will include the animals, the birds, the creatures that move along the ground, and the nations. It will establish a period of security and peace for every living thing on earth. All weapons will be destroyed. <u>Adulterous</u> Israel will be forgiven, taken back, and **betrothed** to God forever. As Israel's <u>husband</u>, the Almighty will establish a new relationship with the nation based upon his **righteousness**, **justice**, **love**, and **compassion**. This wonderful relationship will not be the result of Israel's merits. Rather, it will come about because of God's faithfulness—his unwavering commitment to keep the promises he has made. He will bless Israel and cause the land to be fruitful and the people to prosper. They will have the best of everything in abundance. He will be their God, and they will be his people.

KEY POINT

Four characteristics of God underlying the restoration of Israel are righteousness, justice, love, and compassion.

betrothed: *engaged to be married*

righteousness: *his ability to do right*

justice: *his ability to give each person their due*

love: *his ability to be gracious, tender, affectionate*

compassion: *his ability to be merciful*

☞ **GO TO:**

2 Samuel 7:4–17;
1 Chronicles 16:15–18;
Jeremiah 31:31–34
(covenant)

Hosea 1:2 (adulterous)

Jeremiah 3:14–18;
31:32 (husband)

Duane A. Garrett: It would seem, in fact, that faithfulness sums up the other four qualities in a single word. Because God is consistently good ("righteousness and justice"), one can rely upon him to do good consistently to his people. And because God is consistently merciful ("love and compassion"), one can rely upon him to show mercy consistently to his people. The consistent goodness of God, his faithfulness (in contrast to the capriciousness of Baal), is the basis for Israel's salvation.[3]

Some do not believe the Jews are God's chosen people, but to deny that fact is to deny the faithfulness of God. And to deny his faithfulness is to misunderstand his nature.

Nature will turn against humanity during the Tribulation Period, war will be a common thing, and the Jews will be despised. But this will be reversed during the Millennium. Nature will turn the earth into a paradise, peace will prevail, and the Jews will be respected.

Fulfillment: The current restoration of Israel is taking the nation toward the fulfillment of these things. The Jews are not more righteous than other people, but by the time the Millennium arrives, the faithfulness of God will prevail.

Something
to Ponder

Remember
This . . .

Unfulfilled
Millennium

> **Hosea 3:4–5** For the Israelites will live many days without king or prince, without sacrifice or sacred stones, without ephod or idol. Afterward the Israelites will return and seek the LORD their God and David their king. They will come trembling to the LORD and to his blessings in the last days.

Give Us A King

Because they committed spiritual adultery (Hosea 1:1–11) by departing from the Lord, he decreed that the Jews would live many days without a king or prince to rule over them, without priests to offer sacrifices or erect **sacred stones**, and without spiritual symbols such as an __ephod__ or **idol**. After the many days have ended, the Jews will abandon their spiritual adultery, seek the Lord their God (Jehovah) and David their king (a <u>king</u> in the line of <u>David</u>—Jesus). They will do this in the **last days** (that period of time that will end with the Second Coming of Jesus).

☞ **GO TO:**

Exodus 28:1–43
(ephod)

sacred stones: pillars of stone erected in honor of pagan gods

ephod: sacred garment worn by a priest

idol: statue or image used to represent a god (false god)

last days: the last days of the "times of the Gentiles"

Robert T. Boyd: After the worldwide dispersion under Titus and Hadrian, the Jews had no place to worship and offer sacrifices. They built synagogues and observed some feasts, had Rabbis, and offered chickens on the Day of Atonement. But they were a wandering, scattered people until Israel became a nation in 1948. They still have no king, no temple, no scriptural sacrifices, and no priests. And Hosea predicted this over 2,700 years ago.[4]

Duane A. Garrett: This "David" cannot be the historical king, who was long dead, but is the messianic king for whom he is a figure. As D. A. Hubbard states, returning to David implies the reunion of the two kingdoms (1:11), an end to dynastic chaos (8:4), and an end to seeking protection through alliances with pagan states (7:11). Unity and security can come to Israel only when they seek God and his Christ.[5]

It is important to notice that this prophecy was uttered about 2,700 years ago which was before Israel split into two kingdoms (Northern and Southern) and before the Temple was destroyed. In other words, it was given at a time when Israel had a king, priests, and many spiritual symbols. Apart from a revelation from God, how else could anyone foretell these things?

Fulfillment: God put the Jews off the land. Then he restored the nation and sent the **Messiah**. But the Jews rejected him. So God put them off the land a second time. He is now restoring the nation again and the Jews are returning, but they are not returning to accept Jesus. According to the Bible, they will not do that until after the Tribulation Period when Jesus comes a second time. The Millennium will start, he will rule as their king, and they will worship him.

> **Hosea 6:1–3** "Come, let us return to the Lord. He has torn us to pieces but he will heal us; he has injured us but he will bind up our wounds. After two days he will revive us; on the third day he will restore us, that we may live in his presence. Let us acknowledge the Lord; let us press on to acknowledge him. As surely as the sun rises, he will appear; he will come to us like the winter rains, like the spring rains that water the earth."

What Others are Saying:

☞ **GO TO:**

Psalm 2:1–12; 10:15–16; Jeremiah 23:3–8; Zephaniah 3:15; Zechariah 14:9, 16–17 (king)

Something to Ponder

Unfulfilled
Millennium

Messiah: Jesus

☞ **GO TO:**

1 Chronicles 17:7–15; 2 Samuel 7:14–17; Jeremiah 23:3–8; 33:14–16; Ezekiel 34:22–31; 37:1–28; Luke 1:32–33 (David)

repentance: turning
toward God, away from
wrong

☞ GO TO:

Ezekiel 37:1–28 (Israel)

Psalm 90:4; 2 Peter 3:8
(thousand)

**Remember
This . . .**

KEY POINT

The Second Coming is
a sure thing.

WARNING

☞ GO TO:

2 Peter 3:3–4 (last days)

Daniel 9:24 (sin)

Unfulfilled

Second Coming

Hosea acknowledges the fact that the Jews left the Lord and called on them to join him in **repentance**. He predicted God's deathlike destruction of Israel and the fact that God will eventually heal and resurrect the nation. This resurrection of <u>Israel</u> begs for a date which Hosea said would be after two days and on the third day. As God counts time, one day to him is a <u>thousand</u> years to us. Thus, it is revealed that the revival of Israel as a nation would come after two thousand years of our time had passed and before three thousand years of our time was gone. Hosea calls on the Jews again, asking them to repent. He tells them that the return of Christ is as certain as the rising of the sun and the coming of the seasonal rains.

Time is an essential element in the lives of most people, but God is not subject to time like we are. When he said he would revive Israel after two days and raise her up in the third day, he was speaking in terms of his own view of time. He was saying two thousand years would pass before he revived Israel and it would take place within the next one thousand years.

Looking back on history, the Northern Kingdom of Israel fell around 721 B.C., more than 2,700 years ago, and the Southern Kingdom of Judah fell around 586 B.C., more than 2,500 years ago. Two "God days" have passed and we are now in the third "God day" for both kingdoms, as God reckons time.

The Bible predicts that the <u>last days</u> will be characterized by moral decay with scoffers ridiculing the Second Coming. Evildoers will ask, *"Where is this 'coming' he promised?"* And they will say, *"Ever since our fathers died, everything goes on as it has since the beginning of creation"* (2 Peter 3:4). But God doesn't break his promises and the Second Coming of Christ is as sure as the rising of the sun.

Fulfillment: The resurrection and national restoration of Israel has begun, but the Jews will not abandon their <u>sin</u> until the Tribulation Period (seventieth week of Daniel). The Tribulation Period will trigger repentance and the Second Coming of Christ.

The Scattering of the Jews	Scripture
God will stop loving Israel.	Hosea 1:6
God will stop their celebrations and ruin their crops.	Hosea 2:11–12
The Jews will reject sound teaching and forget the law of God.	Hosea 4:6
The Jews will be arrogant.	Hosea 5:5
God will be like a moth and lion to Israel, like rot and a great lion to Judah.	Hosea 5:12–14
Israel will be swallowed up among the Gentiles.	Hosea 8:8
The Jews will have to eat unclean (defiled) food in a foreign land.	Hosea 9:3
Many Jews will die in foreign lands.	Hosea 9:6
Israel's glory (God) will abandon them.	Hosea 9:11
God will reject the Jews for their disobedience.	Hosea 9:17
Because the Jews planted wickedness, they will reap evil.	Hosea 10:13
The Jews will be punished according to their deeds.	Hosea 12:2
The Jews will be like mist, dew, chaff, and smoke that disappears.	Hosea 13:3
Because of rebellion, Jewish children and pregnant women will die.	Hosea 13:16

Dig Deeper

JOEL

Joel 1:15–20 Alas for that day! For the day of the Lord is near; it will come like destruction from the Almighty. Has not the food been cut off before our very eyes—joy and gladness from the house of our God? The seeds are shriveled beneath the clods. The storehouses are in ruins, the granaries have been broken down, for the grain has dried up. How the cattle moan! The herds mill about because they have no pasture; even the flocks of sheep are suffering. To you, O Lord, I call, for fire has devoured the open pastures and flames have burned up all the trees of the field. Even the wild animals pant for you; the streams of water have dried up and fire has devoured the open pastures.

A Snapshot Of Things To Come

When Joel wrote his prophecy, Israel was in the midst of the greatest <u>locust</u> plague the nation had ever experienced. Dark clouds of locusts covered the land causing the prophet to say, *"What the locust swarm has left the great locusts have eaten; what the great locusts have left the young locusts have eaten; what the young locusts have left other locusts have eaten"* (Joel 1:4). The vineyards were destroyed; the bark and leaves were stripped off the trees; there was no pasture for the animals, no crops to harvest, no sacrifices for the priests to offer, no ground that was not barren, no farmer that was not in poverty and despair, and no joy in the land.

The devastating effects of this unprecedented plague caused Joel's mind to skip far into the future to another desperate time the Bible calls the **day of the Lord**. Trouble will come like a judgment from the Almighty. Food will vanish; <u>famine</u> will grip the land; the absence of <u>sacrifice and offering</u> will leave nothing for the priests in the house of God to rejoice about; seeds will rot in the ground; barns will ruin because they will not be needed; granaries will break down because they will not be used; cattle and sheep will cry because they will have nothing to eat or drink; even the wild animals will suffer. The devastation wrought by the swarms of locusts in Joel's time is just a glimmer of the greater destruction to come in the day of the Lord (see GWRV, pages 128–132).

day of the Lord: another name for the Tribulation Period

☞ **GO TO:**

Revelation 9:3–11 (locust)

Revelation 6:5–8 (famine)

Daniel 9:27 (sacrifice and offering)

What Others are Saying:

Irving L. Jensen: Five times in Joel the phrase "the day of the Lord" appears. As we shall see in the next lesson, Joel is looking with his prophetic telescope to the end of time. Even when the New Testament writers referred to that day, it was still in the future.[6]

Duane A. Garrett: This portrayal of starvation and drought gives the reader a sense that creation itself is dying. The "good" order of seedtime and harvest (Genesis 1:14–18; 8:22) has been disrupted; and the variety of plants, creeping things, and beasts is receding into a chaos of dust and death.[7]

Unfulfilled
Tribulation Period

Fulfillment: This is something that will take place during the Tribulation Period.

Joel 2:1–11 These verses call for an alarm to be sounded announcing the arrival of the day of the Lord. It will be a time of darkness, gloom, clouds, and blackness. A great army will march on the fertile land of Israel destroying everything in its path. It will be like the plague of locusts described in Joel 1. The locusts looked like horses, galloped like a cavalry, jumped over mountains, and consumed everything. The sight of this great army will make people afraid and sick. Troops will charge like brave soldiers—scaling walls, marching in line, staying on course, breaking through defenses, rushing into cities, and breaking into houses. The earth will quake, the heavens will be disturbed, and the heavenly bodies will grow dim. God will issue a command to his great army. The day of the Lord will be terrible, and we are asked, *"Who can endure it?"*

A Call To Arms

The word "like" appears nine times in these eleven verses which means the language is **symbolic**. It would be unwise to be **dogmatic** about this event. Joel is using his memories of the plague of locusts to illustrate what a coming military invasion of Israel will be like during the day of the Lord. He calls for the trumpet to be blown on the **holy hill** to signal the coming Tribulation Period— a time of cloudiness and thick darkness like the time when great swarms of locusts filled the skies over Israel. A large and mighty army will spread across the mountains of Israel like the millions of locusts in Joel's day. In front of this army, Israel will be like the garden of Eden; behind it Israel will be like a desert. There has never been anything like it before and will never be anything like it again. Everything this army encounters will be destroyed. The troops will move like galloping cavalry. They will produce a noise like chariots leaping over the mountaintops, like a crackling fire burning everything in its path. The sight of this great army will make people afraid and sick. It will be a well-trained force—charging, scaling walls, marching in line, focused on the target, and plunging through defenses without pulling back. Troops will rush into Jerusalem, breaking into houses and seizing whatever they want. The earth will quake, the sun and moon will be darkened, and the stars will not shine. If God doesn't cut this great and terrible time short, no one will survive.

symbolic: *words that represent something else*

dogmatic: *positive or assertive*

holy hill: *another name for Jerusalem*

☞ **GO TO:**

Joel 1:15–20 (locusts)

Revelation 11:13; 12:16; 16:18 (quake)

Amos 8:9; Matthew 24:29 (sun and moon)

Matthew 24:21–22 (great)

Some critics contend that these verses deal with a past plague of locusts instead of a future military invasion of Israel. But swarms of locusts move in a disorganized, haphazard manner. Joel calls this force *a large and mighty army* (verse 2), and he paints a picture of a well-trained, efficient military force marching in line, not swerving or jostling each other. It is unreasonable to believe locusts have moved like this in the past.

**Remember
This . . .**

Joel gives us an important clue when he refers to this great army as *the northern army.* We know that there will be a future invasion of Israel by a group of nations from the <u>far north</u> (Russia and her allies); that the <u>king of the North</u> will attack the Antichrist in the Middle East; and that there will be a war between Israel and Syria resulting in the destruction of <u>Damascus</u> and Northern Israel. Incidentally, Russia, the king of the North, and Syria will all be defeated and so will this northern army.

☞ **GO TO:**

Joel 2:20 (northern)

Fulfillment: This invasion of Israel is associated with the day of the Lord. That ties it to the coming Tribulation Period.

Unfulfilled

Tribulation Period

> **Joel 2:28–29** "And afterward, I will pour out my Spirit on all people. Your sons and daughters will prophesy, your old men will dream dreams, your young men will see visions. Even on my servants, both men and women, I will pour out my Spirit in those days."

☞ **GO TO:**

Ezekiel 38:1–39:16
(far north)

Daniel 11:40
(king of the North)

Isaiah 17:1–14
(Damascus)

A Bountiful Supply

"Afterward" reveals when this prophecy will be completely fulfilled: it will be after what Joel just said about the defeat of the <u>northern army</u> and after what he said about Israel beginning to <u>praise</u> the name of the Lord. After these things, God will pour out **his Spirit** on all people. "Pour out" means give his Spirit with great abundance and "all people" means all those who praise him regardless of their age, gender, race, nationality, or status in life. And God's reason for doing this will be so that people will be able to: (1) **prophesy**, (2) receive revelations in **dreams**, and (3) receive messages in **visions**. In short, the time is coming when an abundant supply of God's <u>Spirit</u> will be given to all of his people and it will not matter if they are young or old, male or female,

his Spirit: *the Holy Spirit*

prophesy: *foretell events*

dreams: *images that occur while one is asleep*

visions: *images that occur while one is in a trance*

Gentile or Jew, rich or poor. These gifts will verify the presence of the Holy Spirit and identify those who possess them as God's people.

> Although Joel said God will give these prophetic gifts to his people, the Bible warns us to beware of <u>false prophets</u> who use <u>dreams</u> and false <u>visions</u> to pull people away from God.

Fulfillment: The apostle Peter made it plain that God began fulfilling this on the day of <u>Pentecost</u>. But that was just a hint of things to come. The northern army had not yet attacked Israel and the Jews as a nation were not praising the name of the Lord. This prophecy will not be completely fulfilled until the Millennium.

Unfulfilled
Millennium

☞ **GO TO:**

Joel 2:1–11, 20 (northern army)

Joel 2:26 (praise)

Ezekiel 36:27; 39:29 (Spirit)

Matthew 24:24–25 (false prophets)

Deuteronomy 13:1–5; Jeremiah 23:25 (dreams)

Jeremiah 14:14 (visions)

Acts 2:1–18 (Pentecost)

Psalm 2:1–12; Micah 4:11–13; Obadiah 1:15–16 (nations)

Revelation 16:13–14 (evil spirits)

> **Joel 3:9–16** Proclaim this among the nations: Prepare for war! Rouse the warriors! Let all the fighting men draw near and attack. Beat your plowshares into swords and your pruning hooks into spears. Let the weakling say, "I am strong!" Come quickly, all you nations from every side, and assemble there. Bring down your warriors, O Lord! "Let the nations be roused; let them advance into the Valley of Jehoshaphat, for there I will sit to judge all the nations on every side. Swing the sickle, for the harvest is ripe. Come, trample the grapes, for the winepress is full and the vats overflow—so great is their wickedness!" Multitudes, multitudes in the valley of decision! For the day of the Lord is near in the valley of decision. The sun and moon will be darkened, and the stars no longer shine. The Lord will roar from Zion and thunder from Jerusalem; the earth and the sky will tremble. But the Lord will be a refuge for his people, a stronghold for the people of Israel.

D-day (Or Should It Be "A-day" for Armageddon)

This passage calls for unnamed messengers to fan out all over the world to advise the <u>nations</u> to prepare for war. The text does not say so, but these messengers are probably the three <u>evil spirits</u> mentioned in the book of Revelation. They are told to wake up

Valley of Jehoshaphat:
it means "the valley of
God's judgment"

sickle: a large knife used
for harvesting crops

deliver: save the Jews
from this great army

☞ **GO TO:**

Zechariah 14:1–21;
   Luke 21:20–22
   (Jerusalem)

Revelation 19:11–16
   (armies)

Zechariah 14:5 (Lord)

the "*warriors*" and "*fighting men*," and to assemble them for an attack. This war will exempt no one. Those who would normally be excused from military service will not be excused from this great battle. Troops will be mobilized from all over the world. They will gather to attack <u>Jerusalem</u> and to challenge the <u>armies</u> of the <u>Lord</u>. They will assemble in a place called the **Valley of Jehoshaphat**. The heavenly hosts will be told to swing the **sickle** because the earth is ripe for harvest. They will be told to trample the armies because the world is overflowing with wickedness. Multitudes, great multitudes will be there. They will have to face their Maker. It will be the day of the Lord. The <u>sun and moon</u> will grow dim and the stars will cease to shine—darkness will cover the land. Jesus will rush out of Jerusalem to meet this great army. There will be a terrible earthquake and vibrations in the sky. The Messiah will **deliver** his people. The text does not tell us what will happen to the troops, but elsewhere we learn that their dead bodies will provide a great feast for the <u>birds</u> of prey (see GWRV, pages 285–290).

What Others
are Saying:

☞ **GO TO:**

Joel 3:1–2 (Jehoshaphat)

Joel 2:30–31; Amos
   8:9; Matthew 24:29
   (sun and moon)

Revelation 19:17–18
   (birds)

Isaiah 2:4; Micah 4:3
   (swords)

Thomas Ice and Timothy Demy: According to the Bible, great armies from the east and the west will gather and assemble on this plain. There will be threats to the power of the Antichrist from the south, and he will also move to destroy a revived Babylon in the east before finally turning his forces toward Jerusalem to subdue and destroy it. As he and his armies move on Jerusalem, God will intervene and Jesus Christ will return to rescue His chosen people, Israel.[8]

Randall Price: Earthquakes happen frequently in the Jerusalem area, and evidence indicates that the Mount of Olives is set to split should an earthquake of sufficient size strike the region.[9]

Micah 4:3 says the people will "*beat their <u>swords</u> into plowshares and their spears into pruning hooks.*" But we must remember that that is something to be done during the Millennium when Christ reigns on earth and the nations are at peace. Until then, the nations should do the opposite so they can be prepared to defend themselves. Why? Because we live in a time of "wars and rumors of wars."

Remember
This . . .

Fulfillment: There is wide agreement among prophetic scholars that this prophecy refers to the Battle of Armageddon that will take place during the Tribulation Period.

The Millennium	Scripture
Israel will have crops, rain, and food in abundance.	Joel 2:21–27
Because of God's presence Israel will prosper.	Joel 3:17–21

Dig Deeper

AMOS

> **Amos 5:16–20** Therefore this is what the Lord, the LORD God Almighty, says: "There will be wailing in all the streets and cries of anguish in every public square. The farmers will be summoned to weep and the mourners to wail. There will be wailing in all the vineyards, for I will pass through your midst," says the LORD. Woe to you who long for the day of the LORD! Why do you long for the day of the LORD? That day will be darkness, not light. It will be as though a man fled from a lion only to meet a bear, as though he entered his house and rested his hand on the wall only to have a snake bite him. Will not the day of the LORD be darkness, not light—pitch-dark, without a ray of brightness?

KEY Symbols:

The Tribulation Period

Like running from a hungry lion

Like bumping into a ferocious bear

Like leaning on a poisonous snake

Out Of The Frying Pan Into The Fire

Some say there won't be a Tribulation Period, but the Lord says people everywhere—people in all the streets and public places (cities, towns), the farmers (those in the country), the hired mourners (those paid to cry or <u>lament</u>), and those in the vineyards (laborers)—will **wail**. There will be bitter weeping when God passes through their midst in judgment.

Many do not understand the seriousness or severity of the day of the Lord. Some very piously wish that it would arrive. But that is a mistake. The Tribulation Period will be a day of darkness, not light; a period of <u>distress</u>, not joy; it will be a time when danger will surround every person, encircle every human being, and there will be no way for anyone to escape. People will flee one danger and encounter another greater peril. Every place on earth will be under siege. It will be like running from a hungry lion and falling

wail: a loud, painful cry (the death wail)

☞ **GO TO:**

2 Chronicles 35:25 (lament)

Jeremiah 9:17 (wail)

Matthew 24:21–22 (distress)

into the clutches of a ferocious bear, like leaning upon a wall to rest and putting your hand upon a poisonous snake.

What Others
are Saying:

Thomas Ice: Armageddon is the last major event on the prophetic timeline before the establishment of the Millennial Kingdom, Christ's 1000-year reign on Earth. Armageddon isn't an event people should desire or anticipate with joy because it will bring death and destruction. It is, however, a definite future military conflict that will not, and cannot, be avoided by any amount of negotiation.[10]

Unfulfilled
Tribulation Period

Fulfillment: Among prophetic scholars there is no disagreement on the timing of this prophecy. It is plainly stated that this is a reference to the day of the Lord.

KEY POINT

We should not delude ourselves about the Tribulation Period because it will be a time of unparalleled and inescapable danger.

> **Amos 8:9** "In that day," declares the Sovereign LORD, "I will make the sun go down at noon and darken the earth in broad daylight."

A Short Day

Millennium: the thousand-year reign of Christ on earth

"In that day" is a phrase often used in the Bible to refer to the day of the Lord or to the **Millennium**. The day of the Lord will be a time of unusual events. One of those unusual events will be a noon sunset. The earth will go from broad daylight to total darkness at midday.

Remember
This . . .

1. God is the One who separated light from <u>darkness</u> (Genesis 1:3–4).
2. God covered the land of Egypt with total darkness for three days (Exodus 10:21–23).
3. God made the sun and the moon stand still in the middle of the sky for a <u>full day</u> (Joshua 10:12–13).
4. God covered the <u>land</u> of Israel with darkness for three hours when Jesus was crucified (Matthew 27:45).

☞ **GO TO:**

Genesis 1:14–18;
Exodus 10:21–23
(darkness)

Joshua 10:12–14
(full day)

Matthew 27:45 (land)

When the fifth angel pours out his vial during the Tribulation Period, darkness will cover the kingdom of the Antichrist causing his followers to gnaw their tongues in pain. This will be appropriate punishment for those who use their tongues to blaspheme God (Revelation 16:9-11).

Critics offer many different interpretations of this verse. Some say this darkness is just a **metaphor**. Some say it refers to an eclipse during the lifetime of Amos. One writer says smoke will darken the sun. Another thinks this is a reference to the darkness of sin coming into young lives. Still another thinks this refers to the untimely death of the ungodly. But all of these interpreters overlook the plain truth of what Jesus and several of the prophets said: *"The sun will be darkened and the moon will not give its light"* (Matthew 24:29). Where is the explanation for the moon not giving its light in all of these different interpretations?

Fulfillment: Jesus placed the darkened sun at the end of the Tribulation Period when he said, *"Immediately after the distress of those days the sun will be darkened, and the moon will not give its light; the stars will fall from the sky, and the heavenly bodies will be shaken"* (Matthew 24:29).

> **Amos 9:11–15** "In that day I will restore David's fallen tent. I will repair its broken places, restore its ruins, and build it as it used to be, so that they may possess the remnant of Edom and all the nations that bear my name," declares the LORD, who will do these things. "The days are coming," declares the LORD, "when the reaper will be overtaken by the plowman and the planter by the one treading grapes. New wine will drip from the mountains and flow from all the hills. I will bring back my exiled people Israel; they will rebuild the ruined cities and live in them. They will plant vineyards and drink their wine; they will make gardens and eat their fruit. I will plant Israel in their own land, never again to be uprooted from the land I have given them," says the LORD your God.

Hope For The Future

Here, *"in that day"* refers to the Millennium. God will do four things at that time: (1) he will restore David's fallen tent which means he will restore the <u>house of David</u> (a reference to the reign of Christ on earth); (2) he will repair its broken places, which means he will correct the mistakes the leaders of Israel have made while ruling the nation; (3) he will restore its ruins, which means

WARNING

metaphor: *a literary device, when one thing stands for something else*

☞ **GO TO:**

Isaiah 13:9–10; Joel 2:30–31; 3:15; Revelation 8:12 (sun)

Unfulfilled
Tribulation Period

☞ **GO TO:**

2 Samuel 7:4–17; Luke 2:4–7 (house of David)

he will rebuild the towns and cities; and (4) he will build it as it used to be which means he will rebuild Israel according to the instructions he gave to David when he reigned.

"Possess the remnant of Edom and all the nations that bear my name" is usually interpreted to mean God will elevate Israel to the head of the nations. To emphasize the certainty of this, the writer adds that this is a declaration of the Lord. It will be a time of bountiful crops and abundant harvests. The Jews will return to the land—they will rebuild the cities, live in them, and never be put off again.

Billy K. Smith and Frank S. Page: God's forgiveness of Israel will be permanent. His blessing will be constant. Restoration of covenant blessings is an unconditional promise. Once and for all time God promised to plant Israel on their ground, never to be uprooted again. The land would be theirs as a gift from God. "Says the Lord your God" is the closing messenger formula, guaranteeing the promises based on the sure word of Israel's covenant God.[11]

exiled: *removed from Israel*

God says, *"I will bring back my **exiled** people Israel,"* and he says, *"I will plant Israel in their own land, never again to be uprooted from the land I have given them."* If the return of the Jews is God's doing and if he has declared that the land belongs to them, what should happen to those nations that oppose him? If the nations choose to be willingly ignorant of God's will, is a Tribulation Period justified?

***THE LAMPLIGHTER,* NOVEMBER 1998 . . .**

And so it has been in war after war—the War of Independence in 1948, the Suez War in 1956, the Six Day War in 1967, the Yom Kippur War in 1973, the Lebanon War in 1982, and the Gulf War in 1991. When you add to these wars the Arab Intifada (Uprising) that lasted from 1987 to 1993, it is truly a miracle of God that the nation of Israel continues to exist—a tiny Jewish state of 5 million Jews surrounded by a host of 21 Arab nations with a population of 200 million.[12]

Fulfillment: Such famous Bible cities as Ashdod, Ashkelon, Beersheba, Jaffa (now Tel Aviv), and Jerusalem have already been rebuilt. Flowers, grain, cotton, tomatoes, peppers, and more are now growing on rich farm land that was barren just a few years ago. Trees loaded with lemons, limes, oranges, grapefruit, tangerines, and other fruit now cover the once bleak hills. The stage is being set for the fulfillment of this prophecy.

OBADIAH

> **Obadiah 1:15–16** "The day of the LORD is near for all nations. As you have done, it will be done to you; your deeds will return upon your own head. Just as you drank on my holy hill, so all the nations will drink continually; they will drink and drink and be as if they had never been."

All Nations Will Reap What They Sow

These verses identify three **principles** about God's judgment of the nations during the Tribulation Period. First, "*the day of the Lord is near*" means the time when God will <u>judge</u> the nations is approaching. Nations will go too far in their mistreatment of Israel, causing God to intervene in the affairs of the world. Second, "*is near for all nations*" means no nation will be spared. When his wrath is kindled it will fall upon every <u>nation</u> on earth. And third, "*as you have done, it will be done to you*" means that God will take into account how the nations have treated his people. Those who kill will be <u>killed</u>. Those who make Israel drink a <u>cup</u> of suffering will be made to <u>drink</u> from that same cup. They will perish from the earth and be remembered no more.

MESSAGE OF THE CHRISTIAN JEW, MARCH/APRIL 1999 . . .

```
In 1994, Martin Agyare, an African from Ghana,
lost a leg when he was thrown off a train by neo-
Nazis. He now carries a tear-gas pistol and a
knife for protection, and says his friends are
also armed. Martin lives in Belzig, Germany. He
fears victimization and endures daily insults and
prejudice. He is not alone. Things are getting
worse in Germany. Right-wing (neo-Nazi) activity
```

☞ **GO TO:**

Matthew 7:2 (judge)

Psalm 2:1–12; Joel 3:2, 9–16; Micah 4:11–13; Zechariah 14:1–21; Luke 21:20–22 (nation)

Revelation 13:10 (killed)

Matthew 10:40–42; 26:39 (cup)

Matthew 25:31–46 (drink)

principles: fundamental truths

RELATED CURRENT EVENTS

is increasing. Some 11,700 offenses (a post-war record) were recorded in mid-1997, including 790 attacks.[13]

Unfulfilled
Tribulation Period

KEY POINT

When the Tribulation Period arrives, all nations will pay for their anti-Semitism.

KEY Symbols:

The Day of the Lord Is Near

God's judgment is approaching

last days: *the last days of "the times of the Gentiles"*

topography: *earth's surface*

☞ **GO TO:**

Zechariah 14:10 (Jerusalem)

Zechariah 14:4–5 (mountains)

Isaiah 2:1–22; Ezekiel 43:10–12 (Temple)

Fulfillment: One purpose of the Tribulation Period is to punish all nations for their mistreatment of the Jews. Those who are particularly cruel (goat nations) will be destroyed before the Millennium.

MICAH

Micah 4:1–7 In the last days the mountain of the LORD's temple will be established as chief among the mountains; it will be raised above the hills, and peoples will stream to it. Many nations will come and say, "Come, let us go up to the mountain of the LORD, to the house of the God of Jacob. He will teach us his ways, so that we may walk in his paths." The law will go out from Zion, the word of the LORD from Jerusalem. He will judge between many peoples and will settle disputes for strong nations far and wide. They will beat their swords into plowshares and their spears into pruning hooks. Nation will not take up sword against nation, nor will they train for war anymore. Every man will sit under his own vine and under his own fig tree, and no one will make them afraid, for the LORD Almighty has spoken. All the nations may walk in the name of their gods; we will walk in the name of the LORD our God for ever and ever. "In that day," declares the LORD, "I will gather the lame; I will assemble the exiles and those I have brought to grief. I will make the lame a remnant, those driven away a strong nation. The LORD will rule over them in Mount Zion from that day and forever.

The Future Kingdom

"In the last days" is a Bible term referring to that period of time that ends with the Second Coming of Christ. In the **last days** Jesus will return. The **topography** of Jerusalem will change. The Temple Mount will be elevated above the surrounding mountains. The Millennial Temple will be built and become the most sacred place on earth. Multitudes will stream to that place like a mighty rushing river.

Even people from foreign countries will go there. They will visit the house of the **God of Jacob** (Israel). The Word of God will be taught there and people will live by those teachings. God's law and God's Word will come out of Jerusalem. This will be the Millennial Kingdom (see illustration, below).

Jesus will sit as a judge and he will settle disputes among the nations. His reign will produce world peace, **disarmament**, and the end of military training. It will also produce safety and prosperity. This is what God himself says.

Today, all people walk in the name of their own God, but in the future their devotion will be given to Israel's God. He will gather the lame, the exiled, the afflicted and rule over them from the Temple in Jerusalem. And his kingdom will never end.

During the Millennium there will be no need for the United Nations and the World Court because nations and leaders will place themselves under the rule of Christ. There will be no poverty, no theft, no war, only one God, and pure worship. With Jesus on the throne, this world will be the wonderful place God always intended.

Fulfillment: We are already in the last days of "the times of the Gentiles" (see Acts 2:14–21), but the events described in this passage are still future. They will begin with the Second Coming of Christ and carry over into the Millennium.

God of Jacob: *Israel's God*

disarmament: *the destruction of weapons*

☞ **GO TO:**

Genesis 28:13–15 (Jacob)

Something to Ponder

| Unfulfilled |
| Second Coming |
| Millennium |

Bible Kingdoms

SECOND COMING

RAPTURE

DAVID'S KINGDOM	MYSTERY KINGDOM	KINGDOM OF CHRIST	MILLENNIUM KINGDOM	ETERNAL KINGDOM
	CHURCH AGE	TRIBULATION PERIOD	1000 YEARS	BEYOND THE MILLENNIUM

> **Micah 4:11–13** But now many nations are gathered against you. They say, "Let her be defiled, let our eyes gloat over Zion!" But they do not know the thoughts of the LORD; they do not understand his plan, he who gathers them like sheaves to the threshing floor. "Rise and thresh, O Daughter of Zion, for I will give you horns of iron; I will give you hoofs of bronze and you will break to pieces many nations." You will devote their ill-gotten gains to the LORD, their wealth to the Lord of all the earth.

Don't Count Your Chickens Before They Hatch

In Micah 4:1–7 we learned about the future kingdom. But the establishment of that kingdom will be preceded by a planned attack on <u>Jerusalem</u>. Many <u>nations</u> will gather against the chosen city. The great number of attackers will be gloating about what they think will happen to the Jews and will plan to **defile** the Holy City. But they will be unaware of the thoughts and plans of God. They won't know that he has <u>gathered</u> them there to be destroyed. The whole area will be like a giant **threshing floor**, the enemy troops like freshly cut grain, and Jerusalem like a powerful animal with horns of iron and hoofs of bronze. The foreign armies will be pulverized. Israel will gather their ill-gotten wealth and give it to God. Everything will be done for his glory.

Charles L. Feinberg: The besiegers will look with delight on the calamities of the Jews. . . . They do not comprehend the love, wisdom, and grace of God which will overrule Israel's calamities for good. In their venomous hatred against Zion the nations will believe that they have hit upon a plan which will successfully deliver to Israel a death-dealing blow.[14]

Kenneth L. Barker and Waylon Bailey: The nations that are enemies of both God and his people do not know or understand that he is in complete control of everything that is happening, carrying out his own sovereign purpose, plan, and will—including even the siege of Jerusalem. They also do not realize what he has in store for them, to gather them "like sheaves to the threshing floor" to be threshed.[15]

☞ **GO TO:**

Joel 3:1–2, 9–16; Zechariah 14:1–21; Luke 21:20–22 (Jerusalem)

Psalm 2:1–12; Obadiah 1:15–16; Revelation 19:11–16 (nations)

Revelation 16:13–14 (gathered)

What Others are Saying:

defile: *to corrupt*

threshing floor: *a place where grain was beaten or pounded to separate the kernels from the chaff*

Some critics say these verses refer to the Assyrian army attacking the Northern Kingdom of Israel. Others say they refer to the Babylonian army attacking the Southern Kingdom of Judah. Still others say they refer to the Roman army attacking Jerusalem after the death of Jesus. But this is a prophecy about *"many nations"* attacking Jerusalem, not just one nation. And these *"many nations"* are not victorious—they lose.

Fulfillment: Here we have more information about the Battle of Armageddon. The troops will gather late in the Tribulation Period. And they will be destroyed at the Second Coming of Christ.

The Millennium	Scripture
The future Ruler of Israel will come out of Bethlehem Ephrathah.	Micah 5:2–4
The Jews will be a source of blessing for many people.	Micah 5:7
Israel's weapons, fortresses, witches, idols, and sacred stones will be destroyed.	Micah 5:10–15
God will forgive Israel because he made covenants with Jacob and Abraham.	Micah 7:18–20

Dig Deeper

ZEPHANIAH

Zephaniah 1:14–18 "The great day of the Lord is near—near and coming quickly. Listen! The cry on the day of the Lord will be bitter, the shouting of the warrior there. That day will be a day of wrath, a day of distress and anguish, a day of trouble and ruin, a day of darkness and gloom, a day of clouds and blackness, a day of trumpet and battle cry against the fortified cities and against the corner towers. I will bring distress on the people and they will walk like blind men, because they have sinned against the Lord. Their blood will be poured out like dust and their entrails like filth. Neither their silver nor their gold will be able to save them on the day of the Lord's wrath. In the fire of his jealousy the whole world will be consumed, for he will make a sudden end of all who live in the earth."

calamities: famine,
pestilence, earthquakes,
war

☞ **GO TO:**

Matthew 24:21–22
(distress)

Amos 8:9;
Matthew 24:29
(sun and moon)

Deuteronomy 28:29
(blind)

Haggai 2:6–7 (nation)

There's Nothing On TV But A Lot Of Bad News

The time for God's judgment of the earth is approaching and it will arrive quicker than most people realize. Zephaniah describes what it will be like. It will be a time of bitter crying. Even battle-hardened warriors will weep uncontrollably. During this time, God will loose his fierce anger on the world. The **calamities** that follow will produce distress and anguish such as the world has never seen. People will be surrounded by trouble and ruin—loved ones will be killed, houses will be destroyed, jobs will be lost. Even the heavenly bodies—the sun and moon—will be affected and the earth will be covered with thick clouds and intense darkness. The sound of the trumpet and the battle cry will be heard everywhere, signaling the beginning of war. The strongest places will be attacked, great cities will be captured, and fortified places will fall. The distress will be so great people will appear to be blind, feeling their way around wherever they go. God will do this because the people have sinned against him. He will show them no mercy. Their blood will be poured out like unwanted dust. Their insides will be poured out like something dirty and worthless. Every nation will be affected, not just Israel. All who have angered him will come to a sudden end.

What Others are Saying:

J. A. Motyer: The day of the Lord is not arbitrary; it is the logical outgrowth of what humankind is (1:17b); it will bring what humankind deserves (1:17), and it will expose the uselessness of what humans trust (1:16, 18).[16]

David Reagan: The Bible clearly teaches that society will degenerate in the end times, becoming as evil as it was in the days of Noah (Matthew 24:37–39). The Apostle Paul, speaking as a prophet, says that society will descend into a black pit of immorality, violence, and paganism (2 Timothy 3:1–5). He asserts that men will be "lovers of self, lovers of money, and lovers of pleasure." People will be "boastful, arrogant, and unholy," and children will be "disobedient to parents." Sounds like the evening news, doesn't it? In short, we have arrived.[17]

Unfulfilled
Tribulation Period

Fulfillment: The day of the Lord will be an actual event of tragic proportions. It's no wonder that people call it the Tribulation Period.

ZECHARIAH

> **Zechariah 12:1–14** In this passage, God reminds the people that he created the heavens, the earth, and the spirit of man and that he intends to use Jerusalem to make the nations stagger and fall. Judah and Jerusalem will come under siege by all nations, but God will strengthen the Jews and cause their enemies to injure themselves. He will smite the attackers with fear, madness, and blindness. The Jewish leaders will know that God has strengthened them. Those who attack Israel will be playing with fire. Jerusalem will not be destroyed, but God will save the people of Judah first, so the leaders and inhabitants of Jerusalem will not gloat. God will help the Jews who live in Jerusalem by giving them supernatural courage and strength. He will destroy all nations that attack Jerusalem, but he will pour out a spirit of grace and supplication upon the Jews, and they will recognize the One they pierced. All Israel will weep.

A National Hot Potato

This passage begins with a reminder that the following prophecy comes from an all-powerful God, the Creator of all things. Out of love, God offers the nations a warning before they make a terrible mistake—they should not doubt that he can do, or will do, these things. God will cause **Judah** and <u>Jerusalem</u> to occupy center stage at the end of the age. He will use that area to judge the nations and deal a staggering blow to his enemies. It will be the entire world's problem. **Gentile** <u>nations</u> will respond by gathering a great army to attack the West Bank and the Holy City. But God will strengthen the Jews. Attacking them will be the same as attacking God. He will strike the enemy with fear, insanity, and blindness. Afflicted with terror, confusion, ignorance, and stupidity, they will injure themselves and seal their own doom.

In order to reach Jerusalem, the enemy will have to pass through Judah. That is where the first great victory will come. A victory in the outlying settlements before Jerusalem is delivered will prevent the inhabitants of Jerusalem from becoming proud.

God will help the Jews by infusing the Israeli army with supernatural abilities. Jewish soldiers will be exceptionally courageous and strong. They will eventually overcome those who attack them. Then God will instill a spirit of **grace** and **supplication** in the

KEY POINT

During the Tribulation Period, attacking Israel will be the same thing as attacking God.

☞ **GO TO:**

Zechariah 14:1–21; Luke 21:20–22 (Jerusalem)

Psalm 2:1–12; Micah 4:11–13; Obadiah 1:15–16 (nations)

Judah: *the West Bank, Judea*

Gentile: *non-Jewish*

grace: *a desire to follow the Holy Spirit*

supplication: *prayer*

☞ **GO TO:**

Isaiah 53:1–12; John 19:28–37 (pierced)

What Others are Saying:

followed: obeyed

Jewish people. They will realize that they have not **followed** him. They will understand what they have not understood before: their Messiah is the One who was <u>pierced</u>. They will go through a time of national mourning and intense sorrow. Every person will go into seclusion to be alone with God, to grieve over their own sins, and to mourn their past rejection of Jesus.

Grant R. Jeffrey: Israel, with only eight thousand square miles and a population of five million citizens, contains less than one-tenth of one percent of earth's population. Despite its insignificant size, a multitude of debates, conferences and resolutions focus on this small country every year. The leaders of the nations recognize that if Armageddon comes it will undoubtedly start here.[18]

Noah Hutchings: As Zechariah prophesied, Jerusalem is a problem to all nations, a sign that Israel will soon recognize the Messiah at His coming by the nail prints in His hands (vs. 10).[19]

Gary Hedrick: From Megiddo, the world's military forces—probably UN or NATO troops, the European Union, or some combination of these—will begin to make their way southward toward Jerusalem. One can easily imagine how difficult and costly the invasion will be. The attackers cannot use air strikes or artillery on any large scale because of the damage that could be done to ancient religious sites. Jerusalem must be taken the old-fashioned way—on the ground. No wonder John uses the metaphor of blood running up to the horses' bridles to describe the unspeakable carnage that will result (Revelation 14:20).[20]

PA: Palestinian Authority

RELATED CURRENT EVENTS

INTERNATIONAL INTELLIGENCE BRIEFING, JULY 1998 . . .

The **PA** has applied to the UN for an upgraded status as a "state minus." The move would not only have symbolic consequences. It has tangible ones, since the Palestinians would be able to draft resolutions and participate in all debates on the Middle East. Israel has been boxed out of regional groupings at the UN. As a result, it can never dream of full representation on the Security Council or other prestigious UN bodies. An enhanced status for the Palestinian delegation would give "Palestine" more clout at the UN than Israel.[21]

• • •

INTERNATIONAL INTELLIGENCE BRIEFING, MARCH 1999 . . .

The United Nations General Assembly (UNGA) has overwhelmingly passed a resolution calling for a special summit of signatories to the Geneva Convention on July 15 to discuss "illegal Israeli actions in occupied 'East Jerusalem' and the rest of the 'occupied Palestinian Territory' [Judea, Samaria and Gaza]. According to the UN, Israel is in violation of the Geneva Convention in its policies concerning the Gaza strip.[22]

• • •

MIDNIGHT CALL, SEPTEMBER 1998 . . .

Jerusalem, according to the will of the Vatican, should become the capital city of the world. The one-sided claim through Israel as the Jewish capital doesn't properly justify the significance for Muslims and Christians, according to Cardinal Secretary Angelo Sodano. Already in 1947, a plan of separation, under the British mandate, proposed the internationalization of Jerusalem.[23]

• • •

THE JERUSALEM POST, DECEMBER 28, 1998 . . .

For those who take Israel's "special" relationship with the US for granted, the images of President Bill Clinton embracing **Yasir Arafat** and his Palestinian Authority in Gaza last week were a wake-up call. . . . And indeed, the relationship is changing. Clinton's journey to Gaza gave the Palestinian-state-in-the-making American legitimacy. "True, I am Israel's good friend," Clinton told the Palestinians in not so many words, "but I want to be your good friend as well." That symmetry is bad for Israel.[24]

Yasir Arafat: *head of the PLO*

Since the God who created all things—including the heavens, the earth, and humans—also destroyed the Egyptian the Babylonian armies, wouldn't it be a terrible mistake to make him angry? An attack on the tiny nation of Israel would be a big gamble. Is that really the best way to find out if God exists?

Something to Ponder

Unfulfilled

Tribulation Period

Second Coming

Some people believe that there is a God who created all things, but they also believe that he does not intervene in what goes on here on Earth. This chapter refutes that. It reminds us that there is a Creator, that he is involved in the affairs of the world, and that he is going to have the final say on matters concerning Israel.

Fulfillment: The beginning of this battle will be in the Tribulation Period, just before the Second Coming of Christ. After it starts, Christ will return, he will destroy Israel's enemies, and the Jews will recognize him by his wounds.

> **Zechariah 13:1–5** "On that day a fountain will be opened to the house of David and the inhabitants of Jerusalem, to cleanse them from sin and impurity. "On that day, I will banish the names of the idols from the land, and they will be remembered no more," declares the LORD Almighty. "I will remove both the prophets and the spirit of impurity from the land. And if anyone still prophesies, his father and mother, to whom he was born, will say to him, 'You must die, because you have told lies in the LORD's name.' When he prophesies, his own parents will stab him. On that day every prophet will be ashamed of his prophetic vision. He will not put on a prophet's garment of hair in order to deceive. He will say, 'I am not a prophet. I am a farmer; the land has been my livelihood since my youth.'"

There Is A Fountain Filled With Blood

These verses pick up where Chapter 12 left off. Following a brief period of national mourning and repentance, a fountain will be opened to all Jews, and God will forgive their sins including the rejection of Jesus as their Messiah. This forgiveness will be followed by the abolition of false worship, the destruction of idols, and the elimination of <u>false prophets</u>. In many cases, false prophets will be killed by their own parents. Some false prophets will be ashamed of what they have done. And some will try to disguise themselves and deceive people by pretending they are farmers (see GWRV, pages 194–202).

☞ **GO TO:**

Matthew 7:15;
  24:4, 11, 24
  (false prophets)

Charles L. Feinberg: Israel now enters into the provision of God at Calvary. . . . The provision of God will avail for both sin and uncleanness. Zechariah has in mind moral not ceremonial uncleanness. Justification is here and sanctification as well. Judicial guilt and moral impurity will be removed at the same time.[25]

Ed Hindson: A true prophet—

1. must speak in the name of the Lord, not some other god.
2. must have a message that is in accord with God's revealed truth in Scripture.
3. must give predictions of future events that come true *exactly* as stated.[26]

There will be a multiplication of false prophets and a surge in idolatry during the Tribulation Period. Multitudes will worship the <u>image</u> of the beast (the Antichrist); and <u>evil spirits</u> from the mouth of Satan, the mouth of the Antichrist, and the mouth of the False Prophet will gather the nations for the Battle of Armageddon.

Remember This . . .

Fulfillment: The forgiveness will take place at the Second Coming of Christ. The abolition of false worship and the destruction of idols will begin immediately and carry over into the Millennium.

Unfulfilled
Second Coming
Millennium

The Millennium	Scripture
God will have mercy on Israel and build his house in Jerusalem.	Zechariah 1:16–17
Jerusalem will be a great city protected by God.	Zechariah 2:1–5
When God lives in Jerusalem many nations will accept Christ.	Zechariah 2:10–13
Christ will rule with wisdom and remove Israel's sin in one day.	Zechariah 3:8–9
Israel will succeed and the Temple will be built by the power of the Holy Spirit.	Zechariah 4:1–14
Christ will build the Temple and sit upon the throne in Israel.	Zechariah 6:11–12
God will live in Jerusalem, bless it, and cause the Jews to return.	Zechariah 8:1–8

Dig Deeper

☞ **GO TO:**

Revelation 13:14–15 (image)

Revelation 16:13–14 (evil spirits)

Dig Deeper

The Millennium	Scripture
Many Gentiles will visit Jerusalem and join the Jews in worshiping God.	Zechariah 8:20–23
Israel's borders will be expanded to encompass all the returning Jews.	Zechariah 10:8–11

> **Zechariah 13:7–9** "Awake, O sword, against my shepherd, against the man who is close to me!" declares the LORD Almighty. "Strike the shepherd, and the sheep will be scattered, and I will turn my hand against the little ones. In the whole land," declares the LORD, "two-thirds will be struck down and perish; yet one-third will be left in it. This third I will bring into the fire; I will refine them like silver and test them like gold. They will call on my name and I will answer them; I will say, 'They are my people,' and they will say, 'The LORD is our God.'"

A Purifying Holocaust

Zechariah looked into Israel's future and saw the **striking** of God's **shepherd**. The death of the shepherd would be followed by the <u>scattering</u> of Israel. A long period of time would pass, and Israel would return to the land. This much has happened in history, but the rest is yet future. A great **calamity** will come upon the land, says Zechariah, and two-thirds of Israel's people will be killed. The other third will be purified. The result of this national calamity will be that the purified will **call** upon the name of God, and they will be heard by him. He will accept them and they will accept Jesus as their Messiah.

Jimmy DeYoung: This will mark the beginning of the most horrible time for God's chosen people in Jewish history. Satan and Antichrist will unleash unprecedented persecution on Israel. This period, known as the Great Tribulation, will see two of every three Jews killed (Zechariah 13:8). Jesus warned Israel to flee to the wilderness for protection during this time.[27]

Charles L. Feinberg: The purpose of the refining is to purify and develop faith in the remnant. Physical deliverance will be followed by conversion. Thus will the new covenant be fulfilled.[28]

☞ **GO TO:**

Psalm 23:1; John 10:11, 14 (shepherd)

Matthew 26:31 (scattering)

What Others are Saying:

striking: *crucifixion*

shepherd: *Jesus*

calamity: *the Tribulation Period*

call: *pray*

GOD'S WORD FOR THE BIBLICALLY-INEPT

Notice that the returning Jews need to be purified. This is because they are making the same mistake as those who struck the shepherd. They are returning in unbelief. Out of his mercy God will send great tribulation to change this.

Fulfillment: The shepherd was struck in A.D. 30 when Jesus was crucified. Israel was scattered in A.D. 70 when the Romans destroyed the nation. The return is now underway. Two-thirds of Israel's Jews will die during the Tribulation Period. The remainder will accept Jesus at his Second Coming.

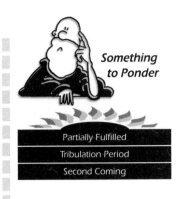

Something to Ponder

Partially Fulfilled
Tribulation Period
Second Coming

THE BIG PICTURE

> **Zechariah 14:1–21** The day of the Lord is approaching. When it arrives the nations will unite, gather an army, attack Jerusalem, capture the city, plunder the houses, rape the women, and cause half the Jews to flee into exile. Those who escape will not be prevented from reentering the city. Then the Lord will enter the battle on Israel's side. He will return to the Mount of Olives, a great earthquake will cause it to split in half, a valley will be created, and many Jews will escape through it. The Lord will have his saints with him; the heavenly bodies will be darkened; Jesus will reign as king over all the earth; the land of Palestine will be leveled out; Jerusalem will be elevated, inhabited, and made secure. Jesus will use a terrible plague to defeat those who attack Jerusalem. He will cause his enemies to fight among themselves, and Jews in the surrounding area will also fight against them. The attackers will be defeated, their valuables will be collected and taken to Jerusalem, their animals will die, and the whole world will turn to Christ. Those who disobey him will be punished, and the Jews will dedicate everything they have to the Lord.

Never Bite Off More Than You Can Chew

Here Zechariah presents more information about the Tribulation Period and the Battle of Armageddon. A world army will capture the city, but it will not be destroyed, and half the Israeli citizens will <u>flee</u> to safety (possibly to a place called Petra; see GWRV, pages 169–180). Enemy soldiers will enter the city, seize valuables and rape the women, but they will not prevent Jews who escape from returning to the city.

☞ **GO TO:**

Matthew 24:15–16 (flee)

Mount of Olives: a mile-long ridge on the east side of Jerusalem

Azel: a village lying just east of the Mount of Olives

Living water: fresh, pure running water

eastern sea: Dead Sea

western sea: Mediterranean Sea

Geba: modern Jeba, a town about six miles north of Jerusalem

Rimmon south: a town about thirty-five miles southwest of Jerusalem

Feast of Tabernacles: a feast of praise, rest, and thanksgiving

☞ **GO TO:**

Revelation 19:11–21 (armies)

Jeremiah 30:8–9; Hosea 3:4–5; Zephaniah 3:15 (king)

Leviticus 23:33–36 (Feast of Tabernacles)

What Others are Saying:

These events will trigger the Second Coming of Jesus. He will return to fight on Israel's side and he will make his first appearance at the **Mount of Olives**. He will temporarily stand on the mountain, there will be a tremendous earthquake, and the mountain will split from east to west. Half of the mountain will shift toward the north and half toward the south, leaving a great valley in between for the Jews to escape through. This valley will extend to **Azel**.

Jesus will bring the <u>armies</u> of heaven with him and the very creation will be affected. There will be no light, but its absence which normally causes a temperature drop, will not cause the weather to turn cold or frost to appear. At night, when it should be dark, the light will return. **Living water** will begin to flow from Jerusalem in two directions—half toward the **eastern sea** and half toward the **western sea**—and it will flow year round.

The attitude toward Jesus will change. He will be <u>king</u> over all the earth. He will have worldwide recognition, and he alone will be called God.

The topography in that area will also change. All the land from **Geba** to **Rimmon south** (as opposed to the city by the same name in the north) will become a plain, but Jerusalem itself will be elevated. The Jews will return to the city and finally have peace and safety.

Concerning the defeat of Israel's enemies, Jesus will smite them with a plague. Their flesh, eyes, and tongues will immediately rot away. They will panic and fight each other, and a similar plague will strike their animals. Because they plundered Jerusalem, their wealth will be collected and taken there.

Survivors living in the nations that attack Jerusalem will visit the Holy City to worship Jesus and celebrate the **Feast of Tabernacles** (see GWRV, page 85). If a nation withholds its worship, God will withhold its rain (their spiritual drought will be answered with a physical drought). Everything in Jerusalem will be dedicated to the Lord. And only those who are true believers will be allowed to serve at the Temple.

Thomas Ice and Timothy Demy: Armageddon prophecy is not literary allegory or myth. Armageddon will be a real event of tragic proportions for those who oppose God.[29]

John Hagee: The first time He came He was nailed to a bitterly rugged cross where He suffered and bled and died alone. The next time He comes He will put His foot on the Mount of Olives and it shall split in half. He will walk across the Kidron Valley and through the eastern gate and set His throne up on the temple mount, and from there He shall reign for one thousand years in the Millennium.[30]

HOPE FOR TODAY, SEPTEMBER 1998 . . .

An artificial deadline has been created targeting May 1999 as a critical mass moment. The date was selected by Yasir Arafat as the date on which he will declare a Palestinian State unless Israel meets his (and others') demands. He promises a destructive war against Israel, with "many nations" joining in the battle led by the Palestinians which will eclipse all of the previous defensive wars fought by Israel since 1948. Sadly, with the ready availability of state-of-the-art missiles, and other sophisticated weapons, including biological weapons, he and his Arab colleagues, with the support of much of the world, probably are capable of bringing such destruction about.[31]

RELATED CURRENT EVENTS

• • •

THE JERUSALEM POST, MARCH 19, 1999 . . .

Both Prime Minister Benjamin Netanyahu and Labor Party leader Ehud Barak denounced as unacceptable the European Union's refusal to treat Jerusalem as part of Israel. German Ambassador Theodor Wallau, whose country holds the rotating presidency of the EU, wrote in a letter that the EU deems Jerusalem a separate entity from Israel, and that European diplomats are not constrained by Israeli political directives there. . . . In addition, Netanyahu said he planned to suggest a resolution by the cabinet rejecting the division of Jerusalem under any circumstances, accompanied by a letter to be sent to the EU explaining that its reliance on UN General Assembly Resolution 181 [which deems Jerusalem a separate entity from Israel] is unacceptable.[32]

• • •

MIDNIGHT CALL, OCTOBER 1998 . . .

Israel fears that the citizens and government
leaders could be put on trial for war crimes over
Jewish settlements in the occupied territories
after the establishment of the International
Criminal Court (ICC). A United Nations conference
in Rome voted to set up the court to prosecute
war criminals for genocide and torture. The definition of war crimes included settling occupied
territories, a policy that has been carried out
by the Israelis in the West Bank and the Gaza
Strip after these areas were captured during the
1967 war.[33]

Remember This . . .

For the real Battle of Armageddon to take place:

1. Israel must be a nation.
2. Jerusalem must be a city.
3. Jerusalem must be controlled by the Jews.
4. The nations must decide to forcefully take Jerusalem away from the Jews.
5. Jesus must return to defeat the nations.

WARNING

This prophecy does not refer to the attack on Jerusalem
by the Romans in A.D. 70. They literally wiped the city off
the face of the earth and killed or carried off all the Jews.
In this case, the city will not be destroyed, not all of the
Jews will be killed, and some will be allowed to reenter
the city.

Unfulfilled
Tribulation Period
Second Coming

Fulfillment: The vast majority of prophetic scholars agree
that this is a prophecy about the Battle of Armageddon and
the Second Coming of Christ. And it will be fulfilled late in
the Tribulation Period.

STUDY QUESTIONS

1. Can a wicked nation be redeemed and restored to the Lord? Explain.
2. What are some of God's judgments mentioned in the book of Joel?

3. What is wrong with wishing the day of the Lord would arrive?

4. According to the prophets Obadiah and Zephaniah, what nations will be affected by the judgments of God during the Tribulation Period?

5. What prophecies refer to Christ in the book of Zechariah?

CHAPTER WRAP-UP

- Hosea had an adulterous wife, but he loved her very much. Her unfaithfulness pictured Israel's attitude toward God. And Hosea's love mirrored God's attitude toward Israel. He will forgive the unfaithful nation, the people will abandon their spiritual adultery, and Jesus will be their King. (Hosea 1:16; 2:18–23; 3:4–5; 6:1–3)

- The great locust plague that laid waste to Israel during Joel's life pictured a much greater destruction that is coming during the Tribulation Period. The millions of locusts that stripped the land are just a glimmer of what a great army will do when it invades Israel and Jerusalem during the day of the Lord. But this great army will be destroyed at what is commonly called the Battle of Armageddon. (Joel 1:15–20; 2:28–29; 3:9–16)

- When the Tribulation Period arrives, God will pass through Israel with great wrath to punish the Jews for their sins. But that does not mean he has stopped loving Israel. He will send Jesus to reign on earth there, correct the mistakes of Israel's leaders, rebuild Israeli towns and cities, restore the nation, cause the crops to flourish, and see that the Jews are never put off the land again. (Amos 5:16–20; 8:9; 9:11–15)

- Those who harm Israel during the Tribulation Period will find that their sins will come back to haunt them. Those who attack Israel will be destroyed. Because of sin, God will send great distress upon the world. When he is through, Jesus will reign in Israel and the nation will prosper. (Obadiah 1:15–16; Micah 4:1–7, 11–13; Zephaniah 1:14–18)

- God will deal a staggering blow to Israel's enemies during the Tribulation Period. They will harm and kill many Jews, but God will use Israel's calamities to bring repentance and salvation to the nation. When it is surrounded, Jesus will return and deliver his people. He will pour out his spirit upon the Jews and forgive their sins. They will accept Jesus as their Messiah, and God will accept them as his people. (Zechariah 12:1–14; 13:1–5, 7–9; 14:1–21)

Part Two

PROPHECIES IN THE NEW TESTAMENT

REVEREND FUN

I really feel that I've been blessed with the gift of prophecy even though I have been coming up with such confusing and odd visions as "Email," "Internet," and "World Wide Web."

Silently Looking Forward

After God gave the prophecies found in the Old Testament books, most scholars believe he went silent for about four hundred years. This period of silence is often referred to as the **Intertestamental Period**. During this time, the Old Testament books were collected, copied, and **validated** by Jewish authorities as meeting the standard of divine inspiration. They were assembled into a single collection, accepted as the Word of God, and kept in a safe place.

The fact that most scholars believe God was silent during the Intertestamental Period does not mean that there were no religious writings. Fourteen short books have been found and assembled into a collection called the **Apocrypha**. But they are not recognized as authoritative because, in most cases, their authors are unknown, and/or they contain false statements, inaccuracies, or inconsistencies. They do not meet the standard of divine inspiration, so they are kept for their historical value, not because anyone believes they are God's Word.

Shortly after the Old Testament was written, the Greeks took over the world and their language became the common language on earth. Tradition says a man called Ptolemy Philadelphus assembled seventy scholars who were experts in both Hebrew and Greek and commissioned them to translate the Old Testament writings into the Greek language. This translation, which is called the **Septuagint**, meaning seventy, was in use when God began to speak again and the New Testament came into being.

KEY POINT

Jesus quoted from the Old Testament many times, but never from the Apocrypha.

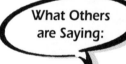
What Others are Saying:

Irving L. Jensen: The thirty-nine books of the Old Testament . . . were God's total written revelation during that time. God was preparing his world for the coming of his Son, the Messiah, the central promise of the Old Testament. Then it happened, Jesus actually came, to live and die for the sins of the world. After that, God inspired new writers to complete the Bible by telling the New Testament story of Jesus and what his coming means for us.[1]

Remember This . . .

Jesus often quoted from the books found in the Old Testament, but he never quoted from the Apocrypha. The same can be said of the New Testament writers. They quoted from the Old Testament over and over again, but there is only one questionable instance of the Apocrypha being quoted. This seems to be evidence that Jesus and the New Testament writers accepted the authority of the Old Testament writings but not the authority of the Apocrypha.

6 PROPHECIES IN THE GOSPELS AND ACTS

CHAPTER HIGHLIGHTS

- Matthew
- Mark
- Luke
- John
- Acts

Let's Get Started

The first segment in the New Testament is a group of four books called the gospels. The word **_gospel_** comes from the Greek language and it means good news or glad tidings. These books present the "good news" about Jesus: his death, burial, resurrection, ascension, and Second Coming. They also contain several prophecies, of which many were given by Jesus, and some are recorded more than once by the different gospel writers (see GWBI, pages 161–164).

The second segment in the New Testament is a single book commonly called Acts. Some refer to Acts as the fifth gospel because it picks up where the four gospels leave off and takes us to the next book—one of the many letters written by the Apostle Paul. Without this transition we wouldn't understand many things about the early church, including its beginning, doctrines, power, and phenomenal growth.

The gospels teach many important truths about man and his relationship with God. Some of the most important truths include:

1. Man is a sinner.
2. Jesus' death is payment for man's <u>sin</u>.
3. Apart from Jesus the human race is fallen and without hope.
4. Jesus' death offers hope to the whole <u>world</u>.
5. God wants us to live our lives according to his <u>will</u>.
6. Prophecies reveal that histroy is moving toward the <u>end of the age</u>, to a time when Jesus will sit on a throne and rule over a kingdom here on earth.

gospel: "good news"

☞ **GO TO:**

1 Corinthians 15:1–58 (gospel)

☞ **GO TO:**

John 1:29 (sin)

John 3:14–18 (world)

Matthew 6:5–13 (will)

Matthew 24:1–51 (end of the age)

The first five truths are very important, especially if one wants to know who God is and how to have a personal relationship with him, but for this study, we are chiefly concerned with the sixth truth.

What Others are Saying:

Henry H. Halley: The Four Gospels are, by all odds, the Most Important part of the Bible: more important than all the rest of the Bible put together: more important than all the rest of the books in the whole world put together: for we could better afford to be without the knowledge of everything else than to be without the knowledge of Christ.[1]

MATTHEW

> **Matthew 5:3–12** "Blessed are the poor in spirit, for theirs is the kingdom of heaven. Blessed are those who mourn, for they will be comforted. Blessed are the meek, for they will inherit the earth. Blessed are those who hunger and thirst for righteousness, for they will be filled. Blessed are the merciful, for they will be shown mercy. Blessed are the pure in heart, for they will see God. Blessed are the peacemakers, for they will be called sons of God. Blessed are those who are persecuted because of righteousness, for theirs is the kingdom of heaven. Blessed are you when people insult you, persecute you and falsely say all kinds of evil against you because of me. Rejoice and be glad, because great is your reward in heaven, for in the same way they persecuted the prophets who were before you.

Prophecy On The Mount

This section of Scripture is part of the **Sermon on the Mount** preached by Jesus. It is commonly called the **Beatitudes** and it is one of the most popular passages in the Bible. It contains high **ethical** standards and is a favorite of many preachers. Some who never deliver a prophetic sermon preach from these verses over and over again. But these Beatitudes are more than an amazing set of principles to live by. They also have a prophetic nature.

The <u>poor</u> in spirit are people who know they are sinners and are convinced they have no way to pay for the sins they have committed. Because they are unable to settle their own sin debt,

Sermon on the Mount: a famous sermon preached by Jesus on a high hill near Capernaum

Beatitudes: a declaration of blessedness in the Sermon on the Mount

ethical: moral

☞ **GO TO:**

2 Corinthians 6:10 (poor)

they humble themselves and seek a Savior to pay in their place. Those who do this are made members of the kingdom of heaven. Their membership becomes effective as soon as they sincerely profess their faith in Jesus, but they will not realize the full benefits of it until the Millennium begins.

The meek are people who profess faith and have received the nature of Jesus. They are <u>gentle</u> people who practice self-control and tolerance, a <u>fruit of the Spirit</u>. They are <u>God's children</u> and, as such, will possess the earth when the Millennium arrives.

Those who are persecuted because of **righteousness** are the ones who try to live right and seek to spread right living around the world. They have accepted Christ as their Savior, are God's children and want others to be God's children too. Because of this they are ridiculed, shunned, and in some cases physically harmed. God has made them members of the kingdom of heaven.

Being a Christian in this life will cost a person. Those who try to do the will of God will be insulted, persecuted, and falsely accused. But God will give them a great reward in heaven.

☞ **GO TO:**

Matthew 11:29 (gentle)

Galatians 5:22 (fruit of the Spirit)

Romans 8:16–17 (God's children)

righteousness: justice, peace, right doing

John F. Walvoord: A careful reading of the Sermon on the Mount supports the conclusion that what Christ was dealing with were the ethical principles of the kingdom which will come into play in the future millennial kingdom but to some extent are applicable now. Accordingly, in the Sermon on the Mount there are frequent references to the present and how the principles He is annunciating should be applied. At the same time there is the distant view of the realization of these ethical principles when Christ will be reigning on earth.[2]

What Others are Saying:

Life Application Bible Commentary: According to Revelation 21–22, believers will enjoy a new heaven and a new earth. God will one day freely give his true disciples what they did not grasp for themselves on earth.[3]

Fulfillment: These are ethical principles that spell out the way God wants us to live now, but they will have a greater application in the Millennium and beyond. Those who try to live by them now will receive great rewards in the future.

Continuously Being Fulfilled
Millennium
After the Millennium

> **Matthew 13:24–30** Jesus told them another parable: "The kingdom of heaven is like a man who sowed good seed in his field. But while everyone was sleeping, his enemy came and sowed weeds among the wheat, and went away. When the wheat sprouted and formed heads, then the weeds also appeared. The owner's servants came to him and said, 'Sir, didn't you sow good seed in your field? Where then did the weeds come from?' 'An enemy did this,' he replied. The servants asked him, 'Do you want us to go and pull them up?' 'No,' he answered, 'because while you are pulling the weeds, you may root up the wheat with them. Let both grow together until the harvest. At that time I will tell the harvesters: First collect the weeds and tie them in bundles to be burned; then gather the wheat and bring it into my barn.'"

parables: stories about familiar things that teach or illustrate unfamiliar things

Son of Man: Jesus

children of God: the saved

children of the devil: the lost

☞ **GO TO:**

Matthew 13:24–30 (The Parable of the Weeds)

Matthew 13:37 (Son of Man)

Matthew 13:38 (sons of the kingdom)

Matthew 13:39 (world)

Revelation 21:8 (fiery)

From The First Coming To The Second Coming

Matthew 13 is a well-known chapter in the Bible because it contains a series of **parables** about the kingdom of heaven (see illustration, page 147). These parables give insight into the course of events in heaven between the first and second comings of Jesus. One of them is called <u>The Parable of the Weeds</u>.

The kingdom of heaven can be compared to a man (the **Son of Man**) who sowed good seed (<u>sons of the kingdom</u>, or the **children of God**) in his field (the <u>world</u>). But while everyone was sleeping, his enemy (the devil) came and sowed weeds (sons of the evil one, or the **children of the devil**) among the wheat (children of God), and went away. When the wheat (children of God) sprouted and formed heads (when they began to grow and produce), then the weeds (children of the devil) also appeared. When that happened, servants of the owner (Jesus) asked if they should remove the weeds (children of the devil) from the field (world). The owner said no. To do so might harm some of the wheat (children of God). He said let them grow together until the harvest (end of the age). Then he will send the harvesters (angels); they will collect the weeds (children of the devil), tie them in bundles, and they will be burned (in the <u>fiery</u> furnace).

Jesus is revealing the fact that there are two sowings going on in the kingdom of heaven—one is of God, and the other is of the devil. The children of God and the children of the devil are growing alongside each other in the world. Some would like to have the children of the devil removed, but God does not want that to happen until the end of the age. When the time arrives, God's angels will remove them. They will be restrained until the judgment and then burned.

What Others are Saying:

Thomas Ice and Timothy Demy: Actually, since Matthew 13 surveys this present age in relation to the kingdom, the parables cover the period of time between Christ's two advents—His first and second comings. This includes the tribulation, Second Coming, and final judgment after the rapture.[4]

Life Application Bible Commentary: [The weeds] may be people in the church who appear to be believers but who never truly believe. The apostles later battled the problem of false teachers who came from within the ranks of the believers (see, for example, 2 Peter 2:1–3, 13–22). . . . God will not eliminate all opposition until the end of the age.[5]

KEY POINT

The kingdom of heaven contains both children of God and children of the devil.

The Church Age and the Kingdom of Heaven

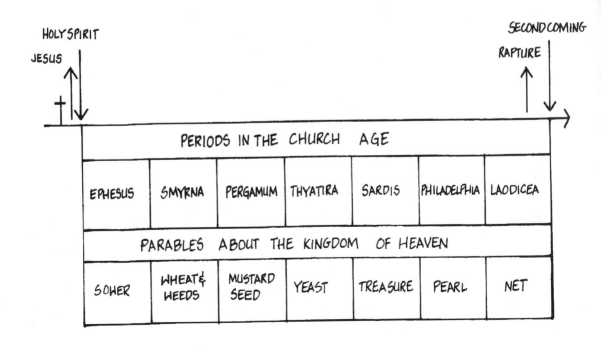

Mike Gendron:

- What is apostasy?
  The falling away from the faith.

- Where will apostates come from?
  The Church. *Even from your own number men will arise and distort the truth in order to draw away disciples after them* (Acts 20:29).

- What will apostates look like?
  Servants of righteousness (2 Corinthians 11:15).

- Where will apostates fall away "to"?
  Not to atheism but to a false Christianity (Matthew 7).[6]

Continuously Being Fulfilled

Tribulation Period

Second Coming

☞ **GO TO:**

Revelation 7:4–8
(144,000)

Revelation 11:3–12
(two witnesses)

Revelation 14:6
(Gospel)

Revelation 16:13
(False Prophet)

Matthew 13:4, 19
(birds)

Matthew 13:1–23 (The
Parable of the Sower)

Many people make the mistake of thinking this harvest is the Rapture. But the Rapture removes the Church from the earth and takes it to heaven. This harvest removes the children of the devil from the earth and binds them for burning. The Rapture occurs before the Tribulation Period. This harvest occurs after the Tribulation Period.

Fulfillment: The wheat and the weeds represent people in the kingdom of heaven. The wheat represents saved Gentiles and Jews. The weeds represent lost Gentiles and Jews, but many of them will claim to be saved. Christians are sowing the gospel today, but after the Rapture the 144,000 Jews, the two witnesses, and an angel will sow the Gospel for God. And the Antichrist and False Prophet will sow for the devil. The harvest is the Second Coming.

> **Matthew 13:31–32** He told them another parable: "The kingdom of heaven is like a mustard seed, which a man took and planted in his field. Though it is the smallest of all your seeds, yet when it grows, it is the largest of garden plants and becomes a tree, so that the birds of the air come and perch in its branches."

What Happened To The Shrub I Planted?

The kingdom of heaven can be compared to a tiny mustard seed that grows into a tree and becomes the resting place for birds. Ordinarily, the mustard seed would grow into a large shrub. It should never grow into a tree. So there is something unusual here. And birds represent the wicked in The Parable of the Sower.

Jesus is saying the kingdom of heaven will experience abnormal growth. It will begin small like a tiny mustard seed and grow much larger than it should. And wicked people will flock to it.

This is consistent with <u>The Parable of the Weeds</u> where Jesus taught that there are two sowings—one of God and one of the devil. If the kingdom of heaven had only true believers, it would be like a shrub, but because of the corruption introduced by the devil, it is more like a tree. In fact, it will be like a tree that has become the resting place of many unbelievers.

☞ **GO TO:**

Matthew 13:24–30
(The Parable of the
Weeds)

David Reagan: The perversion of Bible prophecy by most churches is due to spiritualizing what the Bible says. Just as many Christians spiritualize the days of creation by arguing that they were really eons of time in length, they likewise spiritualize the Millennium to be the Church Age, and they argue that the eternal abode of the redeemed, the new earth, is nothing but code language for heaven.[7]

What Others are Saying:

Mike Gendron:

- Who will fall away?
  Professing Christians who have not been justified (1 John 2:19).

- What will the great apostasy look like?
  A revival in the form of "godliness without power" (2 Timothy 3:5).

- What is the major cause of apostasy?
  For the time will come when men will not put up with sound doctrine. They will turn their ears away from the truth and turn aside to myths (2 Timothy 4:3–4).[8]

Some scholars refer to the kingdom of heaven as professing Christendom or the organized church. Those who use these terms believe there are true Christians and false Christians, a true church and a false church, true believers and make believers. They believe it is the false church or make believers that turn the kingdom of heaven into a monstrosity, a perch for the wicked, etc. This is partly true. The kingdom of heaven does include professing Christendom, but it also includes all those (good and bad, Christians and Jews) who will claim to be people of faith after the Church is Raptured.

Remember This . . .

RELATED CURRENT EVENTS

In his lectures at Iliff [a School of Theology] and in Chicago, Borg [a Jesus Seminar Fellow], renounced his belief in such things as Jesus' virgin birth, the feeding of the 5,000, and Jesus' walking on the water, amongst other things. According to Borg, Jesus never claimed divinity for himself or believed that his death would be a sacrifice for the sins of the world. His belief that the resurrection did not happen follows naturally. For Borg, Jesus was a Jewish prophet and mystic, who died a martyr's death because he opposed the power structures of his day.[9]

Continuously Being Fulfilled

Tribulation Period

Second Coming

Fulfillment: The kingdom of heaven began small with just one person—Jesus. Twelve were added when the disciples joined him. More were added when crowds began to follow and believe. Many true believers (Christians and Jews) will be added after the Rapture, but most of them will be killed. The false church will add large numbers of New Agers, Satan worshipers, cults, and the like. This is why some will be weeded out at the Second Coming and cast into the <u>fiery</u> furnace.

☞ **GO TO:**

Matthew 13:40–42 (fiery)

Exodus 13:3; Matthew 16:6–12; Mark 8:15; 1 Corinthians 5:6–8; Galatians 5:7–10 (yeast)

Revelation 2:20–21; 17:1–8 (woman)

Matthew 13:38 (seed)

Premillennial: *the view that Christ will return before the Millennium*

Postmillennial: *the view that Christ will return after the Millennium*

Gospel: *good news of Jesus Christ*

> **Matthew 13:33** He told them still another parable: "The kingdom of heaven is like yeast that a woman took and mixed into a large amount of flour until it worked all through the dough."

A Perplexing Parable

Commentators are divided over the interpretation of this parable. The **Premillennial** view is that Jesus was saying the kingdom of heaven is like <u>yeast</u> (false teachings) that a <u>woman</u> (the false church) took and mixed into a large amount of flour (processed grain or <u>seed</u>, sons of the kingdom, the children of God) until it all worked through the dough (until the kingdom was corrupted). The **Postmillennial** view is that Jesus was saying the kingdom of heaven is like yeast (the **Gospel**) that a woman took and mixed into a large amount of flour until it all worked through the dough (until the Gospel had impacted the whole world). The Premillennial view is compatible with the teaching that Satan is sowing weeds in the kingdom and that birds (wicked people) will flock to it. And the Postmillennial view is compatible with the teaching that the kingdom of heaven will start small and become great (see GWRV, pages 245–260).

John F. Walvoord: Most interpreters, influenced by the postmillenarian view which was so dominant in the latter nineteenth and early twentieth centuries, identified the yeast as the Gospel which spreads throughout the world. The concept that the yeast is the Gospel, however, is an arbitrary deduction, since throughout Scripture yeast always refers to something contrary to holiness and representing evil.[10]

Mike Gendron: Four Steps to Apostasy (in 2 Timothy)

- They turn away from apostolic teaching (1:15), and they reject the standard for truth (1:13).
- They teach error mixed with truth (2:18), upsetting the faith of some.
- They oppose the truth (3:8), and are rejected in regards to the faith.
- They depart from the faith (4:10).[11]

Jesus was speaking to some religious leaders when he said, *"You hypocrites! Isaiah was right when he prophesied about you: 'These people honor me with their lips, but their hearts are far from me. They worship me in vain; their teachings are but rules taught by men'"* (Matthew 15:7–9). Could it be said that modern religious leaders who teach "Political Correctness" instead of Bible doctrine are teaching the rules of men?

The prophecies in Scripture do not have their origin in the will of man. Since they come from God, it is always right to let the Bible interpret them and never right to impose our own interpretations. The word "yeast" appears in the Bible almost a hundred times. Over and over again it is identified as a symbol of evil, but it is never identified as a symbol of the Gospel. For this reason, we should choose the Premillennial view.

What Others are Saying:

☞ **GO TO:**

Matthew 13:24–30 (weeds)

Matthew 13:4, 19 (birds)

Matthew 13:31–32 (small)

Matthew 15:7–9 (teachings)

2 Peter 1:20–21 (will)

Something to Ponder

Remember This . . .

KEY Symbols:

Yeast
False teachings

Fulfillment: False doctrines are being introduced into the Church and the kingdom is being corrupted. More than once Jesus warned the disciples about this. The true church will be Raptured and the false church will be left behind to enter the Tribulation Period. The kingdom will continue to grow with God's servants taking in more believers and Satan's servants taking in more pretenders. At the Second Coming what's left of the false church will be removed by the angels of God and bound for burning.

> **Matthew 13:44** "The kingdom of heaven is like treasure hidden in a field. When a man found it, he hid it again, and then in his joy went and sold all he had and bought that field."

redeemed: bought, purchased

☞ **GO TO:**

Exodus 19:5–6 (treasure)

Matthew 13:38 (field)

Amazing Grace

Here Jesus says the kingdom of heaven is like a <u>treasure</u> (Israel) hidden in a <u>field</u> (the <u>world</u>). When a <u>man</u> (Jesus) found it (Israel), he hid it again (<u>scattered</u> Israel around the world) and then in his joy went and sold all he had (Jesus left the glories and riches of heaven) and bought (**redeemed**) that field.

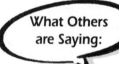

Premillennialists say this means the kingdom of heaven is like a valuable treasure found in a field. It is so valuable we should be willing to give up everything we possess to purchase it. The problem with this is that the kingdom of heaven cannot be bought.

What Others are Saying:

☞ **GO TO:**

John 3:16 (world)

Matthew 13:37 (man)

John 11:49–52 (scattered)

1 Peter 1:18–19 (redeemed)

J. Dwight Pentecost: The purpose of this parable is to depict the relationship of Israel to this present age. Although set aside by God until this age is completed, yet Israel is not forgotten and this age does have reference to that program.[12]

Arno Froese: Never must we be so naive to think that God has rejected Israel and replaced her with the Church. The erroneous conclusion is being made that all the promises given in the Old Testament now belong to the Church. Unfortunately, this teaching is widely accepted among established Protestant denominations and reinforced under the leadership of the Roman Catholic Church. This false doctrine, however, is easily refuted because the prophets clearly write about the return of the Jewish people from the dispersion to the land of Israel, giving an abundance of literal geographic references.[13]

Fulfillment: The Jews have been blinded in <u>part</u> and scattered around the world, but they have not been forgotten by God. Jesus redeemed them when he died on the cross for the sins of the world. They are lost and blind, but by the grace of God they will be saved at the end of the Tribulation Period when they accept Jesus at his Second Coming.

| Partially Fulfilled |
| First Coming |
| Continuously Being Fulfilled |
| Tribulation Period |
| Second Coming |

☞ **GO TO:**

Romans 11:25–29 (part)

> **Matthew 13:45–46** "Again, the kingdom of heaven is like a merchant looking for fine pearls. When he found one of great value, he went away and sold everything he had and bought it."

From Heav'n He Came And Sought Her

This parable is similar to others in this chapter in that Premillennialists and Postmillennialists differ on how it should be interpreted. According to Premillennialists, Jesus is saying the kingdom of heaven is like a merchant man (Jesus) seeking beautiful pearls, who, when he had found one pearl of great price (the Church), went and sold all that he had (gave up everything in heaven) and bought (redeemed) it. But according to Postmillennialists, Jesus was saying the kingdom of heaven is like a merchant (the sinner) seeking beautiful pearls, who, when he had found one pearl of great price (Jesus, or the kingdom, or salvation), went and sold all that he had (wanted that pearl more than anything else) and bought it.

J. Dwight Pentecost: Thus the Lord is showing that within this present age, in addition to acquiring the treasure, Israel, He will also acquire for His personal possession that which was born through injury, the church. We observe (1) that the church, like the pearl, becomes the possession of the "merchantman," Christ, by purchase; (2) the church, like the pearl, is to be formulated by gradual **accretion**; (3) the church, like the pearl, can only become His adornment by being lifted out of the place in which it was formed.[14]

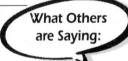

What Others are Saying:

accretion: addition

KEY POINT

The Church was born through injury (the crucifixion of Jesus) and a pearl begins when foreign matter irritates an oyster.

Partially Fulfilled
First Coming
Continuously Being Fulfilled

It is unthinkable that anyone could buy Jesus, the king-dom, or salvation. God <u>gave</u> his Son to die on a cross. Salvation and membership in the kingdom are <u>gifts</u> God gives to those who believe in Jesus.

Fulfillment: Here is really "good news." The kingdom of heaven is for <u>Gentiles</u> as well as Jews. Jesus treasures the church, and he gave up everything at his First Coming to purchase it. It is continually growing.

> **Matthew 13:47–50** "Once again, the kingdom of heaven is like a net that was let down into the lake and caught all kinds of fish. When it was full, the fisher-men pulled it up on the shore. Then they sat down and collected the good fish in baskets, but threw the bad away. This is how it will be at the end of the age. The angels will come and separate the wicked from the righ-teous and throw them into the fiery furnace, where there will be weeping and gnashing of teeth."

Good Fish In, Bad Fish Out

More than just a few commentaries say this parable means the kingdom of heaven is like a net (the Church) that is let down into the lake (the world) where it catches or gathers in all kinds of fish (Christians and pretend Christians). They say it means Jesus will return at the end of the Church Age with his angels, and they will separate the good fish (true Christians) from the bad fish (pretend Christians).

But this cannot be. The net is not the fish. It is what pulls in the fish. The Church (true Christians) will not be separated from the wicked (pretend Christians) at the judgment. The Church will be removed in the Rapture before the judgment. Moreover, the Jews have been ignored in this explanation and excluded from the kingdom of heaven.

It makes more sense to say the kingdom of heaven is like a net (the Word of God) that is let down into the lake (from heaven to the world) where it catches or gathers in all kinds of fish (people). When the net is full (has gathered in all it can), Jesus will come with his angels and they will separate the good from the bad (the saved from the lost). This is how it will be at the <u>end of the age</u> (at the end of the Tribulation Period). The <u>angels</u> will separate the bad fish from the good fish and cast

☞ **GO TO:**

John 3:16 (gave)

Romans 6:23 (gifts)

Matthew 12:15–21;
   Acts 15:13–18
   (Gentiles)

☞ **GO TO:**

Matthew 13:39
   (end of the age)

Matthew 13:41;
   2 Thessalonians 1:7;
   Matthew 25:31–46
   (angels)

the bad into the Lake of <u>Fire</u> where there will be weeping and <u>gnashing</u> of teeth.

Billy Graham: So angels will not only accompany Christ when He returns, but will be assigned the responsibility of gathering out of His kingdom all things that offend and work iniquity, that they might be judged.[15]

J. Dwight Pentecost: We may summarize the teaching as to the course of the age by saying: (1) there will be a sowing of the Word throughout the age, which (2) will be imitated by a false counter sowing; (3) the kingdom will assume huge outer proportions, but (4) be marked by inner doctrinal corruption; yet, the Lord will gain for Himself (5) a peculiar treasure from among Israel, and (6) from the church; (7) the age will end in judgment with the unrighteous excluded from the kingdom to be inaugurated and the righteous taken in to enjoy the blessing of Messiah's reign.[16]

> This parable does not teach that Satan has been bound during the Church Age as the Amillennialist believes. And it does not teach that the world will be totally Christianized before the Second Coming as the Postmillennialist believes. It teaches just the opposite of these two views.

The loving Jesus is warning us in this parable that there will be weeping and gnashing of teeth in hell. He is clearly letting us know that the lost person is making a terrible mistake—hell is forever.

Fulfillment: The age described in this parable is that period of time between Christ's birth and the Second Coming. Between these two great events, Jesus will add multitudes to his kingdom and Satan will infiltrate it with multitudes more. The age will end with Satan's people being removed and cast into the Lake of Fire.

What Others are Saying:

☞ **GO TO:**

Revelation 20:11–15 (Fire)

Matthew 13:42 (gnashing)

WARNING

Something to Ponder

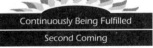

Continuously Being Fulfilled

Second Coming

> **Matthew 21:28–32** "What do you think? There was a man who had two sons. He went to the first and said, 'Son, go and work today in the vineyard.' 'I will not,' he answered, but later he changed his mind and went. Then the father went to the other son and said the same thing. He answered, 'I will, sir,' but he did not go. Which of the two did what his father wanted?" "The first," they answered. Jesus said to them, "I tell you the truth, the tax collectors and the prostitutes are entering the kingdom of God ahead of you. For John came to you to show you the way of righteousness, and you did not believe him, but the tax collectors and the prostitutes did. And even after you saw this, you did not repent and believe him."

KEY POINT

Some religious leaders are lost.

repented: turned toward God, away from sin

John: John the Baptist, a cousin of Jesus

righteousness: justice, peace, right doing

☞ **GO TO:**

Isaiah 5:1–7 (vineyard)

Matthew 3:1–2 (John)

John 14:6 (way)

Two Bad Boys

Jesus said *there was a man* (the Father, God) *who had two sons* (two groups of Jewish citizens). *He* (God) *went to the first* (the common people—tax collectors, prostitutes) *and said, "Son, go and work today in the* vineyard" (Israel). *"I will not," he answered, but later he changed his mind* (**repented**) *and went. Then the father* (God) *went to the other son* (Jewish religious leaders) and made the same request. *He answered, "I will sir," but he did not go.* Jesus asked, *"Which of the two* (the common people or the religious leaders) *did what his father* (God) *wanted?" "The first"* (the common people), *they answered.* Jesus explained that this was why the common people would enter the kingdom of God instead of the Jewish religious leaders. **John** preached the way of **righteousness** and the common people repented and believed, but the religious leaders did not (see GWBI, pages 168–170).

What Others are Saying:

Remember This . . .

William Barclay: This parable teaches us that promises can never take the place of performance, and fine words are never a substitute for fine deeds.[17]

The false prophets of Israel were religious, but lost. The Antichrist will be religious, but lost. This is also true of cults and false religions. Doing religious things is not necessarily synonymous with serving God.

Fulfillment: The Church began with Jewish common people: the twelve disciples, more than a <u>hundred</u> followers, and several <u>thousand</u> who were saved early in their ministry. The Romans destroyed Israel in A.D. 70 including most of the religious leaders.

Continuously Being Fulfilled
First Coming

☞ **GO TO:**

Acts 1:15 (hundred)

Acts 2:41; 4:1–4 (thousand)

> **Matthew 24:1–2** Jesus left the temple and was walking away when his disciples came up to him to call his attention to its buildings. "Do you see all these things?" he asked. "I tell you the truth, not one stone here will be left on another; every one will be thrown down."

A House Of Cards

While Jesus was leaving the **Temple** for the last time before being crucified, his **disciples** approached him to point out its buildings (see GWBI, page 174). They were built with extremely large stones of granite weighing several tons each. Together they made a massive structure that appeared to be indestructible. But Jesus said the Temple would be so thoroughly destroyed that not one stone would be left on top of another.

Temple: main religious center of the Jews

disciples: the chosen twelve

Solomon's Temple: the Temple built by King Solomon

William Barclay: It may well be that at least some of the disciples had not been very often to Jerusalem. They were Galileans, men of the highlands and of the country, fishermen who knew the lakeside far better than they knew the city. Some of them at least would be like country folk come up to London for a visit, and they were staggered by what they saw; and well they might be, for there was nothing quite like the Temple in the ancient world.[18]

What Others are Saying:

Zerubabbel: a governor of Judea who did so much to rebuild the Temple it was named for him

This was not the Temple Solomon built (see 1 Kings 5-8). Because there was so much sin in the land and no repentance, God allowed Babylon to destroy that Temple in 586 B.C. This is the Temple Ezra helped rebuild. It was very small at first and often called **Zerubabel**'s Temple. Later, it was remodeled and expanded. This work was completed under the reign of King Herod and the structure was called Herod's Temple.

Remember This . . .

☞ **GO TO:**

Ezra 3:1–8; 4:1–14 (Zerubabbel)

Fulfillment: In A.D. 70 a powerful Roman general named Titus captured Jerusalem and set it on fire. He planned to save the Temple, but his troops harbored such great hatred for the Jews they set it on fire too. Gold decorations on the building melted and the hot liquid flowed into cracks between the Temple stones. After the stones cooled, soldiers pried them apart to get the gold out. Not one stone was left unfettered.

> **Matthew 24:3–5** As Jesus was sitting on the Mount of Olives, the disciples came to him privately. "Tell us," they said, "when will this happen, and what will be the sign of your coming and of the end of the age?" Jesus answered: "Watch out that no one deceives you. For many will come in my name, claiming, 'I am the Christ,' and will deceive many."

Mount of Olives: a very high hill about ¾ mile east of Jerusalem

the ruler who will come: a title referring to the Antichrist

many: probably the United Nations or leaders of many nations

Antichrist: against the Christ, the anti-Messiah

☞ **GO TO:**

Acts 1:10–12 (heaven)

Zechariah 14:4 (stand)

Matthew 24:1–2 (buildings)

Matthew 24:8 (beginning)

Daniel 9:21–27 (Gabriel)

Revelation 6:2 (white horse)

Revelation 13:1–10 (beast)

False Christs

Now we come to some of the most famous prophecies in the Bible. They were given on the **Mount of Olives** and for this reason they have been given a special name: the Olivet Discourse. This is the place from which Jesus ascended into heaven when he left the earth after his First Coming, and it is also the place where he will stand when he returns at his Second Coming.

He went to the Mount of Olives and sat down. Four of his disciples approached him, wanting to know when the Temple buildings would be destroyed and what would be the signs of his Second Coming and the end of the age. He began his answer by identifying several that he compared to "the beginning of birth pains." It is well known that an expectant mother's birth pains get closer together, harder, and more painful as the birth of her child nears. By analogy, Jesus was saying that these signs are things that always occur, but they will get closer together, harder and more destructive as my Second Coming draws near.

The first sign mentioned is false Christs. This sign is significant because the angel Gabriel told Daniel that the Tribulation Period will begin when **the ruler who will come** confirms a covenant with **many** to protect Israel for seven years (see GWDN, pages 253–258). This ruler will be the ultimate false Christ and he is the one Christians call the **Antichrist**. He is the rider on the white horse mentioned in the book of Revelation. He's called a beast because he will be so evil (see GWRV, pages 183–194); he will be possessed by Satan. And Jesus is saying that the Antichrist is a false Christ who will come during the Tribulation Period, but there will be many false Christs before he arrives and none of them will be as wicked.

Dave Hunt: It is essential to note that the very *first sign* (and thus the most important one) Jesus gave in response to His disciples' query was *religious deception*: "take heed that no man deceive you." It is significant, too, that His revelation of this primary sign was phrased as a warning: "take heed," or *beware*. He repeated this sign two more times for emphasis and explained the nature of the coming deception: it would involve *false Christs, false prophets,* and *false signs and wonders.*[19]

Charles Halff: For more than 30 years since I have been preaching on the radio, I have tried to show people that Satan's program is to make this world religious without Christ. The Word of God is very clear on this point. Satan loves to operate in the field of religion.[20]

THE UNITED METHODIST REPORTER, OCTOBER 10, 1997 . . .

Pope John Paul II described Mary as "mediatrix of prayer, Mother of God and mother of all humanity." His address reflected a recent controversy in the Roman Catholic Church over the pope's devotion to Mary. His personal view has been amplified by a global petition effort to have him declare Mary "co-redemptrix" with Christ despite the strong rejection of such a dogma by a papal theological commission.[21]

RELATED CURRENT EVENTS

These signs (false Christs, wars, famine, earthquakes) have a twofold nature. First, they are pre-Rapture signs. And second, they are post-Rapture or Tribulation Period signs. These four signs will occur in a lesser degree before the Rapture of the Church. And they will occur in a greater degree after the Rapture of the Church.

Remember This . . .

Fulfillment: Jim Jones, Sun yung Moon, and David Koresh are just a few of the people who claimed to be Christ in the latter half of the twentieth century. It has even been estimated that there are now more than ten thousand false Christs in the U.S. alone. And there will be many more as we approach the end of the age and the arrival of the Antichrist at the beginning of the Tribulation Period.

> **Matthew 24:6–7a** "You will hear of wars and rumors of wars, but see to it that you are not alarmed. Such things must happen, but the end is still to come. Nation will rise against nation, and kingdom against kingdom."

Wars And Rumors Of Wars

Battle of Armageddon:
the last and greatest war

☞ **GO TO:**

Daniel 9:26
(Anointed One)

Revelation 6:3–4
(red horse)

Joel 3:9–16; Zechariah
14:1–21 (nations)

Matthew 24:8
(birth pains)

This is not only a prophecy given by Jesus, it is also part of a previously mentioned prophecy that the angel Gabriel gave to Daniel (Daniel 9). Gabriel predicted the death of the <u>Anointed One</u> (crucifixion of Jesus), the destruction of the city and the sanctuary (Jerusalem and the Temple), and even that war will continue to the end. The war to end all wars will be when the fiery <u>red horse</u> is released, peace is removed from the earth, and the <u>nations</u> gather against Jerusalem for the **Battle of Armageddon**.

But a close reading of what Jesus said here reveals that it is actually a loving warning. He is saying there will be many wars and rumors of wars before the end arrives. Those who thought WWI, WWII, or the Vietnam War was the end of the world had a right to be concerned, but the beginning of a war is not sufficient reason to think the end has come. Keep in mind that wars will be like <u>birth pains</u>. They will get closer together and more destructive as the end of the age approaches.

What Others are Saying:

Jack Van Impe: By the year 2000, according to U.S. intelligence sources, as many as twenty-four Third World nations will have acquired long-range ballistic missiles. Half of them may have a nuclear capability. . . . Furthermore, there are now forty countries that have in their arsenals cruise-type missiles capable of hitting U.S. cities if fired from a ship or submarine.[22]

The Antichrist will present himself as a man of peace. He will falsely claim to be the Prince of Peace (Jesus). But God will expose this fake to the world by causing his phony peace programs to fail. World leaders who follow him will be rejecting the true Christ and the only solutions to world problems.

Remember This . . .

MIDNIGHT CALL, JUNE 1996 . . .

According to a report prepared by the National Defense Council Foundation located in Washington, D.C., conflicts around the world have doubled since 1989 when Communism collapsed. The foundation calculated seventy-one wars or conflicts around the world in 1995, including those resulting from drug-related violence.[23]

RELATED CURRENT EVENTS

• • •

ENDTIME, JULY/AUGUST 1998 . . .

Scientists quickly moved the world's "doomsday clock" five minutes closer to midnight [after Pakistan and India tested nuclear weapons in 1998]. The minute hand of the clock—a measure of how close humankind is to destroying itself—was moved to nine minutes before midnight, with midnight representing a worldwide nuclear holocaust. Since 1995, the clock has been set at 14 minutes until midnight. The adjustment, made on June 11th, is the closest to "doomsday" the clock has been since 1988, before the collapse of the Soviet Union.[24]

Continuously Being Fulfilled
Tribulation Period

Fulfillment: According to the April 1999 issue of the *Prophetic Observer*, "In the course of human history, man has fought 4,535 wars, up to the last count, and 600 million men have been killed in these conflicts. . . . and compare this statistic with the fact that half of these—300 million casualties—have been in wars which occurred in the twentieth century. In other words, there have been as many people killed in war since 1914 as in the previous 5,500 years."[25]

Bread of Life: *Jesus*

the two witnesses: *two powerful men of God who will preach during the Tribulation Period*

☞ **GO TO:**

John 6:35
(Bread of Life)

Revelation 6:5–6
(black horse)

Revelation 11:1–6 (rain)

What Others
are Saying:

☞ **GO TO:**

Matthew 24:6–7
(warfare)

Remember
This . . .

Continuously Being Fulfilled
Tribulation Period

> **Matthew 24:7b** "There will be famines . . . in various places."

Famine

The Antichrist will come on the scene predicting an era of economic growth for the world. His promises will include plenty of food and an abundance of goods for all people. But he will be a false **Bread of Life** and God will not let his false claims succeed. The rider on the black horse will be loosed bringing economic collapse and causing the price of wheat and barley (food) to soar. Multitudes will not be able to afford the excessive prices. And **the two witnesses** will come on the scene with power to shut up the sky so that it will not rain during their 3½ year presence on earth.

Jack Van Impe: Warfare from earliest times has also been a primary contributor to the destruction of crops and animals, and subsequent blockades and attacks on cities and ports have been responsible for countless famines.[26]

Texe Marrs: It is the plan of these super-rich plotters to gain total world power through their control of the production, storage, distribution, and sale of food. Food, they are convinced, translates into empire and is the ultimate weapon in the seduction of mankind.[27]

Jesus is coming back to put an end to the Antichrist, to false worship, to war, to those who will use their control of food and water to subjugate people, to the wicked who persecute and kill Christians, and to failed policies that starve people and enslave.

Fulfillment: Famine is an enormous problem in the world today, especially in many African countries. And with thousands dying every day, some nations including the United States are cutting back on food contributions to starving people. But as bad as it is, things will be much worse during the Tribulation Period.

> **Matthew 24:7b** "There shall be . . . pestilences . . . in divers places" (KJV).

Pestilence

The prophet Zechariah said God will strike all those nations that fight against Jerusalem during the Tribulation Period with a <u>plague</u>. The Apostle John said the rider on the <u>pale horse</u> will be loosed with power to kill one-fourth of the earth with war, famine, **diseases**, and wild animals. The two witnesses will have power to stop the rain and <u>strike the earth</u> with every kind of plague as often as they want.

But what about today? Scientists and doctors are constantly reporting outbreaks of new, unknown and more deadly diseases. Drug use, sexual activity, natural disasters, and other problems are causing explosive and dangerous outbreaks. In some African countries, as much as one-fourth of the population is now HIV-positive. The disease is **mutating**, and many types and subtypes are now spreading among both homosexuals and heterosexuals. The production of **biological weapons** is given top priority in several nations. And some producers are selling to anyone who has the money.

Prophetic Observer: What if 100 million people in just India alone die of starvation? This would be equal to all the people in the United States west of the Mississippi River starving to death. We cannot begin to imagine the carnage, the filth, the contamination, and the spread of deadly diseases that would result. There would not be enough doctors or vaccination serum in the world to fight it.[28]

YAHOO! NEWS, NOVEMBER 1998 . . .

As the death toll climbed steadily toward 11,000, with another 13,000 missing across devastated parts of Honduras, Nicaragua, El Salvador and Guatemala, Hurricane Mitch became the most destructive Atlantic storm since The Great Hurricane of 1780, blamed for 22,000 deaths in the eastern Caribbean. But even while bodies surfaced from the mud, the desolated populations of Central America—one of the poorest regions of the world—faced new threats: malaria and dengue epidemics as mosquitoes multiplied by stagnant

☞ **GO TO:**

Zechariah 14:12–15 (plague)

Revelation 6:7–8 (pale horse)

Revelation 11:3–6 (strike the earth)

diseases: *pestilence or plague*

mutating: *changing, taking on a new form*

biological weapons: *weapons containing harmful diseases and organisms*

What Others are Saying:

RELATED CURRENT EVENTS

ponds, hunger as food supplies ran out and land mines from former civil wars, now brought back to the surface by floodwaters. "Desperation, hunger, diarrhea, and the pestilence of cholera in some parts has arrived," said Nicaraguan President Arnoldo Aleman in an interview with Mexican broadcaster Televisa, making an impassioned plea for medicines. "We are told by fishermen that the stench of death near the coast is sickening," Aleman added.[29]

Continuously Being Fulfilled
Tribulation Period

Fulfillment: Just fifty years ago, scientists and doctors were confidently predicting the soon eradication of terrible diseases from the earth, but things changed and they now say the spread of diseases is a major problem in the world. Medical experts, health agencies, the CIA and others are trying to warn the world about possible outbreaks of pestilences on a massive worldwide scale. This problem will become more serious as the Tribulation Period approaches. Then it will reach a horrifying peak.

> **Matthew 24:7b** "There will be. . . earthquakes in various places."

Earthquakes

Mount of Olives: a very high hill about ¾ mile east of Jerusalem

☞ **GO TO:**

Zechariah 14:3–5 (Mount of Olives)

Isaiah 13:13 (shake)

Joel 3:16 (tremble)

Revelation 16:18 (earthquake)

The prophet Zechariah predicted that a massive earthquake will split the **Mount of Olives** in two when Jesus returns; the prophet Isaiah said the earth will <u>shake</u> from its place at that time; the prophet Joel said the earth and sky will <u>tremble</u>; and the book of Revelation says there will be a tremendous <u>earthquake</u> unlike any that *"has ever occurred since man has been on earth"* (Revelation 16:18). Skyscrapers and bridges will fall, islands will sink into the sea, entire mountains will drop into the earth, and houses will splinter and collapse.

But what about today? At the beginning of the twentieth century, between 1900 and 1910, there was only one earthquake measuring 7.2 or higher on the Richter scale. Between 1950 and 1960, there were nine. There were 125 in just five years, between 1990 and 1995 (see illustration, page 165). And every year scientists tell us a "big one" is on the way.

John Hagee: There were 378 recorded earthquakes in the seventeenth century, 640 in the eighteenth, and 2,119 in the nineteenth. Someone might try to explain this away by thinking that there are no more earthquakes today than in the past, and it's just that our ability to detect them has improved. But the number of earthquakes recorded has risen from 2,588 in 1983 to 4,084 in 1992.[30]

Billy Graham: There have been famines, plagues, and earthquakes for thousands of years, but seldom so many all at once and seldom so concentrated in time and space.[31]

NEWSWEEK, OCTOBER 4, 1999 . . .

Taiwan's biggest earthquake in more than a century registered 7.6 on the Richter scale, leaving more than 2,200 people dead, 6,500 injured and 100,000 homeless. It was the world's third major seismic shock in a month, following a 7.4 blast in Turkey on Aug. 17 (which killed 15,000) and a smaller quake in Greece on Sept. 7 (139 dead).[32]

**RELATED
CURRENT
EVENTS**

Earthquakes 6.0 and Above

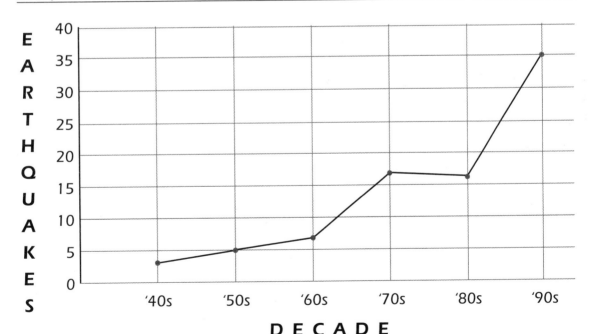

DECADE

SOURCE: 1999 World Almanac

Continuously Being Fulfilled
Tribulation Period

The various examples of "birth pain"–type increase in both frequency and the intensity of these signs is a vivid reminder that the Tribulation Period is drawing near. And the fact that these signs are occurring simultaneously makes it even more sure.

There is overwhelming evidence on the occurrence of these things—false Christs, wars, famine, pestilence, and earthquakes—that would be hard for anyone to deny. This evidence demands the most serious consideration possible.

Fulfillment: God is sending the world a message every time an earthquake rattles the earth. He is using their increased frequency and intensity to tell us the Tribulation Period is approaching and we need to be prepared for eternity.

> **Matthew 24:9** "Then you will be handed over to be persecuted and put to death, and you will be hated by all nations because of me."

Persecution

Verses 1 and 2 in Matthew 24 deal with fulfilled prophecy: the destruction of the Temple in A.D. 70. Verses 3 through 8 deal with prophecy that is continuously being fulfilled: birth pain–type false Christs, war, famine, pestilence, and earthquakes. Here, the word "then" signals a change in the Olivet Discourse. Verses 9 through 51 deal with future events: the Tribulation Period, Second Coming, judgment. Although those who accept Christ after the Rapture will be affected by these things, the events described in these verses refer primarily to Israel and the Jews.

During the Tribulation Period, the <u>nations</u> will hate Israel and lay siege to Jerusalem. In the whole land <u>two-thirds</u> of the Jews will be killed. Concerning both Christians and Jews, those who refuse to take the **Mark of the Beast** will be <u>killed</u>. The Antichrist and his corrupt followers will try to wipe out God's true people before Jesus returns to establish his earthly kingdom.

Mark of the Beast: the mark, number or name of the Antichrist

---

☞ **GO TO:**

Zechariah 12:1–3 (nations)

Zechariah 13:8 (two-thirds)

Revelation 6:11; 13:15 (killed)

David Hocking: These signs will actually occur—exactly as Christ foretold—only during the Tribulation. And though we believe we will escape the great sufferings of the Tribulation by being with Christ in heaven, this is very serious stuff.[33]

J. Vernon McGee: The affliction He is talking about is anti-Semitism on a worldwide scale.[34]

Randall Price: Once Israel asserts her independence from the rule of Antichrist, anti-Semitism will explode on a worldwide scale, and Israel will truly be "hated by all nations."[35]

When conservative Christians express biblical views that oppose politically correct ones, they are criticized as mean-spirited extremists, fundamentalists, enemies of world peace, and **homophobes**. When this occurs, who is spreading the hate?

Fulfillment: Israel has been restored as a nation, but the people have not been restored spiritually. Unfortunately, preparing them will require a great deal of persecution. During the Tribulation Period, the Jews will be seen as a threat to world government, world religion, and world peace. The world's desire for ethnic cleansing will produce another **Holocaust**.

> **Matthew 24:10** "At that time many will turn away from the faith and will betray and hate each other."

Betrayal

What Jesus said here can be applied to Christians, but his primary reference is to Jews living during the Tribulation Period. Doing the will of God will be more than frowned upon, it will be dangerous, and it will even get many killed. When <u>buying or selling</u> basic necessities such as food, water, medicine, and electricity becomes illegal for all who refuse to take the Mark of the Beast, dissension and <u>hatred</u> will develop not only with the civil and religious authorities, but also with those who are normally one's most faithful allies. To curry the favor of the authorities, to secure safety for themselves, and to acquire goods and services, people will <u>betray</u> their parents, brothers, relatives, and friends to death.

What Others are Saying:

KEY POINT

Hatred of Christians and Jews will greatly accelerate and include terrible acts of betrayal and violence during the Tribulation Period.

Something to Ponder

Unfulfilled
Tribulation Period

homophobes: people who are afraid of, mean to, or prejudiced against homosexuals

Holocaust: mass destruction of the Jews during World War II

 **GO TO:**

Revelation 13:16–17 (buying or selling)

Mark 13:12–13 (hatred)

Luke 21:15–19 (betray)

What Others are Saying:

Judas: a disciple who betrayed Jesus

disciples: Jesus' followers

Remember This . . .

Something to Ponder

Unfulfilled

Tribulation Period

☞ **GO TO:**

Matthew 26:47–50 (Judas)

Matthew 25:31–46 (people)

false prophets: people God did not send who claim to have a message from God

Union Gospel Press: As persecution increases, believers and unbelievers will be separated. There will be some who, like **Judas**, will be fellow travelers for a while. When things do not go as they expect, however, these people will turn on friends and family.[36]

Concerning anti-Semitism, Christians should remember that the **disciples** were Jewish, the Apostle Paul was Jewish, and the Old and New Testaments were written by Jews. Most importantly, a Jew named Jesus died for our sins. He will return to Israel in the near future, judge the nations, and separate <u>people</u> in accordance with their treatment of his followers.

When God's people abandon him, ignore the Bible, and worship false gods, they must repent or he will eventually withdraw his protection. Without his help, they will face disease, fear, injustice, oppression, poverty, tyranny, violence, and a host of other problems. He is patient, but eventually it will come down to this: repent or perish.

Fulfillment: More Christians and Jews have been persecuted and killed this century than in all of history. Some want to deny the death of six million Jews in Germany during WWII. Millions of Christians have been killed in Africa this decade and President Clinton has turned a blind eye to it. Current apathy will explode into bitter hatred during the Tribulation Period.

> **Matthew 24:11a** "And many false prophets will appear."

False Prophets

There have been many **false prophets** in the history of the world, but the Rapture of the Church will leave a vacuum the false church will rapidly try to fill and explain. This vacuum will produce an explosion of pretenders who will claim to speak for God. But their God will not be the God described in the Bible; the salvation they proclaim will not be the death of Jesus on the cross; many of the moral standards they espouse will contradict what the Bible says, and their "feel good" predictions of love, justice, peace, and prosperity will turn into rubbish.

Thomas Ice and Timothy Demy: While the next event for the true church—the body of Christ—is **translation** from earth to heaven at the rapture, those unbelievers left in the organized church as an institution will pass into the tribulation and form the base of an apostate super-church that the **False Prophet** will use to aid the worldwide rule of the Antichrist (Revelation 13; 17–18).[37]

Charles Halff: A true prophet magnifies Christ. A false prophet doesn't. A true preacher will always point you to the Word of God. A false preacher will point you to visions, dreams, maybe rituals or ceremonies. Some will point you to mind reading, astrology, and a thousand and one other things.[38]

Mike Gendron: Satan's Devices for Apostasy

- Counterfeit gods—2 Thessalonians 2:3–4
- Counterfeit Jesus(es)—2 Corinthians 11:4
- Counterfeit Christs—Matthew 24:24
- Counterfeit spirits—1 John 4:1; 1 Timothy 4:1
- Counterfeit apostles—2 Corinthians 11:13; Revelation 2:2
- Counterfeit prophets—2 Peter 2:1; 1 John 4:1
- Counterfeit ministers—2 Corinthians 11:15
- Counterfeit gospels—Galatians 1:6–9
- Counterfeit miracles—2 Thessalonians 2:9; Revelation 16:13
- Counterfeit worship—John 4:24[39]

ENDTIME, JANUARY/FEBRUARY 1999 . . .

A brand of Christianity is coming our way like nothing we've ever seen before, nor heard preached. But it sounds good, and it's awfully close to the real thing. Worse yet, it's approaching us with blistering speed like a fire-breathing dragon dressed like Mary's little lamb. It's called United Religions, and, no matter how pretty their words of denial are and however sincere they may be or may come across, it appears almost certain this organization will be the structure used by the False Prophet's endtime global religion.[40]

RELATED CURRENT EVENTS

Something to Ponder

Unfulfilled
Tribulation Period

Astrologers, fortune tellers, psychics and witches are predicting a new age of peace and prosperity, but Bible signs indicate that we are on the brink of the Tribulation Period. World leaders predicted a comprehensive peace in the Middle East by the year 2000, but the Bible teaches that there will be no peace until Christ returns. President Clinton is predicting there will be no more armies, just peacekeeping forces, but the Bible predicts a two hundred million–man army will invade the Middle East. Clinton is predicting no more wars, just peacekeeping operations, but the Bible predicts a Russian invasion of Israel and a Battle of Armageddon. Clinton is predicting the era of big government is over, but the Bible predicts a coming world government led by the Antichrist. Who or what should we believe?

Fulfillment: There is nothing wrong with wanting to know the future, but we should realize that there are many false prophets in the world and there will be a myriad more when the Tribulation Period arrives, especially in the false church and in Israel.

> **Matthew 24:11** "False prophets will appear and deceive many people."

Religious Deception

☞ **GO TO:**

Exodus 32:1–35 (calf)

Matthew 26:3–5 (kill)

Matthew 26:14–16 (twelve)

Matthew 24:4 (watch out)

It was a priest named Aaron who sinned against God by building a golden <u>calf</u> in the wilderness; corrupt priests and elders who plotted to <u>kill</u> Jesus; one of the <u>twelve</u> disciples who betrayed Jesus; a United Methodist theologian who said, "God is dead"; a Presbyterian Bishop who said, "The virgin birth is a myth"; an Anglican Bishop who said, "Hell does not exist"; and an Episcopal Bishop who said, "There is no God." Good people making mistakes and unbelievers teaching error for truth are not new. This is why Jesus said, "<u>Watch out</u> that no one deceives you." In our day, many religions are flourishing (see illustration, page 171). Jesus knew that the winds of deceit will reach gale force during the Tribulation Period.

What Others are Saying:

Joe Chambers: Satan's chief attack against the church has always been to produce a counterfeit. After Satan has produced his counterfeit preachers and prophets, he uses the world to talk about how crazy all Christians are by pointing out the false crowd. How clever and double-tongued the devil and his spirits are in their evil design.[41]

During the Tribulation Period, the Antichrist and his corrupt religious followers will try to reinvent Christianity and Judaism. Powerful and very popular religious figures will make a strong effort to dilute and redefine the long-held beliefs of conservative Christians and Jews. It will be their goal to shift people from the Scriptural teachings of true Christianity and Judaism to the false teachings of a global secular society.

DISCERNING THE TIMES, FEBRUARY 1999 . . .

While overseeing a multimillion dollar research effort on the effects of acid rain and global warming on our nation's forests, Dr. [Michael S.] Coffman became aware that science was being corrupted to advance a political agenda. As he investigated this agenda it became increasingly clear that it was based in deceit, and was being driven by pantheistic beliefs that had as a goal world government and religion.[42]

Remember This . . .

KEY POINT

During the Tribulation Period, political and religious leaders will be anti-Christian and anti-Semitic.

RELATED CURRENT EVENTS

Religions of the World in 1995

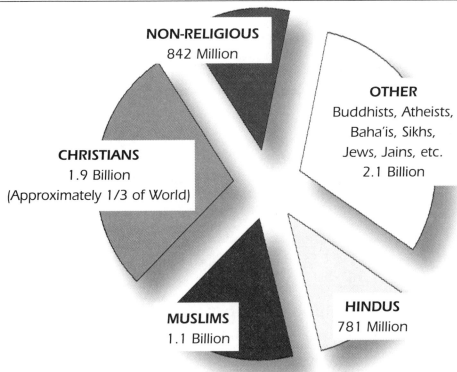

NON-RELIGIOUS
842 Million

OTHER
Buddhists, Atheists, Baha'is, Sikhs, Jews, Jains, etc.
2.1 Billion

CHRISTIANS
1.9 Billion
(Approximately 1/3 of World)

MUSLIMS
1.1 Billion

HINDUS
781 Million

Something to Ponder

Unfulfilled
Tribulation Period

☞ **GO TO:**

Revelation 23:3, 8
(deception)

KEY POINT

It will be difficult to be a Christian during the Tribulation Period.

sin: missing the mark, wrongdoing

Unfulfilled
Tribulation Period

Gospel: good news of Jesus Christ

Political correctness appears to be an effort to bend the Word of God, an effort to substitute a form of godliness for true Christianity and Judaism, an effort to produce an unscriptural set of government-approved religious and social values. Could this kind of religious deception be the underlying cause of the coming persecution of Christians and Jews?

Fulfillment: Religious <u>deception</u> can prosper only in the presence of religious ignorance. It is one of Satan's favorite tools. People use it for gain when the truth is an obstacle. The Antichrist and his corrupt religious leaders will use it during the Tribulation Period to gain religious support and secure peace treaties, and so forth.

> **Matthew 24:12** "Because of the increase of wickedness, the love of most will grow cold."

A Falling Away

The effect of religious deception will be **sin** in the religious community and a turning away from God. In some cases, it will be the Antichrist and his corrupt religious leaders instigating the persecution of true believers causing those on the fringe to abandon the faith for fear of their lives. In other cases, it will be weak morals stemming from false teachings that will cause people to go astray. But the end result will be the same: during the Tribulation Period widespread sin will drive many from God.

Fulfillment: Tolerance of false doctrines leads to moral confusion. Out of that comes immoral decisions, the eroding of society, and the eventual collapse of social order. And, without God, this is exactly what will happen during the Tribulation Period.

> **Matthew 24:14** "And this gospel of the kingdom will be preached in the whole world as a testimony to all nations, and then the end will come."

Preaching The Gospel

False Christs, false prophets, betrayal, and persecution will take a toll, but they will not prevent the **Gospel** from going all over the world during the Tribulation Period. Wicked men have never been allowed to stop the spread of God's Word, and they will not be permitted to do it in the future. After God Raptures the Church, he will do three things:

- **Seal** 144,000 Jews to preach the Gospel to the world
- Send <u>two witnesses</u> to prophesy to the world
- Send an <u>angel</u> to preach to every nation, tribe, language, and people on earth

Dave Breese: The message of the gospel of the grace of God is to be preached in the Gentile world. On the occasion of the Rapture, however, it is the gospel of the kingdom that shall be the message from God. This is the announcement that *"the kingdom of heaven is at hand."*[43]

Grant Jeffrey: The Bible has now been translated in more than 3,850 languages in every nation, tribe and dialect on this planet. Electronic communication transmits the message of hope in Jesus Christ through the air waves worldwide.[44]

Fulfillment: In 1993, the Gospel of grace was being broadcast worldwide, twenty-four hours a day and in ninety different languages. In 1995, Dr. Billy Graham preached to the entire world over television, 70 percent of the world's population had the opportunity to hear him, interpreters were used, and it is estimated that as many as one billion people listened in their own language. In 1996, with the assistance of one million pastors and churches on every continent, Billy Graham preached to the entire world again, and it is estimated that approximately 2½ billion people listened this time. Christians are also now sending the Gospel of grace all over the world electronically via the Internet. Clear evidence supports that the Gospel of the kingdom can go all over the world in our time.

> **Matthew 24:15** "So when you see standing in the holy place 'the abomination that causes desolation,' spoken of through the prophet Daniel . . . "

Defilement Of The Temple

The *"holy place"* will be the future Jewish **Temple**. *"The <u>abomination</u> that causes desolation"* will be the Antichrist who will rise to power over a reunited Europe. He will visit the Temple, declare

☞ **GO TO:**

Revelation 7:1–8 (seal)

Revelation 11:3–12 (two witnesses)

☞ **GO TO:**

Revelation 14:6–7 (angel)

Unfulfilled
Tribulation Period

seal: a mark or symbol to identify and protect

Temple: main religious center of the Jews

☞ **GO TO:**

Daniel 9:27; 11:31; 12:11 (abomination)

☞ **GO TO:**

2 Thessalonians 2:1–4
(God)

Temple Mount: *the hill where all of the Jewish Temples have been built*

covenant: *a comprehensive Middle East peace agreement*

RELATED CURRENT EVENTS

Unfulfilled

Tribulation Period

that he is <u>God</u>, and set up an idol on the wing of that holy building. This will happen 3½ years after he has signed a seven-year covenant with many to protect Israel. Hence, this prophecy is implying several future events:

- The existence of Israel as a nation
- The rebuilding of the Jewish Temple
- Jewish control over the **Temple Mount** (partial, if not complete)
- The reuniting of Europe
- The existence of the Antichrist as a world leader
- The existence of a seven-year **covenant** to protect Israel as a nation
- A visit by the Antichrist to Israel and the Temple at the Tribulation Period midpoint

PERSONAL UPDATE, JULY 1997 . . .

We understand that the Vatican has offered to "internationalize" the Temple Mount: let the Muslims use it on Friday (their holy day); the Jews use it on Saturday (Shabbat), and the Christians on Sunday. This appears consistent with their ambition and agenda to lead the worldwide "ecumenical" movement. . . . However, the Coming World Leader, who ultimately is destined to desecrate this Temple himself, is first going to prove attractive to *both* the Jews and the Muslims, while posing as a replacement for Christ.[45]

Fulfillment: The existence of Israel and Jerusalem are undeniable facts. The existence of a united Europe in the form of the European Union is also a fact. There will be some changes, but Europe is now united. The existence of the Antichrist can neither be confirmed nor denied because the Holy Spirit will not permit him to be revealed until after the Rapture, but many authorities believe he is alive today. The existence of a comprehensive Middle East peace treaty is not a fact, but negotiations have reached their final stages. The existence of the Temple is not a fact, but most of the preliminary work has been done and it can be constructed in as little as six months. It will be constructed and defiled by the middle of the Tribulation Period. It is time for people to wake up. The stage is rapidly being set for the fulfillment of this prophecy. And the Rapture of the Church will occur before we get there.

> **Matthew 24:16–20** "Then let those who are in Judea flee to the mountains. Let no one on the roof of his house go down to take anything out of the house. Let no one in the field go back to get his cloak. How dreadful it will be in those days for pregnant women and nursing mothers! Pray that your flight will not take place in winter or on the Sabbath."

Many Will Run For Their Lives

Here Jesus is warning the Jews about when the Antichrist defiles the Temple during the Tribulation Period. They are the ones who live in **Judea**, the ones who observe the Sabbath. The nations of the earth will gather against <u>Judah</u> and Jerusalem, capture the <u>city</u>, ransack the houses, and rape the women. Defilement of the Temple will be the last major event to occur before this attack takes place and should be seen as a signal to flee (see GWRV, pages 173–174).

Most prophetic scholars believe the Jews will flee to the ancient city of Petra. It is located in a mountainous area of Jordan about twenty miles south of the Dead Sea. About twenty-five hundred years ago, the Edomites carved a large city with business buildings, houses, and caves out of the white and red sandstone there. They eventually deserted the city, but it is an ideal place to hide—it would be easy to defend because of the narrow passages leading to it, and it can be quickly reached by the residents of Judea. Isn't it interesting that a new road to Petra is under construction today, that utilities are being installed there, and that Israel is even storing supplies there?

Sol Scharfstein: Before the [1967 War] began Israel promised King Hussein of Jordan that no harm would come to his country if he stayed out of the fighting. Hussein ignored the peace overture and attacked Jerusalem. Israel counterattacked, and within a few days had defeated the Jordanians. Israeli forces were now in control of the West Bank (Judea and Samaria), and had captured the Old City of Jerusalem. The Temple Mount was under Jewish rule for the first time in almost 2,000 years.[46]

KEY POINT

The moment the Temple is defiled the residents of Judea should instantly flee to the mountains.

Judea: the southernmost part of Israel. Two thousand years ago, it was occupied by the tribes of Judah and Benjamin

☞ **GO TO:**

Zechariah 12:1–9 (Judah)

Zechariah 14:2 (city)

Something to Ponder

What Others are Saying:

ENDTIME, NOVEMBER/DECEMBER 1998 . . .

```
Judea is the West Bank—the territory captured by
Israel in the 1967 War—the area that the Pales-
tinians and the United Nations insist must be
returned to Palestinian control—the area where
approximately 144,000 Jews now live—the area of
which 40% has now been placed under the authority
of Yasir Arafat as a result of recent Mideast
peace negotiations.⁴⁷
```

. . .

HOPE FOR TODAY, SEPTEMBER 1998 . . .

```
One would have to be blind, or totally uninformed
not to see the preparation taking place, the
mounting opposition against Israel, the increas-
ingly radical rhetoric, the proliferation of mis-
sile technology, increasingly ominous weaponry,
the threats, and the lining-up of coalitions de-
scribed in the Scripture. It is unmistakable.⁴⁸
```

Unfulfilled
Tribulation Period

Fulfillment: Jewish priests have been identified and every-thing needed for conducting animal sacrifices and worship services at the Temple has been prepared. This includes a meeting place for the Sanhedrin (the highest legal and religious authority of the ancient Jewish nation), clothing for the priests, furniture for the Temple, and musical instruments for the services. In addition, archaeologists have uncovered an exact full scale replica of the Temple on **Mount Gerizim**, so all the building materials for a new Temple can now be precut and fabricated for rapid assembly when the proper time comes. Since the Temple only has to be present by the middle of the Tribulation Period, for all practical purposes everything is now ready.

Mount Gerizim: a high mountain near the Mediterranean Sea in Israel where the Samaritans worshiped God

Holy Spirit: the Spirit of God or God Himself

Raptured: when the church is removed from the earth

> **Matthew 24:21** "For then there will be great distress, unequaled from the beginning of the world until now—and never to be equaled again."

☞ **GO TO:**

2 Thessalonians 2:1–12 (Evil)

Great Distress (Tribulation)

It is important to remember that the **Holy Spirit** will be removed from the earth when the church is **Raptured** before the Tribulation Period. Evil will no longer be restrained and the Antichrist will go on a violent rampage. Then at the Tribulation Period mid-point, Satan will lose his place in heaven and be <u>hurled</u> down to the earth. As if that isn't bad enough, there will be an outpouring of God's <u>seal</u>, <u>trumpet</u>, and <u>bowl</u> judgments upon the Antichrist and his followers. Crisis will follow crisis like a raging storm that cannot be stopped. Except for the intervention of God, no one would <u>survive</u>.

Dave Breese: It will be the time of the worst carnage and the most despicable situations and the most overwhelming impact of the judgment of God that the world will ever see. If you think that God doesn't see, that He doesn't notice, that He won't judge the world one day, think again. The judgment of God during the Great Tribulation will be absolutely indescribable.[49]

David Reagan: We are told in Zechariah 13:8–9 that two-thirds of the Jewish people will die during this holocaust (another 9.3 million people).[50]

> The group of people called Preterists teaches that Matthew Chapter 24 was fulfilled in A.D. 70 when the Romans destroyed Jerusalem and the Temple. But Jesus said, *"there will be great distress, unequaled from the beginning of the world until now—and never to be equaled again."* The destruction of Jerusalem was terrible, but there have been other destructions as bad or worse.

Fulfillment: The <u>distress</u> in this passage is a reference to the coming Tribulation Period. "Great distress" refers to the second half or the last 3½ years of the Tribulation Period, that period of time immediately after the Antichrist defiles the Temple.

> **Matthew 24:24** "For false Christs and false prophets will appear and perform great signs and miracles to deceive even the elect—if that were possible."

Signs And Miracles

Some ask, Why would anyone follow the Antichrist, false Messiahs, or false prophets? When Jesus walked this earth, he performed great <u>miracles</u> and what he did attracted great <u>crowds</u>. John said,

☞ **GO TO:**

Revelation 12:8–9 (hurled)

What Others are Saying:

☞ **GO TO:**

Revelation 6–16 (seal/trumpet/bowl)

Matthew 24:22 (survive)

WARNING

Unfulfilled
Tribulation Period

☞ **GO TO:**

Daniel 12:1–3; Luke 21:20–23 (distress)

John 2:1–11; 3:2 (miracles)

John 6:1–15 (crowds)

GO TO:

John 2:23 (believed)

"many people saw the miraculous signs he was doing and *believed* in his name" (John 2:23). This is one reason why so many people will make such a terrible mistake. They will fall prey to religious deception backed up by signs and miracles.

What Others are Saying:

Billy Graham: The Bible promises that this line of false christs will grow longer and longer until the final embodiment of antichrist appears at the head of the procession. He will be Satan's man.[51]

heresy: false teaching

occult: Satanic practices

delusions: false beliefs

Dave Hunt: The teaching that non-Christians can create miracles by following "God's laws of faith" or the "laws of the fourth dimension" is a serious **heresy**. Tragically, this tempting lie opens the door into the **occult**, where evil spirits gladly respond with a seeming "miracle" in order to deceive and seduce the unsuspecting into further **delusions**.[52]

WARNING

Without question God can perform signs and miracles. But Satan and his crowd of false Christs, witches, and mystics can do some pretty amazing things too and they will be out in full force during the Tribulation Period.

Unfulfilled
Tribulation Period

Fulfillment: During the Tribulation Period the Antichrist will display "all kinds of *counterfeit* miracles, signs and wonders" (2 Thessalonians 2:9). The False Prophet will perform great and miraculous *signs*, and the spirits of *demons* will perform miraculous signs to gather the leaders of the world for the Battle of Armageddon.

GO TO:

2 Thessalonians 2:9 (counterfeit)

Revelation 13:13 (signs)

Revelation 16:12–14 (demons)

> **Matthew 24:28** "Wherever there is a carcass, there the vultures will gather."

proverb: a short, wise saying

eagles: the Palestinian eagles are actually vultures or birds of prey

Birds Of Prey

This is an ancient **proverb** that Jesus applied to the Battle of Armageddon. A carcass is a dead body. Job noted that the **eagles** gather where the slain are. The main idea of this sign is that the death of many people will cause a gathering of the birds of prey in Israel.

Charles Capps: This plainly reveals it to be the same event as described in Revelation 19:17–18. When the angel will cry with a loud voice for all of the fowls of the earth to come and feast on kings and great men of the earth. The carcass to which Jesus gives reference is of the Antichrist, as well as the armies that follow him. These will all be slain when Christ comes back with His saints at the end of the Tribulation.[53]

DISPATCH FROM JERUSALEM, SEPTEMBER/OCTOBER 1998 . . .

The recent poisoning of vultures in the Ramat HaGolan with organic phosphorus touched a chord with many Israelis, who gave up their time to help save these rare birds.[54]

• • •

DISPATCH FROM JERUSALEM, MAY/JUNE 1999 . . .

There are only 1000 cranes left in the world, and 10% of them are in Israel. Most of them are in the Hula Valley area north of the Sea of Galilee, while others are in the Negev in the south.[55]

• • •

THE JERUSALEM POST, AUGUST 19, 1995 . . .

Capt. Ronen Lev, 24, of Haifa, and navigator, Capt. Yaron Vivante, 22, of Givat Olga, were killed last Thursday morning when their F-15 slammed into migrating storks during a low-altitude training flight over the Negev. The accident, the second fatal crash within a month, occurred as they were flying at approximately 1,000 feet, when a small flock of storks approached the group of four planes undetected.[56]

Fulfillment: Before the Jews started returning to Israel in great numbers, the land was barren and wild animals and birds of prey avoided the area. Along with the returning Jews came the greening of the land, the blossoming of the desert, the reforestation of the hills, the return of wild animals, and the arrival of the birds. During the migration season, birds of prey now fly over Israel by the hundreds of thousands. Thus, they will be there when this great feast is prepared at the Battle of Armageddon.

Dig Deeper

Second Coming	Scripture
The wheat (the saved) will be separated from the chaff (the lost).	Matthew 3:12
The lost will not be allowed to enter the kingdom.	Matthew 7:21–23
Those who did not receive or listen to God's people will suffer terribly.	Matthew 10:14–15
Those who confess or deny Jesus will be acknowledged or denied before God.	Matthew 10:32–33
Those who help God's people in the name of Jesus will be rewarded.	Matthew 10:40–42
Jesus will return with his angels and reward the faithful.	Matthew 16:27
Only those who are prepared (the saved) will enter the kingdom.	Matthew 25:1–13
People will be judged for their faithfulness to Jesus.	Matthew 25:14–30
Good nations will enter the Millennium, but wicked nations will be destroyed.	Matthew 25:31–46

> **Matthew 24:29** "Immediately after the distress of those days 'the sun will be darkened, and the moon will not give its light; the stars will fall from the sky, and the heavenly bodies will be shaken.'"

Heavenly Signs

At the very end of the **distress** there will be great disturbances in the heavenly bodies. The sun will turn black, there will be no light for the moon to reflect, the stars will fall like figs dropping from a fig tree, and the heavenly bodies will shake like they are being rolled up inside a great scroll. Luke adds that there will be anguish and **perplexity** on earth, and people will faint from terror and apprehension over what is happening to the world.

Life Application Bible Commentary: Coming persecutions and natural disasters will cause great sorrow in the world. But when believers see these events happening, they should realize that the return of their Messiah is near and that they can look forward to his reign of justice and peace.[57]

☞ **GO TO:**

Joel 2:30–31; Amos 8:9 (sun)

Isaiah 13:9–13 (moon)

Revelation 6:12–13 (figs)

Revelation 6:14 (scroll)

Luke 21:25–26 (anguish)

distress: Tribulation Period

What Others are Saying:

perplexity: confusion, not knowing what to do

If you are here when this happens, what will you do? How will you protect yourself when there is no place to hide? The stress, anxiety, and terror will be so great that people will have heart attacks and fall in their tracks. Those who put their trust in Jesus Christ now won't have to worry about it.

Something to Ponder

In the late seventies, comet Kohoutek passed by the earth and some thought that was a fulfillment of this prophecy. It happened again when Shoemaker-Levy 9 crashed into Jupiter in 1995, again when Hyakutake passed by in 1996, and again when Hale-Bopp appeared in 1997. But this is not a prophecy about comets flying near the earth or crashing into other planets.

WARNING

Fulfillment: It is impossible to say just what will happen, but this appears to be a Nova, or a partial Nova, of the sun. Scientists see about thirty of these in our galaxy each year. When a star does this it gets very bright, it collapses, and then its light fades somewhat. This would account for both the sun and the moon going dark, and something like this will happen at the end of the Tribulation Period.

Unfulfilled
Tribulation Period

> **Matthew 24:30** "At that time the sign of the Son of Man will appear in the sky, and all the nations of the earth will mourn. They will see the Son of Man coming on the clouds of the sky, with power and great glory."

The Second Coming

"*At that time*" refers to Matthew 24:29. When the sun is darkened, the moon fails to shine, and hundreds of stars start falling out of the sky, then the sign of Jesus will appear in the sky; and people all over the earth will see it and experience great distress. They will be people who mocked, <u>scoffed</u>, and refused to believe in the Second Coming. But when this sign appears, reality will set in and the tears will flow as Jesus returns in the <u>clouds</u> with power and great glory.

☞ **GO TO:**

2 Peter 3:3–7 (scoffed)

Matthew 26:64; Mark 14:62; Acts 1:9–11 (clouds)

Oliver B. Greene: There will be no further need for the sun and the moon because Jesus, who will be brighter than the sun, will shine forth in all of His glory, with the glory of His Father and of the angels.[58]

What Others are Saying:

Billy Graham: The good news for Christians who have remained faithful through trials and persecution will be bad news indeed for everyone who has denied Christ, slandered His people, and followed after false gods.[59]

Charles Capps: Not many years ago, people were saying, "This couldn't happen! It's impossible for everyone to see Him!" But with satellite news coverage as competitive as it is today, I believe CNN as well as many other TV networks will be there to broadcast Christ's Second Advent live via satellite and it will be seen around the world.[60]

shekinah glory: glory
brighter than the
noonday sun

**Something
to Ponder**

What is the sign of Jesus? The Bible does not say, but some commentators think it is something called the **shekinah glory**. When John saw Jesus on the Isle of Patmos, our Lord's <u>face</u> *"was like the sun shining in all its brilliance"* (Revelation 1:16; see GWRV, page 22). It will be so bright *"all the nations of the earth will see it."* People who scoffed at the Second Coming will suddenly realize their sin and weep. But it will be too late to repent.

Unfulfilled

Second Coming

Fulfillment: This is not the Rapture which will remove the Church from the earth and catch the unbelieving world by surprise. This is the Second Coming of Christ in power to put down evil on earth and to establish justice, peace, and righteousness. It will happen at the end of the Tribulation Period, not before.

☞ **GO TO:**

Revelation 1:16 (face)

> **Matthew 24:31** "And he will send his angels with a loud trumpet call, and they will gather his elect from the four winds, from one end of the heavens to the other."

Gathering The Elect

☞ **GO TO:**

Hebrews 1:14 (angels)

Numbers 10:1–7;
Leviticus 23:23–24
(trumpet)

God often uses <u>angels</u> to do great things and he often uses <u>trumpet</u> blasts to assemble his people. Here we are told that Jesus will use angels and trumpet blasts to gather his people. The *"four winds"* and *"from one end of the heavens to the other"* simply means from wherever they are on earth or in heaven. No one will be ignored or forgotten.

Billy Graham: The empire of angels is as vast as God's creation. If you believe the Bible, you will believe in their ministry.[61]

Arnold G. Fruchtenbaum: Since the Jewish prophets had predicted in great detail the worldwide regathering of Israel, Jesus did not spend much time with this, but only pointed out that it will occur after His Second Coming.[62]

John F. Walvoord: At that time Old Testament saints will be resurrected and believers from the tribulation will be raised from the dead. Living Christians will also be gathered. The millennial kingdom will extend to all believers, and at its beginning all the saved will be resurrected.[63]

> **Fulfillment:** The angels of heaven will scour the earth immediately after the Second Coming of Christ. This will be one of the first events to take place in the Millennium.

The Millennium	Scripture
Those following Jesus will be rewarded in the Millennium.	Matthew 19:27–30
God is preparing rewards for the faithful.	Matthew 20:20–23

> **Matthew 24:32–33** "Now learn this lesson from the fig tree: As soon as its twigs get tender and its leaves come out, you know that summer is near. Even so, when you see all these things, you know that it is near, right at the door."

The Nation of Israel

The prophet Jeremiah used good <u>figs</u> to represent good Jews who had been taken captive to Babylon, and he used bad figs to represent bad Jews who had escaped the captivity. The prophet Hosea compared Israel's fathers (Abraham, Isaac, and Jacob) to the <u>early fruit</u> of a fig tree. So Israel is the Bible "fig tree." And Jesus, in effect, was saying, "Watch Israel and when you see all these things happening, understand that the end of the age is near."

What Others are Saying:

KEY POINT

This verse refers primarily to the Jews, but, depending upon its use, the word "elect" (God's faithful people) in the Bible refers to both Jews and Gentiles.

Unfulfilled
Millennium

Dig Deeper

☞ **GO TO:**

Jeremiah 24:1–10 (figs)

Hosea 9:10 (early fruit)

Gary Hedrick: In fact, all the events in Matthew 24 center around Jerusalem. Jerusalem and Israel are the point of reference for anyone who wants to know what time it is on God's prophetic calendar. In Matthew 24, our Lord is saying, "Keep your eyes on Israel. Israel is your point of reference. Israel is the indicator. Watch the fig tree and when you see the branches begin to blossom, when you see the nation begin to come to life again, then you will know the end is approaching."[64]

NEWS FROM ISRAEL, JULY 1998 . . .

**RELATED
CURRENT
EVENTS**

```
A six-year study recently presented to President
Weizmann predicts that by the year 2020, the
population of Israel will exceed 8,100,000, mak-
ing Israel by far the most densely populated
developed country in the world. Israel will be
more than 2.5 times more densely populated than
Japan and the Netherlands, and there will be a
serious shortage of land for residential con-
struction.[65]
```

☞ **GO TO:**

Matthew 24:3, 30
(sign)

Remember
This . . .

The disciples asked, "*What will be the <u>sign</u> of your coming and of the end of the age?*" Jesus said the sign of his coming will appear in the sky, and he said we will know the end of the age is near, right at the door, when we see the rebirth of Israel and all these other things happening.

Something
to Ponder

There is much criticism of those who try to relate current events to Bible prophecy. If this practice is wrong, why did Jesus give the signs and have the Holy Spirit record them, and why did ~~he indicate that~~ we can watch and know when the end of the age is near? Who would not want us to watch?

WARNING

Jesus said, *"When you see ALL THESE THINGS"* [emphasis mine]. This tells us that we should look at the whole picture. Those who think just one earthquake, one war, one terrible disease is a sign are not looking at the complete picture. It is the increase in earthquakes, plus the increase in wars, plus the increase in terrible diseases, plus everything else that is an indicator.

Fulfillment: Jesus gave us these signs. He wants us to understand them and to know what all of them happening at the same time means. The end of the age could not have happened until Israel came back into existence. But the rebirth of that nation has occurred and it has occurred at a time when all the other signs are on the scene. There is only one way to interpret it.

> **Matthew 24:34** "I tell you the truth, this generation will certainly not pass away until all these things have happened."

One Generation

The end will come within one generation. But how long is that? The following are a few opinions one can expect to find when studying this bewildering subject:

1. The word *generation* comes from the Greek word *genea*, meaning race, family, or breed; so this prophecy means the Jews will be preserved as a distinct race until everything is fulfilled.

2. The generation living on earth when Israel became a nation in 1948 will not all pass away before everything is fulfilled.

3. A generation lasts approximately twenty years because young people get married and start a new generation at about that age.

4. A generation lasts <u>forty</u> years because one generation of Jews died during forty years of wandering in the wilderness.

5. A generation lasts <u>seventy</u> years because the normal length of life is seventy years.

6. A generation lasts anywhere from thirty to seventy years because it was <u>fourteen</u> generations (almost a thousand years) from Abraham to David, fourteen generations (a little more than four hundred years) from David to the exile in Babylon, and fourteen generations (about six hundred years) from the Babylonian exile to the birth of Jesus.

 GO TO:

Numbers 32:11–13 (forty)

Psalm 90:10 (seventy)

Matthew 1:17 (fourteen)

**Remember
This . . .**

**Something
to Ponder**

Unfulfilled
Tribulation Period

KEY POINT

It was the wicked who
were removed from
the earth by drown-
ing in Noah's day, and
it was the righteous
who were put into an
ark of safety until they
could be used to re-
populate the earth.

☞ **GO TO:**

2 Peter 2:5 (preacher)

Genesis 6:1–7:24
(flood)

*righteousness: justice,
peace, right doing*

scoffed: ridiculed

*spiritual things: things
about God*

If anyone can figure out how long a generation is, they will still need to figure out when the terminal generation begins. Some say May 1948 when Israel became a nation. Others say June 1967 when Israel captured the Temple Mount. There are a variety of unprovable opinions.

Everyone wants to know "how long is a generation?" There have been many efforts to figure this out, but the answer appears as elusive as the identity of the Antichrist (he cannot be identified until after the Rapture). Could it be that God deliberately made this vague to prevent us from figuring out when the Second Coming will be? We are not supposed to know the day or hour of that.

Fulfillment: There is good reason to believe that this present generation is the generation that will see the complete fulfillment of all these prophecies, but it is impossible to be dogmatic about this belief.

> **Matthew 24:37–39** As it was in the days of Noah, so it will be at the coming of the Son of Man. For in the days before the flood, people were eating and drinking, marrying and giving in marriage, up to the day Noah entered the ark; and they knew nothing about what would happen until the flood came and took them all away. That is how it will be at the coming of the Son of Man.

Like The Days Of Noah

Noah was a preacher of **righteousness** at a time when people **scoffed** at messages from God. When Noah foretold the flood, the people refused to listen. Because of this lack of interest in **spiritual things**, they lived as they pleased right up until the very day the great flood started. That awesome day began just like every other day, but it wasn't long until it started to rain, and the floodwaters began to rise, and in a matter of days, except for Noah and his family, everyone perished.

Jesus is saying, "this is the way it will be at the end of the age. People will scoff at messages about the Tribulation Period, refuse to listen to prophecies about the Second Coming, and do as they please right up until the very last day. That day will begin like every other day with people eating, drinking, attending weddings, etc. But it will be the day their doom is sealed.

186

GOD'S WORD FOR THE BIBLICALLY-INEPT

John Hagee: If you open your morning paper at breakfast tomorrow, you're likely to lose your appetite. Murders, rapes, kidnapping, assault, child abuse, spouse abuse, parental abuse—these are common headlines for even small town newspapers. [People] are thinking <u>evil</u> all the time. And just as the floodwaters caught them unaware, so the end of the earth will catch these deceived sleepers. The Messiah will come, the thread of history will snap, and those who were unprepared will be caught up in the Tribulation which is to follow.[66]

Charles Capps: In Matthew 24, Jesus refers to "Noah's day," because Noah and his family represented all of the righteous on the earth at that time. They were taken into the safety of the ark before the judgment of God was released on the earth. Notice that His emphasis is really on the fact that the wicked didn't know what was coming until after Noah had escaped to safety. Then the flood came and took the wicked away.[67]

Fulfillment: Our generation has witnessed unparalleled spiritual apathy and ignorance. Most people are ambivalent toward what is happening on the prophetic front. This may well be the group of people that is caught completely off guard.

> **Matthew 24:40–41** "Two men will be in the field; one will be taken and the other left. Two women will be grinding with a hand mill; one will be taken and the other left."

The Great Separation

Many people make the mistake of thinking this is the Rapture, but it has nothing to do with that mysterious event. It is a continuation of what Jesus was saying about the Days of Noah and all those who were removed from the earth by drowning in the great flood. Here he is telling us two men will be in the field; one will be removed for judgment and the other left. It will be that way for women also: two women will be grinding with a hand mill; one will be removed for judgment and the other left. Those who are left will help repopulate the earth during the Millennium.

What Others are Saying:

☞ **GO TO:**

Genesis 6:5 (evil)

Unfulfilled

Second Coming

What Others are Saying:

John F. Walvoord: The context indicates that the one who is taken is taken in judgment, much like the people who perished outside the ark, as illustrated in the previous context (Matthew 24:39). Also, according to Luke 17:37, those who are taken are killed, and vultures eat their bodies. This is exactly the opposite of the Rapture.[68]

In the Parable of the Weeds, the field is the world. That parable teaches that Jesus will send his angels out at the end of the age to collect the weeds (wicked people) and throw them into the fiery furnace, where there will be weeping and gnashing of teeth.

Fulfillment: God intends to remove the wicked from the earth at the end of the age so they cannot enter the Millennium. At the Second Coming they will be taken away and held for judgment before the Great White Throne of God.

Remember This . . .

Unfulfilled
Second Coming

☞ **GO TO:**

Matthew 13:24–43 (Parable)

Matthew 13:38 (field)

Matthew 13:38 (weeds)

Revelation 20:11–15 (Throne)

MARK

> **Mark 9:42–48** "And if anyone causes one of these little ones who believe in me to sin, it would be better for him to be thrown into the sea with a large millstone tied around his neck. If your hand causes you to sin, cut it off. It is better for you to enter life maimed than with two hands to go into hell, where the fire never goes out. And if your foot causes you to sin, cut it off. It is better for you to enter life crippled than to have two feet and be thrown into hell. And if your eye causes you to sin, pluck it out. It is better for you to enter the kingdom of God with one eye than to have two eyes and be thrown into hell, where 'their worm does not die, and the fire is not quenched.'"

KEY Symbols:

Field
 World

Weeds
 Wicked people

millstone: a large round, flat stone (doughnut-shaped) used for grinding corn, wheat, or other grains

A Sobering Word

After explaining to his disciples the fact that every act of kindness toward his people will be greatly rewarded, Jesus focused on children and taught that anyone causing them to sin will be severely punished. The punishment will be so harsh, those who experience it would be better off if they had a large **millstone** tied around their neck and were cast into the sea where they would surely drown. He then taught that we should be willing to go to extremes to avoid sinning because it will be a terrible thing to be cast into the eternal <u>fire</u> of <u>hell</u> where the worms never die (Note: KJV mentions worms, but NIV does not).

Think about who it is that is saying this. It is Jesus, the Son of God, the **Omniscient One**, the One who loves us so much he literally left heaven and willingly died a cruel death. Why do you think he warned us about the horrors of hell? Could it be that he knows what hell is like? Is it wise to ignore this?

The word *hell* is a translation of the word *Gehenna*, a form of a Hebrew word that means Valley of <u>Hinnom</u>. This is a valley southeast of Jerusalem where, at one time, wicked Jews burned their children as sacrifices to the false gods they were worshiping. When the good king Josiah took the throne, he declared that place unclean and would not let anyone <u>sacrifice</u> their children there anymore. Then the residents of Jerusalem started dumping their garbage there, the place became infested with worms, and fires burned there day and night. In effect, Jesus is saying, "stop sinning because you do not want to spend eternity in a place like that."

Fulfillment: This is a warning to unbelievers about their judgment before the Great White Throne of God. All who have not accepted Jesus as their Savior will be cast into the Lake of Fire.

LUKE

> **Luke 1:32–33** "He will be great and will be called the Son of the Most High. The Lord God will give him the throne of his father David, and he will reign over the house of Jacob forever; his kingdom will never end."

A King Forever

God sent the angel Gabriel to visit a **virgin** named Mary, to tell her that she had found **favor** with God, and that she had been

☞ **GO TO:**

Revelation 20:11–15 (fire)

Matthew 5:22; 10:38 (hell)

Something to Ponder

Remember This . . .

☞ **GO TO:**

2 Chronicles 28:3; Jeremiah 7:31; 32:35 (Hinnom)

2 Kings 23:10 (sacrifice)

Unfulfilled

After the Millennium

Omniscient One: *the One who knows everything*

virgin: *she had never had sexual relations with a man*

favor: *obtained God's approval*

Son of the Most High: Son of the Supreme God

given a throne: become a king

Jacob: the nation of Israel

chosen to bear a very special child. The angel told her to name this special child Jesus. He said Jesus would be called the **Son of the Most High**. Jesus would be **given a throne** and would rule over the house of **Jacob**; he would rule forever.

The angel is quite clear: Jesus will have a very special Father-Son relationship with God. He will someday sit on the throne of Israel. And his rule will never end. Other kings have come and gone, but this <u>King</u> will not.

What Others are Saying:

John F. Walvoord: The throne of David was a political throne, the house of Jacob encompassed the literal descendants of Jacob, and the prediction that Jesus' kingdom would never end was a repetition of the perpetuity of the Davidic kingdom.[69]

☞ **GO TO:**

1 Samuel 2:10; Jeremiah 23:3–8; Ezekiel 37:1–28; Hosea 3:4–5; Zechariah 14:9–17 (King)

Mark 5:1–20 (Legion)

David Hocking: In 2 Samuel 7, God told David that Messiah would come out of his "body," and that God would establish his throne forever. In Psalm 132:10–11, God confirmed that He would set on David's throne the fruit of his "body." So when we say that Jesus is of the house of David, we are saying that He is the One who fulfills all the hopes of the Jewish people.[70]

In this passage, we note that it was an angel that referred to the coming Jesus as the Son of the Most High. After Jesus was born, he encountered a demon-possessed man in the region of the Gerasenes and the demon whose name was <u>Legion</u> called Jesus "Son of the Most High God." Could it be that this is his title in the unseen world of angels and demons?

Something to Ponder

Unfulfilled
Millennium

Fulfillment: It is almost certain that Mary expected great things of Jesus, but, as great as he was, he did not completely fulfill this prophecy at his First Coming. The Jews rejected him as their king and managed to have him crucified. Therefore, this must be fulfilled in the future. Almost 2000 years have passed since the angel Gabriel told Mary that Jesus would rule in Israel. For most of this time the nation did not exist and no earthly king was needed. But things have changed. Everyone knows the nation has been restored. It only remains for the King to return and take his throne.

The Millennium	Scripture

Those who practice humility and
tenderness toward the weak will be great. ...... Luke 9:48

Those who seek the kingdom will receive it. ...... Luke 12:31–32

Those who are faithful until the end will be
rulers in the kingdom. .... Luke 12:42–44

Those wanting to enter the kingdom will
have to completely trust God. .... Luke 18:17

Those willing to give up everything for
God will receive great rewards. .... Luke 18:29–30

The original disciples will occupy a
special place in the kingdom. .... Luke 22:29–30

> **Luke 12:45–48** "But suppose the servant says to himself, 'My master is taking a long time in coming,' and he then begins to beat the menservants and maidservants and to eat and drink and get drunk. The master of that servant will come on a day when he does not expect him and at an hour he is not aware of. He will cut him to pieces and assign him a place with the unbelievers. That servant who knows his master's will and does not get ready or does not do what his master wants will be beaten with many blows. But the one who does not know and does things deserving punishment will be beaten with few blows. From everyone who has been given much, much will be demanded; and from the one who has been entrusted with much, much more will be asked."

Live Like His Return Is Soon

This **parable** deals with the attitudes of two groups of people who know the will of God, but do not believe Jesus will return anytime soon, and a third group that does not know the will of God and, therefore, is not looking for the return of Jesus. The first group is warned about abusing their authority—those who fail to look for the Lord's return and start abusing their weaker fellowmen will be caught by surprise when he returns and suffer the most terrible of fates. The second group is warned about being lazy—those who know the will of God and ignore the opportunity to serve him will be subjected to a series of harsh punishments in the life to come. The third group is composed of those

parable: a story about familiar things that teaches or illustrates unfamiliar things

KEY POINT

Watch for the return of Jesus, do the will of God, and be good to those around you.

☞ **GO TO:**

Revelation 20:11–15
(Lake of Fire)

who do not know the will of God—if they use the little knowledge they have to do things worthy of punishment, they will be punished and it will be a series of minor punishments in the life to come.

What Others
are Saying:

Remember
This . . .

Unfulfilled
Second Coming
After the Millennium

William Barclay: Knowledge and privilege always bring responsibility. Sin is doubly sinful to the man who knew better; failure is doubly blameworthy in the man who had every chance to do well.[71]

There are degrees or grades of punishment in the life to come. Notice that the first group will be cut in pieces and assigned a place with the unbelievers (<u>Lake of Fire</u>); the second group will be beaten with many blows; and the third group will be beaten with few blows.

Fulfillment: Some live like they think the Second Coming will never arrive. Without question it has taken longer than most people thought, but that does not mean it will never happen. Jesus will come again and the skeptics will find themselves standing before the Great White Throne.

The Great White Throne	Scripture
People will be held responsible for hearing and rejecting God's Word.	Luke 8:16–18
Cities will be held responsible for hearing and rejecting God's Word.	Luke 10:10–16
Every secret sin will be exposed.	Luke 12:2–3

*Dig
Deeper*

> **Luke 17:22–24** Then he said to his disciples, "The time is coming when you will long to see one of the days of the Son of Man, but you will not see it. Men will tell you, 'There he is!' or 'Here he is!' Do not go running off after them. For the Son of Man in his day will be like the lightning, which flashes and lights up the sky from one end to the other.

With Lightning Speed

This is something Jesus said to his disciples, but the text shows that it not only applied to them, but also to those followers who will be alive at the end of the age. There will be great <u>distress</u> on

☞ **GO TO:**

Matthew 24:21–22
(distress)

earth during the Tribulation Period with people longing for the Second Coming of Jesus to make things better. But he will not return until the time is right. In the meantime, there will be false sightings and the appearance of <u>false Christs</u>, but they will not be credible. When Jesus returns, it won't be to visit different sites on earth. It will be like a flash of <u>lightning</u> streaking across the sky.

The return of Jesus will be without warning and the over-whelming judgments will begin in the blink of an eye. What changes can one make in the blink of an eye? Wouldn't it be wise to make things right with God beforehand and not be caught off guard?

Fulfillment: The first time Jesus came he spent about thirty-three years on earth. Even that was not enough time for some to recognize him and repent of their sins. He will return at the end of the Tribulation Period and it will be so fast that there will be no need to go looking for him and no time to change anything.

> **Luke 17:28–30** "It was the same in the days of Lot. People were eating and drinking, buying and selling, planting and building. But the day Lot left Sodom, fire and sulfur rained down from heaven and destroyed them all. It will be just like this on the day the Son of Man is revealed."

Like The Days Of Lot

When Jesus returns things on earth will be very much like they were in the days of Lot. The cities of <u>Sodom and Gomorrah</u> stood on the brink of a fiery destruction from heaven, but the people went about their daily **pursuits** as though nothing bad would ever happen to them. They partied, bought and sold, built houses, etc., right up to the last day of their existence, the day Lot left Sodom. On that day, fire and brimstone fell from heaven and destroyed them all.

The Pulpit Commentary: The cities are trading and feasting, and lo! the fires of heaven come down and consume them. They who trifle with the most sacred things are sure to find that, suddenly, in such an hour as they think not, the end arrives. The business plans are broken off; the brilliant career is concluded; the flow of pleasures is arrested. Death suddenly appears, and

☞ **GO TO:**

Matthew 24:23
(false Christs)

Matthew 24:27 (lightning)

Something to Ponder

Unfulfilled
Second Coming

KEY POINT

There will be no need to go here or there because the Second Coming will be as sudden as a bolt of lightning.

☞ **GO TO:**

Genesis 19:1–29
(Sodom and Gomorrah)

pursuits: activities

What Others are Saying:

deals his fatal blow. . . . The soul awakes from its long lethargy to see that its powers have been wasted and that its chance is gone![72]

Fulfillment: Many people act like nothing bad will ever happen to them. They refuse to let world events open their eyes. During the Tribulation Period there will be some who fancy themselves safe right up to the last day of their existence on earth. But just as surely as fire fell from heaven to destroy Sodom and Gomorrah, Jesus will return to deal with them.

> **Luke 17:32–33** "Remember Lot's wife! Whoever tries to keep his life will lose it, and whoever loses his life will preserve it."

She Needed An Attitude Adjustment

Unfulfilled
Second Coming

☞ **GO TO:**

Matthew 6:24
(two masters)

Genesis 19:17–26
(Lot's wife)

Jesus said, *"No one can serve <u>two masters</u>. Either he will hate the one and love the other, or he will be devoted to the one and despise the other"* (Matthew 6:24). The point is that people should develop the right attitude about God and the things of this world; to put off doing so is foolish.

<u>Lot's wife</u> is an example. God sent angels to get her out of Sodom before he destroyed that city with fire and brimstone. The angels told her to flee and not look back, but she did not listen; she disobeyed and lost her life when she was turned into a pillar of salt. Apparently she loved Sodom, did not want to leave it, did not want to give up her worldly goods, and did not believe God would destroy that loathsome place. So while fleeing, she hesitated, looked back, and perished—she ended up losing everything anyway.

This goes to the heart of people's attitude toward worldly things. We should always be ready to give up our possessions for the things of God. Those who seek to save their life (refuse to turn it over to Jesus) will lose it, and those who are willing to lose their life (give it up for Jesus) will save it.

What Others are Saying:

Henry M. Morris with Henry M. Morris III: Christ accepted the historicity of Adam and Eve (Matthew 19:4–5), of Abel (Matthew 29:35), of Noah (Luke 17:26), of Abraham (John 8:56–58), and Lot (Luke 17:28). . . . He believed in the supernatural destruction of Sodom and Gomorrah (Luke 17:29) and the calamity of Lot's wife.[73]

Can you give up your vehicles, your house, and all your other possessions for Jesus? During the Tribulation Period, those who want to keep everything will lose; and those who are willing to lose everything will gain. The decision should not be tough and a person should not hesitate, but many will. What will you do?

Fulfillment: We all know that we can die on a moment's notice, but most people think they have plenty of time to prepare for that. It will not be that way during the Tribulation Period when approximately three-fourths of the world's population will die, and most of the others will be caught by the surprising return of Jesus.

Something to Ponder

Unfulfilled
Tribulation Period
Second Coming

The Second Coming	Scripture
If anyone is ashamed of Jesus, he will be ashamed of them at his coming.	Mark 8:38
Be prepared because the Second Coming will catch the lost by surprise.	Luke 12:35–40

> **Luke 21:20–22** "When you see Jerusalem being surrounded by armies, you will know that its desolation is near. Then let those who are in Judea flee to the mountains, let those in the city get out, and let those in the country not enter the city. For this is the time of punishment in fulfillment of all that has been written."

Dig Deeper

The End Is Near

Jesus talked about <u>wars</u> and rumors of wars and he said, "*but the end is still to come*" (Matthew 24:6). Here he speaks of a war that will signal the approach of the end. He warned that hostile armies will encircle <u>Jerusalem</u>, that when it happens the people of **Judea** should immediately flee to the mountains (probably **Petra**), that the people in Jerusalem should evacuate the city, and that those in the surrounding area should stay away from there. Terrible events will follow and most of the area will be made <u>desolate</u>.

Judea: the southernmost part of Israel, it was occupied by the tribes of Judah and Benjamin

Petra: an ancient city in the mountains of Jordan

☞ **GO TO:**

Matthew 24:6 (wars)

Zechariah 14:1–21; Joel 3:9–16 (Jerusalem)

Daniel 9:26 (desolate)

Irvin Baxter Jr.: The pressure will build on Israel to either share Jerusalem or place it under international control. Israel will refuse. International condemnation will come against Israel because of her actions concerning Jerusalem. Finally, a resolution will be passed

What Others are Saying:

on the UN Security Council demanding that Israel comply to the directives of the International Community. Israel will refuse.[74]

PERSONAL UPDATE, DECEMBER 1998...

```
Regardless of the short-term outcome of the
"peace process," one thing is almost certain: the
fate of the peace process will hinge on the fu-
ture of the city of Jerusalem. Israel has claimed
Jerusalem as its capital and is tightening its
grip on the city by extending its boundaries to
increase the Jewish proportions. The Palestinians
are making the claim that Al Quds (the Arabic
name for Jerusalem) will also be the capital of a
newly declared Palestinian state.[75]
```

• • •

DISPATCH FROM JERUSALEM, MARCH/APRIL 1999...

```
The Palestinians, who have openly and repeatedly
laid claims over eastern Jerusalem, also have
demands on the western part as well. Palestinian
Authority senior, Abu Allah, declared on March
12th that the PA will insist on discussing west-
ern Jerusalem in the final-status negotiations.
Abu Allah, who appeared before a gathering of the
Fatah Youth movement, said he was speaking in the
name of Yasir Arafat. Abu Allah also cited the
recent European Union letter implying that Israel
has no sovereignty over any part of Jerusalem.[76]
```

The Tribulation Period serves four purposes:

1. To <u>punish</u> the people of the earth for their sins, for the blood shed upon the earth (war, murder, abortion, etc.)
2. To restore to Israel their land which other <u>nations</u> lay claim to
3. To uphold <u>Zion's</u> (Jerusalem's) cause, a recompense to the nations for their mistreatment of Israel
4. To allow Jews to bear the Lord's <u>wrath</u> for sinning against him

RELATED CURRENT EVENTS

Something to Ponder

☞ **GO TO:**

Isaiah 26:19–21 (punish)

Ezekiel 36:1–38 (nations)

Isaiah 34:8 (Zion's)

Micah 7:9 (wrath)

The Battle of Armageddon will occur because the nations have

> scattered the Jews,
>
> seized land belonging to the Jews, and
>
> divided up the land of Israel.

God is returning the Jews to the land of Israel, and any nation that tries to put the Jews off the land is going against what he is doing. The Jews and the land go together. God will punish those nations that oppose what he is doing by drawing them into the Battle of Armageddon. Isn't it clear what side the United States should be on?

Fulfillment: Israel will not be able to stand up against the superior forces of the Antichrist and his UN or world army at first. But attacking Jerusalem is a step toward the Battle of Armageddon. Just when it appears that everything is hopeless for Israel Jesus will return, the Jews will accept him as their Messiah, and you can kiss the world army goodbye.

☞ **GO TO:**

Joel 3:2 (scattered)

Jeremiah 12:14–17 (seized)

Joel 3:2 (divided)

Something to Ponder

Unfulfilled
Tribulation Perod

☞ **GO TO:**

Amos 9:13–15 (Israel)

JOHN

> **John 5:43** "I have come in my Father's name, and you do not accept me; but if someone else comes in his own name, you will accept him."

How Could You Do That?

Jesus was talking to a group of Jews and he reminded them that, as a nation, they had rejected him. He was the Messiah and he came to them in the name of God, but they wanted to get rid of him. Someday there will be someone else who will come to them as a great leader in his own name, and the Jews as a nation will eagerly accept him. This verse does not identify that person, but virtually all prophetic writers agree that he will be the Antichrist.

David Reagan: But the Bible does not teach that the Jews will receive the Antichrist as their Messiah. It teaches they will accept him as a great political leader and diplomat and that they will put their trust in him as the guarantor of peace in the Middle East.[77]

What Others are Saying:

RELATED CURRENT EVENTS

DISPATCH FROM JERUSALEM, MARCH/APRIL 1999...

Over 350,000 Orthodox Jews attended a prayer vigil/rally on Sunday, February 14th. It was the largest demonstration in Jerusalem history. . . . Rabbi Elimelech Tirnoyer, one of the main organizers and the announcer at the rally, summed up the event: "The participants filled the streets. . . . This was great, an awesome spectacle! I can only describe it as a preparation for the coming of the Messiah into the gates of Jerusalem."[78]

Remember This . . .

Jesus came in his Father's name. He called God his <u>Father</u> and said he could do what he saw the Father do, that the Father <u>sent</u> him, and that his works were testimony to that. But the Antichrist will come to honor his own name and to boast of his own works.

| Unfulfilled |
| Tribulation Period |

Fulfillment: Jesus warned that <u>false Christs</u> will appear and perform great signs and miracles to deceive even the very elect. The Antichrist cannot come on the scene until after the Rapture, but when he arrives the Jewish nation will love him. They will accept him as the great leader they have been looking for.

☞ **GO TO:**

John 5:17–19 (Father)

John 5:30 (sent)

Matthew 24:24 (false Christs)

Dig Deeper

The Great White Throne	Scripture
Unbelievers are already under the condemnation of God.	John 3:18
The wrath of God abides on those who reject Jesus.	John 3:36
The lost will be raised from the dead and condemned forever.	John 5:28–29
Those who reject Jesus will be judged by the words he spoke.	John 12:48

> **John 11:25–26** Jesus said to her, "I am the resurrection and the life. He who believes in me will live, even though he dies; and whoever lives and believes in me will never die. Do you believe this?"

The Dead Will Be Raised

When a man named Lazarus became seriously ill his two sisters sent for Jesus, but he did not go immediately and Lazarus died. Jesus finally arrived four days after Lazarus was buried, Lazarus' sister Martha was distressed. Jesus told Martha that her brother would rise again. She thought he was talking about a future resurrection. Jesus explained that she was right to believe in a future resurrection, but that was not what he was talking about. He called himself "the resurrection and the life" which means he is the One who raises the <u>dead</u>, the One who gives spiritual life and physical life. He also said the living who believe in him will never die, meaning they will never die the **second <u>death</u>**. Jesus then raised Lazarus from the dead (see GWWB, pages 260–269).

W. Herschel Ford: He was saying that those who believed in Him, even if they were dead like Lazarus, would again be brought to life.[79]

Is it possible that Jesus was also revealing the **Rapture** in these verses? In essence he said those who are dead will live again and those who are alive will never die. When Paul revealed the Rapture he said, *"the dead in Christ will rise first"* (1 Thessalonians 4:16). In other words, the dead will live. Then Paul said, *"we who are alive and are left will be <u>caught up</u> together with them in the clouds to meet the Lord in the air"* (1 Thessalonians 4:17). Believers who are alive when Jesus comes for his Church will go directly to heaven and not die.

Fulfillment: There will be two future resurrections (John 5:28–29): a resurrection of life, and a resurrection of damnation. This passage not only refers to the resurrection of Lazarus, but it also refers to one phase of the resurrection of life known as the Rapture (see GWRV, page 298).

The Millennium	Scripture
There will be just one group of believers in the future.	John 10:16
Jesus was born to be a king.	John 18:37

☞ **GO TO:**

Ephesians 2:1–7 (dead)

Revelation 1:18; 2:11; 20:14–15 (death)

second death: spiritual death, being cast into the Lake of Fire

What Others are Saying:

Something to Ponder

Rapture: when the Church is removed from the earth

Unfulfilled
Rapture

☞ **GO TO:**

1 Thessalonians 4:13–18 (caught up)

Dig Deeper

> **John 14:2–3** "In my Father's house are many rooms; if it were not so, I would have told you. I am going there to prepare a place for you. And if I go and prepare a place for you, I will come back and take you to be with me that you also may be where I am."

It's The Rapture

Frequently read at funerals, this is one of the most beloved passages in the entire Bible. Few people associate it with the Rapture, but that is what it actually refers to.

Jesus was going away, but he promised to return to take us back with him. He is not talking about collecting us when we die. His <u>angels</u> take care of that. Rather, he is talking about returning to raise the dead in Christ and to gather those who are <u>alive</u>. This is what Christians call the Rapture.

☞ **GO TO:**

Luke 16:22 (angels)

What Others are Saying:

1 Thessalonians 4:13–18 (alive)

saints: believers

Remember This . . .

Unfulfilled
Rapture

KEY POINT

The Rapture is when Jesus returns for his saints, and the Second Coming is when he returns with his saints.

W. Herschel Ford: One day, when we least expect it, Jesus will come in the air as we are told in 1 Thessalonians 4:13–18. He will take all of His people, those who are dead and those who are living, up to heaven with Him.[80]

Hal Lindsey: We are snatched away before we even know what hit us. We are then taken to His Father's House where He has already prepared a place for us (John 14:1–4). So the Rapture literally could occur at any moment.[81]

There is a difference between Jesus coming *for* his **saints** and Jesus coming *with* his saints. His coming for his saints is the Rapture (see 1 Thessalonians 4:17) and his coming with his saints is the Second Coming (see Revelation 19:11–14).

Fulfillment: Without question, the soul and spirit of a believer goes to be with God when the Christian dies. But the day will soon come when Jesus will bring that soul and spirit back so he can raise the believer from the dead with a new body. He will receive the resurrected believer unto himself and take him or her back to heaven with him.

The Rapture	Scripture

Those who win souls for Jesus will
be rewarded. .... John 4:36

The saved will be raised from the dead
to live forever. .... John 5:28–29

Jesus will not lose any of his, and all will
be raised from the dead. .... John 6:39, 44, 54

Dig Deeper

ACTS

> **Acts 1:6–7** So when they met together, they asked him, "Lord, are you at this time going to restore the kingdom to Israel?" He said to them: "It is not for you to know the times or dates the Father has set by his own authority."

You Don't Need To Know

The disciples grew up with the Old Testament Scriptures. They were rightly taught that **Messiah** will return to establish a kingdom, that the kingdom will be centered in Israel, that Messiah will be the king, and that he will sit on the throne of David in Jerusalem.

The event in this passage took place after Jesus was raised from the dead. He had returned to visit his disciples and teach them, but they seemed to think he had returned to establish his earthly kingdom. They wanted to know if the time for him to do that had arrived. Jesus did not deny that the kingdom will be restored. He simply pointed out that God did not want him to reveal the time to them.

Some people criticize those who are interested in Bible prophecy. But the disciples were interested in it and Jesus did not rebuke them for that. He said, in fact, we should watch for his coming.

The question the disciples asked Jesus has nothing to do with signs of the Rapture, with the time of the Rapture, or anything else about the Rapture. They asked about the earthly kingdom of Jesus. But many mistakenly think they asked about the Rapture. Actually, they probably didn't even know what the Rapture is.

Messiah: the Christ, the coming King and Deliverer (Jesus)

☞ **GO TO:**

Luke 1:32–33 (kingdom)

Jeremiah 23:3–8; Hosea 3:4–5; Zephaniah 3:15; Zechariah 14:9, 16–17 (king)

Matthew 24:42 (watch)

Remember This . . .

WARNING

Fulfillment: We now know that God decided to establish his Church and call out a people before he restores the kingdom to Israel. But after the Church is Raptured, and after the Tribulation Period, Jesus will return to restore a kingdom that will exist through the Millennium.

Dig Deeper

The Millennium	Scripture
God plans to restore everything. .... Acts 3:19–21	

> **Acts 1:9–11** After he said this, he was taken up before their very eyes, and a cloud hid him from their sight. They were looking intently up into the sky as he was going, when suddenly two men dressed in white stood beside them. "Men of Galilee," they said, "why do you stand here looking into the sky? This same Jesus, who has been taken from you into heaven, will come back in the same way you have seen him go into heaven."

He'll Be Back

This event took place when Jesus appeared to his disciples for the last time. He walked around on earth talking to them and then suddenly he began to rise into the <u>clouds</u>. He went up and disappeared from sight. The disciples were still looking at the clouds when two **angels** said Jesus had gone to heaven. He is now seated at the right hand of God and will one day return in the *same* way he left.

☞ **GO TO:**

Daniel 7:13–14;
Matthew 24:30;
Revelation 1:7
(clouds)

John Hagee: Jesus Christ, the Prince of Glory, will appear suddenly in the heavens, brilliantly, in a way that no one will be able to miss.[82]

What Others
are Saying:

angels: *heavenly beings that serve God, usually messengers*

Remember
This . . .

Jesus was taken up into heaven in a body that his disciples could see and talk to which means he will return in a body that people can see and talk to. This is important because some people do not believe in a bodily resurrection of the dead and some people wonder what Jesus will be like when he sits on his throne in Jerusalem. Just remember that Jesus was raised with a body, he went away with a body, and he will return with a body.

The return being referred to here is the Second Coming, not the Rapture.

Unfulfilled
Second Coming

Fulfillment: Jesus was on the **Mount of Olives** (Acts 1:12; Zechariah 14:4; Matthew 24:3) with his disciples when he ascended into heaven and he will return there at his Second Coming. This also happens to be the same place where he taught his disciples about his Second Coming and the end of the age.

Mount of Olives: *a very high hill about ¾ mile east of Jerusalem*

> **Acts 15:14–17** Simon has described to us how God at first showed his concern by taking from the Gentiles a people for himself. The words of the prophets are in agreement with this, as it is written: "After this I will return and rebuild David's fallen tent. Its ruins I will rebuild, and I will restore it, that the remnant of men may seek the Lord, and all the Gentiles who bear my name, says the Lord, who does these things."

God's Threefold Program

Church leaders had gathered in Jerusalem for a very important meeting. After much discussion, a man named James began to speak. What he said reveals God's threefold program for the future beginning almost two thousand years ago: (1) James agreed with Simon (Peter) that God is currently working among the **Gentiles** to select a group of people for himself. This select group is called the Church; (2) after God has taken out his Church, Jesus will return to reestablish the **house of David**. This means Jesus, a descendant of David, will come back to restore the nation of Israel and rule over it; and (3) then the remnant of Jews that is left, and all the Gentiles who call themselves Christians, will serve Christ.

Gentiles: *non-Jews*

house of David: *the family, lineage, or descendants of King David, a great Jewish king*

☞ **GO TO:**

Amos 9:11–12;
  2 Samuel 7:14–17;
  Luke 2:4–7
  (house of David)

J. R. Church: James said Cornelius, the Roman centurion, was the first convert among Gentiles—the first of millions to come. He proclaimed that God was calling out of the Gentiles a people who would be called by His name. Then he quoted the Amos passage, which predicted the raising up of the tabernacle of David, at which time a remnant of Jews would seek after the Lord, along with all the Gentiles who are called by His name.[83]

What Others are Saying:

Dig Deeper

It is important to notice that James pointed out that what Peter had said conformed to the words of the prophets. The claims of religious people should always be compared to the Scriptures. This will be especially critical when the Antichrist and his false prophets are in control.

Fulfillment: Step one: the establishment of the Church has been underway for almost 2,000 years. Step two: the return of Jesus to rule over Israel is future, but it appears to be getting close because of the reestablishment of that nation. Step three: a remnant of Jews and Gentile believers will survive the Tribulation Period and repopulate the earth during the Millennium.

The Tribulation Period	Scripture
God will pour out the Holy Spirit on people from every class or rank.	Acts 2:17–18
The sun will be darkened and the moon will turn to blood.	Acts 2:19–20

The Rapture Period	Scripture
Jesus will judge the living and the dead.	Acts 10:42
The resurrection of Jesus is assurance that God will judge believers.	Acts 17:31
There will be a resurrection of the just (believers).	Acts 24:15
Christians have forgiveness and an inheritance.	Acts 26:15–18

The Great White Throne	Scripture
The resurrection of Jesus is assurance that God will judge unbelievers.	Acts 17:31
There will be a resurrection of the unjust (unbelievers).	Acts 24:15

STUDY QUESTIONS

1. Whom does Jesus call blessed?
2. What is the name of the famous sermon Jesus preached about the end of the age and why is it called that? What does it have to do with his ascension into heaven and his Second Coming?
3. What connection did Jesus make between sin and hell? Name two things that will never cease to exist in hell.

4. Will there be different degrees of punishment in hell? Explain.

5. Who raises the dead, and when will Christians be raised?

CHAPTER WRAP-UP

- Matthew recorded a series of prophecies Jesus gave about the kingdom of heaven. He taught that the kingdom of heaven contains a mixture of saved and unsaved, but angels will remove the unsaved at the end of the age. He revealed many signs that can be interpreted to mean the end of the age is near if these signs are being simultaneously fulfilled. (Matthew 5:3–12; 13:24–50; 21:28–32; 24:3–41)

- Mark recorded a warning Jesus gave about causing children to sin and an exhortation he gave to go to extremes to avoid sinning. Jesus taught that it will be a terrible thing to be cast into hell. (Mark 9:42–48)

- Luke recorded what the angel Gabriel told Mary—that Jesus would be a king with a kingdom. Luke also recorded: (1) a parable Jesus told that taught we should live like the Second Coming is near; (2) a revelation of Jesus that predicts things will eventually get so bad, many will long for the Second Coming; (3) another revelation that others will live like nothing bad will ever happen to them; (4) a teaching that we should be ready to give up everything for God; and (5) a revelation that armies surrounding Jerusalem suggest all the prophecies are about to be fulfilled. (Luke 1:32–33; 12:45–48; 17:28–33; 21:20–22)

- John records Jesus' prediction that many Jews will eagerly accept the Antichrist and believers will be raised from the dead. John also tells us that Jesus is preparing places in heaven for believers. (John 5:43; 11:25–26; 14:2–3)

- In the book of Acts we learn that God wants to keep secret the time and date he has chosen for restoring the kingdom to Israel. We are also given details of Jesus' ascension into heaven and told that he will return in the same way. And we learn that God plans to include the Church in the kingdom, restore the nation of Israel under Jesus, and include a remnant of Jews and Gentiles who survive the Tribulation Period. (Acts 1:6–7, 9–11; 15:14–17)

7 PROPHECIES IN THE LETTERS WRITTEN BY THE APOSTLE PAUL

CHAPTER HIGHLIGHTS

- A Time to Reap Rewards
- A Time to Bow and Confess
- A Time of Wrath
- A Time of Trouble
- A Time for Great Things

Let's Get Started

The New Testament contains twenty-seven books and there is wide agreement that the Apostle Paul authored thirteen of them. Many scholars also believe Paul wrote a fourteenth, the book of Hebrews. But since this cannot be proven, the prophecies in Hebrews will be treated in the next chapter. Nine of the thirteen books accepted as Paul's are addressed to churches and four to individuals. The nine addressed to churches are placed in the Bible before the four addressed to individuals and all are organized according to length—the longest appear first in each category and the shortest appear last. The only book that seems out of order is the book of Galatians and for that we have no explanation.

The nine books addressed to churches are: Romans, 1 and 2 Corinthians, Galatians, Ephesians, Philippians, Colossians, and 1 and 2 Thessalonians. The four books addressed to individuals are: 1 and 2 Timothy, Titus, and Philemon.

Remember This . . .

ROMANS

Romans 2:5–6 But because of your stubbornness and your unrepentant heart, you are storing up wrath against yourself for the day of God's wrath, when his righteous judgment will be revealed. God "will give to each person according to what he has done."

☞ **GO TO:**

Romans 3:4 (kindness)

John 3:36; Romans 1:18–20; Ephesians 5:3–7; Colossians 3:5–6 (wrath)

What Others are Saying:

wrath: God's firm intent to punish sin and sinners

Something to Ponder

A Treasure You Don't Want

Paul was talking about the coming judgment of God when his thoughts turned to those who reject the treasures of God: his <u>kindness</u>, tolerance, and patience. People ought to recognize the goodness of God and repent of their sins, but many will not do that. They receive his blessings daily, but will not change their wicked ways. When the record books are opened, they will receive a different kind of treasure (see illustration, this page). It will coincide with the evil they have done and come out of the **wrath** of God (see GWBI, pages 229–231).

Noah Hutchings: In 1 Corinthians 3 we are informed about the treasures of the children of God which have been laid up in Heaven, but here in Romans 2:5 Paul says that the ungodly are likewise laying up treasures to be revealed in the day of wrath at the "revelation of the righteous judgment of God." From verse six we know the latter refers to the Great White Throne judgment.[1]

Dave Breese: So the fund of human iniquity and consequent divine judgment is building in a kind of cosmic bank. While this is the day of grace and God is not moving in devastating judgment, it is also the time that iniquity is being recorded in a book that will one day be opened.[2]

Those who respond to the goodness of God, repent of their sins, and accept Jesus as their Savior are storing up treasure also: rewards in heaven. What kind of treasure do you want in your account?

Judgment of Believers and Unbelievers

		SECOND COMING		
	RAPTURE	BELIEVERS BEFORE JUDGEMENT SEAT OF CHRIST. (1 CORINTHIANS 3:9-15)		UNBELIEVERS BEFORE GREAT WHITE THRONE OF GOD. (REVELATION 20:11-15)
CHURCH AGE		TRIBULATION PERIOD	MILLENNIUM	AFTER THE MILLENNIUM

Fulfillment: After the Millennium those who have died without accepting Jesus as their Savior will be raised from the dead and made to appear before the Great White Throne of God. The <u>books</u> will be opened and they will be judged according to what they have done. And all of them will wind up in the Lake of Fire.

☞ **GO TO:**

Revelation 20:11–15
(books)

The Great White Throne	Scripture
People will be judged even if they do not know what the Bible says, but those who have heard the Word will be judged more severely.	Romans 2:12–13
The judgment will include secret thoughts, motivations, and intentions.	Romans 2:16

Dig Deeper

> **Romans 2:8–9** But for those who are self-seeking and who reject the truth and follow evil, there will be wrath and anger. There will be trouble and distress for every human being who does evil: first for the Jew, then for the Gentile.

trouble and distress: suffering and affliction, the Tribulation Period

Those Who Don't Learn From History Are Doomed To Repeat It

Those individuals and nations that have the wrong attitude toward God, the self-seeking ones who live to glorify themselves, and those who reject the truth of God's Word—the ones who follow sin instead of Jesus—will receive <u>wrath</u> and anger. There will be a time of **trouble and distress** for every human being who sins. It will begin with the Jews, but it will include the Gentiles.

☞ **GO TO:**

Zephaniah 1:14–15
(wrath)

Zephaniah 1:14–18;
Matthew 24:21, 29
(trouble and distress)

Noah Hutchings: But when Israel rejected that light, God's wrath was shed upon that nation as He warned through the prophets. And now that the Gentile nations are in danger of committing the same, God's wrath is upon them, and it will be poured out without measure as is so vividly described in the Book of Revelation.[3]

What Others are Saying:

The power of God to save people is found in the Gospel. It was given to the Jews (nation of Israel) first and then it was given to the Gentiles. And that is the way the judgment of God will fall. The nation of Israel will be first in line, but the Gentile nations will be right behind them.

Remember This . . .

Fulfillment: The Gentile world seems to have forgotten that God allowed the Northern Kingdom of Israel to fall to the Assyrians in the eighth century B.C., that he allowed the Southern Kingdom of Judah to fall to the Babylonians in the sixth century B.C., and that he allowed the Romans to defeat Israel in 70 A.D. Gentile nations have failed to learn lessons about how God deals with wayward countries from these historical events, so we are doomed to go through what Israel went through.

Dig Deeper

The Tribulation Period	Scripture
God will bruise Satan.	Romans 16:20

The Millennium Period	Scripture
Jesus will rule over the Gentiles.	Romans 15:12

> **Romans 9:27–29** Isaiah cries out concerning Israel: "Though the number of the Israelites be like the sand by the sea, only the remnant will be saved. For the Lord will carry out his sentence on earth with speed and finality." It is just as Isaiah said previously: "Unless the Lord Almighty had left us descendants, we would have become like Sodom, we would have been like Gomorrah."

Something To Cry About

Here we have three verses and three different thoughts about Israel and the Tribulation Period:

1. In verse 27, Paul is saying that the prophet <u>Isaiah</u> was crying over Israel when he said even though there will be a great number of Jews, only a **remnant** will be saved. It grieved Isaiah to know that out of a very large number of Jews only a small percentage will be saved.

2. In verse 28, Paul is expressing the certainty or the determination of God to execute his judgments swiftly and completely.

3. In verse 29, Paul is saying that it will be like the prophet Isaiah said once before: "*If the <u>Lord Almighty</u> does not intervene to save a remnant the nation will be like Sodom and Gomorrah.*" The startling truth here is that God will be

☞ **GO TO:**

Isaiah 10:22–23 (Isaiah)

Isaiah 1:9
  (Lord Almighty)

remnant: *the few within Israel who trust God*

forced to intervene to keep the entire nation from being corrupted and destroyed.

What Others are Saying:

The Pulpit Commentary: Hence the relevance of the passage, not only as showing God's way of dealing with his people in times of old, but also as an intimation of how it should be when the Messiah should come.[4]

Noah Hutchings: The work will be finished during a very short time of great tribulation, and those Jews during the tribulation who come to a knowledge of the truth that Jesus Christ is the Messiah who is coming back, will be saved to enter the kingdom age. All others will be killed.[5]

Some ask, Why would God allow the world to go through the Tribulation Period? But look at what will happen if he doesn't. All Israel will be corrupted and destroyed. Is it not an act of love and grace that he refuses to let that happen?

Something to Ponder

Unfulfilled

Tribulation Period

Fulfillment: The things the Bible predicts will happen to all the earth during the Tribulation Period are horrible indeed. But the awesome truth is that even worse things will happen if the world should somehow escape that terrible time. Even though the Tribulation Period will only last seven years, the percentage of Jewish survivors will be small. This will include the 144,000 sealed <u>servants</u> of God plus those who <u>flee</u> to the mountains when the Antichrist defiles the Temple.

☞ **GO TO:**

Revelation 7:3–8 (servants)

Matthew 24:15–16 (flee)

> **Romans 11:25–27** I do not want you to be ignorant of this mystery, brothers, so that you may not be conceited: Israel has experienced a hardening in part until the full number of the Gentiles has come in. And so all Israel will be saved, as it is written: "The deliverer will come from Zion; he will turn godlessness away from Jacob. And this is my covenant with them when I take away their sins."

Don't Get A Big Head

It is clear to Christians that Jesus is the Messiah, but unclear why most Jews—not all because the early Christians were Jews—will not accept him as their Messiah. It was a **mystery** in Paul's life-

mystery: hidden truth

remnant: *the few within Israel who trust God*

Gentiles: *non-Jews*

☞ **GO TO:**

Revelation 7:3–8 (seal)

Revelation 11:3–12 (two witnesses)

Revelation 14:6 (angels)

Zechariah 13:7–9 (perish)

Matthew 24:15–22 (flee)

Isaiah 59:20; Joel 3:16–17 (Zion)

Isaiah 59:21; Jeremiah 31:31–34 (covenant)

Ezekiel 36:24 (people)

time, but it is not one now because Paul chose to explain it. The main points are as follows:

1. *"Israel has experienced a hardening in part"* means part of the nation has been hardened. The *"hardening in part"* is not a partial or incomplete hardening of every Jew. It is a definite hardening of most of the Jews, but no hardening of some of them. This explains why a few in every generation accept Jesus as their Messiah and how there is always a **remnant** in existence.

2. *"Until the full number of the Gentiles has come in"* means the *"hardening in part"* is not permanent. The end of the hardening depends upon when God receives all the **Gentiles**. In other words, the *"hardening in part"* will continue until the Church is Raptured. At that point, God will <u>seal</u> the 144,000, call the <u>two witnesses</u>, and use his <u>angels</u> to evangelize the nation.

3. *"All Israel will be saved"* does not mean everyone who calls himself a Jew will be saved. It means everyone that God recognizes as a Jew will be saved. Think of it like this: not everyone who calls himself a Christian is a Christian by God's reckoning and, in like manner, not everyone who calls himself a Jew is a Jew by God's standards. With God it is a matter of faith and not ancestry. During the Tribulation Period most of the Jews will <u>perish</u> in the wars against Israel. But 144,000 sealed Jews, all those who obey Jesus and <u>flee</u> into the mountains when the Antichrist defiles the Temple, and a few out in the country, will be saved. But obedience to Jesus is the key.

4. Verse 26 can be linked to several Old Testament passages. The deliverer is Jesus and <u>Zion</u> is Jerusalem. This means Jesus will establish his throne in Jerusalem and issue his decrees concerning Israel and the world from there.

5. Verse 27 tells us that God will remove the hardening because he made a <u>covenant</u> to take away Israel's sins. He promised to make the Jews his <u>people</u> and to be their God, and that will happen.

What Others are Saying:

John F. Walvoord: The answer to the question of whether God rejects His people (v. 1) is answered by the fact that God has not rejected them but will carry out His purposes as indicated in prophecy.[6]

Noah Hutchings: If the Jewish nation today was converted to faith in Jesus Christ as the Messiah, then the Bible would not be true.[7]

J. Dwight Pentecost: Paul has previously declared (Romans 9:6) that God is not numbering all the physical seed of Abraham as descendants, but that the promises are to those who are in faith. Thus we understand the "all Israel" in Romans 11:26 to refer to this believing remnant, the believing Jews at the **second advent** of Christ.[8]

> **Fulfillment:** God is not through with Israel. The nation and the people have a definite role to play in the future. After the Rapture, God will begin to remove the hardening. Those Jews who survive the Tribulation Period will turn to Christ at his Second Coming.

> **Romans 14:10–12** You, then, why do you judge your brother? Or why do you look down on your brother? For we will all stand before God's judgment seat. It is written: "'As surely as I live,' says the Lord, 'every knee will bow before me; every tongue will confess to God.'" So then, each of us will give an account of himself to God.

It's More Than A Genuflect

Paul is asking why one Christian would judge or look down on another. He reminds us that we will all appear before the <u>judgment</u> seat of God and be required to <u>bow</u> down and make confession. Instead of passing judgments on others and condemning them for their failures, he is suggesting that we instead concentrate on cleaning up our own lives. This means each one of us.

> The judgment of Christians is not the same as the judgment of non-Christians. Christians will appear before the judgment seat of Christ. Our eternal destiny will be secure because of our faith in Christ, but our works will be judged to determine what heavenly rewards we will receive. Non-Christians will appear before the <u>Great White Throne</u> of God. Their eternal destiny will not be secure because they have not had their name recorded in the <u>Lamb's Book of Life</u> for accepting Jesus.

Fulfillment: Many Christians never go to the altar at church to bow in the presence of God. But when we get to heaven, we will be compelled to do so and to account for such lapses. It would be much better to start now and avoid the excuses.

Dig Deeper

The Rapture	Scripture
Following Jesus (doing good) will be rewarded with eternal life.	Romans 2:7
Glory, honor, and peace will be given to all who do good (follow Jesus).	Romans 2:10
The blood of Jesus will deliver the saved from God's wrath.	Romans 5:9
Believers who suffer for Christ will share in the glory of Christ.	Romans 8:17–18

1 CORINTHIANS

> **1 Corinthians 3:10–15** By the grace God has given me, I laid a foundation as an expert builder, and someone else is building on it. But each one should be careful how he builds. For no one can lay any foundation other than the one already laid, which is Jesus Christ. If any man builds on this foundation using gold, silver, costly stones, wood, hay or straw, his work will be shown for what it is, because the Day will bring it to light. It will be revealed with fire, and the fire will test the quality of each man's work. If what he has built survives, he will receive his reward. If it is burned up, he will suffer loss; he himself will be saved, but only as one escaping through the flames.

The Right Stuff

missionary: *a person sent by a church to do religious work and spread the Gospel*

Paul was a **missionary** and an expert at starting and building churches. He compared what he did to building a building and warned that all buildings should be built with great care, especially spiritual buildings like the Church. God laid the foundation for his Church when he sent his Son Jesus. Anyone who tries to build on any other foundation is rejecting the one God has already laid, and that will not work with God.

Anyone who builds a building must choose the kind of materials to build with—steel, brick, wood, straw—and some materials are better than others (brick is better than straw, etc.). Those who want to build a spiritual building (the Church, their life) must choose between indestructible high-quality materials like gold, silver, and costly stones (sound Bible doctrines like the death, burial, and resurrection of Jesus, holy living) and destructible low-quality materials like wood, hay, and straw (unsound, feel-good, no-demand doctrines). All structures face the test of high winds, hard rains, heat, or cold. And all spiritual buildings face the day of judgment. These will test the quality of the builder's work.

Builders who want their buildings to stand should use the best materials. Builders of spiritual buildings who have used indestructible high-quality materials will receive a reward in heaven because what they did will survive the day of judgment. Builders of spiritual buildings who have used destructible low-quality materials will survive, but suffer great loss and have no reward.

Arnold G. Fruchtenbaum: The concern of this judgment is whether the believer followed what God's will was for him or not. If a believer is doing the will of the Lord, obeys His commandments, and fulfills the ministry for which he received his spiritual gifts, then he is building on the foundation with gold, silver, and precious stones. But where he falls short of these things, he is building wood, hay, and stubble.[9]

Jesus told a story about two men who built themselves a house. One man dug deep and built his house upon a rock. But the other man built his house on top of the ground. Later, a storm came, it rained, the river got out of its banks, and floodwaters beat vehemently upon both houses. The house built upon the rock stood. But the house built upon the ground collapsed. A giant flood cannot do much to a large rock, but it can turn the ground into mud and wash it away. Building materials are very important from the foundation to the top of the building.

Notice that the main issue is the quality of the building materials, not the quantity. A small amount of gold, silver, and costly stones will survive a fire, but a huge mansion of wood and straw will not. Some believers will receive a reward in heaven, even though they didn't build very much, because they used the right materials. Other believers will receive no reward in heaven, even though they built all their life, be-

☞ **GO TO:**

2 Corinthians 5:10 (judgment)

What Others are Saying:

☞ **GO TO:**

Luke 6:46–49 (house)

1 Corinthians 10:4 (rock)

Remember This . . .

Something to Ponder

☞ **GO TO:**

2 John 1:8 (rewarded)

KEY Symbols:

Foundation
Jesus
HIS BIRTH, TEACHINGS, DEATH,
ETC.

☞ **GO TO:**

1 Corinthians 6:1
(disputes)

Jude 6; 2 Peter 2:4
(angels)

What Others
are Saying:

*Lucifer: one of Satan's
names*

cause they didn't use the right materials. What kind of building materials are you using?

Fulfillment: Many people give no thought to their heavenly
reward, but God wants us to build the biblical way so we can
be <u>rewarded</u> fully. That which honors Jesus is worthy of a
full reward; that which doesn't honor him is worthless. This
principle will be very important when the believer stands
before the throne on the day of judgment.

> **1 Corinthians 6:1–4** If any of you has a dispute with
> another, dare he take it before the ungodly for judg-
> ment instead of before the saints? Do you not know
> that the saints will judge the world? And if you are to
> judge the world, are you not competent to judge trivial
> cases? Do you not know that we will judge angels? How
> much more the things of this life! Therefore, if you have
> disputes about such matters, appoint as judges even
> men of little account in the church!

I Can't Believe You Didn't Know That

Believers are told to settle their <u>disputes</u> with each other within
the Church. Those who go to court against each other are often
asking unbelievers to rule on their problems. More often than
not, this shames the Church. Knowing that some may think
Church members are not qualified to settle the disputes of others,
Paul asks, "Don't you know that believers will judge the world,
and if God trusts us to do a great task like that, don't you think
believers are qualified to judge trivial matters? Don't you know
that believers will judge <u>angels</u>?"

Dave Breese: The devil, as you know, is an angel. Therefore, the
devil will be a part of this group that is judged by you, and by
me. . . . We will be a part of that tribunal that makes right everything that is wrong in the world.[10]

Billy Graham: Is it not stranger still that angels themselves will
be judged by believers who were once sinners? Such judgment,
however, apparently applies only to those fallen angels who followed **Lucifer**.[11]

Fulfillment: Believers are going to be given <u>authority</u> over the nations during the Millennium. We will <u>reign</u> with Christ, solve problems, and pass judgment on fallen angels. This may seem like an impossible task to some, but the **Holy Spirit** will help us with it.

Unfulfilled
Millennium

Holy Spirit: the Spirit of God, or God himself

The Second Coming	Scripture

The tragic events in Israel's history are given to prevent others from making the same mistakes. .... 1 Corinthians 10:11

Dig Deeper

> **1 Corinthians 9:24–25** Do you not know that in a race all the runners run, but only one gets the prize? Run in such a way as to get the prize. Everyone who competes in the games goes into strict training. They do it to get a crown that will not last; but we do it to get a crown that will last forever.

☞ **GO TO:**

Revelation 2:26 (authority)

2 Timothy 2:12; Revelation 20:4 (reign)

I Want A Real One

Most scholars think Paul loved sporting events because he often used them to illustrate the things of God. This illustration refers to the fact that many contestants entered the Greek races, but only one came in first; also, that even though the contestants trained very hard for those races, the winner's crown of laurel leaves soon dried out. Then Paul plainly states that Christians are striving for crowns that will last forever.

Incorruptible Crown: a crown that lasts forever

temptation: an inward pull to doing wrong

soul winners: those who win others to Christ

Theodore H. Epp: The word "crown" implies a kingdom. A crown is not just something beautiful to look at; it speaks of a reward in connection with a kingdom. A crown is placed upon a king because he has dominion over a certain area. Christ's rewards have to do with sharing the rulership of His kingdom.[12]

What Others are Saying:

☞ **GO TO:**

2 Corinthians 1:14 (Rejoicing)

Believers can win five crowns:

1. **Incorruptible Crown** for those who overcome **temptation** (1 Corinthians 9:25)

2. Crown of <u>Rejoicing</u> for **soul winners** (1 Thessalonians 2:19–20)

3. Crown of Life for those who give up their life for Christ (James 1:12; Revelation 2:10)

Remember This . . .

4. Crown of Righteousness for those who have longed for the Second Coming (2 Timothy 4:8)

5. Crown of Glory for faithful teachers and preachers (1 Peter 5:2–4)

Considering that believers will be given valuable rewards in heaven, isn't it wise to discipline ourselves and to use our lives to honor Jesus? Isn't it foolish to aimlessly drift through life doing things that dishonor him?

Fulfillment: Those Christians who use their lives to serve Christ are storing up treasure in heaven. Their treasure will be given to them shortly after the Rapture of the Church.

Dig Deeper

The Rapture	Scripture
The faithful will not be found lacking at the Rapture.	1 Corinthians 1:6–8
Rewards beyond our imagination await the faithful.	1 Corinthians 2:9
Every believer will be judged fairly and receive praise from God.	1 Corinthians 4:5
Satan can harm the flesh, but not the spirit of an unfaithful believer.	1 Corinthians 5:5
God raised Jesus from the dead and he will raise his people also.	1 Corinthians 6:14
The Lord's Supper looks to the death of Jesus and the Rapture of his church.	1 Corinthians 11:26
Death entered the world by a man (Adam) and it will be removed by a man (Jesus).	1 Corinthians 15:21–22
Not everyone will die, but everyone will receive a new body.	1 Corinthians 15:51
The Rapture will take place in a split second.	1 Corinthians 15:52
Our new bodies will be immortal.	1 Corinthians 15:53

> **1 Corinthians 15:24–26** Then the end will come, when he hands over the kingdom to God the Father after he has destroyed all dominion, authority and power. For he must reign until he has put all his enemies under his feet. The last enemy to be destroyed is death.

☞ **GO TO:**

1 Corinthians 15:22 (Adam)

Genesis 3:1–19 (die)

Revelation 19:11–21 (Lord)

Revelation 20:1–6 (reign)

Revelation 20:7 (thousand)

Revelation 20:10 (Lake)

Revelation 20:14; 21:4 (death)

The End

Because <u>Adam</u> and Eve sinned people <u>die</u> and their bodies return to the dust. But the dead will be raised in the Rapture and taken to heaven with those believers who are alive at that time. That will be followed by the seven-year Tribulation Period and the Second Coming of our <u>Lord</u>. We will <u>reign</u> with him while Satan is bound for a thousand years during the Millennium. After the <u>thousand</u> years have passed, Satan will be released for a short time, but he will eventually be cast into the <u>Lake</u> of Fire. Finally, even <u>death</u> will be destroyed and it will exist no more.

The end of things on earth will come after Jesus turns the kingdom over to his Father. But that will not happen until after Jesus puts down all of our enemies. He must reign until that happens. And the last enemy to be destroyed will be death, not Satan.

William Barclay: As God sent forth His Son to redeem the world so in the end God will receive back a world redeemed, and then there will be nothing in heaven or in earth outside the love and power of God.[13]

Fulfillment: Anytime Satan is free there will be sin and death on earth. But Jesus will put an end to them all: Satan, sin, and death. Then he will turn this creation back over to God and subordinate himself to the Father.

What Others are Saying:

Unfulfilled

After the Millennium

2 CORINTHIANS

> **2 Corinthians 4:14** Because we know that the one who raised the Lord Jesus from the dead will also raise us with Jesus and present us with you in his presence.

We Go, Too

Paul knew that death was not the end of Jesus. Our Lord had been raised from the dead when he talked to Paul on the road to <u>Damascus</u>. So Paul was absolutely sure that the resurrection of Jesus

☞ **GO TO:**

Acts 9:1–19 (Damascus)

☞ **GO TO:**

Colossians 1:19–22 (God)

What Others are Saying:

Unfulfilled
Rapture

Dig Deeper

was an accomplished fact. And because of this he was persuaded that we will be raised from the dead too and that we will be taken into the very presence of <u>God</u>.

William Barclay: He was able to speak with such courage and such disregard of personal safety because he believed that even if death took him, the God who raised up Jesus Christ could and would also raise him up. He was certain that he could draw on a power which was sufficient for life and greater than death.[14]

Fulfillment: Multitudes are going to beat death and the grave. Following the Rapture, we will be presented holy in the sight of God, without blemish and free from accusation.

The Rapture	Scripture
The things on earth are temporary, but the things in heaven last forever.	2 Corinthians 4:17–18
If a believer's earthly body is destroyed, he will receive a heavenly body.	2 Corinthians 5:1–4
If a believer's spirit leaves its body, it goes to be with Jesus.	2 Corinthians 5:6–8
Every believer must go before Jesus to receive or lose rewards.	2 Corinthians 5:10
Sorrow that causes repentance leads to salvation; otherwise to judgment.	2 Corinthians 7:10
The Church will be presented to Jesus as the Bride of Christ.	2 Corinthians 11:2

GALATIANS

Galatians 6:7–9 Do not be deceived: God cannot be mocked. A man reaps what he sows. The one who sows to please his sinful nature, from that nature will reap destruction; the one who sows to please the Spirit, from the Spirit will reap eternal life. Let us not become weary in doing good, for at the proper time we will reap a harvest if we do not give up.

The Law Of The Harvest

Every farmer knows if he sows corn, he will harvest corn; if he sows wheat, he will harvest wheat. The crop is determined by the kind of seed sown. This is an immutable law of nature. We should not deceive ourselves about life because we are unable to deceive God. If a person's life doesn't please God, then he will die without pleasing God—his harvest will be destruction. But if a person's life pleases God, then he will die pleasing God—his harvest will be eternal life. So it is with the Law of the Harvest: the one who uses all of his time, talent, and resources to satisfy himself will be destroyed; but the one who uses some of it to do things for God will reap eternal life. Hence, we should keep sowing and be patient because there will be a harvest.

Theodore H. Epp: Galatians 6:7–9 tells us that to sow to the flesh, to use our resources to fulfill selfish personal desires, will result in spiritual decay. But to yield ourselves to the Holy Spirit in our thinking, planning, praying and believing will result in abundant living.[15]

William Barclay: If a man allows the lower side of his nature to dominate him, in the end he can expect nothing but a harvest of trouble. But if a man keeps on always walking the high way, and always doing the fine thing, he may have to wait long, but in the end God repays.[16]

Paul is not teaching salvation by works. The only _way_ to please God with your life is to serve Christ.

Fulfillment: A farmer cannot sow seed one day and harvest a crop the next. And the size of the harvest depends on the amount of seed sown. A good harvest takes time and lots of seed. The judgment may not be as soon as we think, and it may seem like we will never be rewarded, but it is a law that cannot be broken. Wait patiently for the Rapture and keep on sowing.

The Rapture	Scripture
It is the will of God that Jesus deliver us from this world.	Galatians 1:4

What Others are Saying:

☞ **GO TO:**

John 14:6 (way)

WARNING

Unfulfilled Rapture

Dig Deeper

Dig Deeper

The Great White Throne	Scripture
Those who teach false doctrines will pay a terrible penalty.	Galatians 5:10
The list of sins that will send a person to hell is long.	Galatians 5:19–21

EPHESIANS

> **Ephesians 5:5–6** For of this you can be sure: No immoral, impure or greedy person—such a man is an idolater—has any inheritance in the kingdom of Christ and of God. Let no one deceive you with empty words, for because of such things God's wrath comes on those who are disobedient.

A Sure Thing

sin: missing the mark, wrongdoing

Some rightly argue that **sin** in this life has its own rewards. The alcoholic often loses his job, health, and family. The drug addict often loses his money, property, health, and life. Premarital sex results in more than one million teenage American girls getting pregnant out of wedlock each year. Divorce results in 35–40 percent of America's children living in single parent homes. Crime results in American taxpayers having to shell out $10–20 billion per year. No one can deny the terrible consequences of sin in this life.

☞ GO TO:

Matthew 5:27–30 (hell)

John 3:36 (wrath)

Matthew 5:21–22 (judgment)

But the problem is that some wrongly say the tragic price of immorality ends for each person when they die. There are many in the world, and even many in the Church, who say there is no such thing as a place called **hell**, and no such thing as the <u>wrath</u> or <u>judgment</u> of God. Their words are **empty** and should not be believed. Sin upsets God and we can be sure that morally impure people will be excluded from the kingdom of heaven.

What Others are Saying:

hell: a place of eternal punishment

empty: meaningless

William Barclay: The gravest disservice that any man can do to a fellow man is to make him think lightly of sin. Any teaching which belittles the horror and the terror of sin is poisonous teaching. Paul besought his converts not to be led away and deceived with those empty words which took the terror and the sting from the idea of sin.[17]

The Pulpit Commentary: Scripture tells us plainly that sins of impurity entail exclusion from "the kingdom of Christ and of God" (Ephesians 5:5); that he will judge whoremongers and adulterers (Hebrews 8:5), and that "the abominable, and murderers, and whoremongers, and sorcerers, and idolaters, and all liars, shall have their part in the lake that burneth with fire and brimstone" (Revelation 21:8).[18]

What Others are Saying:

This does not mean a person can enter the kingdom by living a morally pure life. But it does mean that those who have truly accepted Jesus as their Savior will give up their greed and idolatry. When Christ is Lord of a person's life, it shows.

WARNING

Fulfillment: Jesus warned that false prophets will arise and <u>deceive</u> many. Those who listen to them will come under the wrath of God, be excluded from the kingdom when Jesus <u>comes</u> back, and be made to stand before the Great White Throne of God.

Unfulfilled

Tribulation Period

After the Millennium

The Millennium	Scripture
History is moving toward the reign of Jesus over all things in heaven and on earth.	Ephesians 1:10

Dig Deeper

> **Ephesians 5:25–27** Husbands, love your wives, just as Christ loved the church and gave himself up for her to make her holy, cleansing her by the washing with water through the word, and to present her to himself as a radiant church, without stain or wrinkle or any other blemish, but holy and blameless.

☞ **GO TO:**

Matthew 24:11, 24 (deceive)

Matthew 25:31–46 (comes)

Ephesians 2:1–2 (gave)

Matthew 27:32–56 (crucified)

Your Past, Present, And Future

This passage is really a teaching about what God wants in the relationship between a husband and wife, but it also contains great truths about the past, present, and future of the Church. The past event: Jesus died for the Church. His life was not taken from him, he <u>gave</u> it up because he loves us. It was an unselfish sacrifice for our benefit and it was accomplished when he was **crucified**.

The present event: his **holy** Church is being cleansed by the "*washing with water through the word.*" True Church members are constantly undergoing change for the better and the agent of that

crucified: *nailed to a cross*

holy: *separated or set apart*

☞ **GO TO:**

John 15:3; 17:17 (Word)

stain: *sign of sin*

wrinkle: *sign of old age*

blemish: *scars, wounds, or imperfections*

What Others are Saying:

Partially Fulfilled
Rapture

Dig Deeper

change is the Bible. The <u>Word</u> of God is read or proclaimed and people respond by abandoning their sins, worshiping God, and doing acts of charity.

The future event: the Church will be presented to Jesus radiant—without **stain**, **wrinkle** or **blemish**—holy and blameless. On earth the Church has many flaws, but in heaven the flaws will be eliminated, the Church will take on the glory of Christ, and it will be accounted blameless before God.

John F. Walvoord: The cleansing "by the washing with water through the Word" refers to the cleansing power of the Word of God, not to the baptismal ceremony as some have taken it. This is the basic reason for expository preaching and the study of Scripture. The goal is not simply to comprehend the truth but to apply it in its sanctifying power to the individual life.[19]

Fulfillment: Jesus is not acting haphazardly. His ultimate goal is to redeem a people, help them change their ways, and have them presented to himself in heaven in such a way that no harm can ever come to them.

The Rapture	Scripture
The Holy Spirit is the beginning of what Christians will receive and a sign of more to come.	Ephesians 1:14
Christians have a great inheritance in the Lord.	Ephesians 1:18
Christians will be exhibits of God's grace in the ages to come.	Ephesians 2:7
The Holy Spirit is evidence of our salvation until we are presented to Jesus.	Ephesians 4:30

PHILIPPIANS

Philippians 2:9–11 Therefore God exalted him to the highest place and gave him the name that is above every name, that at the name of Jesus every knee should bow, in heaven and on earth and under the earth, and every tongue confess that Jesus Christ is Lord, to the glory of God the Father.

The Real CEO

Paul is saying that because Jesus humbled himself and died on a cross, God honored him by giving him the highest place in the kingdom. Other Scriptures say Jesus is seated at the <u>right hand</u> of God. God has also given him a <u>name</u> greater than the name of any other being who ever lived. In fact, the time will come when every knee will bow at the mention of his name. This includes everyone in heaven (Christians, angels), everyone on earth (the Jews, others), and everyone under the earth (Satan, demons, the lost). Everyone will also confess that Jesus is **Lord**.

☞ **GO TO:**

Romans 8:34;
  Colossians 3:1;
  Hebrews 10:12;
  1 Peter 3:22
  (right hand)

Matthew 1:21 (name)

Oliver B. Greene: The tongue of the atheist, the tongue of the pagan, the tongue of the blasphemer, the tongue of the ungodly—ALL will one day confess that Jesus is God's Christ—*to the glory of God.*[20]

What Others are Saying:

Lord: *the One who is over everything*

Billy Graham: The wicked angels would never want to call God "Father," though they may call Lucifer "father," as many Satan worshipers do. They are in revolt against God and will never voluntarily accept His sovereign lordship, except in that Day of Judgment when every knee will bow and every tongue confess that Jesus Christ is Lord.[21]

David Hocking: The greatest thing we can do as believers is praise Jesus Christ as Lord to the glory of God the Father. And when we proclaim Him as Lord, let no one misunderstand—we are proclaiming Him as the Lord Jehovah of the Old Testament, the Almighty God in human flesh![22]

☞ **GO TO:**

Matthew 7:22–23 (Lord)

Fulfillment: Those sincere believers who confess Jesus is Lord here on earth will do it again in heaven shortly after the Rapture. Those pretenders who call him <u>Lord</u> and all those who have never called him Lord will be forced to do so at the Great White Throne judgment following the Millennium.

Unfulfilled
Rapture
After the Millennum

The Rapture	Scripture
God will complete his purpose in the life of every believer.	Philippians 1:6
Christians who spread the Word of God will not lose their reward.	Philippians 2:16

Dig Deeper

The Rapture	Scripture
Being raised from the dead in the Rapture should be more important than anything in life.	Philippians 3:11
Christians are citizens of heaven who should wait for Jesus to return, to give them a new body, and to subdue all things.	Philippians 3:20–21

Dig Deeper

COLOSSIANS

> **Colossians 3:23–25** Whatever you do, work at it with all your heart, as working for the Lord, not for men, since you know that you will receive an inheritance from the Lord as a reward. It is the Lord Christ you are serving. Anyone who does wrong will be repaid for his wrong, and there is no favoritism.

☞ **GO TO:**

Ephesians 1:13–14; Colossians 1:12 (inheritance)

Galatians 6:7–10 (God)

2 Corinthians 5:10 (Judgment Seat of Christ)

Revelation 20:11–15 (Great White Throne)

You Have Inherited A Great Fortune

This passage was addressed to Christians who were slaves in Paul's lifetime, but the teachings are still applicable to all Christians. Slaves worked long and hard for little or no pay. Inheriting anything was out of the question. Yet Paul advised them to work without grumbling or complaining, to work enthusiastically and cheerfully, to do it like they were working for the Lord instead of people. Christians know they will receive an <u>inheritance</u> from Jesus in heaven. They are his representatives here on earth, and any good is done for him. Those who wrong Christians will be repaid by <u>God</u>. They are in his hands and he will show no partiality or favoritism when he judges them.

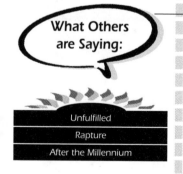

What Others are Saying:

Unfulfilled
Rapture
After the Millennium

Life Application Bible Commentary: Christians work first for the Lord Jesus Christ and second for the companies that write their paychecks. No matter what the job, our first goal is serving Jesus.[23]

Fulfillment: Christians will appear before the <u>Judgment Seat of Christ</u> and receive or lose rewards shortly after the Rapture. Non-Christians will go before the <u>Great White Throne</u> of God after the Millennium.

The Rapture	Scripture
The Christian's hope (rewards, eternal life) is in heaven.	Colossians 1:5
Christians are partakers in the inheritance of all who belong to Jesus.	Colossians 1:12
Christians will go before Jesus holy and free of blame.	Colossians 1:22
When Jesus returns, Christians will be raised and appear with him in glory.	Colossians 3:4

The Tribulation Period	Scripture
Because of sexual sins, impurity, lust, and idolatry God will send tribulation.	Colossians 3:5–6

Dig Deeper

1 THESSALONIANS

> **1 Thessalonians 4:13–17** Brothers, we do not want you to be ignorant about those who fall asleep, or to grieve like the rest of men, who have no hope. We believe that Jesus died and rose again and so we believe that God will bring with Jesus those who have fallen asleep in him. According to the Lord's own word, we tell you that we who are still alive, who are left till the coming of the Lord, will certainly not precede those who have fallen asleep. For the Lord himself will come down from heaven, with a loud command, with the voice of the archangel and with the trumpet call of God, and the dead in Christ will rise first. After that, we who are still alive and are left will be caught up together with them in the clouds to meet the Lord in the air. And so we will be with the Lord forever.

The Rapture

The Thessalonian believers seemed to think that Christians who died before the Rapture should somehow be separated from Christians alive during the Rapture. They were worried that they might not see their deceased loved ones again. This was a misunderstanding that Paul sought to clear up. He did not want them worrying about those who had died (or those who had "*fallen asleep*"); and he did not want them grieving over their loved ones like "*oth-*

☞ **GO TO:**

John 11:1–16 (asleep)

☞ **GO TO:**

Ephesians 2:12 (hope)

Romans 10:9–13 (believe)

1 Corinthians 15:52 (trumpet)

Lord: Jesus

archangel: a leader or angel of the highest rank

caught up: Raptured

What Others are Saying:

ers which have no <u>hope</u>" (the lost). He pointed out that we <u>believe</u> Jesus died and rose again, and we believe that when he returns he will bring with him the souls and spirits of believers who have died. Paul assured the Thessalonian believers that he had a direct promise from Jesus that those who are living when Jesus returns will not displace or hinder the resurrection of those who have died.

After addressing the misunderstanding, Paul gave an explanation of what will happen. He said the **Lord** will descend from heaven and give a very loud command. His voice will sound like the voice of an **archangel**. The <u>trumpet</u> of God will sound and the dead in Christ will rise first. This will include every Christian that has died since the beginning of Christianity. After that, all Christians who have not yet died, the ones who are alive at the time the dead are raised—will be **caught up** with the resurrected believers to join Jesus in the air.

Oliver B. Greene: The early Christians called their burial grounds "cemetery." (The Greek word means *dormitory* or *sleeping chamber*.) In the true sense of the word, the believer's body is put in a grave ("dormitory")—a crypt or sleeping chamber in a mausoleum—and it will remain there until the resurrection.[24]

Charles Capps: The "trump of God" in 1 Thessalonians 4:16 and Revelation 4:1 is not the same as the seventh angelic trumpet mentioned in Revelation 11:15. The trumpet of the seventh angel signals a series of events which will take place over several days. The trump of God signals an event which will take place in the twinkling of an eye. So they can't be the same.[25]

Norbert Lieth: [This passage] isn't referring to a general resurrection. Only the dead in Christ and those who are alive in Christ will be raised or transformed. All the other dead will remain in their graves until the day of judgment.[26]

Hal Lindsey: We will suddenly one day just blast off into space. Faster than the eye of the unbeliever can perceive, every living believer on earth will disappear. The world will probably hear a great sonic boom from all our transformed immortal bodies cracking the sound barrier.[27]

Dave Breese: The Rapture is important for many things, but its chief importance is that it marks the end of the epoch of grace and the beginning of the dispensation of the Tribulation.[28]

Do not confuse the Rapture with the Second Coming. Jesus comes *FOR* his church at the Rapture. He comes *WITH* his church at the Second Coming. The Rapture will take place *BEFORE* the Tribulation Period. And the Second Coming will take place *AFTER* the Tribulation Period.

 WARNING

The word *Rapture* is not in the English translations of the Bible, but the concept is. The original New Testament text was written in the Greek language and it used the Greek word *harpazo*. When the Greek was translated into Latin, *harpazo* became *rapere*. When the Latin was translated into English, *rapere* could not be translated into just one word. The combination of words used was "caught up." But the word *rapere* has been Anglicized into the word Rapture and this is the word most Christians now use.

 Remember This . . .

Apart from the grace of God none of us would make it to heaven. But the age of grace will be over when the Rapture occurs. Wouldn't it be wise to accept the grace of God before he completes his Church and turns back to Israel and the Law?

 Something to Ponder

Fulfillment: There are no specific signs of the Rapture. The Bible teaches that it can happen at any time and without any advance notice. However, we do know about many things that will happen after the Rapture and there are signs that all those things are approaching. Therefore, we know that the Rapture is getting close.

Unfulfilled
Rapture

> **1 Thessalonians 5:1–9** Now, brothers, about times and dates we do not need to write to you, for you know very well that the day of the Lord will come like a thief in the night. While people are saying, "Peace and safety," destruction will come on them suddenly, as labor pains on a pregnant woman, and they will not escape. But you, brothers, are not in darkness so that this day should

surprise you like a thief. You are all sons of the light and sons of the day. We do not belong to the night or to the darkness. So then, let us not be like others, who are asleep, but let us be alert and self-controlled. For those who sleep, sleep at night, and those who get drunk, get drunk at night. But since we belong to the day, let us be self-controlled, putting on faith and love as a breastplate, and the hope of salvation as a helmet. For God did not appoint us to suffer wrath but to receive salvation through our Lord Jesus Christ.

Keep Your Eyes Peeled

day of the Lord: the
Tribulation Period

☞ **GO TO:**

Daniel 9:24–27
(covenant)

Jeremiah 6:14; 8:11
(peace)

Joel 2:2; Amos 5:18–20
(darkness)

John 12:36 (light)

Zephaniah 1:14–16;
1 Thessalonians 1:10
(wrath)

Romans 5:8–9 (blood)

Matthew 25:1–13
(asleep)

Revelation 16:15
(awake)

Luke 12:37 (watching)

Hebrews 10:25
(approaching)

This passage addresses the question, When will the **day of the Lord** take place? We are told that we do not need an answer because we already have it. "*The day of the Lord will come like a thief in the night.*" This means it will come unexpectedly.

Notice what the people will be saying when the day of the Lord arrives: "*Peace and safety.*" The peace movement will be very strong and the seven year covenant signed by the Antichrist with many to protect Israel will create a false sense of peace and safety in the world. It will be like it was in Jeremiah's day when people said they had peace, but there was no peace.

Notice also two things about what will happen to unbelievers when the day of the Lord arrives: (1) destruction will come suddenly upon *them*, the unbelievers who are proclaiming peace and safety; and (2) *they*, the unbelievers, will not escape.

Notice four things about believers: (1) believers will not be caught by surprise. They know the signs. They are watching and will not be caught off guard; (2) believers do not belong to the darkness. The day of the Lord is a day of darkness. Believers are children of light; (3) believers are not appointed to suffer wrath. Not one drop of floodwater fell on Noah. Not one spark of fire and brimstone fell on Lot. And not one iota of wrath will fall on believers; and (4) believers are appointed to receive salvation. The blood of Jesus does this.

Finally, notice four things about how believers should react: (1) believers should not fall asleep. All of our life many of us have heard the Second Coming is near. We have heard it so much it would be easy for us to fall asleep. But we should stay awake; (2) believers should watch. Some are critical of Christians who study the prophetic signs, but Jesus wants us to be watching. The Bible says we can see the day approaching; (3) believers should be alert and self-controlled. Some go overboard one way, selling everything, and sitting down to wait on his coming. Others go overboard the other way and scoff at the idea of his <u>coming</u> again. Both attitudes are errant. We should stay busy and never scoff because it will happen when God is ready; and (4) believers should put on faith, love, and hope. Faith comes from hearing the Word. Lovingly anticipating his appearing will be rewarded with a crown of righteousness. And the Second Coming is our <u>hope</u>.

☞ **GO TO:**

2 Peter 3:3–4 (coming)

Titus 2:13 (hope)

William T. James: One day, perhaps quite soon, a leader will step from the ranks of his contemporaries, and through guile, persuasion, and diplomatic acumen unparalleled in the world's long, war-torn history, he will convince even the most skeptical Israeli hard-liner to trust him to ensure Israel's security. It will be the *covenant made with death and hell* foretold by the prophet Daniel, which Isaiah the prophet said God Himself will annul (Isaiah 28:18).[29]

What Others are Saying:

Hal Lindsey: The Rapture delivers believers from this period of destruction.[30]

KEY POINT

Believers will not go through the Tribulation Period.

Jack Van Impe: Never in twenty-five centuries has there been an Israel that could sign a world peace contract with the one who comes to power, whoever he is and whenever it is. . . . The clock is ticking. The end of time as we know it is fast approaching. The signs are everywhere—even in the heavens.[31]

THE JACKSON SUN, JULY 22, 1999 . . .

In a communiqué distributed by the Government Press Office (GPO) Sept. 11, the death toll of terrorism victims in the five years since the Oslo agreement [a peace accord between the PLO and Israel] is compared to that of the preceding years. The statistics show that more people have been killed by Palestinian terrorists in the 5 years since the first Oslo agreement was signed in September 1993 (279) than in the 15 preceding years (254).[32]

RELATED CURRENT EVENTS

• • •

Remember
This . . .

Unfulfilled

Rapture

Tribulation Period

DISPATCH FROM JERUSALEM, NOVEMBER/DECEMBER 1998 . . .

On Wednesday March 3rd after a visit to Israel, in a speech on the floor of the Senate, Florida Senator, Connie Mack pointed out that, "The Palestinian leadership does not want peace, but rather a state it can use to 'eliminate the State of Israel,' in keeping with the still legally unchanged PLO National Council. While the government of Israel makes good faith efforts to reach a peace agreement, the Palestinian Authority teaches children hatred.[33]

• • •

HOPE FOR TODAY, MAY 1999 . . .

The Palestinians insisted Wednesday that a permanent peace agreement with Israel be concluded by May, rejecting a later target date floated by Israeli Prime Minister Ehud Barak. Palestinian Planning Minister Nabil Shaath said that in exchange for the Palestinians' decision to forgo a unilateral declaration of statehood in May 1999—the original deadline for a peace accord—they were assured by the European Union and the United States that an extension should not exceed one year.[34]

Because peace negotiations have been going on for many years, some do not realize the significance of what is happening. This is because they do not understand that the negotiations are going through stages. Most of the current agreements are just steps toward a final settlement. The important thing now is the fact that negotiations have now reached the final stage and a comprehensive agreement is on the horizon.

Fulfillment: Peace negotiations in the Middle East have now reached a fever pitch. Experts say it is just a matter of time until a comprehensive agreement is signed. This is the kind of situation that will prevail when the Tribulation Period arrives. But the Rapture will occur first.

The Rapture	Scripture
Jesus rescues Christians from God's forthcoming wrath.	1 Thessalonians 1:10
Saved souls are the joy of Christians.	1 Thessalonians 2:19–20

Dig Deeper

2 THESSALONIANS

> **2 Thessalonians 1:6–10** God is just: He will pay back trouble to those who trouble you and give relief to you who are troubled, and to us as well. This will happen when the Lord Jesus is revealed from heaven in blazing fire with his powerful angels. He will punish those who do not know God and do not obey the gospel of our Lord Jesus. They will be punished with everlasting destruction and shut out from the presence of the Lord and from the majesty of his power on the day he comes to be glorified in his holy people and to be marveled at among all those who have believed. This includes you, because you believed our testimony to you.

Trouble For Trouble

The wicked understand practically nothing about the nature of God. He is a God who judges sin and all his judgments are just. If he acted unjustly in any way, he would sin, but he is holy and cannot do that. So his very nature requires him to send trouble upon those who trouble his people. If someone enslaves his people during the Tribulation Period, they will be enslaved. If someone kills his people, they will be <u>killed</u>.

It is also the nature of God to give relief to his people. He will do this when he comes in judgment at the end of the Tribulation Period. His powerful <u>angels</u> will be with him to gather those who have afflicted his people and bind them for judgment. Jesus will pour out his diving anger upon them: (1) because they did not take the opportunity to know God, and (2) because they refused to obey the **Gospel**. These will be people who heard the Gospel, but refused to respond.

The result of the Lord's divine anger will be horrible for the lost: "*They will be punished with everlasting destruction,*" which means they will be cast into the <u>Lake of Fire</u>. They will also be "*shut out from the presence of the Lord,*" which means they will be expelled from his kingdom. And they will be shut out "*from the*

☞ **GO TO:**

Revelation 13:10 (killed)

Mark 8:38 (angels)

Revelation 20:11–15 (Lake of Fire)

Gospel: *good news of Jesus Christ*

majesty of his power," which means they will be banished from the source of all good things.

Victory will come when he returns to display his church at the end of the Tribulation Period. Then people will marvel at what he has done for his followers.

What Others are Saying:

Billy Graham: For the Christian believer, the return of Christ is comforting, for at last men and women of faith will be exonerated. They will be avenged. The nonbeliever will see and understand why true Christians marched to the sound of another drum. But for the sinful unbeliever, the triumphant return of Christ will prove disastrous, because Christ's return ensures final judgment.[35]

WARNING

Unfulfilled
Second Coming

Everlasting destruction does not mean total annihilation or ceasing to exist. It means being cast into the Lake of Fire and being cut off from the goodness of God forever.

Fulfillment: Terrible calamities await all who harm those who turn to God after the Rapture. The wicked will receive affliction for affliction, misery for misery, woe for woe. Those who harm God's people will be repaid at the Second Coming.

> **2 Thessalonians 2:1–12** Concerning the coming of our Lord Jesus Christ and our being gathered to him, we ask you, brothers, not to become easily unsettled or alarmed by some prophecy, report or letter supposed to have come from us, saying that the day of the Lord has already come. Don't let anyone deceive you in any way, for that day will not come until the rebellion occurs and the man of lawlessness is revealed, the man doomed to destruction. He will oppose and will exalt himself over everything that is called God or is worshiped, so that he sets himself up in God's temple, proclaiming himself to be God. Don't you remember that when I was with you I used to tell you these things? And now you know what is holding him back, so that he may be revealed at the proper time. For the secret power of lawlessness is already at work; but the one who now holds it back will continue to do so till he is taken out of the way. And then the lawless one will be revealed, whom the Lord Jesus will overthrow with the

> breath of his mouth and destroy by the splendor of his coming. The coming of the lawless one will be in accordance with the work of Satan displayed in all kinds of counterfeit miracles, signs and wonders, and in every sort of evil that deceives those who are perishing. They perish because they refused to love the truth and so be saved. For this reason God sends them a powerful delusion so that they will believe the lie and so that all will be condemned who have not believed the truth but have delighted in wickedness.

Do Not Be Deceived

This passage was written to correct several mistaken beliefs that cropped up in the early Thessalonian church. Apparently someone created an erroneous document or report, falsely attributed it to Paul, and circulated it among the believers there. Some church members thought it was true and wrongly believed Jesus had already come to Rapture his Church, that they had somehow missed this great gathering in the sky, that the Antichrist had already arrived, and that they had entered the Tribulation Period.

Paul warned them not to become alarmed and not to let anyone deceive them about these things. He pointed out that there will be a great **rebellion** against God before the Tribulation Period arrives. This rebellion will precede the Tribulation Period and pave the way for the appearance of the **man doomed to destruction**.

One of the things this wicked man (the Antichrist) will do is to think he is greater than everything that is worshiped. He will go to the Temple and announce that he is God. Daniel called this terrible act "the abomination that causes desolation" and Jesus himself spoke of it. From what they said it is obvious that this will take place at the Tribulation Period midpoint and it implies that the Temple in Jerusalem will be rebuilt. When the Jews see this, many of them will flee into the mountains.

Paul reminded the Thessalonians that he told them all these things when he was with them. He rebuked them because they had been taught and should not have allowed themselves to be so easily led astray. He reminded them that they knew what is holding the Antichrist back, and that it is being done to prevent this wicked man from being revealed before God's appointed time.

rebellion: apostasy

man doomed to destruction: the Antichrist

☞ **GO TO:**

Daniel 9:27; Matthew 24:15 (the abomination that causes desolation)

Matthew 24:16 (flee)

☞ **GO TO:**

Revelation 19:19–20
(capture)

Paul assured the Thessalonians that the **secret power of law-lessness** was already with them, and working among them but that the Antichrist himself will continue to be held back. Hence the power of rebellion is working in the world, but it is partially restrained and it will remain partially restrained until the Holy Spirit is taken out of the way. This will happen when the Church is Raptured. The indwelling presence of the Holy Spirit in the Church is helping to check the great rebellion and also prevent-ing the appearance of the Antichrist.

After the Church is Raptured, and the Holy Spirit is removed with it, God will let the Antichrist be revealed. He will rule until Jesus returns at his Second Coming to <u>capture</u> and destroy him. Jesus will do this to the Antichrist because the Antichrist's reign will be brought about by the work of Satan. The Antichrist will use the power of Satan to perform many kinds of counterfeit miracles, signs, and wonders, and to do all kinds of evil things to deceive people. Multitudes will perish because they will not lis-ten to the Word of God when they are exposed to it, and they refuse to be saved while they have the opportunity. God will make sure they are deceived by the Antichrist to punish them for not listening and being saved. He will judge them for rejecting the truth about his Son and for enjoying their life of sin.

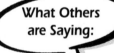

What Others are Saying:

John F. Walvoord: 2 Thessalonians 2:1–4 offers remarkable evi-dence that the rapture of the church occurs before the end-time prophecy. Paul is demonstrating that they are not in the day of the Lord as false teachers have taught them, because the man of law-lessness has not appeared.[36]

Dave Hunt: These apostates, however, will not leave the church and announce themselves as atheists. They will not convert to Buddhism or Hinduism. While there are always some exceptions, it is important to understand that the apostasy doesn't represent a massive defection from Christianity but a turning away from the truth within the professing church.[37]

Dave Breese: Here Paul introduces a character that will be of consequence during the days of the Tribulation. And what does he call him? The great benefactor of mankind? No. The "man of sin" will be revealed, the man whose fundamental nature is sin. He is the embodiment of sin.[38]

What Others are Saying:

Bill Perkins: God currently allows a delicate balance of good and evil in the universe. . . . For every depraved act, there is a righteous deed. As evil builds upon evil, Christianity builds on the Rock. Both evil and good are increasing proportionately on the scales until the day when God removes the counterweight, leaving evil no restraint.[39]

RELATED CURRENT EVENTS

GOOD NEWS, MAY/JUNE 1999 . . .

```
Most U.S. pastors pray fewer than 30 minutes a
day. A study of 572 pastors by church growth
expert C. Peter Wagner showed that 57 percent
pray fewer than 20 minutes a day; about 34 per-
cent spend between 20 minutes and an hour praying
daily.⁴⁰
```

| Unfulfilled |
| Rapture |
| Tribulation Period |
| Second Coming |

Fulfillment: The great rebellion has begun and the Rapture will soon follow. Then there will be two supernatural comings: the first will be the Antichrist and the second will be Jesus. The Antichrist will appear at the beginning of the Tribulation Period and Jesus will appear at the end. In between these two comings will be a seven-year period of great evil, great deception, and great death. When the Temple will be rebuilt is unknown, but most scholars think it will be after the Rapture and all agree that it will be before the Tribulation Period midpoint.

1 TIMOTHY

> **1 Timothy 4:1–4** The Spirit clearly says that in later times some will abandon the faith and follow deceiving spirits and things taught by demons. Such teachings come through hypocritical liars, whose consciences have been seared as with a hot iron. They forbid people to marry and order them to abstain from certain foods, which God created to be received with thanksgiving by those who believe and who know the truth. For everything God created is good, and nothing is to be rejected if it is received with thanksgiving.

Church Age: the time
the true church is on
earth before the Rapture

☞ **GO TO:**

2 Thessalonians 2:3
(rebellion)

Matthew 24:9–11
(persecution)

Matthew 24:12 (love)

1 John 4:1–3 (spirits)

Colossians 2:16 (eating)

What Others
are Saying:

latter times: the last days
of the "times of the
Gentiles"

The Dark Side

There is general agreement that these verses refer to the **Church Age** and especially to the latter part of it leading up to the Rapture. Rebellion against God will increase as the Rapture nears. Persecution and deceit will also increase. The love of many will grow cold. Some will depart from what they once professed to believe and follow other religions (see illustration, page 171). They will be in touch with wandering evil spirits from the sanctuaries of Satan and they will be listening to doctrines taught by demons.

These demonic doctrines will come through hypocritical liars, religious pretenders, false preachers, counterfeit Christians, and the like who will not be grieved by what they do. They will be able to speak demonic doctrines and lies without remorse. Marriage is ordained by God and he created meat to feed his people, but these deluded people will forbid marriage and the eating of animals.

Billy Graham: Demonic activity and Satan worship are on the increase in all parts of the world.[41]

Noah Hutchings: We look over the world today and see the rise of spiritualism, astrology, ESP, mediums talking with the dead, ministers holding seances, devil worship, witchcraft, etc., and we know that we must be living in the **latter times.** Never has there been such a worldwide revival of spiritualism, even in the Dark Ages.[42]

Dave Hunt: No longer clinging to the view that nothing exists except matter, science now admits the reality of a nonmaterial dimension governed by mysterious forces and inhabited by nonmaterial intelligences which it can neither identify nor explain. Every facet of occultism is now being explored as the new hope in medicine, education, psychology, business, military intelligence, and space science. Contact is sought and advice is followed from spirit entities whose trustworthiness cannot be established by scientific means.[43]

Mike Gendron: Our Marching Orders:

- Keep away from every brother who does not live according to apostolic teaching. (2 Thessalonians 3:6)
- Do not associate with anyone who does not obey Paul's instruction (so they will be ashamed). (2 Thessalonians 3:14–15)
- Avoid those who oppose sound doctrine. (Romans 16:17)

- Withdraw from those who advocate a different doctrine. (1 Timothy 6:3–5)
- Be sanctified (set apart) by the truth. (John 17:17)
- Do not be yoked with unbelievers. (1 Corinthians 6:14–17)
- Expose false teachers. (Ephesians 5:11; Revelation 2:2)[44]

☞ **GO TO:**

Ephesians 6:12 (spiritual forces of evil)

When the Sadducees asked Jesus a ridiculous question about marriage, he told them the angels do not marry. And here we have a teaching that demonic spirits will lure people into forbidding marriage in the latter times. Is it possible that the spiritual forces of evil in the heavenly realm are trying to enforce their laws on human beings?

Fulfillment: Interest in the occult is at an all-time high around the world. Pagan religions are promoted under the guise of protecting the environment. Contacting spirits of the dead is no longer taboo and in some circles it is viewed as an act of enlightenment. Cohabitation is common and there are many who wrongly advocate and practice vegetarianism in the name of Christianity (see GWHN, pages 3–4, 156). Many of those involved in these things are religious people and some are associated with the Church.

Something to Ponder

Continuously Being Fulfilled
Church Age

The Great White Throne	Scripture
Some sins are obvious; others become evident only with time.	1 Timothy 5:24

The Rapture	Scripture
Good deeds are obvious, but those that are not cannot be hidden.	1 Timothy 5:25
Christians have a command that must be kept until the Rapture.	1 Timothy 6:11–14
Living or dead, Christians will be judged by Jesus at the Rapture.	2 Timothy 4:1
A crown of righteousness will be given to those who long for his appearing.	2 Timothy 4:8
Christians will be delivered from evil in this world and transferred safely to heaven.	2 Timothy 4:18
The hope of Christians is the appearance of Jesus in glory to Rapture his Church.	Titus 2:13

Dig Deeper

2 TIMOTHY

> **2 Timothy 3:1–5** But mark this: There will be terrible times in the last days. People will be lovers of themselves, lovers of money, boastful, proud, abusive, disobedient to their parents, ungrateful, unholy, without love, unforgiving, slanderous, without self-control, brutal, not lovers of the good, treacherous, rash, conceited, lovers of pleasure rather than lovers of God—having a form of godliness but denying its power. Have nothing to do with them.

☞ **GO TO:**

2 Thessalonians 2:4 (proclaim)

Revelation 18:17 (great wealth)

Daniel 7:8 (boastfully)

Daniel 13:5 (proud)

Matthew 24:9–12 (wickedness)

Mark 13:12 (children)

Daniel 8:25 (stand)

Daniel 8:24; Matthew 24:15 (holy)

1 Timothy 4:3 (forbid marriage)

Matthew 24:12 (love)

Revelation 6:2 (conqueror)

Revelation 13:5–6 (slander)

2 Timothy 3:6 (desires)

Revelation 20:4 (beheaded)

Rough Times

Here Paul offers a partial list of things we can expect in the last days of the Church Age. Evil will prevail and characteristics of the Antichrist will be apparent. Those influenced by the Antichrist will be:

1. Lovers of themselves—the Antichrist will <u>proclaim</u> himself to be God.
2. Lovers of money—world leaders will weep over the loss of their <u>great wealth</u> during the Tribulation Period.
3. Boastful—the Antichrist will speak <u>boastfully</u>.
4. Proud—the Antichrist will utter <u>proud</u> words.
5. Abusive—there will be an increase in <u>wickedness</u> with people hating and betraying each other.
6. Disobedient to their parents—<u>children</u> will rebel against their parents and have them put to death.
7. Ungrateful—Jesus died for the sins of the world, but the Antichrist will take his <u>stand</u> against Christ.
8. Unholy—the Antichrist will kill <u>holy</u> people and defile the holy place with his image.
9. Without love—the false church will <u>forbid marriage</u>, and the <u>love</u> of many will grow cold.
10. Unforgiving—the Antichrist will be a <u>conqueror</u> bent on conquest.
11. Slanderous—the Antichrist will <u>slander</u> the name of God.
12. Without self-control—people will be swayed by evil <u>desires</u> especially sexual desires.
13. Brutal—the Antichrist will have believers <u>beheaded</u> during the Tribulation Period.

14. Not lovers of the good—church leaders should love what is <u>good</u>, hold fast to the message of God and teach sound doctrine, but it will not be so in the last days of the Church Age.

15. Treacherous—the Antichrist will be a liar, breaking his <u>covenant</u> to protect Israel.

16. Rash—the Antichrist will change <u>set times</u> and laws.

17. Conceited—the Antichrist will <u>magnify</u> himself.

18. Lovers of pleasure more than lovers of God—<u>sexual immorality</u> will be a major Tribulation Period sin.

19. Form of godliness—the Antichrist will be a <u>false Christ</u>.

The **spirit of antichrist** is to be against the things of Christ. Notice how this "spirit" and the things the Antichrist himself will do break the Ten Commandments:

1. No other god should be placed before God, but the Antichrist will exalt himself above every god.

2. Idols are forbidden, but the Antichrist will place an image of himself at the Temple.

3. God's name should not be taken in vain, but the Antichrist will call himself God and pretend to be the Christ.

4. The Sabbath day should be kept holy, but the Antichrist will try to change times (the Sabbath) and seasons.

5. People should honor their father and mother, but children will be disobedient to parents, and the Antichrist will show no regard for the gods of his fathers.

6. People should not murder, but the Antichrist will kill the saints.

7. People should not commit adultery, but sexual immorality will be a major sin when the Antichrist reigns.

8. People should not steal, but <u>theft</u> will be a major sin when the Antichrist reigns.

9. False testimony is forbidden, but the Antichrist will be a slanderer.

10. Coveting is forbidden, but people will be lovers of money.

☞ **GO TO:**

Titus 1:6–9 (good)

Daniel 9:27 (covenant)

Daniel 7:25 (set times)

Daniel 11:36 (magnify)

Revelation 9:21 (sexual immorality)

Matthew 24:5, 23–24 (false Christ)

Remember This . . .

spirit of antichrist: any inclination to oppose Christ or be against the things of Christ

☞ **GO TO:**

Revelation 9:21 (theft)

Fulfillment: Some say there is no need for Church members to watch for signs because none have been given to the Church. This is not true. The Church has been told that the spirit of antichrist will prevail and actually pave the way for the arrival of the "man of sin." The current disrespect for the Ten Commandments is a good indication that this is happening.

Dig Deeper

The Church Age	Scripture
The time will come when Church members will not listen to sound doctrine.	2 Timothy 4:3–4

The Millennium	Scripture
If we endure we will reign with him, but if we disown him, he will disown us.	2 Timothy 2:12
When the Millennium begins, Jesus will judge those who turned to him during the Tribulation Period.	2 Timothy 4:1

STUDY QUESTIONS

1. When God judges the lost what will he go by?
2. When will the partial hardening of Jewish hearts cease? What part of Israel will be saved?
3. How is building in the Church with gold, silver, and costly stones different from building with wood, hay, and straw?
4. Name five things that will take place at the Rapture.
5. Will the day of the Lord catch everyone as a thief in the night? Explain.

CHAPTER WRAP-UP

- Paul advised the Galatians to please the Holy Spirit because every man "reaps what he sows." He advised the Corinthians to build on Jesus with sound doctrines and holy living, etc., because the believers' works will be tested and rewards will be passed out for works that last. He also advised the Corinthians to run life's race to win because believers who win will be rewarded with a crown. He advised the Colossians to work with all their heart because believers will receive an inheritance from Jesus as a reward. (Galatians 6:7–9; 1 Corinthians 3:10–15; 1 Corinthians 9:24–25; Colossians 3:23–25)

- Paul advised the Romans not to judge others because they too will be judged and they will have to account to God. He told the Philippians that God has exalted Jesus—every knee will bow and every tongue will confess that he is Lord. (Romans 14:10–12; Philippians 2:9–11)

- Paul said those who reject God's goodness are storing up wrath. All who are self-seeking, who reject the truth and follow evil will receive wrath and anger. The Day of Wrath will come like a thief in the night for those who are not watching for the return of Jesus. When he comes back those who do not know God and do not obey the Gospel will be punished. (Romans 2:5–6, 8–9; 1 Thessalonians 5:1–9; 2 Thessalonians 1:6–10)

- Paul said many who falsely claim to be Christians will abandon the faith and follow deceiving spirits near the end of the Church Age. Terrible times will come and the spirit of antichrist will prevail. This great rebellion will pave the way for the wicked Antichrist who will visit the Temple in Jerusalem and claim to be God. Many will be deceived by his miracles and signs, and they will perish because they refused to love the truth and be saved. We can be sure that the immoral, the impure, and the greedy will not inherit the Kingdom of Christ. (1 Timothy 4:1–3; 2 Timothy 3:1–5; 2 Thessalonians 2:1–12; Ephesians 5:5–6)

- A time will come when the dead in Christ will be raised and all living believers will be raptured; when the Church will be presented to Christ and be found holy and blameless; when the hearts of the Jews will no longer be hardened and the nation will be saved; when Christians will judge the world and angels; when all of God's enemies will be destroyed, including death. (1 Thessalonians 4:13–18; Ephesians 5:25–27; Romans 11:25–27; 1 Corinthians 15:24–26; 1 Corinthians 15:24–26)

8 PROPHECIES IN THE LETTERS WRITTEN BY OTHER APOSTLES

CHAPTER HIGHLIGHTS

- The New Covenant
- Hoarding Wealth
- The Rapture
- Eyewitnesses
- Scoffers and Fallen Angels

Let's Get Started

Following the thirteen New Testament books written by the **apostle** Paul is a series of eight books written by other apostles. These books are sometimes called general **epistles** because they are not directed to a particular person, such as Timothy or Titus, and they are not directed to a particular congregation, such as the one at Corinth or the one at Ephesus. The book of Hebrews is addressed to all Jews who convert to Christianity regardless of where they attend church. And the other seven books are addressed to the **Church** as a whole, not to specific individuals or congregations.

The subject matter is primarily Christian doctrine, but the authors make many appeals for obedience and faithful service. And they include tidbits of prophetic information not found anywhere else in the Bible. God wanted these things included so we dare not neglect them.

apostle: one who is sent out, specifically applied to the twelve disciples, Paul, and other New Testament missionaries

epistles: New Testament letters written by apostles

Church: the followers of Jesus Christ, as opposed to a building where people meet to worship

Larry Richards: Others wrote letters to some of the first century churches, and these are usually called the "general epistles." They include writings of Peter and John, who were apostles, and Jesus' half-brothers James and Jude, who were leaders in the church. They also include the book of Hebrews.[1]

What Others are Saying:

HEBREWS

> **Hebrews 8:7–13** For if there had been nothing wrong with that first covenant, no place would have been sought for another. But God found fault with the people and said: "The time is coming, declares the Lord, when I will make a new covenant with the house of Israel and with the house of Judah. It will not be like the covenant I made with their forefathers when I took them by the hand to lead them out of Egypt, because they did not remain faithful to my covenant, and I turned away from them, declares the Lord. This is the covenant I will make with the house of Israel after that time, declares the Lord. I will put my laws in their minds and write them on their hearts. I will be their God, and they will be my people. No longer will a man teach his neighbor, or a man his brother, saying, 'Know the Lord,' because they will all know me, from the least of them to the greatest. For I will forgive their wickedness and will remember their sins no more." By calling this covenant "new," he has made the first one obsolete; and what is obsolete and aging will soon disappear.

Out With The Old And In With The New

Hebrews: another name for the Israelites, the Jews

Law: all the rules God gave to Moses

grace: the undeserved favor of God

☞ **GO TO:**

Jeremiah 31:31–34 (new covenant)

There were problems with the old covenant God made with Israel when Moses led the **Hebrews** out of Egypt. That covenant was temporary in the sense that it did not permanently deal with sin. It required people to keep the **Law**, but they kept breaking it causing God to find fault with them. So he promised a <u>new covenant</u> with Israel and Judah (see illustration, page 248). This new covenant will not be like the old covenant, the covenant of Law, because the Jews' ancestors failed to keep that one and God finally cancelled it. It will be a new covenant, the covenant of **grace**, written not on tablets of stone like the Ten Commandments, but placed in the minds and written on the hearts of people, giving them a new intimate relationship with God. This inward relationship will mean the Jews will not need priests, such as Aaron was in the wilderness, to teach them because everyone will have a built-in knowledge of God. And this new covenant will be better because God will permanently forgive the people's sins. By calling this a new covenant, God is saying the old covenant made with the Jews is obsolete. Those Jews who accept Christ should go by the new one, not the old one.

GOD'S WORD FOR THE BIBLICALLY-INEPT

John F. Walvoord: The details of the covenant relate primarily to Israel's future in the millennial kingdom. At that time Israel will experience spiritual revival. The knowledge of Christ will be universal, as Christ will be dwelling bodily on earth.[2]

Irving L. Jensen: These promises were better in two respects. First, while the promises of the old covenant pertained mainly to the present life, being promises of length of days, prosperity and national privileges, the promises of the new covenant are principally for spiritual blessings, and they pertain not only to this life but also to the life to come. Second, the promises of the new covenant are not conditional upon man's works, but upon Christ's death. In the old covenant God said, "If ye will." In the new covenant He says, "I will."[3]

People who do not follow God's laws need to have their hearts changed. The indwelling presence of Christ does that. The person who receives Christ has a built-in desire to obey God. Could it be that the reason the Jews failed so often is that they did not have a desire to obey in their heart?

Something to Ponder

Fulfillment: This will be exactly what the writer to the Hebrews says it will be: a new covenant with Israel. The Jews who accept Christ now are under the same covenant of grace the Church is under. And, in the future, the entire nation will be brought under this covenant.

Unfulfilled
Millennium

The Millennium	Scripture
Jesus is God and he will rule in righteousness forever.	Hebrews 1:8
The Jews who accept Jesus will enter the Millennium.	Hebrews 4:6
There will be a Sabbath-rest for the people of God.	Hebrews 4:9
God will make a new covenant with Israel.	Hebrews 10:16–17

Dig Deeper

The Rapture	Scripture
Those who look for Jesus will see him in the Rapture.	Hebrews 9:28

The Second Coming	Scripture
God will destroy all the enemies of Jesus.	Hebrews 11:13

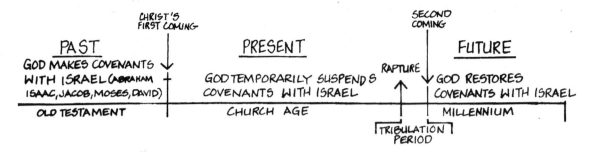

CHRIST'S
FIRST COMING

SECOND
COMING

PAST
GOD MAKES COVENANTS
WITH ISRAEL (ABRAHAM
ISAAC, JACOB, MOSES, DAVID)

PRESENT
GOD TEMPORARILY SUSPENDS
COVENANTS WITH ISRAEL

RAPTURE

FUTURE
GOD RESTORES
COVENANTS WITH ISRAEL

OLD TESTAMENT   CHURCH AGE   MILLENNIUM

TRIBULATION
PERIOD

God's Covenants with Israel

KEY POINT

Two times in the future when wealth will be worthless are during the Tribulation Period and when one stands before the Great White Throne of God.

☞ GO TO:

Revelation 18:1–24 (rich)

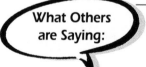

What Others are Saying:

JAMES

> **James 5:1–3** Now listen, you rich people, weep and wail because of the misery that is coming upon you. Your wealth has rotted, and moths have eaten your clothes. Your gold and silver are corroded. Their corrosion will testify against you and eat your flesh like fire. You have hoarded wealth in the last days.

Raise Your Right Hand And Repeat After Me

Everyone who has money would do well to listen to this scathing rebuke of the rich. God is not against people having money, but he is against people permitting money to interfere with their relationship with him. Here he tells the <u>rich</u> who hoard wealth for the last days to cry because misery awaits them. When he says, "*Your wealth has rotted,*" he means the time will come when it will be worthless. Even good clothes and precious metals will be worthless. When the Tribulation Period arrives one's riches will be worthless, and when the judgment comes one's riches could very well be evidence that they did not give to the poor, evidence of greed and selfishness, evidence that will cause the awesome judgment of God to fall on them.

William Barclay: Now the point is that gold and silver do not actually rust; so James in the most vivid way is warning men that even the most precious and even the most apparently indestructible things are doomed to decay and to dissolution. The rust is a proof of the impermanence and the ultimate valuelessness of all earthly things.[4]

Life Application Bible Commentary: Their hoarding will not only demonstrate their wrong priorities, it will also show how their actions deprived the needy of help and resources that could have been given. James has already pointed out that "judgment without mercy will be shown to anyone who has not been merciful" (2:13).[5]

What Others are Saying:

In the last days, people will hoard gold and silver, stocks and bonds, food, and other things in an effort to provide a safety net for themselves during hard times. But the riches they so dearly trust in will become a snare because ultimately only those who trust in God will be safe. Jesus asked, *"What good will it be for a man if he gains the whole world, yet forfeits his soul?"*

Something to Ponder

Fulfillment: It will be useless to hoard treasures during the Tribulation Period. Theft will be a major problem. People will stop buying gold, silver, and fine clothes. A day's wages will not buy enough food. And one's works, not wealth, will be the basis of judgment when the books are opened at the Great White Throne. With the Second Coming looming on the horizon, one would be wise to use his wealth to help the poor and to give to those doing the work of God. The comforts of this world will be short-lived, but the rewards for sharing will last forever.

Unfulfilled	
Tribulation Period	
After the Millennium	

☞ **GO TO:**

Matthew 16:26 (gains)

Matthew 6:19 (treasures)

Revelation 9:21 (theft)

Revelation 18:11–14 (gold)

Revelation 6:5–6 (wages)

The Great White Throne	**Scripture**
Evil desires produce sin, and sin will lead to the second death.	James 1:15
The person who breaks just one Commandment is guilty of breaking all the laws of God.	James 2:10
God will not be merciful to those who have not shown mercy.	James 2:12–13

The Millennium	**Scripture**
Believers who have humbled themselves before God, shown faith, and loved him will inherit the kingdom.	James 2:5

Dig Deeper

> **James 5:7–9** Be patient, then, brothers, until the Lord's coming. See how the farmer waits for the land to yield its valuable crop and how patient he is for the autumn and spring rains. You too, be patient and stand firm, because the Lord's coming is near. Don't grumble against each other, brothers, or you will be judged. The Judge is standing at the door!

Waiting For A Harvest

Every Christian should have patience. When the Bible talks about patience, it usually refers to being patient with people. But here it means being patient about the Rapture. James asks us to consider how the Jewish farmer waits on the land to produce a valuable crop. He sows his crop in the fall and waits for the autumn rain to make the seed sprout. He works long and hard to tend the crop and waits for the spring rain to provide moisture for the grain to fill out. James says this is the kind of patience and endurance that is needed for the Rapture, and he advises Christians to settle their differences because Jesus will return and we will be judged.

What Others are Saying:

Theodore H. Epp: On my desk at work I have a sign which reminds me of this. It says, "Perhaps today." On my desk at home I have a sign which reminds me of this. It says, "Watch and pray." We need reminders to keep our attention focused on the possibility that Christ can come back at any time. Concentrating on this blessed hope will do many things for our attitudes, faithfulness, actions and reactions.[6]

KEY POINT

It takes a long time for seed to sprout and produce a crop, but it happens. Likewise, Jesus will return.

The Pulpit Commentary: Think, he says, of the long-suffering of the farmer. His is a life of arduous toils and of anxious delays. He must wait for the "early rain" in the late autumn before he can sow his seed; and for the "latter rain" in April, upon which his crops depend for the filling of the ear before the harvest ripens. This patience is necessary. Although sometimes sorely tried, it is reasonable. The "fruit" which the farmer desires is "precious"; it is worth waiting for.[7]

Something to Ponder

The concept of the soon return of Christ should impact our lives. It should motivate those who are living in sin to abandon their sin. It should motivate Christians to settle disputes, pray, and do good works. Is the nearness of his return and the approaching judgment affecting you?

Fulfillment: The farmer cannot plant a crop one day and harvest it the next. He must be patient, allowing nature to do its work. Then he receives a valuable reward. In like manner, Christians cannot expect to be saved today and Raptured to heaven tomorrow. We must be patient, have hope, and let Jesus prepare the way. Then he will return and we will receive the treasures we have hoped for.

Unfulfilled
Rapture

The Rapture	Scripture
The Christian who perseveres under trial will receive a crown of life.	James 1:12
The person who chooses to keep God's commandments will be blessed.	James 1:25

Dig Deeper

1 PETER

> **1 Peter 1:3–7** Praise be to the God and Father of our Lord Jesus Christ! In his great mercy he has given us new birth into a living hope through the resurrection of Jesus Christ from the dead, and into an inheritance that can never perish, spoil or fade—kept in heaven for you, who through faith are shielded by God's power until the coming of the salvation that is ready to be revealed in the last time. In this you greatly rejoice, though now for a little while you may have had to suffer grief in all kinds of trials. These have come so that your faith—of greater worth than gold, which perishes even though refined by fire—may be proved genuine and may result in praise, glory and honor when Jesus Christ is revealed.

Something To Rejoice About

This passage begins with seven reasons why Christians should praise God:

1. *"The Father of our Lord Jesus Christ"* is a phrase the apostle Paul used also. It reveals that God holds the position of Father in the **Trinity** and Jesus holds the position of Son.

2. *"In his great mercy"* refers to the fact that we cannot save ourselves, raise ourselves from the dead, take ourselves to heaven, but these things will happen because God decided to have mercy on us.

☞ **GO TO:**

2 Corinthians 1:3;
Ephesians 1:3
(Father)

Luke 1:26–38 (Son)

Trinity: a word not found in the Bible, refers to the idea that God exists in three ways: as God the Father, as God the Son, and as God the Holy Spirit

☞ **GO TO:**

John 3:1–21
(born again)

rescued: Raptured

☞ **GO TO:**

2 Corinthians 4:16–18
(temporary)

Something to Ponder

distress: the Tribulation Period

Unfulfilled

Rapture

☞ **GO TO:**

Matthew 24:21–22
(distress)

3. "*He has given us the new birth*" is something Jesus taught when he told Nicodemus he must be <u>born again</u> if he wanted to see the kingdom of God. Among other things it means God changes lives and allows people to start over again.

4. "*Hope through the resurrection of Jesus*" means we have proof that God can raise the dead and reason to believe he will raise us.

5. "*Inheritance*" refers to eternal life in heaven, a place that can never be defiled, damaged, or destroyed.

6. "*Shielded by God's power*" means no matter what happens to us in this life, God has provided a way to protect us in the future.

7. "*Salvation that is ready to be revealed in the last time*" means he has provided a way to rescue Christians from the time of judgment. We will be **rescued** before the Tribulation Period and protected from judgment at the Great White Throne.

According to Peter, Christians should rejoice for three main reasons: (1) the grief in our trials of life is only <u>temporary</u>. The hardships will be done away with giving us much to look forward to; (2) the trials of life are God's way of testing us. He does not permit them out of a desire to hurt us. He permits them because they will help us grow as Christians and bring more praise to him; and (3) the trials of life will make us stronger, equip us to endure even greater hardships, and prepare us to meet Christ at his coming.

The new birth is something God does for everyone who sincerely accepts Jesus as their Savior. The Holy Spirit works in people's lives to bring about changes according to the will of God. The "born again" person develops a new character, a desire to please God, a new set of priorities and values, and hope for the future. Experience the new birth and you will be brought into the kingdom of God.

Fulfillment: Death delivers all Christians from the hardships and dangers of this world. And the Rapture will deliver living Christians from the greatest period of **distress** the world has ever known. All the signs indicate that this deliverance is near.

The Rapture	Scripture
Believers should prepare for the grace to be given when Christ Raptures the Church.	1 Peter 1:13
All believers will be judged.	1 Peter 4:5
Jesus can return at any moment so believers should be self-controlled and clear minded and should pray.	1 Peter 4:7
The Holy Spirit rests on believers who suffer for Christ; they will receive a future inheritance.	1 Peter 4:13, 14
Believers will be judged first, but unbelievers will suffer more.	1 Peter 4:17
Believers will share in the glory of Christ at the Rapture.	1 Peter 5:1
Believers who remain faithful under trial will receive a crown of glory when Christ returns.	1 Peter 5:4

The Great White Throne	Scripture
All unbelievers will be judged.	1 Peter 4:5

Dig Deeper

2 PETER

> **2 Peter 1:16–19** We did not follow cleverly invented stories when we told you about the power and coming of our Lord Jesus Christ, but we were eyewitnesses of his majesty. For he received honor and glory from God the Father when the voice came to him from the Majestic Glory, saying, "This is my Son, whom I love; with him I am well pleased." We ourselves heard this voice that came from heaven when we were with him on the sacred mountain. And we have the word of the prophets made more certain, and you will do well to pay attention to it, as to a light shining in a dark place, until the day dawns and the morning star rises in your hearts.

We Saw It With Our Own Eyes

Here Peter declares that he and the apostles did not invent stories about the Second Coming of Jesus. He states that he and the apostles were eyewitnesses to what Jesus will be like when he

☞ **GO TO:**

Matthew 17:1–13
(transfigured)

John 8:12 (Light)

transfigured: *his appearance was drastically changed*

What Others are Saying:

apostolic: *from the apostles*

Unfulfilled
Second Coming

Dig Deeper

returns in glory. He was referring to the appearance of Jesus when he was **transfigured** on the mountain. But they not only saw this, they heard God honor and glorify Jesus by speaking from heaven about his love for his Son. Peter continued by reminding us that we not only have the **apostolic** assurances of the Second Coming, we also have the assurances of the prophets. In fact, we have so much evidence, we would be wise to heed these things until the day Jesus returns. He is the Light of the world, the bright Morning Star (Revelation 2:28; 22:16).

Life Application Bible Commentary: Thus all that the apostles taught and wrote, even regarding the awesome *power* of Christ and the promise of his second *coming*, was grounded in experience and fact, without embellishment or speculation. The believers must always remember that the truth they received was truth indeed, passed on by those who had lived with and learned from Jesus.[8]

Fulfillment: The transfiguration of Jesus gave the disciples a brief glimpse into the future. It was God's way of providing them with information about the Second Coming so they could pass it on to the world and assure us it will happen. It is evidence that what the prophets said is true. People would be wise to pay attention.

The Rapture	Scripture
Those who live for God, will receive a rich welcome into his kingdom.	2 Peter 1:11

> **2 Peter 3:3–4** First of all, you must understand that in the last days scoffers will come, scoffing and following their own evil desires. They will say, "Where is this 'coming' he promised? Ever since our fathers died, everything goes on as it has since the beginning of creation."

"Where Is He?"

"First of all" means this is a high-priority item. It may not seem very important, but it is. The last days of the Church Age will be characterized by people mocking the doctrine of the Second Coming of Christ. Their apostasy will generate from evil desires and come in the form of a scoffing question: Why hasn't Jesus returned

☞ **GO TO:**

Jude 18 (scoffing)

like he promised? Then they will pretend to prove that he will not return with a ridiculous argument. Nothing, they will say, has changed since the beginning of the earth (see GWRV, pages 27–58).

Dave Hunt: The apostasy involves claiming that revival rather than the Rapture is imminent and denying that apostasy must come. Again, these days are upon us, and we need not quote the many Christian leaders who ridicule belief in the Rapture, calling it an escape theory. Their books and tapes are readily available.[9]

> Here is one reason why Jesus has not already returned. Peter said, *"But do not forget this one thing, dear friends: With the Lord a day is like a thousand years, and a thousand years are like a day. The Lord is not slow in keeping his promise, as some understand slowness. He is patient with you, not wanting anyone to perish, but everyone to come to repentance"* (2 Peter 3:8–9).

Remember This . . .

Both the Old and the New Testaments repeat the promise of the Second Coming over and over again. At one time, all the major denominations accepted it, believed it, and preached it. But many will not even talk about it today. What does this tell us about the signs of the times?

Something to Ponder

Fulfillment: Apostate teachers have taken over many of our religious institutions. They are denying not only the virgin birth, the inerrancy of the Scriptures, and other long-held beliefs, but also the once esteemed doctrine of the Second Coming. If they do not die first, many of these apostates will be the beginning of the false church that will be so prevalent during the first half of the Tribulation Period.

Continuously Being Fulfilled
Church Age

The Tribulation Period	Scripture
False prophets and teachers will lead many astray and they will be punished.	2 Peter 2:1–10

The Great White Throne	Scripture
God knows how to hold the unrighteous for judgment.	2 Peter 2:9
Severe punishment is reserved for the wicked.	2 Peter 2:17

Dig Deeper

1 JOHN

> **1 John 3:2** Dear friends, now we are children of God, and what we will be has not yet been made known. But we know that when he appears, we shall be like him, for we shall see him as he is.

Like Him

dogmatically: positively, emphatically

We have three great truths here. The first is that believers already are the children of God. We do not *hope* to be saved or *hope* to go to heaven. We can **dogmatically** declare that we are saved and we are going to heaven. We have what some call a "know so" salvation. This is true because God said it.

The second great truth is that "*what we will be has not yet been made known.*" People ask, Will I look like a teenager in heaven, an older person, or what? The answer is, this is something God has not yet revealed so we do not know. We probably wouldn't understand it even if he did.

☞ **GO TO:**

1 Thessalonians 4:13–18 (come down)

Philippians 3:21 (body)

The third great truth is that we will be like the glorified Christ when he returns. He will <u>come down</u> from heaven, raise the dead believers, and transform every believer's body into a glorious <u>body</u> like his. This is something we cannot explain, but we know it will be wonderful.

What Others are Saying:

David Hocking: If we can't get excited about this, we simply don't understand what it means! We will be supernaturally, fantastically, gloriously transformed! Like a caterpillar that possesses the DNA of a butterfly, we will go through a supernatural metamorphosis that will transform us into what He has made our new nature to be.[10]

J. Vernon McGee: This does not mean that all of us are going to be little robots or simply duplicates—it is not that at all. We will be like Him but with our own personalities, our own individualities, our own selves. He will never destroy the person of Vernon McGee. He'll not destroy the person that you are, but He is going to bring you up to the full measure, the stature where you will be like Him—not identical to Him, but like Him.[11]

Following the resurrection of Jesus, he suddenly appeared inside a <u>locked</u> room and showed the disciples his hands and side. On another occasion, he appeared and <u>ate</u> with them. And on yet another occasion, he gave them some instructions and then ascended into <u>heaven</u>. What to *"be like him"* means is a mystery, but it sure sounds exciting.

Fulfillment: Believers are the children of God right now, but new bodies are needed before we can be like Christ. We will receive them when the Church is Raptured.

Something to Ponder

Unfulfilled
Raptured

The Rapture	Scripture
The faithful will not be ashamed when they stand before Christ at his coming.	1 John 2:28
Because believers demonstrate the love of Christ, they will not be afraid at the judgment.	1 John 4:17
Every believer should strive for a full reward.	2 John 1:8

Dig Deeper

The Tribulation Period	Scripture
Believers will know the last days have arrived because of the opposition to Christ.	1 John 2:18
False prophets and teachers will arise and deny that Jesus came from God.	1 John 4:3

☞ **GO TO:**

John 20:19–28 (locked)

Luke 24:36–43 (ate)

Acts 1:4–11 (heaven)

JUDE

Jude 6 And the angels who did not keep their positions of authority but abandoned their own home—these he has kept in darkness, bound with everlasting chains for judgment on the great Day.

An Interesting Day In Court

Many people are concerned about the future of humankind. Satan and his fallen angels are winning spiritual battles all over the planet and some worry that they will win the war. But the Bible teaches that they will be defeated, judged, and stripped of their power forever. It even teaches that some have already been locked in a dark dungeon called the <u>Abyss</u> and that the time will come when believers will <u>judge</u> them (see GWRV, pages 127–132).

☞ **GO TO:**

Revelation 9:1–11 (Abyss)

1 Corinthians 6:3 (judge)

**Something
to Ponder**

Unfulfilled
Millennium

*subterranean: beneath
the earth's surface*

Abyss: *a deep pit where
demons are kept*

***Dig
Deeper***

☞ **GO TO:**

---

2 Peter 2:4 (angels)

---

1 Timothy 4:1
(deceiving)

Matthew 25:41 (Fire)

The Southwest Radio Church: The angels who left their estate in Heaven knew the God who created them. They knowingly and willingly made a choice to follow Satan; therefore, there is no redemption for fallen angels.[12]

Imagine this: It will be spookier than walking through a haunted house at night. No horror film can do it justice. You will be in a courtroom when one of the grossest, most evil demons of the underworld is brought before you to be judged. You will face him and declare his fate.

Fulfillment: There seems to be two classes of fallen <u>angels</u>. The worst have been locked in a **subterranean** dungeon called the **Abyss**. Those not so bad are roaming loose on earth <u>deceiving</u> people and causing great harm. Believers will judge these angels during the Millennium and have them cast into the Lake of <u>Fire</u>.

The Second Coming	Scripture
Jesus will return with thousands upon thousands of saints.	Jude 14
The ungodly will be judged for wrongdoing and speaking against Jesus.	Jude 15

The Great White Throne	Scripture
The apostates will be thrown into hell.	Jude 13

STUDY QUESTIONS

1. How is the new covenant different from the old covenant?
2. Is the accumulation of wealth wrong? What is it about hoarding wealth that will make people miserable in the last days?
3. What warning is given to Christians who grumble against each other? What has the mercy of God done for believers? Who will we be like when the Rapture occurs?
4. What supernatural event underlies Peter's teaching about the Second Coming? Explain.
5. What foolish argument will scoffers set forth in the last days? What does the judgment of fallen angels imply?

- The old covenant of Law has been replaced with a new covenant of grace. This new covenant will be instilled in the minds and hearts of God's people. And it will be better because it will be accompanied by forgiveness of sins. (Hebrews 8:7–13)

- Some will hoard wealth for the last days, reap misery for doing so, and in the end find that their wealth is worthless. This will be presented as evidence of greed and selfishness at their judgment. (James 5:1–3)

- Patience is required of those looking for the rapture. They will receive mercy, hope, and an inheritance, be shielded by God, escape the Tribulation Period, and be protected from the Great White Throne judgment. And most amazingly, we will be like Christ. (James 5:7–9; 1 John 3:2)

- The Second Coming of Christ is not a fable. Jesus performed a miracle on the Mount of Transfiguration to reveal the Second Coming to the disciples. They were eyewitnesses to something the Old Testament prophets predicted long before. (2 Peter 1:16–19)

- People will mock the doctrine of the Second Coming in the last days and use ridiculous arguments in an effort to prove it won't happen. Following the Second Coming believers will judge the fallen angels. (2 Peter 3:3–4; Jude 6)

9 PROPHECIES IN THE BOOK OF REVELATION

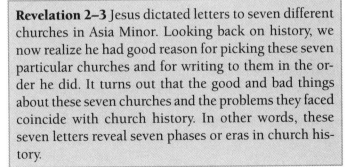

CHAPTER HIGHLIGHTS

- The Church Age
- The Seven Seal Judgments
- The Seven Trumpet Judgments
- The Seven Bowl Judgments
- The Millennium and Beyond

Let's Get Started

Now we come to one of the most awesome books in the entire Bible: the book of Revelation. The word *revelation* comes from a Greek word meaning *uncovering* or *disclosing*. This book contains information about the future, beginning nearly 2,000 years ago, that Jesus disclosed to his disciple <u>John</u>. It is attracting widespread interest today because the daily newspapers are filled with articles that seem to indicate the end of the age is drawing near. If these truly are "signs," and it looks like they are, the world is on the brink of terrible **calamities**. People need to know these things and be prepared.

revelation: an uncovering of something hidden

calamities: war, disasters, etc.

☞ **GO TO:**

Revelation 1:1 (John)

THE BIG PICTURE 🔍

> **Revelation 2–3** Jesus dictated letters to seven different churches in Asia Minor. Looking back on history, we now realize he had good reason for picking these seven particular churches and for writing to them in the order he did. It turns out that the good and bad things about these seven churches and the problems they faced coincide with church history. In other words, these seven letters reveal seven phases or eras in church history.

Church History Before It Happens

There are many ways to interpret the seven letters to the seven churches. Some say they represent seven different spiritual condi-

Seven Churches of Asia

The seven churches men-
tioned in Revelation were
actual churches in Asian
cities.

tions that existed in the churches (see illustration above) of John's
day. Others say they are messages to individuals of all ages and
still others say they are messages to the Church as a whole. Actually, it seems that all of the above are true and, although there is
no verse of Scripture to verify it, it also appears to be true that
they represent seven eras or phases in the Church Age (see GWDN,
pages 27–58).

Tim LaHaye: It is suggested that they also represent the seven
basic divisions of church history. A study of history reveals that
the Church has gone through seven basic periods or stages.[1]

The book of Revelation is a prophecy (Revelation 1:3) and
the seven letters provide a panoramic view of church history
from the first Pentecost to the Tribulation Period midpoint.

Church Age	Scripture	Approx. Historical Date	Prophetic Condition of the Church
Ephesus Period	Revelation 2:1–7	Pentecost to A.D. 100	Will backslide
Smyrna Period	Revelation 2:8–11	A.D. 100 to A.D. 312	Will be persecuted
Pergamum Period	Revelation 2:12–17	A.D. 312 to A.D. 590	Will compromise doctrines
Thyatira Period	Revelation 2:18–29	A.D. 590 to A.D. 1517	Will tolerate heresy
Sardis Period	Revelation 3:1–6	A.D. 1517 to A.D. 1750	Will almost die
Philadelphia Period	Revelation 3:7–13	A.D. 1750 to A.D. 1900	Will be evangelistic
Laodicea Period	Revelation 3:14–22	A.D. 1900 to Trib. Period midpoint	Will be lukewarm

Fulfillment: If it is true, and many prominent authorities believe it is, that seven eras of the Church Age are revealed here, then the Church Age is now in its final hours and the Rapture is imminent.

THE BIG PICTURE

> **Revelation 4–5** John was called up into heaven where he saw Jesus sitting on a throne next to God. He saw a rainbow over the throne, twenty-four elders seated on other thrones around it, seven blazing lamps and a sea of glass in front of it, and four living creatures by it. God was holding a scroll with seven seals and an angel asked, "Who is worthy to break the seals and open the scroll?" Jesus was the only One qualified to do this. Then the four living creatures, the twenty-four elders, multitudes of angels, and everyone else worshiped him.

Let's Go To Heaven

The Church Age (Revelation 2–3) will end with the Rapture. A voice sounding very much like a <u>trumpet</u> will summon the Church into heaven where the saved will appear before a <u>throne</u> occupied by both God and Jesus. The twenty-four <u>elders</u>, the four living <u>creatures</u>, and multitudes of <u>angels</u> will be there. It will be that time between the Rapture and the Tribulation Period and the issue will be "Who is worthy to break the seals and open the scroll?" In other words, Who can qualify as the Redeemer of the world and open the seals? We will learn more about the seals later, but here we learn that Jesus will be the only one in <u>heaven</u> or on earth who is qualified to do this. He is the <u>Lamb</u> that was slain for the sins of the world and his shed blood **purchased** a people to <u>reign</u> on earth.

Continuously Being Fulfilled
Church Age

☞ **GO TO:**

1 Thessalonians 4:13–18; Revelation 4:1 (trumpet)

Revelation 4:2 (throne)

Revelation 4:4 (elders)

Revelation 4:6 (creatures)

Revelation 5:11 (angels)

Revelation 5:3–5 (heaven)

John 1:29; Revelation 5:6–10 (Lamb)

Revelation 5:9–10 (reign)

purchased: *redeemed*

KEY POINT

Jesus will be found worthy to open the scroll.

Unfulfilled

Rapture

☞ **GO TO:**

Revelation 6:1–2
(first seal)

Gary G. Cohen: Once broken, a seal was impossible to repair without leaving tell-tale traces; thus here we are certain that this book with its woes for the earth has never yet been opened. It was certainly not opened prior to the crucifixion as vs. 9 shows; and its contents (Chapters 6–19) do not mesh with these past 2,000 years of church history. The opening is set for the start of the Tribulation Period! The fact that there are seven seals shows that the entire matter—here Tribulation judgments for the ungodly upon earth—will be completely dispatched by these seven seals.[2]

John F. Walvoord: Immediately after the Rapture of the church, there will be a time period which may be called a period of preparation. In this period there will emerge a ten-nation group forming a political unit in the Middle East. A leader will emerge who will gain control first of three and then of all ten (cf. Daniel 7:8, 24–25). From this position of power he will be able to enter into a covenant with Israel, bringing to rest the relationship of Israel to her neighbors (9:27), and beginning the final seven-year countdown culminating in the Second Coming.[3]

Fulfillment: These chapters reveal the Rapture and what will occur in heaven shortly after that. The "shortly after" events will take place during that period of time the Antichrist is rising to power on earth (see GWRV, pages 85–86).

THE BIG PICTURE 🔍

Revelation 6:1–8:1 John watched as Jesus opened the seven seals on the scroll in heaven one at a time (the seventh released seven trumpet judgments). As each seal was opened, a judgment that was being restrained in heaven was released. In between the opening of the sixth and seventh seals a pause occurred while God marked 144,000 Jewish evangelists.

It's Time to Deal With Rebellion On Earth

All of the judgments on earth will be triggered from heaven. The first seven seals will be as follows:

Seal #1—Jesus will open the first seal and the first living creature will release a rider on a white horse that most experts agree is the Antichrist. He will rise to power with great deception saying and doing many good things to give people a false sense of hope. He will wrap himself in piety and respectability and his supporters will not sense the evil in his heart. He will talk peace, but John says he will come forth *"bent on conquest."*

Seal #2—Jesus will open the <u>second seal</u> and the second living creature will release a rider on a fiery red horse. This rider will undo the world's fragile peace treaties and spark a rash of conflicts around the world. God will permit this to show the world that the Antichrist is a false prince of peace.

Seal #3—Jesus will open the <u>third seal</u> and the third living creature will release a rider on a black horse. This rider will surge forth with the terrible consequences of war. These include, among other things, economic disaster and famine. Most currencies will be worthless and food shortages will be common. Misery, poverty, and starvation will prevail. God will permit this to show the world that the Antichrist is a false bread of life.

Seal #4—Jesus will open the <u>fourth seal</u> and the fourth living creature will release a rider on a pale horse. This rider will be named Death, and the color of his horse will be similar to that of spoiled meat. A creature named Hades will follow him and these two ghoulish characters will use war, famine, plagues, and wild animals to harvest the souls of unbelievers as fuel for the fires of hell.

Seal #5—Jesus will open the <u>fifth seal</u> and there will be great persecution and death of those who accept Christ after the Rapture. The media and world leaders will portray these new Christians as enemies of world government, world peace, world religion, and the environment. They will blame these new **converts** for starting religious wars; call for their elimination to preserve the dwindling food supplies and protect the environment; and use food, water, and other things as weapons to force support for a new world government.

Seal #6—Jesus will open the <u>sixth seal</u> and there will be a great earthquake, the sun will turn pitch black, the moon will turn blood red, meteors will fall to the earth, the wind will recede like the rolling up of a scroll, and every mountain and island on earth will move or shake. This appears to be nuclear war throwing debris into the atmosphere and affecting the very universe itself. It will cause worldwide panic, multitudes will try to hide from God in caves and bomb shelters, and many will finally realize that the Tribulation Period has arrived.

The First Interlude—In between the sixth and seventh seals there will be a pause in the coming events. Jesus said the <u>Gospel</u> will be preached in the whole world before the end comes, but at this point the Church will be in heaven because of the Rapture. So God will call "time out" in the judgments to **seal** 144,000 Jews.

☞ **GO TO:**

Revelation 6:3–4
(second seal)

Revelation 6:5–6
(third seal)

Revelation 6:7–8
(fourth seal)

Revelation 6:9–11
(fifth seal)

Revelation 6:12–17
(sixth seal)

converts: new Christians

☞ **GO TO:**

Matthew 24:14
(Gospel)

seal: mark

☞ **GO TO:**

Revelation 8:1–6
(seventh seal)

⬭ What Others
are Saying:

☞ **GO TO:**

Matthew 24:11 (false)

Matthew 24:6–7 (wars)

Matthew 24:7 (famine)

**Something
to Ponder**

Unfulfilled
Tribulation Period

☞ **GO TO:**

Matthew 24:9 (death)

Matthew 24:7
(earthquakes)

Matthew 24:29
(heavenly bodies)

Whatever this seal is, it will protect from harm while they preach to the world and win a great multitude to God.

Seal #7—Jesus will open the seventh seal and this will start a new series of tragedies called the trumpet judgments.

Dave Breese: If we want to know the direction in which the world is going, that direction is ahead of us. We are to anticipate not a utopia or a perfect world, but an era of devastating divine judgment.[4]

J. Vernon McGee: The Great Tribulation is the Devil's holiday. That is the day when he is going to have freedom to do as he pleases. We will see why God is going to grant that: it is a period of the judgment of God upon a Christ-rejecting world.[5]

After the Rapture things will grow progressively worse. The world will go through a false sense of peace (Seal #1); several wars and rumors of wars (Seal #2); economic collapse and famine (Seal #3); the death of millions of unbelievers because of war, famine, and plagues (Seal #4); the persecution and death of believers (Seal #5); earthquakes with disturbances in the heavenly bodies possibly because of nuclear war (Seal #6); and then the trumpet judgments will begin (Seal #7).

Fulfillment: After the church is removed from the earth by the Rapture, there will be a brief period of euphoria followed by a seven-year period of war, famine, pestilence, persecution, and death on a level so intense it staggers the imagination.

THE BIG PICTURE 🔍

> **Revelation 8:2–11:19** John watched as seven angels stood before God and each one sounded a trumpet (the seventh trumpet brought on seven judgments called bowl judgments). One at a time the trumpets sounded and each time a terrible catastrophe took place on earth. In between the sixth and seventh was a pause while John received two other visions.

Judgment Will Come Upon All The World

The judgments found in Revelation appear in sets of seven. For purposes of study, each set of seven can be broken down into four and three. For example, the seal judgments fall into two categories: the Four Horsemen of the Apocalypse and then three additional judgments. In like manner, the seven trumpet judgments will fall into two categories: four "Judgments of One-Third" and three judgments called "Woes." The following is an overview of the trumpet judgments:

Trumpet #1—An angel will sound the <u>first trumpet</u> and hail and fire mixed with blood will fall to the earth and destroy one-third of the plant life. This furious supernatural storm will alter the entire balance of nature, destroy badly needed crops hastily planted to curb food shortages, destroy lumber needed to build houses, destroy grazing land needed for cattle, and kill a tremendous number of people.

Trumpet #2—An angel will sound the <u>second trumpet</u> and something *like* a huge burning mountain—perhaps a blazing meteor, a comet, or a very large missile with a chemical warhead—will be hurled into the sea causing it to turn into blood, killing one-third of the sea creatures and destroying one-third of the ships. The Bible does not say so, but it seems likely that this will cause a great tidal wave that will pollute, damage, and destroy large areas of coastline.

Trumpet #3—An angel will sound the <u>third trumpet</u> and a large burning star will fall from the sky. People will name it after a bitter herb in the Bible called **wormwood** because it will pollute and poison one-third of the earth's fresh water supply (rivers, springs, etc.) and cause many people to die. Fresh water is one of earth's most precious commodities and losing one-third of it will have terrible consequences. Those who think they can submit to God after the Rapture are making a terrible mistake.

Trumpet #4—An angel will sound the <u>fourth trumpet</u> and the light of the sun, moon, and stars will be diminished by one-third. This will affect the weather and every form of plant and animal life on earth. It may even bring about the nuclear winter predicted by many scientists and environmentalists.

Trumpet #5—An angel will sound the <u>fifth trumpet</u> and another star will fall from heaven. This will not be a literal star because it will be given a key and is called "he." Most conservative commentators believe this "he" will be Satan. His key will unlock his subterranean home called the Abyss. He will use it to release multiplied millions of demon-possessed locusts with stings similar to that of a **scorpion**. God will not permit them to kill anyone, but their poison will be so toxic many people will want to die. Some will even try to commit suicide, but they will not succeed.

☞ **GO TO:**

Revelation 8:7
(first trumpet)

Revelation 8:8–9
(second trumpet)

Revelation 8:10–11
(third trumpet)

Revelation 8:12
(fourth trumpet)

Revelation 9:1–12
(fifth trumpet)

wormwood: a bitter, intoxicating, poisonous herb

scorpion: a small spider-like animal with a poisonous sting

These scorpions will be allowed to torture people for five months, and everyone except the 144,000 Jewish witnesses will be tortured.

Trumpet #6—An angel will sound the sixth trumpet and four of Satan's fallen angels will be released and given authority to kill one-third of humankind. They will gather a 200-million-person army—most commentators believe this will be China and her allies, but a few say these will be demonic creatures—to carry out their assigned task.

Trumpet #7—Loud voices in heaven will announce that "*The kingdom of the world has become the kingdom of our Lord and his Christ, and he will reign forever and ever*" (Revelation 11:15). The twenty-four elders will fall down and worship God. Then there will be a great earthquake, a great hailstorm, and the seven bowls of God's wrath will be poured out. These events will happen very fast, and they will come near the end of the Tribulation Period.

The Second Interlude—A mighty angel will descend to the earth with a small book and stand with one foot on the sea and the other foot on dry land. This will be a symbolic way of claiming the planet for God. The angel will announce that the remaining judgments will not be delayed and all of them will be fulfilled exactly as the prophets said.

The Third Interlude—The Jewish Temple will be in existence, but the outer court will be controlled by the Gentiles for forty-two months. Two witnesses will appear and begin to prophesy. No one will be allowed to harm them for forty-two months. They will be able to hold back the rain, turn water into blood, and strike the earth with various kinds of plagues. After the forty-two months have expired, the Antichrist will be permitted to kill them and their bodies will be left in the street for all the world to see for 3½ days. Then they will be raised from the dead and ascend into heaven.

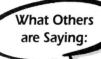

What Others are Saying:

Grant R. Jeffrey: God cannot simply ignore our sin and allow an unrepentant sinner into heaven despite their rejection of God. God's absolute justice makes it impossible for Him to ignore our sins.[6]

John F. Walvoord: These are catastrophic judgments and should not be explained away. In view of the fact that they are supernatural, we should not limit God in what He is desiring to do.[7]

A group of people called **Preterists** teach that most, if not all, Bible prophecy has been fulfilled. They also teach that the really bad things were fulfilled in A.D. 70 when the Romans destroyed Jerusalem. But one-fourth of Earth's population will die in the fourth seal and one-third will die in the sixth trumpet. Nothing like this has ever happened before, but it will happen during the Tribulation Period.

The first plague on Egypt in the days of Moses turned the <u>waters</u> into blood, the seventh was <u>hail</u> that killed people and animals, and the ninth was <u>darkness</u> that covered the land. Since God did these things in the past, isn't it reasonable to assume that he can do them again?

PERSONAL UPDATE, MARCH 1999 . . .

In an overt illustration, Secretary Cohen [U.S. Secretary of Defense William Cohen] appeared on the ABC News program "This Week" and held up a five-pound bag of sugar to show the amount of the biological weapon that could destroy half the population of Washington, D.C. There is no effective treatment for unvaccinated victims of inhalational anthrax. Antibiotics will suppress infection only if administered *before* any symptoms of infection occur—usually within the first 24 to 48 hours. The disease is 99% lethal to unprotected individuals.[8]

Fulfillment: Jesus intends to establish a kingdom here on earth during the Millennium. He cannot allow unrepentant people into that kingdom or they will corrupt it. They must repent or perish before the kingdom is established. The purpose of these judgments is to give people a future and to protect the future of those who follow God.

WARNING

Preterists: a group that teaches that most, if not all, Bible prophecy has been fulfilled

Something to Ponder

RELATED CURRENT EVENTS

☞ **GO TO:**

Exodus 7:14–25 (waters)

Exodus 9:18–26 (hail)

Exodus 10:21–23 (darkness)

Unfulfilled
Tribulation Period

> **Revelation 12:1–17** After the seventh trumpet sounded and before the seven bowls of God's wrath were poured out, John was told to prophesy about some of the peoples, nations, languages, and kings of the Tribulation Period. Then he saw a sun-clothed woman in heaven with the moon under her feet and a crown of twelve stars on her head. She was expecting a male child that would rule the world. A dragon stood before her desiring to destroy the child at birth. The child was born and taken up into heaven. The woman fled into the wilderness, and the dragon went to heaven, but God's angels cast him down to earth. He pursued the woman into the wilderness, but God protected her.

The Dragon Loses

The symbols associated with this woman (the sun, moon, and twelve stars) are all found in a single dream Joseph had in the Old Testament about the nation of Israel. This child who will rule the nations is Jesus and the dragon is identified as Satan. When Jesus first came to this earth as a human child, Satan tried to have him killed. When Jesus began his ministry Satan tried to destroy that by tempting him with the kingdoms of the world. When Jesus was dying on a cross for the sins of the world, Satan tried to stop that by having others encourage him to save his life. Following his death, Jesus was resurrected and he ascended into heaven. In the future, at the Tribulation Period midpoint, Israel will have to flee into the mountains, and Satan will lose his place in heaven and be cast to this earth with many of his fallen angels. They will do as much damage on earth as they can. Satan will also try to destroy all the Jews, but God will not allow that. He will help many of them escape and supernaturally protect them.

☞ **GO TO:**

Genesis 30:22–24; 37:3–4 (Joseph)

Psalm 2:1–9 (nations)

Revelation 12:9 (dragon)

Matthew 2:13–18 (child)

Matthew 4:1–11 (kingdoms of the world)

Matthew 27:42–44 (cross)

Matthew 24:16 (flee)

What Others are Saying:

J. Dwight Pentecost: According to Revelation 12, the object of satanic attack during the tribulation period is "the woman" who produced the child. Since this child is born "to rule all nations with a rod of iron" (Revelation 12:5), it can only refer to Christ, the one whose right it is to rule. The Psalmist confirms this interpretation in Psalm 2:9, which is admittedly Messianic. The one from whom Christ came can only be Israel.[9]

John Hagee: Satan will target Jews and Christians because attacking them is the only way he can retaliate against God. Unable to prevail against God militarily, Satan will seek revenge against Him by targeting the Jewish people, the apple of God's eye, for extermination.[10]

The Bible warns that Israel and <u>Jerusalem</u> will be severely attacked at the end of the age, but God will be watching for this, and all who try to harm this nation will actually be doing injury to themselves. Every nation that attacks Jerusalem will be destroyed.

Fulfillment: The return of Israel as a nation is a clear sign of the approaching Tribulation Period. When the Temple is rebuilt the stage will be set for the Antichrist to defile it and that will signal the casting of Satan and his fallen angels to earth. The implications for all who trust in God are terrifying, but those who defy God will be in greater peril in the long run.

THE BIG PICTURE

Revelation 13:1–18 As John continued to prophesy about some of the main characters who will be on earth during the Tribulation Period, he saw a beast coming out of the sea and a beast coming out of the earth. The beast coming out of the sea became the primary political leader of the Tribulation Period. He received political support from ten other rulers or leaders, but the dragon was his main source of power and authority. This beast was wounded but healed; he was a military genius, a blasphemer, and a persecutor of God's people. Then the beast coming out of the earth appeared and he became the primary religious leader of the Tribulation Period. He pretended to follow God, but his doctrines were like those of the dragon. He gave religious support to the first beast, forced people to worship the first beast, performed miracles, set up an idol of the first beast and caused it to come to life, and killed all who refused to worship it. He also forced people to be identified with a mark on their right hand or forehead the number of the beast coming out of the sea.

The beast coming out of the earth is the False Prophet. He will be the world's most powerful religious leader during the Tribulation Period. He will present himself as a lamb, but will be a wolf in sheep's clothing; and his doctrines will be like the doctrines of

☞ **GO TO:**

Zechariah 12:1–9
(Jerusalem)

Remember
This . . .

Unfulfilled

Tribulation Period

KEY Symbols:

The Woman
The nation of Israel
CLOTHED WITH THE SUN
(JACOB OR ISRAEL)

THE MOON UNDER HER FEET
(RACHEL, ISRAEL'S WIFE)

THE CROWN OF TWELVE STARS
(THE TWELVE TRIBES OF
ISRAEL, JACOB'S TWELVE
SONS)

Satan. At first, his authority will be equal to that of the Antichrist, and he will use it to give full support to that evil man. Multitudes will be deceived and forced to worship an idol he will set up in honor of the Antichrist. He will get a law passed forcing everyone to receive a mark on their right hand or forehead. This mark will be like a license to transact business. Those who have it will be allowed to buy and sell, but those without it will be denied that privilege. This mark will be the number and name of the Antichrist. People cannot figure it out now, but after the Rapture when the Antichrist is revealed people will discover that the numerical value of his name is 666.

Beasts Of Sea And Earth

The beast coming out of the sea is the Antichrist. He will be the world's most powerful politician during the Tribulation Period and is called a beast because he will be filled with evil. This beast will have ten <u>horns</u> which means he will have ten kings (or ten leaders of factions) on earth who will give him political support. And he will have seven <u>heads</u>, which means he will have ties to the seven world governments of past history. The <u>dragon</u>, who was identified in the previous chapter as Satan, will give him power. He will receive what appears to be a fatal wound during his reign, but to the amazement of the world he will be miraculously healed. People will be overwhelmed by his personality, his rise to power, and his ability to win wars. He will boast of his abilities, **blaspheme** God, try to kill everyone who worships God, and gain the worship of multitudes.

Tim LaHaye: Whenever a political leader tries to exterminate religion or the true worship of God, he must use the services of a false religious leader. The Antichrist will be no different. His leader will look "like a lamb" and speak "like a dragon" (verse 11).[11]

Charles Halff: Every year, uncounted billions of dollars change hands in the "underground economy." People avoid paying taxes by working for cash, without making or keeping records. Billions are made in untracked and untaxed revenue from crime and insurance fraud. Drug dealers routinely do business in suitcases of untaxed cash. Certainly, the elimination of cash currency would largely put a stop to such illegal dealings. Believe it or not, the system is already in place.[12]

☞ **GO TO:**

Revelation 17:12 (horns)

Revelation 17:7–11 (heads)

Revelation 12:9 (dragon)

blaspheme: show contempt for God

What Others are Saying:

Terry L. Cook: I.D. technologies are advancing rapidly and someday will trap many because it will sound so reasonable and logical. There are men and women in high places who know exactly what they are doing. And what they want is control of your life.[13]

RELATED CURRENT EVENTS

ENDTIME, MAY/JUNE 1999 . . .

The globalists obviously feel that the time to enact their long-dreamed-of global government has come. And it appears that they are right. The only thing standing between us and world government is the United States of America and its Congress. If America is willing to collaborate in the stripping away of the remaining vestiges of U.S. sovereignty, then the day of the nation-state is over and the era of world government will have dawned.[14]

• • •

ENDTIME, JANUARY/FEBRUARY 1999 . . .

There is a document called the Global Ethic, penned by Roman Catholic theologian Hans Kung. Watch out for it. It appears the Global Ethic may become the Statement of Faith of this new religion which they adamantly claim they are forming. To have a truly sustainable world order, we must sign on to the Global Ethic.[15]

• • •

"POINT OF VIEW" RADIO TALK SHOW, JANUARY 13, 1999 . . .

It [Earth Ethics, the new global religion] literally starts out by saying the earth itself is alive. . . . That's Gaia, that's the belief that the earth is truly a living, thinking, believing, thoughtful entity. And that is how it starts out. And, ironically, if you read the material that goes along with it, if in fact this ever gets into the force of law, what it really requires is that every single person must uphold the very principles of this new earth ethic including pastors of our church. If they want to maintain government sanctioned church, they must pledge some sort of allegiance to this new earth ethic. It's very clearly spelled out in their [the United Nations] documentation.[16]

Something to Ponder

Unfulfilled

Tribulation Period

KEY Symbols:

Beast Out Of The Sea

The Antichrist

☞ **GO TO:**

Revelation 14:1–4
(144,000)

Revelation 6:7–8;
Revelation 9:15
(killed)

Revelation 9:20–21
(humankind)

Revelation 14:6 (Gospel)

Revelation 14:8 (Babylon)

Revelation 13:16–18;
14:9–11 (Mark)

Revelation 14:14–16
(earth)

Revelation 14:17–19
(clusters)

*indignation: another
name for the Tribulation
Period*

The idea of a Global Ethic sounds good. After all, a lot of wars are religious wars. But the establishment of a Global Ethic is the same thing as the establishment of a world religion. And the establishment of a world religion will bring about the persecution of Christians and Jews because they will not comply. Would you switch religions? Would you accept the values of a man who gets his marching orders from Satan?

Fulfillment: Throughout the entire history of humankind, the control of all buying and selling and the tracking of all individuals has been impossible. In fact, for hundreds of years skeptics have said such a day would never come. But now we have entered the computer age and many United Nations bureaucrats are giving this idea serious consideration.

THE BIG PICTURE

> **Revelation 14:1–20** John saw Jesus standing on Mt. Zion with the 144,000 and he heard a heavenly choir singing. The 144,000 had made it through the Tribulation Period unharmed, undefiled, faithful to the teachings of Jesus, and they said nothing but the truth. Then John saw several angels. They first preached the Gospel on earth and urged people to turn to God. The second announced the destruction of Babylon. The third announced that all who took the Mark of the Beast would be cast into the Lake of Fire. The fourth prevailed upon Jesus to remove multitudes of unbelievers from the earth, and the fifth removed wicked nations.

Supernatural Intervention

Considering the fact that more than half the earth's population will have been killed by this time in the Tribulation Period, it will be truly amazing that every one of the <u>144,000</u> Jewish witnesses will still be living. Not even one will be <u>killed</u> by famine, hail, polluted water, nuclear bombs, the Antichrist, or any other disaster that takes place during this **indignation**. And considering all the wicked things <u>humankind</u> will be doing, it is a wonder that God will still love people enough to send an angel to preach the <u>Gospel</u> to all those on earth, but he will. Then one of his angels will announce the destruction of <u>Babylon</u>, another will announce the destruction of those who take the <u>Mark</u> of the Beast, another will announce the removal of unbelievers from the <u>earth</u>, and another will announce the removal of <u>clusters</u> (nations) from the earth.

Billy Graham: It will be a time of nuclear conflagrations, biological holocausts and chemical apocalypses rolling over the earth, bringing man to the edge of the precipice. History will "bottom out" in the battle of Armageddon. We already see its shadow creeping over the earth.[17]

For hundreds of years the ancient city of Babylon did not exist, but here we have a prediction that it will fall during the Tribulation Period. Isn't it interesting that the city has come back into existence in recent years? And isn't it interesting that this is occurring at the exact same time in history that Israel and Europe are being revived? Is this a coincidence?

Fulfillment: When the Battle of Armageddon approaches, many nations, cities, and individuals will be removed from the earth by the terrible weapons we now possess. If the people of earth would heed the preaching of the 144,000 and the angel God plans to send, they could avoid this. But they will not listen and they will not escape the awesome judgments of God.

THE BIG PICTURE

> **Revelation 15:7–16:21** John watched as one of the four living creatures handed the seven bowls filled with God's wrath to seven different angels. As each angel went forth and poured out his bowl upon the earth, a terrible judgment took place. Finally, a voice from the throne of God said, "It is done."

Fast And Furious

During the Millennium, God plans to set up a kingdom here on earth. If the lost were allowed to enter that kingdom, they would corrupt it just like they have everything else. But God will not let that happen again. When Jesus returns at the end of the Tribulation Period, he will send out his <u>angels</u> to gather the lost and cast them into hell. This is not something he will enjoy doing. The apostle Peter said God doesn't want anyone to <u>perish</u>, but he does want everyone to come to **repentance**. So as the end of the age approaches, God will pour out the most severe judgments of all, referred to as "bowls," in one final effort to change the hearts of unbelievers. The first four judgments will affect the earth, the sea, the fresh water, and the sun. The last three will affect the Antichrist and his kingdom.

What Others are Saying:

Something to Ponder

Unfulfilled
Tribulation Period

KEY Symbols:

Beast Out Of The Earth

The False Prophet

KEY POINT

The heavenly angels will be very active on earth during the Tribulation Period.

☞ **GO TO:**

Matthew 13:40–42 (angels)

2 Peter 3:9 (perish)

repentance: turning toward God, away from wrong

*Satanic Trinity: Satan,
the Antichrist, and the
False Prophet*

KEY POINT

Those who take the
Mark of the Beast or
worship the image of
the Antichrist will not
repent and be saved.

**What Others
are Saying:**

Bowl #1—The <u>first bowl</u> will be poured out upon the land. Those who still have a chance to repent will not be affected, but all those who have taken the Mark of the Beast or worshiped his image will be covered with ugly, painful sores. The Antichrist will not be able to heal his own followers and the world will know he is a fake.

Bowl #2—The <u>second bowl</u> will be poured out upon the sea turning it into blood. The pollution will kill every living creature in it.

Bowl #3—The <u>third bowl</u> will be poured out upon all the earth's remaining fresh water, turning that into blood. The angel in charge of it will declare that this judgment is justified because the Antichrist and his followers have been spilling the blood of God's people.

Bowl #4—The <u>fourth bowl</u> will be poured out upon the sun, turning up its heat output and scorching people with fire. They will acknowledge the existence of God, but will curse his name and refuse to repent or give him glory.

Bowl #5—The <u>fifth bowl</u> will be poured out upon the Antichrist and his kingdom, plunging everything into darkness and causing such grave misgivings among his people they will chew their tongues in agony. Their pain will be so intense that they will curse God, but none of them will repent of their sins.

Bowl #6—The <u>sixth bowl</u> will be poured out upon the Euphrates River, causing it to dry up and paving the way for the kings of the East (China and her allies) to move their great army westward toward Israel and the Middle East. The **Satanic Trinity** will respond by sending demonic spirits to gather the other kings of the earth for a great battle. They will assemble at a place called Armageddon.

Bowl #7—The <u>seventh bowl</u> will be poured out and the greatest earthquake the world has ever experienced will take place. Every city on earth except Babylon will be in ruins and that city will be split into three parts. Earth's entire surface will be changed. All the islands will sink beneath the waters, every mountain will be leveled, and people will be crushed by hundred-pound hailstones falling from the sky.

David Jeremiah with C. C. Carlson: Loathsome skin diseases are significant because they are outward signs of inward corruption. Jesus described those who looked good on the outside, but were rotten to the core, when He spoke to the self-righteous leaders of His day.[18]

Both offensively and defensively, Russia is racing toward full military readiness. U.S. authorities report that they have stored "at least 362 million metric tons of grain in nuclear blast and fallout shelters." They are also developing the dreaded binary chemical weapons which can be disguised as ordinary industrial chemicals. Yet they are said to be as powerful as the deadly VX gas. Additionally, and at great expense, they are engineering a so-called "superplague," which could resist all medical treatments.[19]

• • •

DESTINY BULLETIN, MARCH 1999 . . .

[1998] brought approximately 700 catastrophic natural disasters, which killed at least 50,000 people—making 1998 the most calamitous year on record, according to Munich Reinsurance, a German company that monitors natural disasters. Last year's total was *three times* the annual average for natural catastrophes during the 1960's.[20]

• • •

THE COMMERCIAL APPEAL, NOVEMBER 24, 1998 . . .

Water shortages in parts of the world in the next 25 years will pose the greatest threat to food production and human health, according to a study financed by the United States and Japan. At a time when 1.3 billion people have no access to clean water, it also could become a key issue in conflicts, warns the report's author, World Bank vice president and agriculture expert Ismail Serageldin.[21]

God can do anything. If he wants to cover unbelievers with <u>festering</u> sores, turn water into <u>blood</u>, plunge the world into <u>darkness</u>, or crush everything with hundred-pound chunks of <u>hail</u>, he can.

RELATED CURRENT EVENTS

☞ **GO TO:**

Exodus 9:8–12 (festering)

Exodus 7:14–24 (blood)

Exodus 10:21–22; Matthew 27:45 (darkness)

Exodus 9:18–25 (hail)

Remember This . . .

Unfulfilled
Tribulation Period

Because of the similarities some writers think the bowl judgments are a restatement of the trumpet judgments. The similarities are there, but there are also many differences including the fact that the bowl judgments will be much more extensive.

Fulfillment: Many who go to church no longer believe it, and many who never go to church scoff at it, but this world is headed for judgment. God will not accept a Satanic world government, a godless Global Ethic, or a Christ-hating civilization. Whether people believe it or not, the "good old days" are almost over and things are about to change drastically.

JUDGMENT

Bowls	Trumpets	Seals
1 Sores on followers of Antichrist	1/3 of plants destroyed	Antichrist released
2 Seas turned to blood	1/3 of seas polluted	War breaks out
3 Fresh water turned to blood	1/3 of fresh water polluted	Economic collapse, famine
4 Sun scorches unbelievers	1/3 of heavenly bodies darkened	Death of unbelievers
5 Darkness over kingdom of Antichrist	Demonic locusts released	Death of believers
6 Battle of Armageddon earthquake	1/3 of mankind killed	Nuclear war
7 Destroys every city	Bowls dumped	Trumpets sound

THE BIG PICTURE 🔍

☞ **GO TO:**

Revelation 16:17
(seventh)

Revelation 17:1–18:24 After the <u>seventh</u> angel poured out the seventh bowl, there was another pause so one of the angels could explain the mystery of Babylon the Great. She had two identities: a woman and a city. As a woman this evil person was a prostitute and she taught her children to be like her. She conspired with political leaders to merge religion and government. At first, she was rich, supported the beast with seven heads and ten horns, and thrived by persecuting God's faithful people. John was told that the beast (the Antichrist) will come out of the Abyss, rule over a world kingdom divided into ten regions, oppose Christ, and be defeated. But

before he falls, God will put it in his heart to turn against the woman and destroy her. As a city, Babylon will develop strong ties with world government and become the home of world trade. It will be rich and sinful, will persecute God's people, and will be destroyed in one hour. World leaders will cry when they see her destruction. The city will become the home of demons and will never rise again.

Some Mysteries Are Truly Mysterious

The one world government will think it needs a one world religion to prevent religious wars. As a woman Mystery Babylon is the **Global Ethic** that will exist during the Tribulation Period. Being a prostitute means she will commit **spiritual adultery**, a biblical way of saying she will be unfaithful to God. Teaching her children to be that way too means this world religion will influence all the other religions of the world to adopt her wicked beliefs. World political leaders will love her Global Ethics, her set of one world religious values, and the two (the prostitute and the world leaders) will be so infatuated with each other at first they will try to merge church and state. The **beast** will support her for awhile—she will be rich and will help persecute and kill God's true people. The beast, commonly called the Antichrist, will be someone who comes out of the Abyss, the subterranean abode of demons. He will rule over the next world kingdom, the seventh in history, and drastically change it into an eighth—a Satanic New World Order. At the time he takes over the seventh, it will have been divided into ten regions, each region having a ruler and all ten rulers giving him their unqualified support. He will oppose everything associated with Christianity and be defeated by Christ at his Second Coming. But before that happens, God will put it in the beast's heart to destroy all those who supported the one world religion.

As a city, Mystery Babylon will court world leaders and support world trade. Some businessmen will become extremely wealthy. It will be one of the most wicked places on earth and the crimes committed there will not go unnoticed by God. The city will be destroyed in one hour. Her destruction will be worldwide news, political leaders will be terrified, and rich businessmen will grieve over their losses.

Global Ethic: government approved religious values, one world religion

spiritual adultery: abandoned God

beast: the Antichrist

☞ **GO TO:**

Revelation 13:1 (beast)

KEY POINT

Before the Tribulation Period is over, all those involved in this corrupt religious system will be killed by the Antichrist and his political allies.

**What Others
are Saying:**

Hal Lindsey: The seven-headed beast represents the six great powers which have had dominion over the world, and a seventh kingdom which has not yet risen. When it comes it will be a ten-nation revival of the sixth head (the old Roman Empire), and is pictured by the beast's ten horns.[22]

David Jeremiah with C. C. Carlson: When John was given a vision of the world tomorrow where the beast would reign, he saw that this world leader would be supported by two powerful global allies: one will be religious in nature and the other, economic. This unholy alliance will form the final world government—doomed for extinction.[23]

Wim Malgo: Religion, even the Christian religion, without Jesus Christ as its center, is the most corrupt thing there is! This is the great whore, and it is spiritual harlotry when we accept Christianity without accepting Christ as our Savior and Redeemer.[24]

*Remember
This . . .*

Unfulfilled

Tribulation Period

No one will be able to buy or sell during the Tribulation Period without taking the Mark of the Beast and worshiping the Antichrist. Therefore, all of these global traders will be corrupt businessmen under the influence of Satan.

Fulfillment: Church and state are going to be merged during the Tribulation Period and the result will be a corrupt religious system. The two will cooperate to strengthen each other and to persecute and kill true believers. The world government will destroy the world religion and Jesus will destroy the world government.

THE BIG PICTURE

> **Revelation 19:1–21** John witnessed a praise service in heaven, the Second Coming of Christ, and the end of the Antichrist and the False Prophet.

The Second Coming

Armageddon: the last and greatest war on earth

Lake of Fire: the final abode of Satan and his followers

At the end of the Tribulation Period, all those in heaven will begin to praise God for his destruction of Babylon and for avenging the death of true believers. The Church will be united with Christ, heaven will open, and Jesus will return to earth with his Church. He will confront the troops of the Antichrist at **Armageddon** and destroy them. Then he will capture the Antichrist and the False Prophet and throw them into the **Lake of Fire**.

William L. Pettingill: What a terrible picture this is! Let it be remembered that the Artist who painted it is God Himself. He has in His great compassion told us beforehand concerning things not seen as yet, and He tells us that all these things must shortly come to pass.[25]

Wim Malgo: While the Satanic trinity (cf. Revelation 16:13) deceives all the kings of the earth and leads them to Israel (for Armageddon lies in Israel), it is ultimately the Lord Himself who is leading them there, *"And he gathered them together into a place called in the Hebrew tongue Armageddon"* (Revelation 16:16). Here it becomes absolutely clear what is taking place worldwide. The nations do not want to war with God and the Lamb but with Israel. They do not see that in reality they are fighting against God and the Lamb.[26]

KEY POINT

At the Second Coming Jesus will return *with* his church not *for* his church, and his return will be to put an end to all rebellion against God.

Arnold G. Fruchtenbaum: The thing that should be carefully noted here is that the church is already in heaven *before* the second coming. Furthermore, the church has been in heaven long enough to undergo the Judgment Seat of Christ. This clearly means that the Rapture and the second coming cannot be the same thing but must be separated by some duration of time.[27]

Unfulfilled
Tribulation Period

Fulfillment: It is sad that so many so-called brilliant people will go to such a terrible destruction, but it will be the result of their own faulty decisions. What will happen to them will be the result of their own steadfast refusal to abandon their wicked ways and turn to God. They will leave him with no choice.

THE BIG PICTURE

Revelation 20:1–15 John saw an angel seize Satan and throw him into the Abyss for a thousand years. He witnessed the resurrection of those who refused to take the mark and watched as they reigned with Christ for a thousand years. None of them suffered the second death. After the thousand years ended, Satan was released for an unspecified period of time and he led other rebellions against God. This brought destruction upon his followers and got him cast into the Lake of Fire. Then the dead unbelievers were raised, judged, and cast into the Lake of Fire too, which is the second death.

The Millennium And Beyond

Following the Second Coming an angel will be sent from heaven to earth to arrest Satan. He will capture the devil, bind him, and cast him into the Abyss to prevent him from harming the earth for the next thousand years. This thousand-year period is often called the **Millennium**. During this time, the Church will sit on thrones and <u>judge</u> the world. The Tribulation Period saints who were beheaded by the Antichrist will be raised from the dead and they will reign also. They will never be cast into the Lake of Fire. After spending a thousand years in the Abyss, Satan will be released. The Bible does not state it, but the purpose of this seems to be to test those born on earth during the Millennium and to prove that sin is a flaw in the human heart, not something that results from a bad environment. Satan will cause many to sin and they will be destroyed by fire from heaven. Satan will be captured again and this time he will be thrown into the Lake of Fire and will never escape. Having done this, God will set up a throne, raise every unbeliever from the dead, open the books, and judge each person by their record. The Book of Life will be opened, but the names of these people will not be there because they will be people who never accepted Jesus as their Savior. They will be cast into the Lake of Fire.

Millennium: the thousand-year reign of Christ on earth

☞ **GO TO:**

1 Corinthians 6:2–3 (judge)

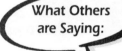

What Others are Saying:

William L. Pettingill: The departure of the Church from the Earth will be but temporary. She will return with her Lord when He comes in the clouds of Heaven with power and great glory to judge the world and reign as King of Kings and Lord of Lords [sic]. Wherever He goes she will go, for she is His bride and the promise is "so shall we ever be with the Lord."[28]

David Jeremiah with C. C. Carlson: The Great White Throne Judgment will not be like any courtroom experience anyone has ever had. There will be a Judge, but no jury; a Prosecutor, but no defender; a sentence, but no appeal. This is the final judgment of the world. God is patient, but at that time there will be no more opportunities to accept Him.[29]

Thomas Ice and Timothy Demy: The lake of fire is the final form of hell from which, once placed there, no one ever leaves.[30]

The day will come when the Book of Life will be checked and anyone whose name is not there will be sent to hell forever. Is your name in the Book of Life?

Some critics do not believe in a Millennium, but a thousand-year period is mentioned six times in Revelation 20. Once is enough, but six times makes it emphatic.

Fulfillment: The things mentioned in this chapter are incredible, but many of them are confirmed by other prophecies in the Bible. The return of Christ to set up a kingdom and judge the world is mentioned over and over again. Christians have much to rejoice about and non-Christians have much to fear.

Something to Ponder

WARNING

Unfulfilled
After the Millennium

THE BIG PICTURE

> **Revelation 21:1–27** John saw a new heaven and a new earth. He also saw the Holy City called the new Jerusalem. God and his church were both there. The Holy City had twelve gates, twelve foundations, and a thick wall, but there was no temple, no sun, and no moon. Visitors flocked there with gifts, but nothing impure was allowed in.

The Holy City

In the future, the current heaven and <u>earth</u> will be replaced. One of the features of the new earth will be the absence of large bodies of water. There will also be a Holy <u>City</u> which will be the future dwelling place of the Church. The throne of God will be there and everything will be new. We will not die, cry, or hurt, and we will have free access to the Holy Spirit. This is our Christian inheritance for overcoming sin through faith in Jesus. And there will be no unbelievers there because they will all be in the <u>Lake of Fire</u>.

The Holy City will descend to the new earth. It will glow with the glory of God, have a high wall with twelve gates, have an angel sitting at each gate, and have the name of one of the twelve tribes of Israel written on each gate. The wall will be sitting on twelve foundations and each foundation will bear the name of one of the twelve apostles. The city will be cube shaped, each side being about 1,500 miles long, and will be made out of pure gold. The wall around the city, comprised of **jasper**, will be about 216 feet thick, and its foundations will be decorated with various kinds

☞ **GO TO:**

2 Peter 3:13 (earth)

Hebrews 11:13–16 (City)

Revelation 20:11–15 (Lake of Fire)

jasper: an opaque, translucent stone such as opal, diamond, or topaz

of precious stones. Each gate will be made of a single pearl and the main street will be pure gold.

The city will not have a Temple in it because there will be no sin there and everyone will have direct access to God and Jesus. The Father and the Son radiate light so their presence will eliminate the need for a sun and moon. In fact the light will be so great, it will even light up the new earth. There will never be any darkness or any need to shut the gates. Visitors will be allowed in, but only those who have accepted Christ.

What Others are Saying:

Wim Malgo: Jerusalem is the opposite of Babylon. The separation of the two is radical and clearly visible, for Jerusalem is situated on the new earth. Today also, the contrast between light and darkness, good and evil, heavenly and earthly, the true bride of the Lamb and the whore, is visible.[31]

Hal Lindsey: This ends the Millennium, and eternity then begins with God destroying the old earth and re-creating a new heaven (universe) and earth. His crowning creation, however, is the New Jerusalem—that beautiful City of God.[32]

Unfulfilled

Tribulation Period

Fulfillment: Some worry about overpopulation and the earth running out of critical resources. But the One who created it in the first place will create another one that will be better and will never be depleted or destroyed.

THE BIG PICTURE 🔍

> **Revelation 22:1–21** An angel showed John a river containing the water of life. Then he showed John the tree of life and told him more about God and heaven. Finally, John heard Christ's final invitation, final warning and final promise.

Lot's Of Good News

The Holy City will have a river called *"the river of the water of life."* This is a symbol of the <u>living water</u> or the Holy Spirit and it will flow from the throne of God. The truth taught here is that there will be a continual outpouring of the Holy Spirit in the New Jerusalem and this outpouring will satisfy the spiritual thirst of everyone there. Rows of the <u>tree of life</u> will grow on each side of the river and bear fruit for the residents of the city. The believer's task will be to serve God, and each one will see God's face, bear his name, and walk in his light.

☞ **GO TO:**

John 4:13–14
(living water)

Genesis 3:22–24
(tree of life)

The angel pointed out to John that the return of Jesus will happen very fast; many commentators say, "in the twinkling of an eye." Also, those who die without Christ as their Savior will never change and never have a Savior, but those who die with Christ as their Savior will belong to him in eternity and receive rewards for their service in this life. One of the blessings will be permission to pass through the gates of the city. Hell, the abode of unbelievers, will be outside the city somewhere. The final invitation is to come and be saved through faith in Jesus. The final warning is that anyone who adds to or takes away from the words in the book of Revelation will suffer the wrath of God. The final promise is that Jesus will come back and it will happen very fast. The last verse in the Bible is a reminder for his people: *"the grace of the Lord Jesus be with God's people. Amen."*

What Others are Saying:

John F. Walvoord: All that spoke of sin and its penalties is wiped away in heaven, and there is nothing left that is a reminder of sin. All are blessed, not cursed. In support of this conclusion, it is revealed that God's throne and that of the Lamb will be in the city.[33]

Larry Richards: We cannot know how wonderful eternity will be for those who have trusted God until we are welcomed into the new heaven and earth God will create. But these last chapters of the Bible tell us that it will be wonderful indeed.[34]

After reading the daily newspaper or watching the daily news on TV, one can easily think the future looks bleak and become discouraged or depressed. But we must remember that many of these troubling events are things Jesus said would happen just before he returns. Today, things may look bleak, but prophetically speaking the future looks bright.

Fulfillment: God gave Bible prophecy for many reasons. One purpose is to warn unbelievers of God's future judgment. Knowing these things will cause some to repent of their sins and accept Jesus as their Savior before it is too late. Another purpose is to let God's people know that he is still in control and has many blessings in store for them in the future. The blessings mentioned in this chapter just scratch the surface of what eternity will be like for the saved.

Something to Ponder

Unfulfilled
After the Millennium

STUDY QUESTIONS

1. What is an interlude and what is revealed during each one of them?
2. What is wormwood and what harm will it do?
3. What are the two identities of Babylon the Great and what do they mean?
4. Identify two symbols that are used to describe the Antichrist. What do they mean?
5. What will the Holy City be like and what is its name?

CHAPTER WRAP-UP

- Many experts believe the seven letters to the seven churches are, among other things, prophecies that foretell seven phases of church history. They are seen as a panoramic view of church history before it happened. According to this interpretation, the Church is now in the seventh and last period, the Laodicean period. This places the Church in its final hours before the Rapture. (Revelation 2–3)

- The Tribulation Period judgments have been written on a seven-sealed scroll in heaven. Jesus will break the seals and open it after the Rapture. The first will release the coming Antichrist; the second will spark a rash of wars; the third will bring economic collapse and famine; the fourth will take the life of untold millions of unbelievers; the fifth will release persecution and death of believers; the sixth will be something, perhaps nuclear war, that will impact the entire universe; the seventh will release the trumpet judgments. (Revelation 6:1–8:1)

- After Jesus breaks the seventh seal, seven angels will stand before God and blow a trumpet one at a time. When the first trumpet sounds, hail mixed with fire will destroy one-third of the plant life; when the second trumpet sounds, a huge burning mountain will kill one-third of the sea creatures and destroy one-third of the ships; when the third trumpet sounds, a large burning star will fall to earth and pollute one-third of the earth's fresh water supply; when the fourth trumpet sounds, the light of the sun, moon, and stars will be diminished by one-third; when the fifth trumpet sounds, multiplied millions of demon-possessed locusts will be released to sting earth's inhabitants; when the sixth trumpet sounds, four of Satan's fallen angels will cause the death of one-third of humankind; the seventh trumpet will cause a great earthquake, a great hailstorm, and the release of the seven bowl judgments. (Revelation 8:2–11:15)

- After the angel sounds the seventh trumpet, seven angels will pour out a bowl of God's wrath one at a time. The first will cause the followers of the Antichrist to be covered with ugly painful sores; the second will kill the sea creatures; the third will pollute earth's fresh water; the fourth will cause the sun to grow hotter and scorch people; the fifth will put the Antichrist and his kingdom in darkness and cause great fear; the sixth will dry up the Euphrates River and set up the Battle of Armageddon; and the seventh will be the greatest earthquake the world has ever seen. (Revelation 16:2–21)

- During the Millennium Satan will be restrained, the Church will serve as judges on earth, and believers who die after the Rapture will be resurrected. After the Millennium Satan will be temporarily released and cause more rebellion on earth; then he will be seized and cast into hell; and then the dead unbelievers will be resurrected, judged, and cast into hell. Following that, God will create a new heaven and new earth. The Holy City will descend to the new earth, and the Church will dwell in the Holy City and move back and forth between it and the new earth. (Revelation 20–22)

APPENDIX A — THE ANSWERS

CHAPTER ONE

1. Prophecy is an important part of the Word of God. It reveals what God plans to do. Up to forty percent of the Bible is prophecy. Because so much prophecy has already been fulfilled, we can logically expect the rest to be fulfilled. (Introduction)
2. Yes. He allowed Satan to tempt Adam and Eve, the world to be corrupted, and Israel to stray. He will allow a Tribulation Period. (Genesis 3:14–19; 6:11–13; Deuteronomy 4:26–31)
3. His covenants are the driving force behind prophecy. They reveal what God plans to do and they are everlasting. (Genesis 12:1–3; 13:14–17; 15:18; 17:19)
4. God will bless us if we bless Israel. Our Messiah came from the nation of Israel. The covenants tell us who the Promised Land belongs to. (Genesis 12:1–3)
5. He will come from the nation of Israel and from the tribe of Judah. (Genesis 28:13–15; Numbers 24:14–19)

CHAPTER TWO

1. It contains the first use of the word "Messiah" or "Christ" in the Bible and it predicts that the Messiah or Christ will also be a king. (1 Samuel 2:10)
2. The phrase "David's house" refers to the dynasty of David and it will last forever because Jesus who is a descendant of David will rule over it. (2 Samuel 7:4–17)
3. It would be one of the consequences of Solomon and/or his descendants abandoning God. If they turned away from God, became unfaithful, lived in sin, and failed to keep his commandments, God would turn away from them and the Temple would no longer be special to him. (1 Kings 9:3–7)
4. Never. They are everlasting covenants. (1 Chronicles 16:15–18)
5. It depends. One's relationship with God through Christ is the determining factor. The saved will celebrate, but the lost will weep. (1 Chronicles 16:31–33)

CHAPTER THREE

1. Instead of having verses that rhyme, Hebrew poetry has thoughts that are repeated. The same thoughts are restated in a slightly different way.
2. He would have flesh, see with his eyes, stand on earth, it will be in the latter days, etc. (Job 19:25–27)
3. It makes him laugh at, scoff, rebuke, and terrify his opposition. (Psalm 2:1–12)
4. They will mock him, pierce his hands and feet, scorn him, despise him, cast lots for his clothes, give him vinegar to drink, and accuse him. (Psalm 22)
5. Everyone on earth. Jerusalem. Israel. (Psalm 22, 48, and 132)

CHAPTER FOUR

1. The Jews will no longer defile themselves; they will obey God and keep his laws. Jerusalem will be called the City of Righteousness and the Faithful City. (Ezekiel 37:23–38; Isaiah 1:24–31)
2. The Tribulation Period. It will begin with a seven-year covenant to protect Israel. It will be half over when the Antichrist sets up the abomination that causes desolation. (Jeremiah 30:5–7; Daniel 9:27)
3. It is a covenant that God will make with Israel during the Millennium. He will bless the nation with rain, good crops, freedom, safety, and a knowledge of him. It will be a covenant of peace and it will be everlasting. (Ezekiel 34:22–31; 37:1–28)
4. The bones represented the entire nation of Israel that had scattered into foreign nations; Israel seemed dead, dried up, and without hope. The joined sticks represented the revival of Israel and Judah as one nation. (Ezekiel 37:1–28)
5. Russia and her allies, Babylon (Iraq), and Damascus (Syria). (Ezekiel 38:1–39:16; Isaiah 13:1–22; 17:1–14)

CHAPTER FIVE

1. Yes. Hosea compared the wickedness of Israel to that of an adulterous wife. He predicted that the nation would be punished, renewed and restored. (Hosea 1:10–11; 6:1–3)
2. A lack of food and water, empty storehouses, dried-up pastures, a military attack against Israel, the sun and moon darkened, and the Battle of Armageddon. (Joel 1:15–20; 2:1–11; 3:9–16)
3. The world will be filled with distress and danger. (Amos 5:16–20)
4. All nations. The entire world. (Obadiah 1:15–16; Zephaniah 1:14–18)
5. The Jews will look upon the One they pierced and weep. He is the shepherd, the One who will return to the Mount of Olives, the One who will return with his saints. (Zechariah 12:1–14; 13:7–9; 14:1–21)

CHAPTER SIX

1. Jesus calls blessed those who are poor in spirit, those who are mournful over sin, those who are meek before God, those who hunger and thirst for righteousness, those who are merciful, those who have a pure heart, and those who are peacemakers. (Matthew 5:3–12)
2. The sermon is called the Olivet Discourse because Jesus was on the Mount of Olives when he preached it. That is also where he was when he ascended into heaven and where he will return. (Matthew 24:3–5; Acts 1:9–11)
3. It is better to stop sinning than to go to hell. The worms never die and the fires are never quenched there. (Mark 9:42–48)
4. The one who knows God's will and does not do it will be punished more than the one who does not know it. More is required of those who know better. (Luke 12:45–48)
5. Jesus. When he returns to receive his people in the Rapture. (John 11:25–26; 14:2–3)

CHAPTER SEVEN

1. He will judge each person according to what he has done. They will receive trouble for trouble. (Romans 2:5–6; 2 Thessalonians 1:6–10)
2. The hardening will cease at the Rapture of the Church when the full number of Gentiles has come in. The Bible says all Israel will be saved, but "all Israel" includes only those people God says are Jews. (Romans 11:25–27)
3. Gold, silver, and costly stones are indestructible materials that represent sound Bible doctrines such as the death, burial, and resurrection of Jesus, holy living, etc. Wood, hay, and straw are destructible materials that represent unsound, feel-good doctrines. Those who build in the church with indestructible materials will receive a reward. (1 Corinthians 3:10–15)
4. Jesus will return in the clouds, he will bring the deceased believers with him, they will be raised from the dead, living believers will be caught up into the clouds with them, and all believers will be with him forever. (1 Thessalonians 4:13–18)
5. No. Believers have been taught so they are not in darkness and will not be caught up by surprise. (1 Thessalonians 5:1–9)

CHAPTER EIGHT

1. The old covenant was faulty, required keeping the Law, required priests, was broken by the Jews, and was cancelled by God. The new covenant is a covenant of grace, is placed in people's hearts, requires no priests, and provides forgiveness of sins. (Hebrews 8:7–13)

2. No. God blesses many people with wealth so they can use it to do his work and glorify him. But hoarding wealth in the last days will make some people miserable because they will lose everything when it becomes worthless. Wealth will not substitute for faith in God. It will not buy his favor or stop his judgment. Rather, it will be used against the lost as evidence of greed and selfishness. (James 5:1–3)

3. Those who grumble against others are warned that they will be judged. The mercy of God has given us new birth, hope, an inheritance, protection, and more. And when the Rapture occurs we will be like Jesus. (James 5:7–9; 1 Peter 1:3–7; 1 John 3:2)

4. The miracle on the Mount of Transfiguration. Jesus took some of his disciples to this mountain, a change came over him, a voice spoke from heaven, and the Second Coming was revealed. (2 Peter 1:16–19)

5. The scoffers will imply that nothing has changed since the beginning of creation. The judgment of the fallen angels implies that all who reject God will be judged. (2 Peter 3:3–4; Jude 6)

CHAPTER NINE

1. An interlude is a pause in the sequence of events. For example, God placed an interlude in between the opening of the sixth and seventh seals to explain the marking of the 144,000. He placed another interlude after the sounding of the seventh trumpet to explain that a mighty angel will claim possession of the earth for Jesus during the Tribulation Period and to explain the two witnesses. Another interlude explains the attacks on Israel, the Antichrist, and the False Prophet. (Revelation 7:10–13)

2. This is the third trumpet judgment, a great star blazing like a torch that will fall to earth and pollute one-third of the fresh water supply. It will be named after a bitter herb in the Bible and those who drink the tainted water will die. (Revelation 8:10–11)

3. She is a mother and a city, a false religion and the home of global trade. As a mother she will commit spiritual adultery with world leaders, merge church and state, and produce a Global Ethic that will be opposed to Christ. Her daughters are the prostitute religions (false religions) of the world. As a city, she will be the home of global commerce, the home of corrupt businessmen who have taken the mark and worshiped the Antichrist. (Revelation 17–18)

4. He will be the first rider to appear on a white horse and the first beast, the one coming out of the sea. As the rider on a white horse, he will be a counterfeit Christ, a fake man of God who will talk peace and produce war. As the first beast, he will be full of evil, blaspheme God, worship Satan, receive authority from Satan, and kill God's people. (Revelation 6:2; 13:1–10)

5. God will dwell with his people, and there will be no death, loneliness, depression, pain, or suffering there. Jesus, the Holy Spirit, the angels, and the Church will be there, but no unbelievers. The city will be square on all sides, have a thick wall, gates of pearl, streets of gold, a river of the water of life, the tree of life, no sun, and no night. It will be called the new Jerusalem. (Revelation 21–22)

APPENDIX B — THE EXPERTS

Wayne Barber, Eddie Rasnake and Richard Shepherd—Pastors at Woodland Park Baptist Church in Chattanooga, TN, conference speakers, and authors. (AMG Publishers, P.O. Box 22000, Chattanooga, TN 37422)

William Barclay—Internationally recognized scholar, teacher, author, and pastor, and the editor of the *Daily Study Bible* series of books. (The Westminster Press, Philadelphia, PA)

Kenneth L. Barker and Waylon Bailey—Seminary professors, authors, and pastors. (Broadman & Holman Publishers, Nashville, TN)

Irvin Baxter, Jr.—Pentecostal minister, editor of *Endtime Magazine*, and author of several books. (Endtime, P.O. Box 2066, Richmond, IN 47375-2066)

Robert T. Boyd—Pastor, author, archaeologist, and conference speaker. (Kregal Publications, Grand Rapids, MI 49501)

Dave Breese—President of World Prophetic Ministry and Bible teacher on *The King Is Coming* television program. (World Prophetic Ministry, P.O. Box 907, Colton, CA 92324)

Charles Capps—Author, teacher, and host of *Concepts of Faith* radio broadcast. (He lives in England, AR)

Joe Chambers—Senior editor of *The End Times And Victorious Living*, pastor, and author of several books. (Paw Creek Ministries, Inc., 5110 Tuckaseegee Road, Charlotte, NC 28208)

J. R. Church—Host of the nationwide television program *Prophecy in the News*. (Prophecy Publications, P.O. Box 7000, Oklahoma City, OK 73153)

Gary G. Cohen—Author and president of Clearwater Christian College. (Cleawater Christian College, Clearwater, FL)

Terry L. Cook—Pastor, author, and lecturer. (Second Coming Ministries, 61535 S. Highway 97, Unit 9, Suite 288, Bend, OR 97702)

Timothy Demy—Navy chaplain and author. (Harvest House Publishers, Eugene, OR 97402)

Jimmy DeYoung—Author, conference speaker, and expert on Israel.

Charles Dyer—Professor of Bible exposition at Dallas Theological Seminary in Dallas, Texas, and author of several books. (He lives in Garland, Texas.)

Theodore H. Epp—Author and host and former Director of *Back To The Bible Broadcast*. (Back to the Bible, Lincoln, Nebraska 68501)

Charles L. Feinberg—Dean emeritus of Talbot School of Theology in California, author, lecturer, and recognized authority on Jewish history. (Moody Press, Chicago, IL)

W. Herschel Ford—Former pastor of several large Southern Baptist churches including First Baptist in El Paso, Texas. (Zondervan Publishing House, Grand Rapids, MI)

Arno Froese—Editor of *Midnight Call* and *News From Israel*. (Midnight Call, Inc., 4694 Platt Springs Road, West Columbia, SC 29170; News From Israel, P.O. Box 4389, West Columbia, SC 29171-4389)

Arnold G. Fruchtenbaum—Founder of *Bible Institute* in Israel and *Ariel Ministries* in the United States with fellowships ministering to Jews in several major cities. (San Antonio, TX)

Arno C. Gaebelein—Pastor, teacher of the Word, and one of the greatest Bible expositors in the history of this country. (Loizeaux Brothers, Neptune, New Jersey)

Duane A. Garrett—Professor at Bethel Theological Seminary and author. (Bethel Theological Seminary, St. Paul, MN)

Mike Gendron—Evangelist and conference speaker. (Proclaiming The Gospel, P.O. Box 940871, Plano, TX 75094, www.pro-gospel.org)

Billy Graham—World famous evangelist and author of several books. (Billy Graham Evangelistic Association, 1300 Harmon Place, P.O. Box 779, Minneapolis, MN 55440-0779)

Oliver B. Greene—Author of several books, radio show host, and former director of The Gospel Hour, Inc.

John Hagee—Founder and pastor of Cornerstone Church and President of Global Evangelism Television. (San Antonio, TX)

Charles Halff—Executive director of The Christian Jew Foundation, host of *Messianic Perspectives Radio Network*, and featured writer for *Message of the Christian Jew*. (Messianic Perspectives, P.O. Box 345, San Antonio, TX)

Henry H. Halley—Author of one of the best-known and most-used Bible study guides in the world, *Halley's Bible Handbook*. (Zondervan Publishing House, 1415 Lake Drive SE, Grand Rapids, MI 49506)

Gary Hedrick—Author, speaker on the *Messianic Perspectives Radio Program*, and writer for *The Christian Jew Foundation Newsletter*. (Messianic Perspectives, P.O. Box 345, San Antonio, TX)

Ed Hindson—Minister of Biblical Studies at Rehoboth Baptist Church in Atlanta, Georgia, vice president of *There's Hope*, dean of the Institute of Biblical Studies at Liberty University in Virginia, and executive board member of the Pre-Trib Research Center in Washington, D.C.

David Hocking—Pastor, radio host, and director of *Hope For Today Ministries*. (P.O. Box 3927, Tustin, CA 92781-3927)

H. Wayne House—Dean and professor at Michigan Theological Seminary in Plymouth, MI, freelance writer and author. (Kregel Publications, Grand Rapids, MI 49501)

Dave Hunt—Internationally known author of more than twenty books with sales exceeding three million copies.

Noah Hutchings—President of *The Southwest Radio Church*, one of the oldest and best-known prophetic ministries in the world, and author of more than one hundred books. (P.O. Box 1144, Oklahoma City, OK 73101)

Thomas Ice—Pastor, author, college teacher, and executive director of the Pre-Trib Research Center in Washington, DC. (Harvest House Publishers, Eugene, OR 97402)

William T. James—Coauthor and general editor of several books presenting a series of insightful essays by well-known prophecy scholars, writers, and broadcasters. (Benton, AR)

Grant R. Jeffrey—Best-selling author and frequent guest on radio and TV programs. (Frontier Research Publications, Inc., Box 129, Station U, Toronto, Ontario, Canada M8Z 5M4)

Irving L. Jensen—Professor emeritus of Bible at Bryan College in Dayton, TN, and author of dozens of books with more than sixty currently in print. (World Wide Publications, Minneapolis, MN 55403)

David Jeremiah with C. C. Carlson—David Jeremiah is president of Christian Heritage College and senior pastor of Scott Memorial Baptist Church in El Cajon, CA, and host of a popular radio program called *Turning Point*. Carol Carlson has authored/coauthored a total of nineteen books, the most famous being *The Late Great Planet Earth* with Hal Lindsey.

Tim LaHaye—Founder and president of Family Life Seminars, author, pastor, counselor, television/radio commentator, and nationally recognized authority on Bible prophecy and family life.

Norbert Lieth—Writer in *News From Israel*. (See Arno Froese)

Hal Lindsey—Many call him the father of the modern day prophecy movement. He is president of Hal Lindsey Ministries, author of many books, and host of a radio and TV program. (P.O. Box 4000, Palos Verdes, CA 90274)

Herbert Lockyer—Author and pastor of churches in England, Scotland, and the U.S. before his death in 1984.

Marlin Maddoux—Host of *Point of View Radio Talk Show* and author. (International Christian Media, P.O. Box 30, Dallas, TX 75221)

Wim Malgo—Former author, pastor, lecturer, evangelist, and founder of *Midnight Call Magazine* and *News From Israel*. (See Arno Froese)

Texe Marrs—Retired military officer, author of more than a dozen books, former university professor, and head of *Living Truth Ministries*. (Living Truth Ministries, Austin, TX)

J. Vernon McGee—Pastor, author, and former host of the popular *Thru The Bible With J. Vernon McGee* radio program. (Thru The Bible Radio, Box 100, Pasadena, CA 91109)

Chuck Missler—An expert on Russia, Israel, Europe, and the Middle East, founder of Koinonia House Ministries, and editor of *Personal Update* newsletter. (Koinonia House, P.O. Box D, Coeur d'Alene, ID 83816-0347)

Henry M. Morris with Henry M. Morris III—Authors of several books and teachers at the Institute for Creation Research. (Master Books, Inc., P.O. Box 727, Green Forest, AR 72638)

J. A. Motyer—Former principal of Trinity College in Bristol, England, editor of *The Bible Speaks Today* commentary series, pastor, and author of several books. (Intervarsity Press, Downers Grove, IL 60515)

Russell L. Penney—Professor of Missions at Tyndale Theological Seminary and author. (Tyndale Theological Seminary, Fort Worth, TX)

J. Dwight Pentecost—Scholar and professor emeritus at Dallas Theological Seminary. (Dallas Theological Seminary, Dallas, TX)

Bill Perkins—Executive Director of Compass International, Inc., and host of *Steeling the Mind of America* conferences (Compass International, Inc. 460 Canfield, Suite 1000, Coeur d'Alene, ID 83815)

William L. Pettingill—Author of more than a dozen books. (Fundamental Truth Publishers, Findlay, OH)

Randall Price—President of World of the Bible Ministries, Inc., and author. (World of the Bible Ministries, Inc., 110 Easy Street, San Marcos, TX 78666-7336)

David Reagan—Founder and senior evangelist of *Lamb & Lion Ministries,* host and teacher of *Christ in Prophecy* radio program, author of several books, and editor of a monthly publication called *The Lamplighter.* (Lamb & Lion Ministries, P.O. Box 919, McKinney, TX 75070)

Larry Richards—Author of more than 175 books and general editor of the *God's Word for the Biblically-Inept* series. (Starburst Publishers, P.O. Box 4123, Lancaster, PA 17604)

Sol Scharfstein—Author of more than one hundred books. (KTAV Publishing House, Inc., 900 Jefferson Street, Hoboken, NJ 07030)

Billy K. Smith and Frank S. Page—Dr. Smith is a former provost and dean at New Orleans Baptist Theological Seminary, and author of numerous articles and books. Dr. Page is a pastor, and the author of numerous articles on Old Testament studies and church administration. (Broadman & Holman Publishers, Nashville, TN)

Charles Stanley—Senior pastor of the 12,000-member First Baptist Church in Atlanta, GA, speaker on radio and television program called *In Touch,* and author of numerous books. (First Baptist Church, Atlanta, GA)

Gary Stearman—Author, conference speaker, and speaker on *Prophecy In The News* television program. (See J. R. Church)

Lee Strobel—Award-winning author, graduate of Harvard Law School, chief legal editor of *The Chicago Tribune.*

Bruce A. Tanner—Writer in *The Bible Expositor And Illuminator.* (See Union Gospel Press)

W. H. Griffith Thomas—Widely recognized before his death as one of the world's outstanding Bible teachers, preacher and lecturer, author of several books. (Wm. B. Eerdmans Publishing Co., 255 Jefferson Ave. S.E., Grand Rapids, MI 49502)

Jack Van Impe—Cohost, along with his wife Rexella, of a worldwide television ministry that analyzes the news in light of Bible prophecy. (Jack Van Impe Ministries International, P.O. Box 7004, Troy, MI 48007)

John F. Walvoord—Theologian, pastor, author, past president and past chancellor of Dallas Theological Seminary, and past editor of the seminary's theological journal called *Bibliotheca Sacra.* (Dallas, TX)

Note: To the best of our knowledge, all of the above information is accurate and up to date. In some cases we were unable to obtain biographical information.
—THE STARBURST EDITORS

ENDNOTES

PROPHECIES IN THE OLD TESTAMENT

Chapter 1

1. *The World Book Encyclopedia*, 1990, Volume P (Chicago: World Book), 274–275.
2. Larry Richards, *The Bible: God's Word for the Biblically-Inept* (Lancaster, PA: Starburst Publishers, 1998), 1.
3. Wayne Barber, Eddie Rasnake, and Richard Shepherd, *Following God* (Chattanooga: AMG Publishers, 1998), 7.
4. Ed Hindson, *Is the Antichrist Alive and Well?* (Eugene, OR: Harvest House Publishers), 22.
5. Bruce A. Tanner, *Bible Expositor and Illuminator* (Fall 1987): 38.
6. Barber, Rasnake, and Shepherd, *Following God,* 19.
7. Robert T. Boyd, *Boyd's Handbook of Practical Apologetics,* (Grand Rapids: Kregel Publications, 1997), 36.
8. Barber, Rasnake, and Shepherd, *Following God,* 44.
9. John F. Walvoord, *Major Bible Prophecies* (Grand Rapids: Zondervan, 1991), 43–44.
10. Henry M. Morris with Henry M. Morris III, *Many Infallible Proofs* (Green Forest, AR: Master Books, 1998), 194.
11. Russell L. Penney, *The Conservative Theological Journal* (December 1998), 458–459.
12. Mike Hughes, *The Jackson (Tennessee) Sun*, 4 December 1998, 1B.
13. Boyd, *Boyd's Handbook of Practical Apologetics,* 102–103.
14. W. H. Griffith Thomas, *Genesis* (Grand Rapids: Eerdmans, 1946), 160.
15. Ibid., 198.
16. Ibid., 238.
17. Barber, Rasnake, and Shepherd, *Following God,* 44.
18. Daymond Duck, *On the Brink* (Lancaster: Starburst Publishers, 1994), 22.

Chapter 2

1. Lee Strobel, *The Case for Christ* (Grand Rapids: Zondervan, 1998), 262.
2. Henry H. Halley, *Halley's Bible Handbook* (Grand Rapids: Regency Reference Library, 1927), 184.
3. Walvoord, *Major Bible Prophecies,* 101.
4. Thomas Ice and Timothy Demy, *Fast Facts on Bible Prophecy* (Eugene, OR: Harvest House Publishers, 1997), 117.
5. Wayne H. House, *Dictionary of Premillennial Theology,* Mal Couch, general editor (Grand Rapids: Kregel Publications, 1996), 315–316.

Chapter 3

1. Charles Stanley, *The Glorious Journey* (Nashville: Thomas Nelson, 1996), 213–214.
2. Arno C. Gaebelein, *The Book of Psalms* (Neptune, NJ: Loizeaux Brothers, 1978), 9–10.
3. The Associated Press, *The Jackson (Tennessee) Sun*, 20 November 1998, 1B.
4. J. R. Church, *Hidden Prophecies in the Psalms* (Oklahoma City: Prophecy Publications, 1986), 43.
5. Thomas Ice and Timothy Demy, *Prophecy Watch* (Eugene, OR: Harvest House Publishers, 1998), 50–51.
6. David W. Breese, letter, *Destiny Bulletin*, November 1998, 3.
7. Ed Hindson, *Approaching Armageddon* (Eugene, OR: Harvest House Publishers, 1997), 231.
8. Charles Halff, *Message of the Christian Jew* (San Antonio: The Christian Jew Foundation), 6.
9. Gaebelein, *The Book of Psalms,* 319–320.

Chapter 4

1. Randall Price, *Jerusalem in Prophecy* (Eugene, OR: Harvest House Publishers, 1998), 229.
2. Dave Hunt, *Occult Invasion* (Eugene, OR: Harvest House Publishers, 1998), 44.
3. Herbert Lockyer, *All the Messianic Prophecies of the Bible* (Grand Rapids: Zondervan, 1973), 61.
4. N. W. Hutchings, *The Persian Gulf Crisis* (Oklahoma City: Hearthstone Publishing, 1990), 104–105.
5. Grant R. Jeffrey, *Prince of Darkness* (New York: Bantam Books, 1995), 163.
6. Gary Stearman, "American Politics Forces Israeli Consessions," *Prophecy in the News*, December 1998, 12.
7. Israel Government Press Office, *Dispatch From Jerusalem*, September/October 1998 (Tulsa: Bridges for Peace), 12.
8. Tim LaHaye, *Understanding the Last Days* (Eugene, OR: Harvest House Publishers, 1998), 83.
9. Wire Service and Staff Reports, "Rosh Hashanah, New Year, Population Statistics," *Dispatch From Jerusalem*, November/December 1998, 1.
10. John Hagee, *Beginning of the End* (Nashville: Thomas Nelson Publishers, 1996), 93.
11. Ice and Demy, *Fast Facts on Bible Prophecy,* 107.
12. Charles Halff, *The End Times Are Here Now* (Springdale, PA: Whitaker House, 1997), 76.
13. "Regathering of Jews to the Promised Land Continues Unabated," *Midnight Call*, November 1998, 36.

14. Arnold G. Fruchtenbaum, *The Footsteps of the Messiah* (Tustin, CA: Ariel Ministries Press, 1983), 282.
15. Walvoord, *Major Bible Prophecies*, 393.
16. Jimmy DeYoung, *Why I Still Believe These Are the Last Days* (Oklahoma City: Hearthstone Publishing, 1993), 31.
17. Clarence H. Wagner Jr., "Wye, O Why?," *Dispatch From Jerusalem*, November/December 1998, 1.
18. Morris with Morris III, *Many Infallible Proofs*, 195.
19. Randall Price, "False Peace: The Pseudo-Storm Shelter," *Forewarning* (Eugene, OR: Harvest House Publishers, 1998), 126.
20. Gary Hedrick, *God's Timepiece* (San Antonio: Messianic Perspectives Radio Network, 1998), GT-74, audiocassette.
21. Price, "False Peace," 135.
22. Chuck Missler, "The Russia, Muslim, Magog Whirlwind," *Forewarning* (Eugene, OR: Harvest House Publishers, 1998), 232–233.
23. Grant R. Jeffrey, *Final Warning* (Toronto: Frontier Research Publications, 1995), 125.
24. Dave Breese, "The Tide of Our Times," *Destiny Newsletter*, December 1998, 3.
25. Randall Price, *Charting the Future* (San Marcos, TX: World of the Bible Ministries, n.d.), 53.
26. Marlin Maddoux, *U.N. Says Water May Be Peace Policy for Future*, "Point of View" Radio Talk Show with Marlin Maddoux (Dallas, TX), 990113, audiocassette.
27. Irvin Baxter, Jr. "Prophetic Fulfillments of 1998—What to Expect in 1999," *Endtime* (January/February 1999), 7.
28. Hal Lindsey, *International Intelligence Briefing*, newsletter, October 1998, 5–6.
29. Ibid., January 1999, 4.
30. Joan M. Veon, *The Women's International Media Group, Inc.*, newsletter, 15 December 1998, 1.
31. J. R. Church, "The Days of Old," *Prophecy in the News*, November 1998, 18.
32. Hindson, *Is the Antichrist Alive and Well?*, 9.
33. Gary Hedrick, *Israel: God's Timepiece* (San Antonio: The Christian Jew Foundation, 1998), 39–40.
34. David Jeremiah with C. C. Carlson, *The Handwriting on the Wall* (Dallas: Word Publishing, 1992), 199–200.
35. Charles H. Dyer, *The Rise of Babylon* (Wheaton: Tyndale, 1991), 188.
36. "India and Pakistan Nuclear Agreement Places Pressure on Israel," *Midnight Call*, December 1998, 31.
37. "Soldier Deaths Underscore Need for Outside Peace Broker," *News from Israel*, January 1999, 25.
38. "Launching of European Money," *Endtime* (January/February 1999), 29.
39. Jack Van Impe, "Britain Pledges Troops for U.N.," *International Intelligence Briefing*, newsletter, November 1998, 5.

Chapter 5
1. Irving L. Jensen, *Minor Prophets of Israel* (Chicago: Moody Bible Institute, 1975), 5.
2. Liat Collins, "PM Expects a Wave of Immigrants," *The Jerusalem Post*, 9 November 1998, International Edition.
3. Duane A. Garrett, *The New American Commentary: Hosea, Joel*, vol. 19A (Nashville: Broadman & Holman Publishers, 1997), 94.
4. Boyd, *Boyd's Handbook of Practical Apologetics*, 112.
5. Garrett, *The New American Commentary: Hosea, Joel*, 104.
6. Irving L. Jensen, *Minor Prophets of Judah* (Chicago: Moody Bible Institute, 1975), 30.

7. Garrett, *Hosea, Joel*, 331.
8. Ice and Demy, *Fast Facts on Bible Prophecy*, 24.
9. Price, *Jerusalem in Prophecy*, 189.
10. Thomas Ice, "What Does the Bible Say About Armageddon?" *Midnight Call*, December 1998, 17.
11. Billy K. Smith and Frank S. Page, *The New American Commentary: Amos, Obadiah, Jonah*, vol. 19B (Nashville: Broadman & Holman Publishers, 1995), 169–170.
12. David Reagan, "50 Miraculous Years," *The Lamplighter*, November 1998, 2.
13. "Surge in Neo-Nazi Violence Fuels Fears in Germany," *Message of the Christian Jew*, newsletter, March/April 1999, 14.
14. Charles L. Feinberg, *The Minor Prophets* (Chicago: Moody Press, 1948), 171.
15. Kenneth L. Barker and Waylon Bailey, *The New American Commentary: Micah, Nahum, Habakkuk, Zephaniah*, vol. 20 (Nashville: Broadman & Holman Publishers, 1998), 93.
16. J. A. Motyer, *The Minor Prophets*, vol. 3 (Downers Grove: Intervarsity Press, 1993), 923.
17. David Reagan, "Living for Christ in the End Times," *The Lamplighter*, February/March 1999, 3.
18. Jeffrey, *Prince of Darkness*, 85.
19. N. W. Hutchings, *Why I Still Believe These Are the Last Days* (Oklahoma City: Hearthstone Publishing, 1993), 15.
20. Gary Hedrick, *The Christian Jew Foundation*, newsletter, November 1998, 2.
21. Hal Lindsey, *International Intelligence Briefing*, newsletter, July 1998, 1.
22. Ibid., March 1999, 2.
23. "Jerusalem Should Become the Most Significant City in the Universe," *Midnight Call*, September 1998, 48.
24. Herb Keinon, "Our Old Friend Has a New Friend," *The Jerusalem Post*, 28 December 1998, International Edition, 3.
25. Feinberg, *The Minor Prophets*, 335.
26. Hindson, *Is the Antichrist Alive and Well?*, 41–42.
27. DeYoung, *Why I Still Believe These Are the Last Days*, 34.
28. Feinberg, *The Minor Prophets*, 339.
29. Ice and Demy, *Prophecy Watch*, 184.
30. Hagee, *Beginning of the End*, 43.
31. David Hocking, "Is It Later Than You Think?," *Hope for Today*, newsletter, September 1998, 2.
32. Danna Harman, "Sharon Attacks EU's Position on Jerusalem," *The Jerusalem Post*, 19 March 1999, International Edition, 1.
33. "Capturing, Occupying Territory Equals War Crimes," *Midnight Call*, October 1998, 42.

PROPHECIES IN THE NEW TESTAMENT
1. Irving L. Jensen, *Simply Understanding the Bible* (Minneapolis: World Wide Publications, 1990), 171.

Chapter 6
1. Halley, *Halley's Bible Handbook*, 414.
2. John F. Walvoord, *Every Prophecy of the Bible* (Colorado Springs: Chariot Victor Publishing, 1990), 364.
3. *Life Application Bible Commentary: Matthew* (Wheaton: Tyndale House Publishers, 1996), 78.
4. Ice and Demy, *Prophecy Watch*, 44–45.
5. *Life Application Bible Commentary: Matthew*, 268.
6. Mike Gendron, *The Great Apostasy*, Pre-Trib Rapture Study Group, 14 December 1998 (Plano, TX: Proclaiming The Gospel, 1998), 1.

7. David Reagan, "What's the Relevance?" *The Lamplighter*, May 1999, 2.
8. Gendron, *The Great Apostasy*, 1.
9. James V. Heidinger II, "The Historicity of Our Faith," *Good News*, May/June 1999, 9.
10. Walvoord, *Major Bible Prophecies*, 213–214.
11. Gendron, *The Great Apostasy*, 2.
12. J. Dwight Pentecost, *Things to Come* (Grand Rapids: Zondervan, 1958), 148.
13. Arno Froese, "European Union in Prophecy," *Midnight Call*, June 1999, 13.
14. Pentecost, *Things to Come,* 148–149.
15. Billy Graham, *Angels* (Waco: Word Books Publisher, 1975), 108.
16. Pentecost, *Things to Come,* 149.
17. William Barclay, *The Gospel of Matthew,* vol. 2 (Philadelphia: Westminster Press, 1956), 287.
18. Ibid., 336–337.
19. Dave Hunt, "Flashes of Falling Away," *Forewarning* (Eugene, OR: Harvest House Publishers, 1998), 28.
20. Charles Halff, "False Prophets in the Last Days," *Message of the Christian Jew,* newsletter, May/June 1984, 3.
21. Cynthia B. Astle, "Methodists' Vatican Visit Cordial But Controversial," *The United Methodist Reporter,* 10 October 1997, Memphis Conference Edition.
22. Jack Van Impe, *2001: On the Edge of Eternity* (Dallas: Word Publishing, 1996), 35.
23. "Wars and Rumors of Wars," *Midnight Call*, June 1996, 31.
24. Irvin Baxter, Jr., "Doomsday Weapons Are Back," *Endtime* (July/August 1998), 16.
25. "The Beginning of Sorrows," *Prophetic Observer,* April 1999, 3.
26. Van Impe, *Edge of Eternity*, 99.
27. Texe Marrs, *Power of Prophecy*, Special Edition, *Days of Hunger, Days of Chaos* (Austin: Living Truth Ministries), 1.
28. "The Beginning of Sorrows," *Prophetic Observer,* April 1999, 3.
29. "World Asked To Assist C. America Hurricane Victims," *Yahoo! News,* 6 November 1998, http://dailynews.yahoo.com/headlines/ts/story.html?s>.
30. Hagee, *Beginning of the End*, 98.
31. Billy Graham, *Storm Warning* (Irving, TX: Word Publishing, 1992), 35.
32. Brook Larmer, "The Night Heaven Fell," *Newsweek*, 4 October 1999, 48.
33. David Hocking, *The Olivet Discourse/Divorce & Remarriage* (La Mirada: Calvary Communications, Inc., 1989), 26.
34. J. Vernon McGee, *Thru the Bible with J. Vernon McGee*, vol. IV (Pasadena: Thru The Bible Radio, 1983), 126.
35. Price, "False Peace," 134.
36. Ken Schafer, *Bible Expositor and Illuminator* (Union Gospel Press, Spring 1981), 47.
37. Thomas Ice and Timothy Demy, *The Truth About the Signs of the Times* (Eugene, OR: Harvest House Publishers, 1997), 26.
38. Charles Halff, "False Prophets in the Last Days," *Message of the Christian Jew,* newsletter, May/June 1984, 8.
39. Gendron, *The Great Apostasy*, 2.
40. Eddie Sax, "Religious Exclusiveness," *Endtime* (January/February 1999), 26.
41. Joe Chambers, "How to Discern False Prophets," *The End Times* (November/December 1998), 2.
42. *Discerning the Times,* newsletter, February 1999, 4.
43. Dave Breese, "The Beginning of Sorrows," *Destiny Newsletter,* June 1999, 2.
44. Grant Jeffrey, *The Signature of God* (Toronto: Frontier Research Publications, 1996), 96.
45. "The Red Heifer," *Personal Update,* July 1997, 11–12.
46. Sol Scharfstein, *Understanding Israel* (Hoboken, NJ: KTAV Publishing House, 1994), 114.
47. Irvin Baxter, Jr., "Time to Negotiate Jerusalem," *Endtime* (November/December 1998), 9.
48. David Hocking, "Is It Later Than You Think?" *Hope for Today,* newsletter, September 1998, 1.
49. Dave Breese, "Cyclone of Apocalypse," *Forewarning* (Eugene, OR: Harvest House Publishers, 1998), 313.
50. David R. Reagan, "The Rise and Fall of the Antichrist," *The Lamplighter,* November 1998, 6.
51. Graham, *Storm Warning*, 143.
52. Hunt, *Occult Invasion*, 120.
53. Charles Capps, *End Time Events* (Tulsa: Harrison House, 1997), 146.
54. "Vulture Population Threatened," *Dispatch From Jerusalem,* September/October 1998, 1.
55. Ibid., May/June 1999, 19.
56. Alon Pinkas, "Two Airmen Killed as Storks Down F-15," *The Jerusalem Post,* 19 August 1995, International Edition, 4.
57. *Life Application Bible Commentary: Matthew,* 478.
58. Oliver B. Greene, *The Gospel According to Matthew,* vol. V (Greenville, SC: The Gospel Hour, 1971), 317.
59. Graham, *Storm Warning*, 38.
60. Capps, *End Time Events*, 148.
61. Graham, *Angels*, 27.
62. Fruchtenbaum, *The Footsteps of the Messiah*, 443.
63. Walvoord, *Major Bible Prophecies*, 263.
64. Hedrick, *Israel: God's Timepiece*, side 2.
65. "Israel Becoming Densely Populated," *News From Israel*, July 1998, 29.
66. Hagee, *Beginning of the End*, 100.
67. Capps, *End Time Events*, 155.
68. Walvoord, *Major Bible Prophecies*, 296.
69. Ibid., 105–106.
70. David Hocking, *The Church Is Born/Who Is Jesus?* (La Mirada, CA: Calvary Communications, 1990), 68.
71. William Barclay, *The Gospel of Luke* (Philadelphia: The Westminster Press, 1953), 172.
72. *The Pulpit Commentary, Mark & Luke*, vol. 16 (Grand Rapids: Eerdmans, 1980), 103.
73. Morris with Morris III, *Many Infallible Proofs*, 58.
74. Irvin Baxter, Jr., "Israel's Future—Through the Eyes of Prophecy," *Endtime* (May/June 1999), 28–30.
75. John Loeffler, "The Case For Jerusalem," *Personal Update,* December 1998, 2.
76. "Palestinians Demand Western Jerusalem, Too," *Dispatch From Jerusalem,* May/June 1999, 8.
77. David R. Reagan, "The Rise and Fall of the Antichrist," *The Lamplighter,* November 1998, 3.
78. Wire Service and Staff Reports, "Prayer Rally: Rehearsal for the Greeting of the Messiah," *Dispatch From Jerusalem,* March/April, 1999, 16.
79. W. Herschel Ford, *Sermons You Can Preach on John* (Grand Rapids: Ministry Resources Library, 1958), 229.
80. Ibid., 293.
81. Hal Lindsey, *Apocalypse Code* (Palos Verdes, CA: Western Front, 1997), 301.

82. Hagee, *Beginning of the End,* 102.

83. J. R. Church, *Raging into Apocalypse* (Green Forest, AR: New Leaf Press, 1996), 184.

Chapter 7

1. N. W. Hutchings, *Romance of Romans* (Oklahoma City: Hearthstone Publishing, 1990), 79.

2. Breese, "Cyclone of Apocalypse," 310.

3. N. W. Hutchings, *Romance of Romans,* 82.

4. *The Pulpit Commentary: Acts & Romans*, vol. 18 (Grand Rapids: Eerdmans, 1980), 270.

5. Hutchings, *Romance of Romans,* 329.

6. Walvoord, *Every Prophecy of the Bible,* 454.

7. Hutchings, *Last Days,* 20.

8. Pentecost, *Things to Come,* 294.

9. Fruchtenbaum, *The Footsteps of the Messiah,* 108.

10. Breese, "Cyclone of Apocalypse," 334.

11. Graham, *Angels,* 39.

12. Theodore H. Epp, *James: The Epistle of Applied Christianity* (Lincoln: Back to the Bible, 1980), 67.

13. William Barclay, *The Letters to the Corinthians* (Philadelphia: Westminster Press, 1954), 169.

14. Ibid., 224.

15. Theodore H. Epp, *Galatians* (Lincoln: Back to the Bible Correspondence School, 1974), 83.

16. William Barclay, *The Letters to the Galatians and Ephesians* (Philadelphia: Westminster Press, 1954), 59.

17. Ibid., 194.

18. *The Pulpit Commentary: Galatians, Ephesians, Philippians, Colossians*, vol. 20 (Grand Rapids: Eerdmans, 1980), 218.

19. Walvoord, *Every Prophecy of the Bible,* 472.

20. Oliver B. Greene, *The Epistle of Paul the Apostle to the Philippians* (Greenville, SC: The Gospel Hour, 1965), 54.

21. Graham, *Angels,* 39.

22. David Hocking, *Israel and Bible Prophecy/Philippians: The Christian's Guidebook to Joy in Christ* (La Mirada, CA: Calvary Communications, 1991), 65.

23. *Life Application Bible Commentary: Philippians, Colossians, & Philemon* (Wheaton: Tyndale, 1995), 225.

24. Oliver B. Greene, *The Epistles of Paul the Apostle to the Thessalonians* (Greenville, SC: The Gospel Hour, 1964), 134–135.

25. Capps, *End Time Events,* 192.

26. Norbert Lieth, "The Rapture," *News From Israel,* March 1999, 10.

27. Hal Lindsey, *The Rapture* (Toronto: Bantam Books, 1983), 46.

28. Breese, "Cyclone of Apocalypse," 318–319.

29. William T. James, *Foreshocks of Antichrist* (Eugene, OR: Harvest House, 1997), 8.

30. Lindsey, *The Rapture,* 143.

31. Van Impe, *Edge of Eternity,* 152–153.

32. "Palestinians: Peace with Israel by May," *The Jackson (Tennessee) Sun,* 22 July 1999, 8A.

33. "More Israelis Have Been Killed in 5 Years Since Oslo," *Dispatch From Jerusalem,* November/December 1998, 12.

34. David Hocking, "You Didn't See It on CNN," *Hope for Today,* newsletter, May 1999, 4.

35. Graham, *Storm Warning,* 278.

36. Walvoord, "Antichrist, Armageddon, and the Second Coming of Christ," *Forewarning* (Eugene, OR: Harvest House Publishers, 1998), 346.

37. Hunt, "Flashes of Falling Away," 28–29.

38. Breese, "Cyclone of Apocalypse," 322.

39. Bill Perkins, "Gathering Clouds of Global Godlessness," *Forewarning* (Eugene, OR: Harvest House Publishers, 1998), 55.

40. "Prayerlessness = Powerlessness," *Good News* (May/June 1999), 10.

41. Graham, *Angels,* 31.

42. N. W. Hutchings, *Studies in Timothy* (Oklahoma City: Hearthstone Publishing, 1990), 75.

43. Hunt, *Occult Invasion,* 567.

44. Gendron, *The Great Apostasy,* 7.

Chapter 8

1. Richards, *Biblically-Inept,* 301.

2. Walvoord, *Major Bible Prophecies,* 187.

3. Irving L. Jensen, *Hebrews* (Chicago: Moody Bible Institute, 1970), 68–69.

4. William Barclay, *The Letters of James and Peter* (Philadelphia: Westminster Press, 1958), 136.

5. *Life Application Bible Commentary: James* (Wheaton: Tyndale, 1992), 123.

6. Epp, *James,* 231.

7. *The Pulpit Commentary: Thessalonians, Timothy, Titus, Philemon, Hebrews, James*, vol. 21 (Grand Rapids: Eerdmans, 1980), 76.

8. *Life Application Bible Commentary: 1 & 2 Peter and Jude* (Wheaton: Tyndale, 1995), 174.

9. Hunt, "Flashes of Falling Away," 36.

10. David Hocking, *Real Truth for True Believers: 1 John* (La Mirada, CA: Calvary Communications, 1990), 37.

11. J. Vernon McGee, *Thru the Bible with J. Vernon McGee*, vol. V (Pasadena, CA: Thru the Bible Radio, 1983), 787.

12. The Southwest Radio Church, *The Whole Realm of Rebellion* (Oklahoma City: The Southwest Radio Church, 1980), 9.

Chapter 9

1. Tim F. LaHaye, *Revelation: Illustrated and Made Plain* (Grand Rapids: Zondervan, 1973), 22.

2. Gary G. Cohen, *Kirban Reference Bible,* Revelation Visualized (AMG Publishers, 1979), 96.

3. Walvoord, *Every Prophecy of the Bible,* 550.

4. Breese, "Cyclone of Apocalypse," 312.

5. McGee, *Thru the Bible,* Volume V, 949.

6. Jeffrey, *The Signature of God,* 271.

7. Walvoord, *Every Prophecy of the Bible,* 564.

8. "Terrorism and Weapons of Mass Destruction," *Personal Update,* March 1999 (Coeur d'Alene, ID: Koinonia House), 5.

9. Pentecost, *Things to Come,* 215.

10. Hagee, *Beginning of the End,* 172.

11. LaHaye, *Understanding the Last Days,* 59.

12. Halff, *The End Times Are Here Now,* 109.

13. Terry L. Cook, "Today's Technology Turns Toward the Mark of the Beast," *Forewarning* (Eugene, OR: Harvest House Publishers, 1998), 114.

14. Dan Barklay, "UN Reform—Preparing for Global Governance," *Endtime* (May/June 1999), 24.

15. Eddie Sax, "Religious Exclusiveness," *Endtime* (January/February 1999), 28.

16. Michael Coffman, *U.N. Says Water May Be Peace Policy for Future,* "Point of View" Radio Talk Show with Marlin Maddoux (Dallas, TX), 990113, audiocassette.

17. Billy Graham, *Approaching Hoofbeats: The Four Horsemen of the Apocalypse* (New York: Avon Books, 1983), 251–252.

18. David Jeremiah, with C. C. Carlson, *Escape the Coming Night* (Dallas: Word Publishing, 1990), 188.

19. "Russia Prepares for War," *Prophecy in the News,* April 1999, 19.
20. Dave Breese, "1998: A Year of Disasters," *Destiny Bulletin,* March 1999, 1.
21. "Study: Global Water Shortage Impending," *The Commercial Appeal* (Memphis), 24 November 1998, A6.
22. Hal Lindsey, *There's a New World Coming* (Eugene, OR: Harvest House Publishers, 1973), 225–226.
23. Jeremiah with Carlson, *Escape the Coming Night,* 167.
24. Wim Malgo, *The Wrath of Heaven on Earth* (West Columbia, SC: *Midnight Call,* 1985), 165.
25. William L. Pettingill, *The Unveiling of Jesus Christ* (Findlay, OH: Fundamental Truth Publishers, 1939), 89.
26. Wim Malgo, *A New Heaven and a New Earth* (West Columbia, SC: Midnight Call, 1985), 73.
27. Fruchtenbaum, *The Footsteps of the Messiah,* 112.
28. Pettingill, *The Unveiling of Jesus Christ,* 93.
29. Jeremiah with Carlson, *Escape the Coming Night,* 217.
30. Thomas Ice and Timothy Demy, *The Truth about Heaven and Eternity* (Eugene, OR: Harvest House Publishers, 1997), 14.
31. Malgo, *A New Heaven and a New Earth,* 146.
32. Lindsey, *There's a New World Coming,* 268.
33. Walvoord, *Every Prophecy of the Bible,* 641.
34. Richards, *Biblically-Inept,* 322.

INDEX

Boldface numbers refer to defined (What?) terms in the sidebar.

Church, J. R.:
    on Gentile Christians, 203
    on New World Order, the, 98
    on Psalm prophecy, 51
Church Age, 3, 5, **238**
    Antichrist during, 240–242
    events during, 240–242
    and the Kingdom of Heaven, illustration
        of, 147
    last days of, 254
    Paul on, 240–242
    Rapture as ending, 263
    seven eras of, illustration, 262
Church Age Temple, 92
City, cities, **101**
    of God (*see* Holy City)
    Holy, 283–285, 287
    of Righteousness, 59
    (*See also* individual cities)
Clan, **72**
Clay, 93
Clinton, Bill (President), 131, 168, 170
Coffman, Michael S., Dr., 171
Cohen, Gary G., on seal, significance of, 264
Cohen, William, U.S. Secretary of Defense,
    269
Collectively, **59**
Colossians, book of, 226–227
    Paul as author, 207
    Rapture prophecy in, 227
Comets, 181, 266
Commandments, **37**
Communism, collapse of, 161
Compassion, **109**
Computer age, 274
Concubines, **20**
Congress (U.S.), 273
Consecrated, **37**
Converts, **265**
Cook, Terry L., on I.D. technology, 273
Cooperation, lack of, 2
Co-regent, **80**
Corinthians, books of, Paul as author, 207
1 Corinthians, book of, 214–219
    Rapture prophecy in, 218
    Second Coming prophecy in, 217
2 Corinthians, book of, 219–220
Corrupt shepherds, **80**
Covenant(s), **13**, **174**
    of Antichrist, with Israel, 104, 230
    Edenic, 14
    God's with Israel, illustration of, 248
    God's, with Isaac, 22–23
    God's, with Israel , fulfillment of, 4–5
    God's, with Jacob, 23–25
    God's, list of, 14
    God's, with Moses, 26–27
    of grace, 246
    of the Law, 246
    New, 246, 259
    old (of Law), 259
Crown, Crowns:
    Crown of Glory, 218
    five that believers can win, 217–218
    Incorruptible, 217
    Crown of Life, 217
    Crown of Rejoicing, 217
    Crown of Righteousness, 218
Crucified, **223**
Crucifixion, 101, 170, 190

Cults, xviii
Cush, Ethiopia, Iraq, Sudan, 88
Cut off, **101**

D

Damascus, 67–**68**, 116
    road to, 219
Dan, tribe of, 91
Daniel, book of, 93–105
    on the Antichrist, 104, 235
    and dream of Nebuchadnezzar, 93
    Gabriel (the angel), and, 100–10, 160, 258
    seventy sevens, 100–105, illustration of, 102
Daniel's prophecy:
    Antichrist, 98–100
    four kingdoms, 93–98
    seventy sevens, 100
Darkness:
    prophesied in Revelation, 276
    the Tribulation Period, during, 230
    (*See under* Sun, darkening)
David, King:
    Amos' restoration prophecy of, 121
    and Ark of the Covenant, 41
    city of, 35
    God's words to, 36
    house of, 65, 203
    as Israel's future king, 85
    as Israel's greatest king, 35
    Jesus as descendant of, 35, 43
    line of, 35
    resurrection of, 80
    as shepherd, 80
    Temple of Solomon and, 43
    throne of, 4–5
Davidic Covenant, 14
David's house, **34**
David's kingdom, 125
David's people, **34**
David's son, **34**
Davos, Switzerland, 95–96
Day of the Lord, **66**, **114**, **230**
    distress on, 128
    (*See also* Tribulation Period)
Dead Sea, 136, 175
Death:
    as rider of pale horse, 265
    second, 199
Decimate, **63**
Decree, **40**
Dedan, 87
Defile, **126**
Deliver, **118**
Delusions, **178**
Demon-possessed man, 190
Demy, Timothy (*see* Ice, Thomas, and Timothy
    Demy)
Depraved, **12**
Devil (*see* Satan)
DeYoung, Jimmy:
    on God's promise to Abraham, 82
    on the Great Tribulation, 134
Disarmament, **125**
Disasters, natural, 277
Disciples, **157**, **168**
    angels appearing to, 202
    background of, 201
    destiny of, 191
    as Galilean, 157
    as Jewish, 168

Diseases, **163**
    skin, 276
Distress, **180**
    Tribulation Period, during, 177, 192–193,
        209
Divination, **61**
Dogmatic, **115**
Dogmatically, **256**
Dogs, **47**
Dominion Now beliefs, 5
Dominion Theory beliefs, 5
Doomsday clock, 161
Dowsing, 61
Dragon, 270
Dream(s), **116**
    Joseph's, 170
    Nebuchadnezzar's, 93–94
Drought, 114
Drug-related violence, 161
Dyer, Charles, on seventy sevens, 102

E

Eagles, **178**
Earth:
    departure of Church from, 282
    end of, 219
    replacement of, 283–284
    wonderful future of, 4
Earth Charter, 97
Earth Ethic, 97, 273
Earthquake(s), 118, 136, 164–166, 268
    recent, illustration of, 165
    Revelation, prophesied in, 164, 265, 276
    scientists' predicting, 164
    as sign, 159
East Jerusalem, 83
Eastern sea, **136**
Ecclesiastes, book of, 45
Economy, global, 94–95
Ecumenical movement, 174
Edenic Covenant, 14
Edom, 27, **56**, 121–122
Edomites, 175
Egypt, 17
    Abraham's move to, 22
    Israelis in, 26
    Jacob's sons in, 26
    plagues of, 269
El Salvador, 163–164
Elah, King, 39
Elam, 74
Elation, **78**
Elect, the, 183
Eli, 33
Empty, **222**
End of time:
    Jesus' prophecy of, 2
    (*See also* Tribulation Period)
England, 95–96
Enmity, **25**
Enoch, 17
Ephesians, book of, 222–224
    Millennium prophecy in, 223
    Paul as author, 207
Ephesus Period, 147, 263
Ephod, **110**
Ephraim (person), 25
Ephraim (place), **85**, **68**
    in Ezekiel's prophecy, 84–85
    Israel as called, 69

God's timetable, secrecy of, 205
Gods, false, 27
Gog, 87–**88**
Gog and Magog, 69
Gold, 93
    in the Holy City, 284
Golden Age, the, 80
Golden calf, 170
Gomer (person), 108
Gomer (place), 87
    Germany, 88
Gomorrah (*see* Sodom and Gomorrah)
Good shepherd, Jesus as, 26
Gospel(s), **143**, **150**, **172**, **233**
    significance in Bible of, 143–144
    truths in, 143–144
Government, world (*see* World government)
Grace, **14**, **129**, **246**
    covenant of, 246
Graham, Billy, 173
    on angels, 183
    on angels, fallen, 225
    on angels, judgment of, 216
    on angels at Second Coming, 155
    on the Antichrist, 178
    on calamities, recent, 165
    on Satan worship, 238
    on the Second Coming, 182, 234
    on Tribulation Period events, 275
Grapes, 121
Great Britain, military of, 104
Great Tribulation Period, **2**–**3**, illustration of, 3
    (*See also* Tribulation Period)
Great White Throne of God, 188–189
    Non-Christians at, 226
Great White Throne prophecy:
    in Acts, 204
    in Galations, 222
    in James, 249
    in Jude, 258
    in Luke, 192, 198
    of Paul in 1 Timothy, 239
    of Paul in Galations, 222
    in 1 Peter, 253
    in 2 Peter, 255
    in Romans, 209
    in 1 Timothy, 239
Greece, 97
    earthquake in, 165
Greek:
    as common language, 142
    New Testament as written in, 4
Greene, Oliver B.:
    on death and resurrection, 228
    on Jesus, brightness of, 181
    on Jesus as Christ, 225
Grief, Christians and, 46
Groaning, **47**
Group of Eight, 95–96
Guatemala, 163–164
Gulf War, the, 94

H

Hades, 265
Hagar, 20
Hagee, John:
    on earthquakes, 164
    on the end time, 187
    on Jesus, First and Second Comings of, 136
    on Russian Jews, 75

on Satan's strategy, 270–271
    on the Second Coming, 202
Hagrites, **56**
Hail, 269
Halff, Charles:
    on the currency system, 272
    on Israel, 56
    on prophets, true and false, 169
    on Satan's program, 159
    on the Tribulation Period, 77
Halley, Henry H.:
    on David, line of, 35
    on the Four Gospels, 144
Handmaids, **24**
Hannah, 33
Heads, seven, of Antichrist, 272
Heaven, replacement of, 283–284
Heavenly bodies, 180
    disturbance of, 266
Heavenly reward, 215–218
Hebrew, **45**
    Old Testament translation from, 142
    poetry, 45
Hebrews (book of), 245
    Millennium prophecy recorded in, 247
    Rapture prophecy recorded in, 247
    Second Coming prophecy recorded in, 247
    uncertain authorship of, 207
Hebrews (people), **246** (*See also* Israelites, Jews)
Hedrick, Gary:
    on God's prophetic agenda, 102
    on Israel, signs of end time in, 184
    on Second Coming, imminence of, 86
    on the siege of Jerusalem, 130
Hell, 188–189, **222**
    location of, 285
    (*See also* Lake of Fire)
Heresy, **178**
Herod, King, 28
Herod's Temple, 92, 157
Hezekiah, King, 39
Hindson, Ed:
    on the Antichrist, 98
    on Armageddon, 53
    on prophets, true, 133
    on Satan's doom, 10
Hindus, 171
Hinnon, Valley of, 189
His eyes and heart, **37**
His Spirit, **116**
HIV virus, 163
Hocking, David:
    on Jesus as of the house of David, 190
    on Jesus as Lord, 225
    on resurrection, bodily, 256
    on Tribulation Period, signs of, 167
Holocaust, **167**
    future, 177
Holy, **90**, **223**
Holy City, 129, 283–285, 287
Holy hill, **115**
Holy One, **47**
Holy Spirit, 116, **176**, **217**
    prophets, and, xvi
    removal at Rapture of, 236
Homophobes, **167**
Honduras, 163–164
Hoofs, 126
Horn(s), 126

Antichrist as, 104
    ten, of Antichrist, 272
Horse(s):
    black, 162, 265
    pale, 163, 265
    red, 160, 265
    white, 158, 264
Hosea, 108, 113, 183
    children of, 108
    Gomer and, 108
Hosea's prophecy, 107–113
    scattering of the Jews, 113
Hoshea, King, 39
House of David, **65**, **203**
House, H. Wayne, on prophecy, 43
Hula Valley, 179
Hunt, Dave:
    on apostasy, 255
    on apostasy, within church, 236
    on dowsing and divination, 61
    on occult and miracles, 178
    on occultism, 238
    on religious deception, 159
Hurricanes, 163–164
Husband, **72**
Hussein, King, 175
Hutchings, Noah:
    on Babylon, doom of, 67
    on God's wrath, 209
    on Israel and the coming Messiah, 130
    on Jews and Jesus, 213
    on judgment of believers and unbelievers, 208
    on spiritualism, 238
Hypocrites, Jesus accusing, 151

I

Ice, Thomas, and Timothy Demy:
    on Armageddon, 120, 136
    on judgment day, 41
    on the lake of fire, 282
    on modern Israel, 75
    on parables of Jesus, 147
    on system of denials, 51
    on Tribulation Period, church and, 169
    on Tribulation Period, military, 118
Identification, mark of the beast and, 272–273
Idiom, **89**
Idol, **170**
Idolatry, **27**, **29**
Incorruptible Crown, **217**
India, 103, 161
Indignation, **274**
Integrity, **37**
Interludes, Revelation, 268
International Criminal Court (war crimes), 96
Intertestamental Period, **142**
Iran, 74
    Persia, 88
Iraq
    as Babylon, 67
    Cush, as part of, 88
    sanctions against, 94
    United Nations and, 94
Iron, 93, 126
Isaac:
    birth of, 16
    God's promises to, 22–23, 40
    Israel as descended from, 16
    twin sons of, 23

Books by Starburst Publishers®

(Partial listing—full list available on request)

God's Word for the Biblically-Inept™ Series:

- ☞ **The Bible** by Larry Richards
- ☞ **Daniel** by Daymond R. Duck
- ☞ **Genesis** by Joyce L. Gibson
- ☞ **Health & Nutrition** by Kathleen O'Bannon Baldinger
- ☞ **Life of Christ, Volume 1** by Robert C. Girard
- ☞ **Men of the Bible** by D. Larry Miller
- ☞ **Prophecies of the Bible** by Daymond R. Duck
- ☞ **Revelation** by Daymond R. Duck
- ☞ **Women of the Bible** by Kathy Collard Miller

(See pages iii–v for purchasing information)

- • **Learn more at www.biblicallyinept.com** •

Announcing Our New Series:
What's in the Bible for . . .™?

The **What's in the Bible for . . .™** series makes the Bible applicable to everyday life. Whether you're a teenager or senior citizen, this series has the book for you! Each title is equipped with the same reader-friendly icons, call-outs, tables, illustrations, questions, and chapter summaries that are used in the **God's Word for the Biblically-Inept™** series. It's another easy way to dig deep into God's Word!

- ☞ **What's in the Bible for . . . ™ Women**
  by Georgia Curtis Ling
- ☞ **What's in the Bible for . . . ™ Mothers**
  by Judy Bodmer
- ☞ **What's in the Bible for . . . ™ Teens**
  by Mark and Jeanette Littleton

On the Brink
Daymond R. Duck

Subtitled: *Easy-to-Understand End-Time Bible Prophecy*. From the author of *Revelation* and *Daniel—God's Word for the Biblically-Inept™*, *On the Brink* is organized in biblical sequence and written with simplicity so that any reader will easily understand end-time prophecy. Ideal for use as a handy-reference book.
(trade paper)   ISBN 0914984586 $11.95

Beast of the East
Alvin M. Shifflett

Asks the questions: Has the Church become involved in a "late date" comfort mode expecting to be "raptured" before the Scuds fall? Should we prepare for a long and arduous Desert Storm to Armageddon battle? Are we ignoring John 16:33, *In this world you will have trouble*? (NIV)
(trade paper)   ISBN 0914984578 $14.95

Grapes of Righteousness
Joseph H. Powell

Subtitled: *Spiritual Grafting into the True Vine*. Dr. Powell uses an analogy that compares and contrasts our development into God's kingdom under His hands, to the cultivating and nurturing of a vineyard by a gardener. Possessing a Ph.D. in Botany, the author uses his extensive study of grafting, pruning, nutrition, and dormancy to illustrate the basic Biblical principles necessary to spiritual birth and subsequent growth and maturity.
(trade paper)   ISBN 0914984748 $10.95

The ***God's Vitamin "C" for the Spirit*™** series has already sold over 250,000 copies! Jam-packed with stories from well-known Christian writers that will lighten your spirit and enrich your life!

God's Vitamin "C" for the Spirit™
by Kathy Collard Miller & D. Larry Miller
(trade paper) ISBN 0914984837 $12.95

God's Vitamin "C" for the Spirit™ of Women
by Kathy Collard Miller
(trade paper)   ISBN 0914984934 $12.95

God's Chewable Vitamin "C" for the Spirit™ of Moms
(trade paper)   ISBN 0914984942 $6.95

God's Vitamin "C" for the Hurting Spirit™
by Kathy Collard Miller & D. Larry Miller
(trade paper)   ISBN 0914984691 $12.95

God's Chewable Vitamin "C" for the Spirit
(trade paper)   ISBN 0914984845 $6.95

God's Vitamin "C" for the Spirit of Men
by D. Larry Miller
(trade paper)   ISBN 0914984810 $12.95

God's Chewable Vitamin "C" for the Spirit of Dads
(trade paper)   ISBN 0914984829 $6.95

God's Vitamin "C" for the Christmas Spirit
by Kathy Collard Miller & D. Larry Miller
(cloth)   ISBN 0914984853 $14.95

The Weekly Feeder: A Revolutionary Shopping, Cooking, and Meal-Planning System
Cori Kirkpatrick

A revolutionary meal-planning system, here is a way to make preparing home-cooked dinners more convenient than ever. At the beginning of each week, simply choose one of the eight preplanned menus, tear out the corresponding grocery list, do your shopping, and whip up each fantastic meal in less than 45 minutes! The author's household management tips, equipment checklists, and nutrition information make this system a must for any busy family. Included with every recipe is a personal anecdote from the author emphasizing the importance of good food, a healthy family, and a well-balanced life.
(trade paper)   ISBN 1892016095 $16.95

God Stories: They're So Amazing, Only God Could Make Them Happen
Donna I. Douglas

Famous individuals share their personal, true-life experiences with God in this beautiful new book! Find out how God has touched the lives of top recording artists, professional athletes, and other newsmakers like Jessi Colter, Deana Carter, Ben Vereen, Stephanie Zimbalist, Cindy Morgan, Sheila E., Joe Jacoby, Cheryl Landon, Brett Butler, Clifton Taulbert, Babbie Mason, Michael Medved, Sandi Patty, Charlie Daniels, and more! Their stories are intimate, poignant, and sure to

inspire and motivate you as you listen for God's message in your own life!
(cloth)   ISBN 1892016117 $18.95

Since Life Isn't a Game, These Are God's Rules: Finding Joy & Fulfillment in God's Ten Commandments
Kathy Collard Miller

Life is often referred to as a game, but God didn't create us because he was short on game pieces. To succeed in life, you'll need to know God's rules. In this book, Kathy Collard Miller explains the meaning of each of the Ten Commandments with fresh application for today. Each chapter includes scripture and quotes from some of our most beloved Christian authors including Billy Graham, Patsy Clairmont, Liz Curtis Higgs, and more! Sure to renew your understanding of God's rules.
(cloth)   ISBN 189201615X $17.95

God's Little Rule Book: Simple Rules to Bring Joy & Happiness to Your Life
Starburst Publishers

Let this little book of God's rules be your personal guide to a more joyful life. Brimming with easily applicable rules, this book is sure to inspire and motivate you! Each rule includes corresponding scripture and a practical tip that will help to incorporate God's rules into everyday life. Simple enough to fit into a busy schedule, yet powerful enough to be life changing!
(trade paper)   ISBN 1892016168 $6.95

Life's Little Rule Book: Simple Rules to Bring Joy & Happiness to Your Life
Starburst Publishers

Let this little book inspire you to live a happier life! The pages are filled with timeless rules such as, "Learn to cook, you'll always be in demand!" and "Help something grow." Each rule is combined with a reflective quote and a simple suggestion to help the reader incorporate the rule into everyday life.
(trade paper)   ISBN 1892016176 $6.95

Promises of God's Abundance
Edited by Kathy Collard Miller

Subtitled: *For a More Meaningful Life.* The Bible is filled with God's promises for an abundant life. *Promises of God's Abundance* is written in the same way as the best-selling *God's Abundance.* It will help you discover these promises and show you how simple obedience is the key to an abundant life. Scripture, questions for growth, and a simple thought for the day will guide you to a more meaningful life.

(trade paper)   ISBN 0914984098 $9.95

Stories of God's Abundance for a More Joyful Life
Compiled by Kathy Collard Miller

Like its successful predecessor, *God's Abundance* (100,000 sold), this book is filled with beautiful, inspirational, real life stories. Those telling their stories of God share Scriptures and insights that readers can apply to their daily lives. Renew your faith in life's small miracles and challenge yourself to allow God to lead the way as you find the source of abundant living for all your relationships.

(trade paper)   ISBN 1892016060 $12.95

More God's Abundance:
Joyful Devotions for Every Season
Compiled by Kathy Collard Miller

Editor Kathy Collard Miller responds to the tremendous success of *God's Abundance* with a fresh collection of stories based on God's Word for a simpler life. Includes stories from our most beloved Christian writers such as Liz Curtis Higgs and Patsy Clairmont that are combined ideas, tips, quotes, and scripture.

(cloth)   ISBN 1892016133 $19.95

God's Abundance for Women:
Devotions for a More Meaningful Life
Compiled by Kathy Collard Miller

Following the success of *God's Abundance*, this book will touch women of all ages as they seek a more meaningful life. Essays from our most beloved Christian authors exemplify how to gain the abundant life that Jesus promised through trusting Him to fulfill our every need. Each story is enhanced with Scripture, quotes, and practical tips providing brief, yet deeply spiritual reading.

(cloth)   ISBN 1892016141 $19.95

Purchasing Information
www.starburstpublishers.com

Books are available from your favorite bookstore, either from current stock or special order. To assist bookstores in locating your selection, be sure to give title, author, and ISBN. If unable to purchase from a bookstore, you may order direct from STARBURST PUBLISHERS. When ordering please enclose full payment plus shipping and handling as follows:

Post Office (4th class)
$3.00 with a purchase of up to $20.00
$4.00 ($20.01–$50.00)
5% of purchase price for purchases of $50.01 and up

Canada
$5.00 (up to $35.00)
15% ($35.01 and up)

United Parcel Service (UPS)
$4.50 (up to $20.00)
$6.00 ($20.01–$50.00)
7% ($50.01 and up)

Overseas
$5.00 (up to $25.00)
20% ($25.01 and up)

Payment in U.S. funds only. Please allow two to three weeks minimum (longer overseas) for delivery. Make checks payable to and mail to:

Starburst Publishers® • P.O. Box 4123 • Lancaster, PA 17604

Credit card orders may be placed by calling 1-800-441-1456, Mon–Fri, 8:30 A.M. to 5:30 P.M. Eastern Standard Time. Prices are subject to change without notice. Catalogs are available for a 9 x 12 self-addressed envelope with four first-class stamps.

NOTES